PRAISE FOR *SOAP OPERA*

"*Wall Street Journal* reporter Alecia Swasy's disturbing yet often hilarious book portrays a neurotic, paranoid company that bears little resemblance to the wholesome consumer products giant that sells such products as Ivory soap, Tide detergent and Crest toothpaste."
  —Gary Strauss, *USA Today*

"Swasy's account of how P&G has become warped and paranoid is fascinating."
  —Susan Chandler, *Chicago Sun-Times*

". . . Swasy has done a fine job of exploring the secretive Procter world . . ."
  —*Business Week*

"If someone had suggested that I spend the weekend reading a book about Procter & Gamble, the soap-and-toothpaste maker, I would have laughed at the idea. But after a few pages of *Soap Opera* by Alecia Swasy, the hook was in deep."
  —Paul D. Clifford, *New York Newsday*

"Well documented. . . . a fascinating history of the company . . ."
  —Gigi Verna, Cincinnati *Business Record*

". . . her investigative reporting, which included interviews with hundreds of current and former P&G employees, provides a highly unflattering portrait of a company that employs nearly 100,000 people and last year had sales of more than $30 billion."
  —*The Economist*

"Her book will be most powerful for readers familiar only with P&G's public image, carefully cultivated from the moment it dubbed Ivory soap '99 44/100 percent pure' in 1881."
  —Jolie Solomon, *Newsweek*

"A chilling look at the corporation as Big Brother . . ."
  —*Publishers Weekly*

"Dirty tricks. Draconian mindset. Cutthroat nature. Paranoid. Oppressive environment. No wonder Procter & Gamble Co. is worried."
  —Jennifer Lawrence *Advertising Age*

"A credible and moving job . . ."
  —David Diamond, *The New York Times Book Review*

"A scathing new book about Procter & Gamble paints the Cincinnati-based consumer products giant as a bully that controls employees, manipulates the government, and unknowingly foots the bill for employee participation in prostitution and drugs."
  —Jennifer Kent and Gary Rhodes, *The Cincinnati Post*

SOAP OPERA

The Inside Story of Procter & Gamble

Alecia Swasy

A Touchstone Book
Published by Simon & Schuster
New York   London   Toronto
Sydney   Tokyo   Singapore

 TOUCHSTONE
Rockefeller Center
1230 Avenue of the Americas
New York, New York 10020

First Touchstone Edition 1994

TOUCHSTONE and colophon are registered trademarks
of Simon & Schuster Inc.

Manufactured in the United States of America

10 9 8 7 6 5 4 3 2 1

Library of Congress Cataloging-in-Publication Data is available.

ISBN 0-671-89781-0 (Pbk.)

For Maribel Allison Swasy,

my mother and friend

Reporter's Note

P rocter & Gamble Company was invited to partici-
pate in this book but declined repeated requests for
interviews and substantive information. In January
1992 I sent a detailed outline of topics I planned to cover in the
book and requested interviews with senior management and others throughout the company. Bob Wehling, vice president of
public affairs, turned me down, saying the company didn't want
anything to do with the book unless it was written like *Moonbeams*, the highly sanitized company magazine.

P&G didn't really need an outline of the book; the company
had obtained a copy of my book proposal when it was sent out to
various publishers. It was leaked to an outside director from a
publisher that didn't buy publication rights. P&G officials denied that they had the proposal, even though Wehling and CEO
Ed Artzt could recite chapter titles and other information found
in the document.

P&G did agree, however, to verify certain facts if I submitted written questions. I tried that. The resulting answers demon-
strated that company officials weren't serious about the offer.
Even trivia proved too much to ask. For instance, I asked about
the Jif and banana and Jif and jelly sandwiches that were served
in the employee cafeteria. The PR department denied that the Jif
and bananas sandwich was ever served. But a menu from May
1985 lists the item for 75 cents. When asked about the team of

women P&G sent to newsrooms to dispel rumors about the dangers of Bounce dryer sheets, P&G officials insisted that never happened. Yet *The Wall Street Journal* reported the event back in 1975 and insiders from the department remember the visits. I asked who started the one-page memo. Wehling responded, "It may have been Plato." On other topics P&G officials simply offered no comment or denied information that numerous other sources inside the company confirmed.

The decision not to cooperate on the book was made by Artzt. He'd talked to the *Journal* for numerous stories and agreed to meet occasionally for off-the-record lunches. He knew from the bootleg copy of my proposal that his chapter was going to be called "The Prince of Darkness." He was angry about the title, even though he's had the nickname for years. Yet he decided that he would break his own no-comment rule and answer some questions about his career to help me "understand the nature of the beast," to use his words.

But he insisted that his answers would be in writing and piped through the public relations staff. That's awfully stilted and doesn't allow for follow-up questions. So we made a deal: If Artzt would sit for an interview, I would tape and transcribe his remarks and allow him to edit his comments.

To be sure, reporters don't usually allow people to edit their remarks. But anything was preferable to written answers filtered through the public relations department, which is well known for sugarcoating everything. Secondly, Artzt routinely suffers interview amnesia after his comments are published. By allowing him to edit the remarks, there was no way he could recant once the book was published. Furthermore, I knew from past experience that he's a talker and wasn't likely to delete much.

In June 1992 he agreed to my offer. During the next few months, Artzt granted me more than twenty hours of interviews in his office and home. Instead of editing the remarks, he added to the transcripts. He did delete a few lines, but they were comments about family or matters irrelevant to the management of P&G.

Despite his candor about his own career, Artzt refused to discuss certain issues, including his battles with retailers or the news media. Furthermore, he continually tried to thwart my work. He ordered his security officers to track down anyone who leaked information to me. I discovered that two months after I began this project. He bullied those who asked permission to talk to me. Some insiders said they were told they would be fired if they met with me. Yet Artzt referred to anyone who speaks anonymously as "chicken shits." Due to his record of searching for news leaks, most insiders aren't named in the book. Those who are named wanted their names to appear. Many gave up their weekends or evenings to discuss their jobs. Some insisted that we meet at night in Newport or Covington, Kentucky, because "we're less likely to be seen over there." Others tape-recorded sessions with intermediaries so their phone records wouldn't reflect a call to me if the Cincinnati police once again investigated phone records for P&G.

Even those who don't work for P&G were nervous about talking, because they have to live in Cincinnati. "If anyone knew I was talking to you," said one business leader, "I'd never serve on another board or do anything in this town." I was constantly amazed at how much P&G terrifies people in the Queen City and everywhere it operates.

Even retirees were hassled. Lou Pritchett, retired vice president of sales, wrote a letter to several of his former colleagues, asking them to talk to me. One forwarded the letter to Artzt, who ordered one of his lieutenants to "do damage control." Others helped too. Charlotte Beers, head of Ogilvy & Mather, secretly tape-recorded what was supposed to be an off-the-record interview. Then she mailed the transcript to Artzt. I found out about that when Artzt pulled it out of a file during one of our interviews. Other advertising agency officials received warning letters that contained thinly veiled threats about losing business if they talked to me.

Even after being castigated in the press for unethically obtaining telephone records in an effort to track down my sources, P&G went to great lengths to keep tabs on me. I know I was followed at some point when I was in Cincinnati during the summer of 1991. P&G kept me under surveillance elsewhere, too. When the company found out about planned interviews, PR officials would call the participants and encourage them not to talk. Even Howard Morgens, a former CEO, was appalled by that tactic. He told me that P&G's Wehling called him prior to my visit. Morgens said he didn't tell P&G that he was talking to me. It's unclear how P&G knew. Wehling said he'd heard it through the grapevine.

Artzt once asked his staff whether I paid people to talk. The answer is no. In fact, only one former employee asked to be paid for his information. As soon as he asked, I ended the interview.

The notes at the end of the book provide detailed documentation of published sources, along with background on interviews. To verify information, especially from unnamed sources, I confirmed the material with multiple sources within and outside P&G. Many of the unnamed sources have proved their credibility again and again, despite angry denials from P&G's PR department.

Besides more than 300 interviews with current and former employees, I interviewed scores of consultants, competitors, and customers. Thousands of court documents and more than 100 years of local and national news coverage were reviewed. In addition, a former P&G market researcher quizzed consumers about what they wanted to read in a book about P&G. The results provided a nationally projectable sample of responses, similar to what he did for P&G and other Fortune 500 clients. The results showed that consumers didn't want the same old fluff offered by the public relations department; they wanted the truth.

Contents

CONTENTS

Prologue

Around the globe Procter & Gamble Co. products take consumers from cradle to grave. Pampers diapers cover babies' bottoms and Ivory soap floats in their bathtubs. Crest toothpaste brushes their teeth and Tide detergent washes their clothes. Folgers coffee starts the workday; Duncan Hines cakes mark each birthday.

The Cincinnati company is an American success story. Founded by two immigrants in 1837 as a manufacturer of soap and candles, Procter & Gamble weathered world wars, depressions, and recessions to become a $30-billion global empire. By Wall Street measures, it is a star performer. A share of P&G stock purchased in 1986 had appreciated 159 percent by 1992—more than double the Dow Jones Average growth rate— and the company has increased dividends to shareholders for thirty-seven years in a row.[1] All told, P&G goods are found in 98 percent of all U.S. kitchens and pantries.[2]

Its management practices have shaped generations of U.S. business leaders. Harvard Business School teaches P&G's heralded brand-management system to each year's crop of MBA students. P&G's invention of selling competing brands has been duplicated to sell everything from Cadillacs to candy bars. P&G alumni are sprinkled throughout the world's leading companies. Many have become CEOs of Fortune 500 companies.[3]

But this Wall Street darling isn't all it appears to be. P&G

has manipulated and controlled consumers, competitors, and the marketplace, while hiding behind the "99$^{44}/_{100}$% pure" image cultivated by years of marketing savvy. This is a company obsessed with control. At times, P&G resorts to guerrilla tactics to squash competitors and anyone deemed an adversary.

I was one of those adversaries. As a reporter for *The Wall Street Journal*, I followed P&G for three years before deciding to write a book about how far the company goes to succeed. Two months into my research, I got my first real taste of P&G's tactics. Searching for news leaks inside the company, P&G convinced the Cincinnati police and Hamilton County prosecutor to get my phone records. Grand jury subpoenas for three months of phone records—about 35 million calls—revealed who was calling my Pittsburgh home or office. [4]

The phone episode is a schoolyard scrap compared to what others have endured. As I listened to the voices inside the company, I discovered that even those who land coveted, high-paying P&G jobs are sometimes harassed. This is not always the benevolent company that was once lauded for being the first to give plant workers Saturday afternoons off with pay and for sharing profits and providing generous benefits. Benevolence has been replaced largely by belligerence. One high-ranking manager who had just left a six-figure salary at P&G spoke of bosses seizing and scrutinizing personal medical records to pry into an employee's personal life. Phone calls are monitored on a regular basis. Those tales and others were corroborated again and again.

Like the radio soap operas P&G first produced in the 1930s, the company image is a fantasy. More than 300 interviews with current and former P&G employees in seven countries—ranging from plant workers and secretaries to two of its CEOs—tell the story of life inside the Ivory Towers. These are not disgruntled employees, as P&G labels anyone who speaks out. Many are highly successful managers who remain on the job. "P&G is like a wonderful ad campaign," said one manager. "But it's a product that doesn't deliver on its claims." Many compare it to a dysfunctional family.[5]

How P&G often bullies many of its 100,000 employees, plus thousands of others at ad agencies plus suppliers and customers, is in itself unsettling. But even more troubling is the far-reaching impact P&G has on American society, from Washington to small-town U.S.A. It dominates the airwaves with its $2-billion advertising budget. Grants from P&G lock up research projects at many major universities. P&G has been a pervasive part of our lives, its advertising equating the American woman's worth with the whiteness of her laundry or the moistness of her layer cakes. At worst, P&G sold dangerous products, such as Rely tampons, despite dire warnings. The company wins environmental awards, but it has destroyed a Florida river with dangerous dioxins and manipulated government officials in order to have its way. Those who have spoken out against the company have been harassed and beaten. One woman was raped, slashed, and burned for taking a stand against P&G. Those who dare to compete against mighty P&G are squashed by a battery of lawyers and costly litigation. Empire building has taken precedence over ethics.[6]

Too often the dark side of P&G is skirted, even by the news media. Likewise, the company has won only praise in the business world because of Wall Street's obsession with ratios and returns. For the first time, insiders help tell the complete story of P&G, without the Ivory finish. Their stories paint a very different picture, one far removed from the utopia relayed to young MBAs in business school or to consumers in advertising campaigns for its cabinet of goods. "We created a lot of folktales," said one brand manager. "They have little to do with reality."

What follows is a collection of stories based on those insider accounts of Procter & Gamble's world, previously so closed that it's been dubbed "the Kremlin." Each one illustrates a different aspect of P&G, whether it's controlling the city of Cincinnati or cracking new markets in Caracas. Each also shows that success often has a very steep price.

SOAP OPERA

1
Proctoids

Mary Jaensch remembers 1985 as the year both Hurricane Gloria and Procter & Gamble swept through her quiet town of Wilton, Connecticut. The storm passed, but the soap company wreaked havoc on her employer, Richardson-Vicks, Inc. Initially P&G seemed like a white knight come to rescue it from an unwelcome takeover bid by Unilever N.V., an Anglo-Dutch consumer products giant. The family-run company chose P&G and its $1.2 billion bid over Colgate, Pfizer, and Unilever because it had the best reputation in the consumer-products industry.[1] Richardson family members, including five who sat on the board of directors, felt P&G would be the best one to preserve the company begun in the 1890s by their forebears, who concocted a brew of menthol, camphor, and eucalyptus oil to make Vicks VapoRub. P&G CEO John Smale had started his career at Vicks, so everyone believed he would take care of them. Employees and family members hoped to preserve traditions such as picnics where everyone heard updates on product developments before playing tennis or watching old family movies. No one in the Richardson family, with its 135 members in five branches, was happy about the sale, according to relatives. But Dick Richardson, chairman at the time, told them to rest easy; they had "stayed a family" despite the sale.[2]

But P&G quickly broke its promises to leave the company

unchanged for five years. In fact, the status quo didn't survive even a year. Senior managers, including the family, were replaced by P&G employees. Or they were "boxed" between two P&G managers so they would learn to do things the P&G way. Those who left for competing drug or cosmetics companies were harassed with threats of lawsuits. "Vicks people were seen as viruses," said Mary Jaensch. "Small and insignificant."

She had to conform to P&G culture. Memos replaced informal meetings and she learned to keep her opinions to herself— they didn't count at P&G. "The decision to sell to P&G was made on a Sunday and it was announced on Monday," recalled Jaensch, then director of Vicks marketing. Immediately, P&G executives began to meddle in every aspect of the business. In one meeting, P&G executives reminded the Vicks sales force they were now "part of the biggest retailing service group in the entire country," she said. "They were totally insensitive to the fact that Vicks was proud of being small and lean."

Ed Artzt, then president of P&G's international business, would drop by the Connecticut headquarters for advertising copy meetings or product development sessions on a new Oil of Olay cream for sensitive skin. "He had no qualms about telling people their ideas were stupid," she recalled. "That's very un-Vicks." The smallest of decisions had to be approved by senior management because "the brass signed off on everything," she said. "There's tremendous pressure to do the process, which tends to wipe out your individuality. I had to buy hook, line, and sinker what P&G believes is right, or I wouldn't succeed in the organization. It was a slap in the face. That's when I truly understood I'd been acquired."[3]

Part of P&G's formula for success is shaping its more than 100,000 worldwide employees into "Proctoids," the nickname wags have given the blue-suited corps. Most come straight from college campuses, but an increasing number land inside P&G through acquisitions such as Vicks and Noxell. "They all get Procterized," said one former officer.

David Cullen, a former P&G brand manager and now a partner at New England Consulting Group, reflected, "P&G would take Michelangelo's statue of David, grind it down to marble dust, and reconstitute it into small ones. Everyone would be exactly the same and be suitable for display on your mantle. The concept is consistency and conformity."[4]

The culture inside P&G is a cross between the marines and the Mormon Church; the higher up you go, the more you know. A paternalistic environment strips employees of privacy and independent thinking. Medical and police records are scrutinized. Phone calls are monitored. Security guards tail managers on business trips. Those who show signs of disloyalty, such as considering a job outside P&G, become pariahs. "It's such an insular corporation," said one longtime manager. "If it had offices on Park Avenue instead of Cincinnati, it wouldn't be that way. But we're in the hinterlands and consumed by our own importance."[5]

The environment has long encouraged lifetime employment by offering hefty stock and benefit packages to those who stay for decades. Even secretaries can retire with more than a half-million dollars in P&G stock. But increasingly, P&Gers stay for a few years of Procter boot camp and then leave the strict culture to rise to the helm at competing firms. "People think it's like going to work at Candyland," said one manager. "You make good money and they take care of you for years. But it's a dysfunctional family."

It wasn't always this way. The roots of P&G's culture go back to 1837. Two brothers-in-law, William Procter, a candle maker, and James Gamble, a soap maker, set up shop in Cincinnati,[6] then nicknamed "porkopolis" because of its dependence on swine slaughterhouses. Candles and soap were made from the leftover fats.[7]

Procter, an Englishman, and Gamble, an Irishman, were Protestants whose faith guided their daily chores. Even during the Civil War, when P&G worked long hours to supply soap to the Union army, the plants would close on Sundays. "The law of the Lord superseded all else," extolled *Eyes on Tomorrow*, the company's official biography. "It was as if Procter & Gamble had a demanding third partner named God."[8]

Indeed, its most famous brand, Ivory soap, was named after Psalms 45:8: "All thy garments smell of myrrh, and aloes, and cassia, out of the ivory palaces, whereby they have made thee glad."[9]

Workers were treated like family. In speeches, company executives still remind employees how P&G came to the aid of stricken families when a cholera epidemic decimated Cincinnati in the 1850s. One Procter employee lost four of his sons in one week to the disease. He stayed home to care for his wife and other children but found his employer still paid him for the time he was off the job.[10]

P&G was the first company to offer comprehensive benefits to employees. In 1885 William Cooper Procter, grandson of the founder, decided the workers would be happier if they had Saturday afternoons off, with pay.[11] "He could've been like J. P. Morgan—lordly and separated from the people," said Hoyt Chaloud, who spent four decades at P&G. "He chose not to."[12]

By 1887 Procter had started a profit-sharing plan, which is the oldest in the country.[13] In 1915 it started a sickness, disability, and life insurance plan.[14] And eight years later the company began its promise of forty-eight weeks of employment a year. When the Great Depression of the 1930s forced other manufacturers to shut down, P&G soap plants remained open.[15] "Whenever we'd see smoke in the valley, we'd know they're making soap at Ivorydale," said Dan Ransohoff, the late Cincinnati historian. "It was wonderful. We knew somebody was working."[16]

William Cooper Procter got the credit for establishing P&G's reputation as a good place to work. He pushed the benefit plans, but he also walked the factory floors to talk to employees.

"His father made him go through all the jobs in the factory and office so he would know the company," recalled Vic Mills, who took a job as a chemical engineer at P&G's labs in the late 1920s.

Employees devoted their lives to P&G. The first employee, Barney Krieger, stayed forty-seven years.[17] Richard Redwood Deupree started as a teenage office boy in the company's treasury department in 1905 and became the first person outside the Procter and Gamble families to ascend to president and chief executive officer. He remained honorary chairman until 1974.[18]

"My dad died when I was twelve, so the company became a father image for me," recalled Lou Pritchett, who began his four-decade P&G career in 1953 as a Mississippi salesman for $275 a month. "I latched on to that institution. The company had a real personality."[19]

P&G had a reputation for taking care of its young as parents would. Gordon Wade worked in brand management. He remembers that his wife, Jill, was given carte blanche to take home a washer and dryer and anything else she needed from a local furniture store, despite the young couple's lack of cash or credit. "She told them I worked at Procter & Gamble," Wade said. Local merchants heard stories about how P&G always made sure bills got paid. The store clerk asked just one question: "Where do you want the stuff delivered?" Wade said.[20]

Even today, the fifth-floor cafeteria at company headquarters offers low-cost meals with company-made ingredients, such as Jif peanut butter in the Jif and jelly sandwiches.[21]

Getting a job at Procter isn't easy. The company's recruiters scour campuses worldwide. The company hires from all majors but recruits most heavily at the big business schools, such as Harvard, Wharton, Stanford, and Northwestern. In the 1960s P&G recruiters convinced Harvard to allow the company to pre-screen its job candidates' résumés, so it could interview only the best prospects. "It made recruiting fifty percent more effective," said Henry Wilson, known as the "dean of recruiting" for the fifteen thousand interviews he did for P&G. "If I hire one in ten, that's very successful." Some candidates are quite persistent: He recalls one student reapplying fifteen times.[22] At universities, professors say P&G gets quite indignant when the best students don't accept offers for interviews and even pesters faculty to lobby the reluctant students.[23]

P&G can't attract all the finance students that it wants, especially those at top schools. "We had trouble appealing to Harvard guys," said James Nethercott, a longtime chief financial officer at P&G. "We didn't pay as much" as Wall Street jobs. Starting salaries in brand management in 1991, for instance, ranged from $27,000 for someone with an undergraduate degree to $53,000 for a master's graduate from a top Ivy League school.[24] Another reason is that many people don't want to live in Cincinnati.

From the start, the P&G philosophy has been to promote from within, so hiring the right people is critical. Everyone starts in an entry-level job and works up through the ranks. P&G typically looks for good grades but also wants campus leaders such as presidents of fraternities or marketing clubs. "We look for the ability to make things happen; people who've risen from the pack," Wilson said. Eighty-one-year-old Howard Morgens, chairman and chief executive officer from 1957 until 1974, said he looked for character above all else:

"There's an esprit de corps that's intangible, and you can't describe it very much. Boy, you can feel it. People were proud to be doing what they were doing. And we wanted everybody in P&G—and this is the thing we looked for mostly in new hires— to have character. We didn't want any people who were just sharp and bright, pretending to be geniuses and that sort of thing."[25]

For his part, Morgens directed musical comedies and wrote short stories while at Washington University in St. Louis. John Smale, chairman and chief executive officer of P&G during the 1980s, showed entrepreneurial flair during his undergraduate years at Miami University in Ohio. He published pamphlets for sororities and fraternities called "Party 'Em Up" and "Party 'Em Up Some More." [26] Current CEO Ed Artzt played basketball at the University of Oregon. Susana Elesperu de Freitas, who now runs P&G's Peru subsidiary, was a geology and French literature major at Dartmouth and spent her summers digging rocks in Guatemala. [27] Doug Hall, who joined P&G in 1980, worked his way through the University of Maine as a magician. He showed up at his P&G interview with his magic show props in a trailer behind his Dodge Coronet. "I did tricks during the interview," he said. [28]

P&G always has more applicants than it needs. One tool used to weed out applicants is P&G's version of the graduate school admission test, known as the M Test. The test measures a candidate's interpretative and reasoning skills. Studies inside P&G show a strong link between high scores on the M Test and success on the job. Many of the high-scoring recruits are now in senior management, though exceptions exist: "Some who are now senior vice presidents had borderline scores," Wilson said. [29]

Some candidates earned distinction for more than just their scores: Kip Knight, who worked at P&G during the 1980s, found a typo in the test. "That really impressed them," he recalled, "but they really freaked that there was a typo." [30]

Managers report that candidates are often given personality tests to find out even more about them. One question asked is: What do you do in your free time? The multiple-choice answers include reading, exercise, and watching television. "We were told the only unacceptable answer was watching TV," said one manager who administered the test. "I thought that was hilarious, considering we're the number-one advertiser in the country and produce our own TV shows." The reason was that "P&G doesn't want any couch potatoes," she said. [31] P&G denies that it gives candidates a personality test.

P&G hires students for finance, manufacturing, marketing,

research, and sales. It has more than one thousand Ph.D.s, more than some universities. [32] But mecca at P&G is a job marketing and advertising its household goods. P&G invented brand management, the notion that different brands within a company should compete against one another as if they were from separate companies. The practice dates back to 1931, a few years after Camay soap was introduced as a competitor to Ivory and given its own advertising agency and manager. Today, among its massive collection of products, P&G in the United States sells eighteen different detergents, seven bar soaps, six shampoos, and three toothpastes. [33]

Brand management is also the center of P&G's competitive environment, where pressures are extreme. A fraction of those who join the brand-management system make it beyond a few years at the company. (One estimate puts turnover at more than 60 percent.) [34] Patrick Hayes started in brand management of bar soaps with about thirty-five others in 1972. Only six of the original group remained after three years. The rest were either fired, or they quit because of the pressure. Hayes himself lost thirty pounds from stress and skipping meals while assisting four different brand managers in sixteen months. "I finally started to gain back some weight because of all the going-away cakes," he joked. Eventually he switched to the public-affairs department. [35]

But those who do succeed can go to the very top. Brand management has launched the careers of most modern-day P&G CEOs. A P&G recruiting brochure shows brand managers as the hub of a wheel, and the spokes are everybody else in the company. [36]

There aren't any career brand managers at P&G; it's up or out. The career path begins at the level of brand assistant, where managers learn to devote their lives to peddling one product. Newcomers start on smaller brands, such as Dreft detergent, rather than the flagship brands, Tide, Crest, or Pampers. They spend their days analyzing the impact a ten-cents-off coupon has on a detergent's volume or planning the next promotion to move more goods. One P&Ger recalled how a brand assistant spent months trying to unload thousands of extra Polaroid cameras ordered by mistake for a promotion. "It took five years to get rid of all the extra cameras."[37]

Another former brand manager said he personalized the success or failure of his brands to a point that became unhealthy. When his brand lost a consumer test against a competing product, "I felt like I'd lost my job, or like I'd run over a pedestrian on the way to work," he said.

Internal competition is one of the biggest motivators. Brand managers treat the competing brands down the hall like their most bitter enemies at Unilever and Colgate. They share little information on brand promotions or advertising with one another. The competition remains intense under P&G's newer plan of managing brands by category rather than single-brand groups, in part because P&G overhires for those jobs and weeds out those who don't make the cut.

"People inside P&G compete with each other. Where do they learn it? From their boss, who competes with them," said one P&Ger. "It's not survival of fittest. It's survival of craziest," said another manager. "You are the abused and become the abuser as you move up the line."

Employees feel the pressure. A report on the top medical claims by P&Gers shows that three of four top claims were stress-related, such as heart attacks. (The fourth was pregnancy.) "If you're a good marketer, you read and learn from the statistics," said one manager. "But P&G doesn't know how to read that kind of data. Instead, if you have a heart attack, you're seen as not being strong enough."

Many women managers find the male-dominated, ultracompetitive environment especially oppressive. "There's a lot of macho here," said one woman. Management announcements used to be posted only in the men's rest room, not the women's. Women ate in a separate part of the cafeteria until the 1960s.

Another common practice of the time was the annual fashion show, at which women employees were asked to be hostesses and serve punch and cookies. "It was largely a white, male company until the early seventies, when somebody said, 'Hey, we need to hire some women, where can we find some?' " she said.

In the early 1970s women were finally allowed to follow the career path and advance from brand assistants to sales training like the men. The term "brand man" was changed to "brand manager." But once they climb the ladder, many women say the prejudice and the abusive, manipulative attitudes of male co-workers only intensify.

Women say they're chastised if they're not "mean enough" on the telephone to outsiders or their coworkers. It's important to sound like the boss. To fit in with the guys, one woman memorized baseball scores and batting averages, but they still didn't talk to her. It's worse for mothers; having a baby while working on the brand-management track equals career suicide. "Stick a fork in you," said one woman. "You're done." Another woman was told to take some additional time to be with her baby when she returned from maternity leave. Her supervisor wasn't eager to have her return, figuring she would be too distracted by motherhood.

Women report that despite clear achievements they are still bypassed by less qualified men. In May 1979 the EEOC sued P&G, prompted by complaints from women employees. The complaint said that P&G failed to allow women to accrue seniority and gain guaranteed employment status on the same basis as men. The practices dated back to at least 1966, according to the complaint. The EEOC office in Cleveland, which handled the complaint, said it was settled on a confidential basis. Despite such actions, apparently little has changed. [38]

Many women who receive the "outstanding" rank in their evaluations are leaving P&G. Some men and women at P&G say it's not a glass ceiling, "it's a concrete bunker." One company survey asked employees to rate on a scale of 0 to 100 whether they agreed that the best people were promoted. Another question asked whether women and minorities received equal chances. Both received scores below 20. One big problem is finding support from male bosses. "If you can't relate to men as a father or lover, you can just forget it," said a woman who worked in brand management. "It took me four years of therapy to realize that."

In 1987 management decided to investigate complaints by women in one P&G division, which at the time had no women in senior positions. When employees in that division were asked to rate the statement "I believe women and minorities have equal opportunities for advancement as men," they gave it a low score. After months of analyzing the survey data, P&G management decided to invite women in the division to discuss the problem. The topic for the lunch meeting was "What nonverbal signals are we sending, if any, that would lead you to believe that you don't have equal opportunities as everybody else?"

But the two male division general managers decided to hold the session at the University Club—one of Cincinnati's traditionally white, male bastions. The meeting took place in a private dining room because women weren't allowed to eat in the club's main dining hall. "We can't join this club, and they're asking us what nonverbal signals they're sending?" scoffed one woman who attended the meeting. "We had a field day with that one." Furthermore, the two GMs sat at the head of the table, rather than taking side seats among the women. The meeting didn't change attitudes in the division or elsewhere in the company, women said. "They don't want to deal with it," said one woman from the division.

The main dining room of the University Club remained off-limits to women until the late 1980s. General Manager Mark Ross doesn't recall when the segregation officially ended. Some women still dine in separate rooms "as a courtesy to their husbands," he said. The club's board has a woman member, and Ross estimates there are somewhere between ten to twenty women out of seven hundred members. The female members say they are mere tokens. To get in, an applicant needs a sponsor. P&G's senior executives still belong to the club. [39]

Procter & Gamble's insensitivity to its women employees persists. At a 1992 awards presentation, management gave out blue sports jackets to recognize top achievers in sales and marketing. The men all replaced their suit coats with the blue jackets as the audience cheered. The few women who were recognized got the men's jackets as well. But they just folded them over their arms and walked off the stage to the sound of polite applause.

As a result of the company's male-dominated culture, no woman has ever reached senior management ranks. Only one member of P&G's board of directors is a woman, Marina Whitman, formerly of General Motors. But like her male colleagues on the board, she does little to challenge management. This group, packed with members of its own senior ranks and sympathetic outsiders, essentially rubber-stamps whatever the CEO wants. While a handful of women now have the title of vice president, they are not considered senior officers who work with the CEO on business strategy. Asked to name his women vice presidents, CEO Ed Artzt can't recall all their names or jobs.

The P&G culture creates a disturbing and at times dangerous workplace for employees. Sexual harassment is tolerated throughout the plants and offices. A consultant who has studied P&G's culture in her work for the company notes that there is no consistent policy on dealing with sexual harassment. "It depends on whether the man is someone the company wants to keep," she said. Scores of women offered stories on how their male boss harassed them and then was promoted or moved to another department. One department had so many complaints—from women both inside and outside the department—that men and women in the department even warn women visitors to avoid being alone with the manager. One consultant reports that when she begins her P&G meetings, "the first question I ask isn't

'Who's the boss?' I ask 'Who is screwing whom?' They are like rabbits. It's considered a perk to screw people."

All of this makes women inside the company question how P&G ever makes those "most admired" lists in magazines or management texts. "When we see those lists, we look at each other and say 'what's going on at the least admired companies?' " said one woman.

Nor does P&G's culture embrace diversity. For all intents it remains a lily-white company, despite court orders to desegregate. In 1977 Judge Sarah T. Hughes ordered the company to come up with an affirmative-action plan for its Dallas plant. Hughes found that P&G gave blacks "the least desirable jobs." That plant was eventually closed as part of P&G's restructuring. [40]

As with other problems, there's little commitment from senior management to embrace diversity. "White men are strategically placed so they can learn what they need to learn to become a vice president," said Marjorie Bradford, a former public-relations manager. She recalls how former CEO Howard Morgens used to keep a book listing the names of young men in the company who showed potential. He either became their personal mentor or assigned someone else to help their careers. "That didn't happen to black folks," Bradford added pointedly. [41] It still doesn't. Floyd Dickens, Jr., a former P&G manager, said the company continues to have a revolving door for blacks because they lack mentors. "They get to midlevel or right above and they leave," he said. "There's no excuse to not have more minorities in decision-making positions." [42] As for black women, very few stay for more than a few months in sales jobs. "We lose one for every new one who comes in," said one manager.

One senior executive, Dick Nicolosi, didn't help P&G's reputation when he told a group of summer interns that P&G had "lowered its standards" when accepting blacks, and that's why the company lost so many. [43] P&G said it doesn't endorse the remarks made by Nicolosi, who left the company in 1992. P&G said it hires people who have qualifications to succeed in the business. Furthermore, the company said the percentages of women and minorities at nearly every level of organization are increasing.

But in a 1993 speech, CEO Ed Artzt acknowledged that the company has a problem dealing with diversity. "Young black managers I've talked with refer to it as the 'pain threshold'—the added burden that results from having one's opinions discounted, from failing to receive deserved credit or recognition, or having to work to a different standard than one's peers," he said.

Still, most say his words at the Martin Luther King, Jr., dinner were mere window dressing. Diversity programs, as well as many other training plans, have been gutted during Artzt's regime. One consultant said some plants still do some training but don't tell senior management. In his defense, Artzt said he has beefed up diversity programs, which were previously a lot of "singing songs and waving diversity flags." For starters, he's pushing a mentoring program and tracking minority progress against that of an average white male. He comes across as remarkably naive when discussing these problems, as if he just discovered the need to correct them. "This guy King was a pretty smart fellow," Artzt once commented.

The WASPy culture of P&G affects Jewish managers too. Former vice president of advertising Bob Goldstein used to visit all new Jewish managers and tell them he would try to help them along. "He felt so out of touch and isolated that he never wanted others to go through that," said one Jewish manager who joined the company in the late 1980s.

Many people who work for CEO Artzt don't realize *he's* Jewish. That's because he tells people he's a Methodist. Artzt, a six-foot bespectacled man, said his family decided to attend the Methodist church in Cincinnati largely because they liked the minister. He bristles at the notion that P&G isn't hospitable to Jews. "This company was founded by an Irish immigrant and an

English immigrant," he said. "They were people of pretty high character and strong principles. Down through the years, there have been people who didn't measure up to that standard and may have contributed to that kind of criticism. I don't know that." [44]

Much of P&G's oppressive culture stems from the tight controls placed on employees regardless of employees' race, sex, or religion. To succeed, you have to be compulsive and a workaholic. A consultant to P&G did a study on company managers and found that at least 40 percent of midlevel managers and above came from dysfunctional families, which made them extremely compulsive and controlling. People who come from that environment will "do anything to keep things smooth," the consultant explained. "That's why kids grow up and go back to drunk fathers and abusive mothers. They are still trying to get them to be real parents." When the consultant showed the findings to P&G managers, they confirmed the results. "The college recruiters said their requirement for hiring is to look for people who are more compulsive than themselves," she said. "That way they know they will succeed." [45]

P&G typically hires young, inexperienced employees, making it easier to mold them. It's an inbred society. Because all promotions come from within, no new blood ever gets into the family at the top. Conforming is more important than performing. "At Procter, if eagles fly alone, they shoot them down," said a former officer.

Indeed, even the architecture of its corporate headquarters sends a message about the company. The older office building is a fortresslike eleven-floor rectangle. When one New York marketing consultant moved to Cincinnati, she noticed the P&G building and asked, "Why is the jail in the middle of town?" The newer additions aren't much better. A twin-tower building added in the 1980s was immediately dubbed the Dolly Parton Towers. Tellingly, the windows in the round towers open into hallways, not offices. "It's indicative of a culture that always looks within," said Thane Pressman, a former brand man.

Inside the fortress, P&Gers learn it's a good idea to dress for success. Blue or gray suits are de rigueur. Managers are scolded if they dress either too well or too casually. One manager, the son of a tailor, was reprimanded for wearing suits that looked too expensive. Another was sent home because his boss said his shoes didn't match his suit. Some departments experimented with "casual Fridays," but most viewed it as sacrilege not to wear suits. A memo from senior management later banned casual Fridays because P&G feared casually dressed employees aren't as productive. "They think we'll all want to start playing Frisbee if we don't have suits on," quipped one manager.

In the 1970s women who wore pants were told to go home and change. Even today, women are discouraged from wearing pants to work. [46] The dress code extends outside the office as well. A *Cincinnati Magazine* article on climbing the corporate ladder offered the following tip from a woman at P&G: "Avoid showing skin—even during off hours." [47]

Management set the tone years ago for the look-alike policy. Walter Lingle, a retired senior vice president, remembers the "fashion police" patrolling the halls back when he joined the company in 1931. "We had a vice president in charge of keeping everybody straitlaced in their dress." The dress code consisted of blue suits and "none of this short-sleeved and sport jacket stuff," Lingle said. The vice president, Herbert G. French, once reprimanded one of Lingle's friends for wearing black-and-white sport shoes to work and sent him home. A couple of days later, the friend asked Lingle if he thought he'd be sent home again. "He showed me his feet—he'd worn two shoes that didn't match," Lingle said with a laugh. "I don't think they caught him." [48]

On occasion P&G has hired outside consultants to coach employees. A Cincinnati beauty college and a Florida consultant have trained some P&Gers on how to behave and dress.[49] Employees get haircuts whenever a boss says their hair is too long.

Many of P&G's tips are outlined in its twenty-four-page manual *You and Procter & Gamble.* "We welcome you as a new member of the Procter & Gamble family," begins the booklet, which covers even the most obscure details. For example, workers are reminded not to disturb other employees or visit other departments, except on official business. "This keeps other employees from doing their work and hinders your own," the booklet warns.

Promptness and neatness are also P&G virtues. Under the heading Good Housekeeping, a few simple rules are offered: "Always keep things in their proper places; space is provided for hats, coats and personal belongings." You're not supposed to eat at your desk, only in the employee cafeteria. (Another understood P&G rule is not to drink at lunch. If you have a drink, you're not to come back to work.)[50]

Employees aren't supposed to decorate their offices with personal artwork. However, managers are allowed to hang artwork issued from P&G's approved collection. One manager recalls that he was reprimanded for having his own lamp on his desk.

Two employees from brand management, Gordon Wade and Chuck Jarvie, poked fun at P&G's strictness by hanging a company-issued painting near brand assistants' desks with a sign that warned: DO NOT LOOK AT OR APPRECIATE THIS PICTURE. YOU ARE IN A CONTROL AREA FOR A TEST ON THE IMPACT OF AESTHETICS ON PRODUCTIVITY. "People would walk by and start to read it," Jarvie said. "Half snapped their eyes away and walked by."[51]

Occasionally the so-called creative people inside the company are humored when they decorate with non-Procter art. Personnel managers show those few unorthodox offices to job candidates "to show new recruits what a progressive place Procter has become," said one manager.

The size and location of your office depends on rank. For instance, you can tell someone's rank by counting ceiling tiles. A twelve-tile-by-twelve-tile ceiling marks the office of a brand manager, and it will have a window. [52]

Procter & Gamble strives for increased efficiency with relentless . . . well, efficiency. In 1985 the company testified before the Cincinnati Board of Health that it didn't want smokers to leave their desks to go to smoking areas because "if each employee who smokes takes six 10-minute smoke breaks per day, that adds up to one hour out of a 7½ hour work day. Mathematically their personal efficiency would be reduced by over 13%." [53]

There were even efficiency studies on the proper use of urinals. One study by the maintenance department determined that the two urinals located closest to the door were being overused. Maintenance workers chained them off, and men were told to use the other urinals. It was the subject of a company memo. The chains were removed when senior men in the company balked about the restriction.

The P&G cafeteria crew once videotaped traffic patterns around the salad bar to study how employees grazed. Nobody questioned this, for it was a "very Procter thing to do," said one manager. One former P&Ger recalls how a brand assistant came to his office visibly shaken because he'd just been scolded by another manager for not walking fast enough. [54]

There's even guidance on how and when to be funny at P&G. *Moonbeams*, the employee magazine, once offered an article on comic-relief strategies that benefit work, but without going too far. The story recommended that workers designate a bulletin board for "humorous contributions." "Post a comical picture or cartoon over your desk." Or better yet: "Pretend something is funny, even when you can't quite feel it." The article noted that the dining room offers "harmony snacks" to stir up fun in the cafeteria. [55] A harmony snack includes trail mix, chocolate-covered peanuts, and gummy bears.

Beyond the tight controls inside the company, the long arm

of P&G stretches well beyond the front door. Newcomers are coached on the "in" places to live in Cincinnati. Mt. Adams is home for scores of brand assistants. As you move up the ranks, it's a good idea to move into eastern suburbs such as Hyde Park. Senior management shoots for the bucolic suburb of Indian Hill. That's where retired vice chairman Tom Laco and current CEO Artzt are next-door neighbors. Living near other P&Gers makes life simpler. Since you're not supposed to talk about Procter business with outsiders, most P&Gers socialize together. Golf and fly-fishing are the politically correct hobbies of management.

Men inside the company are coached on how to manage their spouses so they behave like Proctoid wives. Elinor Artman was one of them. Artman graduated cum laude with honors in chemistry from St. Lawrence University, then attended graduate school at the University of Colorado. There she met her future husband, Neil. They married and moved to Cincinnati in 1955 so he could work as a chemist at P&G.[56]

The young couple rented a home in Greenhills and later moved to Wyoming, both suburbs of Cincinnati. "It's okay to live in Greenhills for a while, but then you're supposed to move to Wyoming or Indian Hill," Artman explained. P&G's conservative ways encouraged attendence at traditional churches: Episcopal or Methodist; nothing liberal, such as Unitarian. The Artmans had five children in ten years, so she filled her days with making beds and cooking meals. They lived in a Cape Cod house, and she joined the PTA.

P&G wives were told never to discuss how much money their husbands made. "There was an air of mystery about pay," recalled the soft-spoken Artman. "P&G was very good to us in a paternalistic, 'yes massuh' way," she said. Husbands had career paths to follow, but she describes the role of spouse as "wandering and worrisome." It was especially difficult for those who didn't have children.

Newcomers' wives joined "classes" of other spouses.

"When enough new people came to your neighborhood, eight would form a bridge club." Get-togethers featured a lot of "surface talk," as she puts it, with questions like "How are the children?"

Those women who joined charitable organizations such as the March of Dimes discovered problems among other P&G wives when they went door-to-door collecting funds. Many would answer in their nightgowns even though it was the middle of the day. "So many of them were aimless, stressed out, and even drunk," Artman reflected. "I couldn't believe this would happen to any of us." Artman was inspired to form a support group called Women Into Tomorrow to rescue what she calls "a lost generation of women."

She invited speakers into the group to discuss feminism, religion, and many other topics. "We had to learn new ways of being with one another," she said. "Not the P&G ways." Many of them began reading Betty Friedan's 1963 feminist classic *The Feminine Mystique.* Friedan "didn't write that book for us," Artman said. "She wrote it *about* us. She must have been peeking into my life."

The death of one of their children, in addition to other strains, shattered the Artmans' marriage; they divorced in 1975. At the age of fifty, Elinor Artman went to theological school and graduated in 1980. She is now a minister in Cincinnati—ironically, at a Unitarian church.

In Procter & Gamble World, it often seems as if the women's liberation movement that swept across America in the 1970s took a detour at Indian Hill. Many P&G executives' wives still tend families full-time. Profiles of executives in *Moonbeams* often feature their wives serving Duncan Hines cakes during the interviews. Many still report that they are scolded if they buy the wrong brands at the grocery store.[57]

P&G's upper echelon apparently wants to influence its employees' choices in politics, too. It's a predominantly Republican group. During the 1960 presidential campaign, company officials posted bulletin-board notices about a stop by John F. Kennedy at Cincinnati's Fountain Square, advising that employees leave at 3:30 P.M. to "avoid the traffic downtown." A week later a notice about a visit by Richard Nixon said employees could leave at 3:30 "to get to the rally in time."[58]

Robert Beeby, who worked at P&G in the 1960s, recalls how he was scolded by his supervisors for joining a protest march outside a downtown dinner at which Nelson Rockefeller, New York's Republican governor, was giving a speech. A P&G officer had escorted Rockefeller to the event and spotted Beeby in the crowd. "I was called in the next day and told, 'This isn't good for your career. You're making waves,' " Beeby recalled.

More recently, company officials make "strong suggestions" to managers about donating to various causes. Ethel Hughes, an executive secretary, said notices were sent to her bosses urging them to donate to various candidates and causes. "It's understood that certain things are built into your salary," she said. Employees at all levels are expected to volunteer for various community causes, and the company donates millions to charities like the United Way agencies. "You're supposed to do more than just go to church on Sunday," said Don Baker, a former package designer at P&G. P&G said it doesn't influence employees' charitable or political contributions.

The pressure to conform at Procter & Gamble is most apparent in its daily operations. One of the biggest differences Mary Jaensch noticed after P&G acquired Vicks was the lack of conversations. "If you didn't articulate an opinion at Vicks, you didn't have a future. They valued your opinion," she said. "At Procter, you never start a sentence with 'I believe.' It's always 'The data suggests.' And unless it's written down in black and white and supported by three rationales, it's untruth." Indeed, P&G keeps a collection of its best memos. Insiders say it's called *The Good Book.*[59]

Learning to write the P&G way takes years. Jack Gordon, a

brand manager on Camay, should win the prize for the most rewrites. In the early 1980s, the company tried a new soap formula to try to bolster the Camay brand, which had been losing sales for twenty-nine years. "Camay had dropped below a three-percent share of the market," recalled the former army officer. "After six months in test, I recommended that the company expand the product. But I was told we didn't have enough test market results." The test Camay was still growing—it had more than 50 percent of the soap sales in the test market. Gordon's bosses kept sending the memo back for rewrites. It took another six months before it reached senior management. At each level, someone would send it back with more questions. So Gordon kept revising the recommendation, all the while watching national sales of Camay drop. "But the management kept saying no, no, no," Gordon said. After a year of testing, "they finally said I could expand it. But I told them I'd lost interest and I walked out." He had rewritten the memo 460 times in six months. [60]

P&Gers learn that memos must begin with "This is to . . ." followed by "recommend," "propose," or "inform." "Typos were verboten," Thane Pressman said. At P&G, those are called "thinkos." And memos should never include words like "very." Problems are referred to as "challenges." "You can take the writings of five hundred men, and in twenty minutes, you can find the P&G guy," Robert Beeby said:

All memos are supposed to be kept to one page, plus exhibits. No one agrees who started the one-page rule; many memos break it. But Tom Laco, then vice chairman, told advertising managers in a 1981 speech that they should adopt a writing style similar to Abraham Lincoln's Gettysburg address:

"It was 275 words long. Two hundred of those words were one syllable. I want to declare that Abraham Lincoln English is the official language of the Procter & Gamble Co., and I want to encourage that kind of simplicity. . . . I think maybe 80% of the memos we write at P&G can be done on one page and maybe one exhibit."[61]

One ad manager tried to cheat a bit and typed the memo on a slightly longer sheet of paper so it would qualify as one page. He got busted when his boss noticed it was longer than all the other papers in his stack. "He was fit to be tied," the manager said.

Many people say the rewriting drills helped them become better thinkers and writers. Others insist it was just another method of control. A senior vice president said his boss sent his memos back because one sentence could be rewritten with seven words instead of eight. He was told to be more concise.

The capriciousness is also seen in annual budget meetings, where brand groups give progress reports on their products and plan for the next year. Failing to impress the boss during these sessions can cost managers their jobs. So they prepare for months, coaching brand assistants on the most obscure facts on their products. For instance, they should know the market share of Cascade dishwashing detergent in Charlotte, North Carolina, or the impact of various humidity levels on a bar of Camay. For days they quiz each other on every possible question that management might ask. They expect the worst because hazing is acceptable.

Brand manager Matt Ariker used to compile between two hundred and three hundred pages of data for budget meetings. "We spent eight or ten weeks straight preparing for that meeting," he recalled. "Saying 'I don't know' when asked a question isn't an option. It was simpler to say 'I resign.' "[62] Vice presidents and senior vice presidents gather for the meeting. Occasionally, even the CEO shows up. "It's like going to the mountain," one manager said. David Williams left his wife at the hospital when she was in labor so he could go to a Crisco Oil budget meeting. "She still reminds me of that one," he said.

All of this trivia goes into a brand book, the brand managers' bible. If you're smart, you keep it with you at all times, just in case you're stopped and quizzed by a senior manager. Nor do you let it out of your sight. Young managers are warned about the time a P&G board member strolled into the Crest brand manager's unlocked office, picked up his brand book, and took it to the CEO's office. The brand manager left the company shortly after that episode.

And it goes beyond brand work. One plant manager said he had to memorize the complete union contract and was quizzed on each clause in the 100-page document. In the sales department, managers are routinely grilled about their products' volumes as well as those of the competing products. One senior sales executive said his wife would quiz him late at night about brand volumes so he could spout off any number during meetings with managers. "I've seen people get decimated for not knowing every detail on why the Spic and Span business was up fifteen percent," said one longtime P&Ger. "They were reduced to tears."[63]

Some say the whole rigorous process builds character. "You have to know your business," said Rowell Chase, a retired executive vice president. He used to do leg exercises in his office while he worked "to keep the blood flowing where it should be." The eighty-nine-year-old retiree still dresses in a blue suit and small bow tie to go to an office just a few blocks from P&G headquarters.[64]

Others offer analyses that reinforce the analogy to a dysfunctional family. CEO Artzt likens the Procter experience to growing up in a family. "Your parents don't do everything right. And if you're lucky, they don't leave permanent scars on you. But if your parents spend your entire childhood being nice to you and ignoring you, maybe you'll be okay. Maybe you won't."[65]

Many say they're not okay in the troubled Procter family. For one thing, junior managers don't make decisions. Even the most basic decisions must travel to the CEO's office. Package-design changes, including details such as the font style and size or color of the letters, are approved by him. When John Smale was CEO, he spent hours deciding whether a new Camay package should be light pink or light, light pink. A Duncan Hines cake mix package change was rejected by senior management because the slice of cake in the photo didn't look right on the plate.[66]

Laco, concerned over the effect this could have on employee morale, warned his fellow senior managers in 1989, about P&G bureaucracy. Too many levels "have to be cleared to get approval," and it's hard to get "even good things done," he said.[67] Some dub it the "P&G minuet": three steps forward and two back. P&Gers at the company's Arkansas office, which sits next to a cow pasture, have another term for the bureaucracy. "This is the only office where we keep some of the bullshit outside," quipped one manager.

Even those who work together in the same department aren't briefed on projects unless there's a "need to know." P&Gers complain there's not enough information shared even inside the company with those who really do need to know. For instance, a February 1989 article in *Moonbeams* reported that 78 percent of the employees said they wanted to hear about the company and "how we're doing against competitors." In addition, 75 percent wanted to know more about how their salaries were determined.[68] Numerous managers said it's taboo to discuss pay. "Your boss would slip a note across the desk to tell you about a raise," David Cullen said. "You were supposed to be excited. Some would slip the note back across the desk and say, 'Hit me again, dealer.'"[69]

Much of the tight control on information stems from fear of competitors finding out too much. There are plenty of companies who would love to find out Procter's plans. Once, in 1964, a manager tried to sell a competitor a Crest budget book, which outlined the brand's plans for the upcoming year. He was arrested as he passed it to an undercover agent posing as the buyer in an airport bathroom stall.[70] But much of it is simple paranoia.

One brand group discovered just how paranoid P&G is when they went to lunch at a Cincinnati restaurant and discussed a commercial that was already on the air. Later that day the brand manager got a call from his boss to discuss "a security violation." He was scolded for talking about the ad at a public restaurant. "Security people go to restaurants because P&G is convinced that corporate spies sit around to hear our conversations," he said. "They hope by harassing you enough, you'll comply with the rules."

Some security officers do little besides ride airplanes between Cincinnati and New York and Chicago to make sure P&G and its advertising agency representatives don't talk shop in flight. Insiders tell a story of a manager who was caught doing company work on the plane. She was told she would be reported. Her response: "Fine. Can I get back to work now?"

In addition, employees are discouraged from making speeches. Only senior management and a select group are allowed to talk publicly on a limited number of topics: naturally, those favorable to company image, such as P&G's environmental efforts. Technical people are told not to join trade organizations out of fear they'll give away trade secrets. Almost comically, P&G tells employees that when traveling, not to use any luggage ID tags that will reveal where they work. [71]

Mary Jaensch recalls that after P&G took over Richardson-Vicks, managers were banned from attending trade shows. "Too much visibility," their new employer declared. When P&G bought the Charmin paper mills, it ended workers' longtime habit of sharing spare parts and supplies with a neighboring paper plant. And P&G built a stronger fence between the two plants. "They were told to never talk to those people again," said one engineer. [72]

Obsession with secrecy goes way back: some of the founding Procters dressed in hunting clothes and carried shotguns so people would think they were hunting quail rather than searching for the new site for a plant north of downtown Cincinnati. [73] Insiders say the paranoia deepened in the late 1960s and early 1970s, when antiwar protests erupted on college campuses nationwide. The burgeoning youth movement's uniform—bell-bottom pants, tie-dyed shirts, and so on; decidedly un-Procter & Gamble—made upper management "freak," said one ex-brand manager. "Managers were told to beware of people with beards."

Former agents of the FBI and CIA, as well as military police, manned the security department. P&G security is currently headed by James Jessee, an ex-FBI man whom even colleagues describe as overzealous. Certain security measures are necessary, such as checking packages before they're sent to the CEO's office. But there are extremes: People can be fired for leaving a company phone book on their desk. [74] Random checks are made to see if office doors are locked during lunch hour and that desks are clean and locked.

One manager recalled how a group of brand assistants played a joke on their brand manager by hiding all his desktop papers and leaving a note telling him to report to security to retrieve them. Security officers scolded him, calling the practical joke "a serious breach of security." He was ordered to turn in the scofflaws, but refused. Within four hours, the security staff had analyzed the typewritten note and narrowed it down to two different brand groups. "They knew the make and model of the typewriter," the manager recalled. P&G said its security department never received a report of the incident.

Morale surveys, which are supposedly anonymous, can come back to haunt managers. One manager, critical of the company in the survey, was reprimanded in an annual performance review for the remarks. "I looked at the survey for any codings or markings that would trace it back to me," he said. "They must have done a handwriting analysis to figure out who wrote it. After that, I always told my people not to be too honest in their answers." [75]

Internal phone calls are monitored too. One former officer

recalls how he was interrogated by his bosses because the phone records showed he had returned a phone call to a Wall Street analyst. P&G said it checks its phone bills in response to a specific allegation of a security violation. Others pegged as troublemakers believe their home and office calls were monitored. One of the women who was pushing for P&G to change some of its policies toward women concluded that her home phone was tapped in the mid-1970s. To confirm her suspicions, she called another woman friend and described a fake meeting that was going to take place later that week. The two women had met in person earlier to stage the call. They were the only two who knew the plan. When the time arrived, a male P&G manager showed up at the meeting place. "The phone call was the only way he could've known," she said.

Walter Donnellon, a longtime union leader at the Baltimore plant, said phone calls were monitored. P&G denies that it eavesdrops on employees' calls. Donnellon said video cameras are also used to monitor employees, especially at plants. In Baltimore, P&G brought in an outside agency to do video surveillance of people suspected of using drugs or alcohol. During the sweep, one employee was fired for taking some paper towels from the plant to clean off his windshield. In most P&G plant towns, the security staff also hires a local police officer to act as a "consultant" to the plant, helping build ties that give P&G access to a lot of police information, such as records of those suspected to be troublemakers.

A newsletter is sent to managers to caution them about any outsiders seeking information, such as headhunters soliciting job applicants for competing firms. One newsletter is called "Good Snakes–Bad Snakes," reporting good and bad security deeds inside and outside the company.

In one particularly chilling episode, security asked all P&Gers to report anyone whom they suspected of abusing drugs or alcohol. Managers were given an internal phone number they could call to leave a message to report the suspects. "They asked us to rat on people under the guise of you're helping them," one manager said in disgust.

Some officials say that security helps managers obtain employees' medical and police records if they want to check out somebody a bit more closely. "I was told by a personnel manager to get one of my people to the company doctors so we could figure out what's really going on with him," a manager said. "Another time he asked me to find out if someone was living with anybody." P&G said corporate security does not have access to police records and has never obtained medical records.

Often, the P&G security guards extend their patrol to outside agencies and suppliers doing business with the company. Ad agencies say they get visits by P&G to make sure no documents are left out on the desks and that binders of information aren't labeled with anything that would reveal any relation to P&G. "What's funny is they usually warn you that they're coming, so you have time to lock up," said one agency manager.[76]

One researcher who worked as a consultant to P&G said she was once followed by P&G security officers after she left the company offices. She learned this when she returned to work the next day and was reprimanded for not having the correct ID badge. "They actually admitted that they followed me home," the researcher said.

Lab workers are watched closely when working on new products such as olestra, P&G's fat substitute. Researchers said they had to account for every milligram used in home tests or face questioning about what they did with it.

Security measures such as surveillance can intimidate, accomplishing P&G's goal of keeping junior employees in line. Beyond that, P&G uses economic pressure to ensure silence in the senior ranks. Stock options are offered only to those managers who vow to keep quiet about company business. When managers reach a level high enough to receive options, they must sign documents promising not to disclose any information about P&G. If they break the vow, P&G revokes the options.[77]

* * *

Such tight control over people helps keep order in P&G's world. Patrick Hayes calls it "organizational fascism." "There's a piece of what Mussolini represented inside P&G," said Hayes, who spent twenty years at the company.[78]

But for those who are loyal, dress correctly, and are deemed a good security risk, the decades of hard work in brands can pay off with a senior management job. It can take twenty years to become a corporate officer and win a place on the hallowed eleventh floor. The P&G executive suite is as quiet as a museum. The wood-paneled walls are covered with oil portraits of the founders and former CEOs, and artwork by Cincinnati artists.

Office doors close with hidden buttons under the executives' desks. A separate elevator carries them to other floors without having to rub elbows with the rest of the staff. They communicate on "bongers," a sort of intercom, rather than walk to one another's offices. It's not very collegial.

A private dining room is one of the perks, although former officers often found the atmosphere uninviting. "There's no backslapping there. It's like attending a luncheon at a wake. But wakes tend to be louder," Lou Pritchett said.[79]

Still, it was important to show up for lunch there, others said, because you don't want to get blackballed in the fraternity. "I played basketball at lunch, and they told me to quit playing," Chuck Jarvie said.

Executives memorized stats on their business results before lunch just in case they were quizzed. First came the obligatory sports chat about the Cincinnati Reds or Bengals. "Between putting the swiss steak on your fork and getting it into your mouth you'd get asked, 'What's your share in Duncan Hines in St. Louis?' " Jarvie said. "It wasn't good for the digestion."

Formal meetings can be even more nerve-racking. Inside the board room officers have assigned seats, with the most junior members sitting farthest from the CEO. "When Ashley Ford, secretary of the company, closed those doors, God, Jesus, Allah, and Buddha were all in the room at the same time," Pritchett said. You are never late. And you speak only when spoken to. And the protocol here tells a lot about how control obsessed P&G really is. The minutes are typed in advance, long before the meeting even begins. "There are no surprises; everything is cleared in advance," Pritchett said.

"Talk pieces," the speeches read by each executive, must be submitted in advance to the CEO, who edits them. Even those get niggled with by the boss. "I used to spend twenty percent to thirty percent of the week preparing for that meeting," Jarvie said.

Relief comes when the food-and-beverage manager brings in a new product. Pritchett recalled one meeting where a new flavor of Pringles was offered to the officers. Even then, they offered no candor, telling management that the chips were "tasty." No decisions are made by the group; only the CEO does that. "This is not a democracy. It isn't even a benevolent dictatorship," Jarvie said.

Some in senior management recognize that the environment is unhealthy. And in recent times, a few have spoken out. Tom Laco, the former vice chairman, told other senior managers in his 1989 farewell address about outside consultants' warnings: The company "won't get the results it deserves until it changes its competitive focus from internal competition to external competition." [80] In an earlier speech, Laco also said: "I don't understand why we hire all these fantastic achievers and then are so parsimonious with our praise. That's ludicrous. We don't dispense enough valid, legitimate praise in our operation." He also said the company was operating at about 20 percent of its potential. [81]

Procter & Gamble is in danger partially because of the pressure that has accompanied its massive growth in the late 1970s and 1980s. Employee ranks swelled to more than 100,000 from fewer than 60,000, as P&G acquired more companies: Vicks, Noxell, Max Factor, and others. The John Smale era, basically the decade of the eighties, also brought increased competition from faster-moving competitors, such as Kimberly-Clark and Colgate. P&G stumbled in several categories, losing market share and profits. P&G was also stung in 1980, when it had to withdraw Rely tampons from the market after that product was linked to the deadly disease toxic shock syndrome. That scared P&G and slowed other research efforts. Furthermore, as P&G faltered in the marketplace, management tinkered with the reward plans for managers and plant workers. The emphasis shifted from long-term growth to short-term returns.

For instance, Smale developed a profit incentive plan that gave managers extra bonuses over a three-year period if they reached certain goals. Managers sacrificed long-term investment in some brands to make their profit forecasts. "On the surface, it worked," said Bill Morgan, a former controller. Bonuses were big, sometimes $50,000 or more. But the system created unrealistic goals, and long-term plans, such as research, were often ditched in favor of quick results. That pinched all areas of P&G but did serious damage in the weakest departments—the food-and-beverage division, for example. The incentive plan has since been cut back, but managers still get a large portion of their pay from meeting goals. [82]

At the same time, plant workers were losing their reward plans. By the 1980s the factory workers lost all their bonuses. It was a lot of money for $35,000-a-year plant workers, because previously they could earn an additional 40 percent of their pay for doing more work. "When the bonus changed, they were asking for same amount of work, but they weren't compensating us," Walter Donnellon said. P&G also began a major plant restructuring during Smale's years, closing sites in Chicago; Long Beach, California; and elsewhere. Many employees were offered transfers and buyouts. But the cutbacks were a sharp blow in a company that prided itself for offering lifetime employment. [83]

Another blow to morale came in the mid-1980s, when P&G

again violated its employment pledge. Engineers were fired and replaced by outside vendors. "People woke up and said, 'Uh-oh, I'm not guaranteed a job for life,' " said one P&G manager. "It caused an uproar in the company." Prior to those cuts, there was more of a consensus style of management under earlier CEOs, such as Howard Morgens. But Smale called the shots alone.

"I got the distinct impression that Smale didn't care for my point of view," said Morgan Hunter, a vice president who left P&G to become a senior executive at American Cyanamid and later became president of RJ Reynolds and Scott Paper. "Dictatorships are fairly efficient," he commented, defining P&G's major weakness as its "just give me the numbers" attitude.[84]

Cincinnati Post business reporter Jolie Solomon, who now writes for *Newsweek,* revealed the engineering cuts. But P&G's public relations department tried to downplay the significance of the move. "We tried to position it as a nonstory," said Marjorie Bradford, the former P&G spokeswoman. But, she conceded, it was significant. "It was an indication that the company was changing the tried-and-true reputation of 'once you work for P&G, you'll never have to worry,' " she said. "There was a quiet revolution going on."

The intense internal competition has only increased under Ed Artzt, who succeeded John Smale in 1990. The short-tempered and blunt CEO tells people he clears out the "deadwood" everywhere he goes. He did that while running the P&G international operation from 1980 to 1990. And it continues in the United States. In late 1992 Artzt sent a videotaped message to all employees to announce a major restructuring of the entire company to get rid of extra layers.

Insiders lament that staying employed now means that style often counts more than substance. And internal politics is eating away at the old meritocracy. "Now it's a burn 'em, churn 'em, and dispose of 'em mentality," one manager said. "We're supposed to hold people responsible for fifty percent business performance and fifty percent people development. But they manage the business side and forget the people side. People are dying to get in here, so they just say, 'We'll get more.' "

One of the more outrageous examples of poor employee relations involved Ethel Hughes, once Artzt's secretary, who'd been with the company longer than its venerable brands, Tide, Crest, and Pampers. In 1991 P&G fired her just weeks before her fiftieth anniversary there because she'd spoken out about the lack of decent raises for secretaries. After current and former managers complained about her dismissal, P&G promised to give her the benefits and profit sharing she would have received had she retired on her fiftieth anniversary, but they didn't want to give her the anniversary watch. Hughes eventually got it after she informed company officials she'd been talking to a reporter. She didn't want one that had P&G's man-in-the-moon logo on it, though. Why not? "I don't want to advertise for them."[85]

Very few are willing to speak up as Hughes did when she saw inequities. Those who manage to make it to the top usually do little to change the often abusive environment. "The attitude is, I'm not going to rock the boat," said Pritchett, the retired sales vice president. P&G consultants say they counsel managers who struggle with a "crisis of conscience" as they climb the ranks. "To stay, you have to be willing to be treated badly," one manager said. A consultant said an increasing number of P&G managers are sent to employee assistance programs for therapy. Some require medication such as Halcion or Thorazine. "We now refuse to make referrals to employee assistance programs when we work with them," the consultant said.[86] Many go to outside counselors for help. "Cincinnati is an overdeveloped market for psychiatric professionals," remarked one manager who sought therapy after leaving P&G.

Many of the best P&Gers tend to leave once they see what it's really like. About one-third of the top executives have left since the mid-1980s. "The best thing I ever did was leave the company," said Bill Morgan, for twenty-four years a P&G controller. "Thank God I'm doing it when I'm forty-eight, not sixty-two."

The exodus is quite a change from the good old days. For generations, P&G never lost anyone it wanted to keep. Junior marketing people began to leave in the 1960s after some left to open their own consulting firms. Now there's a cottage industry of ex-Procter managers, especially in Connecticut. New England Consulting Group and Marketing Corporation of America are full of ex-P&Gers.

The first senior executive to leave was Jack Hanley. When it became apparent that he wouldn't become P&G's CEO, Hanley left to become president of Monsanto. Since then, P&G has lost several vice presidents to other companies. Increasingly, managers at all levels leave after a few years of P&G training because they grow weary of the bureaucracy and manipulation of their lives.

In many cases you're asked to clean out your desk as soon as you submit your resignation. If you're deemed a valuable employee, senior management may try to convince you to stay. "It's like the Mafia," said one manager. "To leave is to display a lack of loyalty, even if you do it for good reasons." P&G rarely calls another job offer a good one, and employees typically face ostracism once they announce they're leaving.

Most companies look at P&G training as better than an MBA. But some ex-P&Gers say it can actually be tough to find a great job if you have *too much* Procter training. Those with ten to twenty years at Procter are often seen as damaged goods by other companies. Employers want P&G "to sort through the cream of the crop and give them good introductory training," said one former officer. "But they don't want robots."

But many graduates rise to great heights outside P&G. The alumni roll includes several dozen CEOs and presidents of companies, among them: Robert Beeby, now retired as head of Frito-Lay; Chuck Berger, president of Weight Watchers International; Jack Balousek, president of the advertising agency Foote, Cone

& Belding; and Chuck Jarvie, who became president of Dr Pepper and now runs his own company in Dallas. Kraft General Foods, Kimberly-Clark, and Johnson & Johnson are full of one-time P&Gers.

Some, such as Dean Butler, leave to follow their entrepreneurial dreams. Butler left to found LensCrafters, a successful chain of optical stores, which he later sold to U.S. Shoe Corp. He now runs a similar chain overseas. "If I'd stayed at P&G and been given wings, we could've done some great things," Butler said.[87]

Doug Hall, who brought nine new products to market at P&G in 1990, took his invention talents to his own firm, Richard Saunders International, named after Benjamin Franklin's pen name. "I wanted to be more like Procter and Gamble were when they started the company," he said.[88]

For some of those who leave, the P&G ties remain strong. John Thomas, an executive recruiter for both manufacturing and marketing, has compiled a directory of more than 1,200 P&G alumni and their current jobs. The group holds occasional reunions. The first one, in the mid-1970s, was hosted by Ted and Vada Stanley, who met and married while at P&G. At their Connecticut home, a giant bar of Ivory soap floated in the pool. Waiters wore T-shirts with pictures of past CEOs such as Howard Morgens and Neil McElroy.

Ex-P&Gers often get a call less pleasant than the one from the alumni reunion committee—from P&G's lawyers. Those who leave for competing firms are harassed and threatened with lawsuits. William Willis, owner of an executive search firm in Greenwich, Connecticut, recalled how a client who tried to leave P&G for another household products company was harassed. "He knew in advance what to expect, because his new boss also was a P&G alumnus," Willis said. "Procter sent out the senior partner at a New York law firm" to warn him about not leaking company secrets to his new employer.[89] At times the talent drain has been severe enough for P&G officials to warn neighboring

Cincinnati companies not to contact their employees. [90] P&G denies that it hassles employees who leave. The company said it does require employees to live up to agreements signed to not engage in competitive employment for a certain period of time.

Some former employees are sued to keep them from divulging "trade secrets," a category quite broad under P&G's definition. Consider Douglas Cowan. After twenty-seven years in product development, he left P&G for a job as vice president of research and development at Drackett Co., another Cincinnati firm, which makes Vanish, Drano, and Windex. P&G filed suit in July 1983 to stop him from taking the new job. [91]

P&G claimed Cowan had access to trade secrets and accepted stock options while at the company; therefore it had a right to stop him from going to work at Drackett for at least several years. The suit sought unspecified damages.

Lawyers for Cowan said in court documents that the majority of P&G employees who have access to trade secrets don't sign any noncompete clauses. Besides, by P&G's own definition, Drackett isn't a primary competitor, according to court documents. Drackett's main products are drain openers, air fresheners, and furniture polishes, among other things. P&G asserted that Drackett's patent activities showed increasing interest in dishwashing detergents, bleaches, and liquid detergents.

In addition, P&G's definition of competitors is too broad in scope. When Cowan resigned, P&G voided his stock options and withheld compensation equal to about 25 percent of his annual pay and threatened to sue to "castigate and humiliate him as an example to other P&G employees and the general public," according to court documents. In October 1983 the court dismissed the lawsuit after the two sides reached an agreement.

Insiders say some who want to work elsewhere simply stay at P&G because their new employer couldn't afford to take on P&G's platoon of lawyers. One former officer was threatened with a lawsuit if he went to work for another consumer products concern, so he switched job plans. "There is implicit and explicit pressure that you can't work anywhere else without P&G taking legal action," the officer said. "I was basically told I could sell shoes in Peoria, but be careful about it. From P&G's perspective, they pretty much own you."

Morgan Hunter, the former vice president, describes his final days at P&G as "the most unpleasant experience of my business career." He told CEO John Smale that he planned to meet with the American Cyanamid board to discuss a job. Smale ordered him not to; he considered Cyanamid a competitor for its product Pine-Sol, which to Smale's way of thinking competed with P&G's hugely successful Comet cleanser. Outraged, Hunter resigned immediately. "It was a horrible experience," he said.

Another manager tried to take a job with a supplier, but his bosses said all contracts with that company would be terminated if he left P&G. "I couldn't be responsible for them losing that money," he said. So he stayed at P&G. "That was the day my career went into hibernation." P&G said it doesn't threaten people who attempt to leave. But a company spokesman said the company does have a policy about suppliers recruiting P&G employees. "We don't recruit suppliers' employees and we expect them not to recruit our employees, as this can create conflicts of interest and concerns about the handling of confidential business information."

One woman, whose husband left P&G for a job at another personal care products company, said her family was harassed. For starters, P&G sent her husband a thirty-five-page document, threatening to sue him for crimes "he might commit" against the company, she said.

Eventually, P&G and the ex-employee reached an agreement, which stated that he could not work on certain products for his new employer. But even after the settlement, he was alerted by friends inside P&G that he was "under surveillance." His wife became frantic when the family's home was photographed by a man in a white van. "I was too frightened to believe P&G was behind this," she said. "It was too bizarre for a respectable company, with a good name built on the caring family image, to condone, much less finance."

The family hired a private investigator to check for bugs or wiretaps at their home. They learned the phone had been tapped, she said, adding, "That was a very sad day for me." [92] P&G denies that it has followed, photographed, or wiretapped former employees.

It was a sad day too for Mary Jaensch when she ended her eleven-year career at Richardson-Vicks after Procter & Gamble's takeover. But looking back, she's glad she did. "People tell me how young I look now that I've left," she said. [93]

2
The Prince of Darkness

After seven months of sales training in Los Angeles, twenty-four-year-old Ed Artzt packed his wife, Ruth, and their two baby daughters into his black-and-red Nash Rambler for the trek to Cincinnati. He was moving to his first brand-management job, on Dash detergent.

The newspaper reporter turned soap salesman was determined to make a good first impression at P&G headquarters. He knew the company was planning one of its first national coupon mailings to consumers, so he figured he should check on retailers' stocks of detergents and soaps as he drove cross-country.

The summer of 1954 brought a heat wave across the family's route through Nebraska, Iowa, and Illinois. The trip took five days because Artzt stopped at sixty grocery stores to talk to managers and check the back rooms for P&G goods. "I'll be back in a minute, honey," he'd tell Ruth as he headed for the grocer's front door. She would wait fifteen minutes or longer with her one- and two-year-olds in 105-degree heat. He didn't leave the car's air conditioner on—that would have burned up the Nash's engine.

After the first few stops, Artzt began to worry about the supply of P&G goods. The coupon mailing would hit after P&G's summer factory shutdowns and sales vacations, and stocks were already low.

When he arrived in Cincinnati, he reported his findings to

his new bosses. "They had never seen anyone conduct a national store check before," he recalled. "I was the only one on earth who had an up-to-the-minute reading on what our store stocks looked like across the country." It was too late to correct the problem, but Artzt's research taught P&G never to mail coupons so close to shutdowns and vacations. "Only a maniac would've done that," he admits. He describes the trip as his wife's "greatest horror"; supermarket parking lots still give her "a cold sweat." She cheered later when the Nash Rambler was destroyed by careening by itself down the driveway into a tree.[1]

As in the trip cross-country, Artzt has been nonstop in his quest to succeed at P&G, regardless of the toll it may take on those around him. To many, the brand man who made it to the CEO's office personifies what's wrong with P&G these days: success at any price and too little attention to people. When Artzt took over as chairman and CEO in 1990, morale plummeted as employees learned why the new boss was nicknamed "The Prince of Darkness."[2]

A look at Artzt helps understand many CEOs and what many do to make it to the top in corporate America. He can be Dr. Jekyll or Mr. Hyde, depending on his mood. There's a self-effacing, funny, and compassionate leader who sends get-well notes to ailing retirees and sympathy cards when a manager has a death in the family. And he often pushes himself harder than anyone else. But there's the dark side of him, the side that seeks revenge and terrorizes those around him.

There's a bit of hypocrisy in this portrait. Consider that Artzt earned his stripes taking the midwestern soap company into foreign lands, yet he openly mocks other cultures. He has referred to men of the Middle East as "guys who wear towels on their heads."[3] He lectures managers about doing their best, yet publicly shreds those who disagree with his ideas. He espouses a belief in the First Amendment and the need for corporate conscience, yet he monitors phone calls to make sure employees aren't leaking information to the press.[4] He admires Attila the

Hun. The barbaric leader's idea of killing those who weren't loyal gives Artzt what he calls "a warm feeling."[5] Subordinates are told not to worry about rank, just make good business moves. Yet he meddles in minutiae, even rewriting employees' advertising copy for toothpaste.[6] He champions diversity with a mentoring program for blacks and women. But insiders say that large numbers of the company's top-ranking women began looking for new jobs after Artzt took over. P&G remains as white, WASPy, and male as ever.[7]

"I have seen Ed be the single most supportive, charming, helpful, and understanding guy in the world," said Alex Keller, who worked for Artzt. "I've also seen him peel the skin off of people a strip at a time and love every minute of it."[8]

The sixty-three-year-old CEO has made some savvy business decisions, such as cutting unprofitable brands, which helps the company's bottom line. But insiders fear that his drive for short-term results so as to achieve his goals before he retires has mortgaged P&G's long-term health, especially in beleaguered U.S. markets. The rank and file hope that popular P&G president John Pepper will still get a chance to run the company when Artzt steps down. The other contender is Durk Jager, who the CEO tapped to run the U.S. operations. Together, Artzt and Jager terrify many and stifle good work. "There's a fair amount of fear in the organization," said one veteran P&Ger. "You keep your nose clean and stay in the middle. Nobody will get you there."[9]

Eventually, however, the disenchanted troops may be the undoing for Artzt and others. Even the CEO has lectured about the dangers of being an unpopular leader. "If people don't like you or don't respect your character," he told a group of students at Wharton Graduate Business School in 1988, "they may help you fail, no matter how brilliant you are."[10]

Edwin Lewis Artzt was born April 15, 1930, in Manhattan, the eldest son of William and Ida Artzt.[11] His grandparents were

Austrian Jewish immigrants who worked as shopkeepers in Philadelphia. A musical prodigy, William Artzt attended the prestigious Royal Music Academy in Vienna at age fourteen. After he arrived, World War I broke out, and Austria interned William because he was an American citizen. Instead of prison, he was allowed to play in the State Opera. But he was still a prisoner of war. The violinist spent three years in captivity before he was released. He contracted rheumatic fever, which left him with an enlarged heart and problems for the rest of his life.

When the war ended, Artzt went to New York to play in the New York Philharmonic Orchestra. But as tastes changed, he switched to dance-band music, playing in shows at the fashionable Waldorf-Astoria Hotel. His music was broadcast live over the radio. Ida Lichtenstein spotted him on stage there one night in 1925. The daughter of a Russian army bandmaster, Ida had grown up practicing the piano and attending the Juilliard School in New York. She accompanied opera singers at Carnegie Hall. Ida and William married and had two sons, Ed and Peter.

When Ed was seven years old, the family moved to Los Angeles, which was fast becoming the hub of the radio industry. They bought a $7,000 house in the still sleepy suburb of Beverly Hills. The musicians' union had a strict one-year residency rule that kept Artzt from working in his profession temporarily. The family lived off their savings, and he spent the time composing new songs and making records. "I admired his courage in pulling up stakes, moving his wife and two kids to California," his son said. "He thought his long-term career would be there."

The house was always full of music. William Artzt often took Ed to the Hollywood Bowl to watch his New York friends perform. His father played with the best, including Benny Goodman, Glenn Miller, and the Dorsey Brothers. He also played for Frank Sinatra's performances, which the youngster would watch from the wings. "We'd go backstage, and they'd exchange old band jock stories about the good old days," he said. "I can remember as a kid being awestruck that my dad was buddies with these guys."

As glamorous as the world of entertainment seemed, the younger Artzt saw how hard his father worked, and it made an impression. His father often worked on musical scores late at night. "I'd leave for school in the morning and he was still at the piano," Artzt recalled. His parents tried to get their son hooked on the piano too, but Ed preferred basketball to music lessons. He'd often stay in the driveway as late as 2 A.M. until he met his goal of shooting twenty-five baskets in a row.[12] The neighbors would complain, but his mother would defend him, pointing out, "At least he's practicing."

Artzt revealed a competitive drive even as a youngster. He and other neighborhood kids would ride their bikes for miles to other parts of Los Angeles in search of a basketball game. They'd bet 25 cents each on the game. "I remember how good it felt to whip those guys and drive home with two bits of their money in my pocket," he said.

He got his first break when his freshman basketball coach at Beverly Hills High School told him he would start the second game of the season. But a few days before the game, Artzt became bedridden with a cold. "You just forget about playing in that game," his father told him. "You're gonna get pneumonia if you try it."

Artzt still had a fever the day of the game, but he couldn't stand missing it. He got dressed, jumped out his second-floor bedroom window, and rode his bike to the high school gymnasium. He played well, despite his illness. As he dribbled toward the basket late in the game, he looked up and saw his father glaring at him from the bleachers. "I just froze," Artzt said. But even his father got caught up in the excitement of the game, which Beverly Hills won. He didn't punish his son. "I wasn't going to be denied," Artzt said. "If I died on the floor, that was okay, as long as I got there. I remember that feeling. It was the highest high I think I've ever had."

He says he was as "difficult a teenager as anyone." Artzt and his father didn't communicate very well, but he praises his mother for always giving him encouragement. "My mother always told me I was great, even though I wasn't," he said. "She filled those up-and-down periods when growing up."

As a ball player, the boy in the number 9 jersey thought he was invincible—until a championship tournament in his senior year. The team had two games in one day. In the first one, he scored twenty-three points against San Bernardino. [13] After the game, Artzt made the mistake of drinking a lot of milk for lunch. His stomach cramped, and he didn't play well in the second game. "I couldn't hit my butt," he recalled. The team lost. Basketball was a big deal at Beverly Hills High. Forty years later at a class reunion, a classmate scolded Artzt for drinking the milk. "I've never forgiven myself for that," he said.

Artzt was a boy of varied interests. He became sports editor of the high school newspaper, *Highlights*. That proved tricky during basketball season, when he'd play the game and then write the story about it. "Occasionally I was confronted with being the high scorer of the game," he said. "I learned about conflict of interest."

As the teenager considered his future plans, his father pushed him to enroll in West Point. A friend had gone to military schools, and the elder Artzt thought that would be a good path for his son to follow. He brought home books about the academy and souvenirs from an Army–Notre Dame football game. But after World War II ended, the idea of a military career lost its appeal. Besides, the younger Artzt already had plans of his own.

He took a journalism class during his senior year and got hooked on writing. He often profiled the people he met backstage with his father. By then, his father was the musical director for CBS Radio's "Blondie" show. Ed's story about Arthur Lake's portrayal of Dagwood Bumstead caught the eye of his teacher, Romaine Pauley. She secretly entered the piece in a journalism scholarship contest. It won first place. "He wrote with a freshness and vigor and a feeling of suitability," said Mrs. Pauley, now ninety-two years old. "He didn't use proverbial terms or worn-out clauses that children in high school are apt to do or the things they learned in advertising. I could always count on him for a novel idea. I think that's the secret to his success." [14]

Artzt credits her with his decision to attend journalism school at the University of Oregon, where he also received a basketball scholarship to wear jersey number 12 on the freshman team of Fighting Ducks. He pledged Sigma Alpha Mu, a Jewish fraternity. There was little choice for him because "in those days, we had segregation on campus," said Larry Black, a fraternity brother. "Ed was very gregarious. He would always go to the dances." [15]

One popular dance was the nickel hop, where men paid 5 cents per dance at the women's dorm. Ruth Nadine Martin, a blond freshman, was at the October dance. "I spotted Ruth at the first dorm I visited," Artzt remembered. "And that was it." The couple met for coffee a couple of days later. She invited him to meet her family at Thanksgiving. His father had died of heart disease that fall, raising questions about whether the nineteen-year-old student would return to campus or go back to Los Angeles to help his mother, who was raising his twelve-year-old brother, Peter. The young couple decided to get married in May 1950, just in case he didn't return to school.

Ruth dropped out of school, but Ed stayed in the journalism program, thriving in both advertising and writing classes. The most valuable class, he found, was radio newswriting. Students were given twenty minutes to write a five-minute newscast, a skill that helped Artzt write concisely.

His basketball career never took off, though. He didn't make the varsity team. Instead, his spare time was devoted to KWAX, the university radio station, where he worked as news editor. The couple also had their first child, Wendy, during his senior year.

After graduation in 1951, Artzt considered a career in broadcasting and interviewed for a job at an Oregon station. They recorded his reading of a script and played it back for him to hear. "*I* would've turned me off," he said. So the young family moved back to live with his mother until they could afford their own apartment in the San Fernando Valley.

Artzt was confused about what career to pursue. He enjoyed writing, broadcasting, and advertising. He decided to try them all at once. His mornings were spent at the *Hollywood Citizen-News,* where he worked as a copyboy and sportswriter. On weekends he worked as associate producer at a local L.A. TV station. He designed stunts and ordered props and wardrobes for shows. Children filled the audience for the show "Hail the Champ," a children's game show. Artzt threw candy bars at them so they would scream on cue. For the show "Wedding Bells," Artzt recruited couples to get married on the air, complete with a fake wedding cake that wouldn't melt under the hot lights.

A public relations firm provided the gifts for the shows, so he also worked part-time for the owner. In that job he delivered prizes for other programs, including "Women Are Wonderful." That introduced him to a fourth job. Grace Glasser, CEO of the Glasser-Gailey ad agency, owned part of the latter show and asked Artzt to write ad copy.

His workday began at about 5 A.M., when he unlocked the newspaper office. Ruth had to rise at dawn to push their black 1947 Ford down the driveway as he tried to start the engine. It belched so much black smoke that the *Citizen-News* used it in a feature photo about L.A. smog. Ruth was not amused by this early-morning ritual. She cursed at him until the car started. "She always had a volatile temper," Artzt recalled. "Her anger was probably what started the car. The goddamn car wanted to get out of there." Eventually the transmission fell out on the freeway.

Artzt worked sixteen hours a day, seven days a week. He often took Ruth with him when it was his turn to write the paper's theater reviews. All reviewers wrote under the pseudonym Lowell Redeling. The senior writers reviewed the hit shows, but Artzt got to cover the comeback of Pinky Lee, a tired burlesque comic. "He was sort of mediocre," Artzt said. "But I felt sorry for him, so I wrote a nice story." Ruth would sleep on the city desk as he worked.

Friends didn't understand why he worked such long hours, but he was running his own test market of careers. "It was a joy to be busy," he said. "I can do things all at once. I'm still doing it. And I always expected others to do that." One day the newspaper editor told him that one of the sportswriters was quitting. He could have a full-time reporter's job. "I went home and I was really sick," he said. "I had to make a decision." He decided to turn down the job and focus on his advertising and television jobs.

The TV shows were later canceled, so Artzt was left with the agency work. His days were spent writing ads for used-car lots and peanut butter. The creative inspiration at the agency wasn't too great: He was given a jar of peanut butter and crackers and told to write. He wasn't even allowed to go to the used-car lot to see what he was writing about.

He decided that he needed to find a better environment to learn advertising and marketing. Artzt's uncle Charlie knew he was restless and showed him a *Los Angeles Times* ad for job openings with Procter & Gamble. "I never would've seen it if it hadn't been for Uncle Charlie," he recalled.

Artzt applied and got the job. His previous work experience allowed him to skip the entry-level brand assistant post, so he started with sales training in December 1953. One of his first assignments was a campaign to get more stores in L.A. to buy more full-page ads to feature P&G brands. The sales units competed to see who could get the most. When Artzt saw the dull promotional materials for the detergents, he designed his own posters. He cut out the Ivory babies from the bar soap labels and put miniature boxes of Oxydol, Tide, and other detergents in their hands. He took the pictures to the Glasser-Gailey agency and asked the art director to paste them to a clothesline. He called the campaign "P&G's Wash Day Sale." He paid for the printing himself and gave the other salesmen the posters. "We sold more full-page ads than anyone else," he said.

He proudly wrote of his success in a memo to his Cincinnati boss. His creativity was rewarded with a bureaucratic and stifling response. The boss scolded Artzt for using his advertising background to create materials for the sales department. "It might have offended someone," he rumbled. He was also mad that Artzt hadn't cleared his use of the Ivory babies with the legal division. "That goes on in big companies," Artzt reflected. The little guy comes up with an idea. It sold a lot of soap. This guy wanted to put me back in my box," he said.

After sales training, he moved his family, including a second daughter, Karen, to Cincinnati. He was quickly noticed for his national store check and assigned to his first brand, Dash detergent. Moving from the West Coast to Cincinnati was an adjustment. "I was one of the Californians who didn't fit into this environment," he said. Coworkers jokingly called him a "hothouse plant."

One way he tried to fit in was to dress the part. Like the rest of the men, Artzt wore a fedora, but colleagues laughed when he walked in with his new hat. Each night he'd find it crumpled on the hat rack. "Somebody is mangling my hat," he complained to his boss, who just laughed at him. On the third day, there was a note attached to the hat. "I did it. Signed, the hat queer." Artzt stopped wearing the hat to work.

Another concession that helped him fit into the conservative P&G culture was his religious preference. Despite Artzt's Jewish heritage, he shunned all aspects of Judaism. Instead, he said his family attended a Methodist church.[16]

Besides the pressure to conform, Artzt realized early in his stay that this job might prove too difficult. The problem was math. He was given the task of calculating a triple-correlation model about the development of automatic washing machines, brand development, and sampling investments. He asked for help from a fellow brand man, who had a background in math. "It's just a simple differential calculus problem," sniffed the other manager. Artzt didn't excel in trigonometry, much less calculus. "It was a chilling thought," he recalled: "I have made a mistake. I've gotten in over my head."

His boss showed him that it was merely simple math, not calculus, and he completed the task. "Every young P&Ger has an experience in those early months," Artzt said. "You come in full of enthusiasm and confidence, and you run into something."

Senior managers were relentless about subordinates knowing every detail of the business. The tough environment prompted some to coin the phrase "mind rubbing" to describe the intense work. "Mind rubbing is what two wild elk do during the mating season when they meet out in the forest," Artzt explained. "They stand one hundred meters apart and at full speed, their two heads collide. That was the early version of mind rubbing at P&G."

When P&G had a smaller staff and headquarters building, everyone ate in a small lunchroom. Over the years, CEOs Richard Deupree, Neil McElroy, and Howard Morgens would sit and discuss the business with junior employees like Artzt. His first real test came when archrival Lever Bros. introduced a liquid detergent called Wisk. It took Procter by surprise, and "all hell broke loose," he said. The company had been experimenting with liquids but, typically, sat on the idea for prolonged tests. Artzt was reassigned to work on getting P&G's liquid detergent Biz to market as fast as possible. It went into test market in a matter of weeks, not the years it usually took to push a product through the company. "It was a classic example of haste making waste," Artzt said in retrospect. The product crystalized in the warehouse, so it had to be reformulated, slowing the test market. Artzt later joked that he was sure that was the end of his career. P&G didn't develop successful liquid detergents until 1975, when it launched Era, followed by Liquid Tide in 1984.

He was shifted for the third time in less than two years to

handle another crisis: Comet cleanser. The brand was responding to Colgate's Ajax, which also had taken P&G by surprise in the 1950s. Comet was in the process of expanding and had problems after a promising test market in Peoria, Illinois. Artzt's boss Bill Snow, a brand promotion manager, summoned him to talk with then CEO Morgens. The chief executive wanted to know how Artzt would fix Comet.

Artzt devised a two-part plan. First, he would resample the product. The company had botched an earlier mailing by distributing the samples before Christmas. Postal carriers dumped millions of the samples in the trash because their loads were too heavy. Second, Artzt suggested spending more for media and promotions in leading counties. Seven major urban markets bought one-third of the cleanser sold, and Ajax concentrated its efforts there. Artzt estimated he'd need $3 million to fix the brand. Without hesitating, Morgens told him to proceed. "I was floored. No memo, no questions, no clearance through channels," Artzt said. Ever since that experience, he has told brand managers who fret about not having much power that knowledge, not rank, *is* power at P&G.

Comet was his favorite assignment because it was his first shot at correcting a serious problem. "That was really an Olympic gold medal kind of thing for me," he said. "If my career had ended or plateaued there, I would have had plenty to feel good about."

Artzt's work paid off. He was promoted to brand manager in less than two years, versus three years for most P&Gers. He continued to move from brand to brand until 1960, when the company put him in charge of the advertising copy section, which was created when P&G was making the transition from radio to TV advertising. The group worked closely with ad agencies to develop ads and research techniques such as day-after recall—a measure of how many people remember a commercial—and execution styles such as slice-of-life commercials.

But Artzt discovered the downside of separating the brand managers from the advertising. The brand folks were closer to the business, followed trends, and had a better perspective on when copy should change. He recommended that the group be disbanded, even though he was in charge of it. The company's senior management agreed, and it was gone a year later.

Artzt's toughness with ad agency creative directors and account representatives earned him the nickname "Prince of Darkness." Morgan Hunter, a P&Ger who rode in a car pool with Artzt, credits an agency creative director for the nickname, which has stuck throughout Artzt's career. "Ed does have good advertising sense," Hunter said. "But when dealing with creatives, you need a surgeon's scalpel, not a carpenter's hammer."

Artzt disagrees about the origin of the nickname. He says it came from his penchant for working late at the office. One Saturday he went to the office and stayed until Sunday morning. The next week his boss Ed Harness called him into his office to question him about his long hours. "If you keep this up, you'll burn out before you're forty," Harness warned him. Artzt promised to change. "That was the last time I ever did that—at the office," he said. [17]

His responsibilities at home grew along with those at the office. By 1966 the family had grown to five children, including a son, William, and two more daughters, Laura and Elizabeth. The youngest daughter had to sleep in a closet for her first two years because they outgrew their home in Cincinnati's Indian Hill suburb. Even vacations couldn't guarantee Artzt's family escape from his chronic workaholism. He once packed his wife and kids into the car for a trip but decided to make a quick stop at the office before leaving town. About three hours later he returned to the car to check on them. "There was a lot of anger in that car," he said. He told them he'd be ready in a short while. Ruth knew better. She suggested that the family go home while he worked and they'd try again the next day.

When the family went to Michigan for fishing trips, Artzt insisted on driving nonstop. His children would plead with him to pull over so they could get something to drink; he'd promise to stop in the next town, where he had heard there was a Dog n Suds, a favorite hot dog and root beer chain. He'd continue to drive for miles.

Once on vacation, the compulsive head of the family scheduled their days like boot camp. He divided the days into "activity units," encouraging the children to pack as many activities as possible into the day. If the children reported an eight-unit day, Artzt would say, "I'm proud of you. Tomorrow we go for ten." He worked out timetables to keep everyone on schedule. He was horrified if he discovered a ninety-minute gap in their plans. Ruth's response was typically a resigned "God help us all."[18]

Occasionally he'd take a P&G outing with other brand managers and ad agency friends. Bart Cummings, retired CEO of Compton Advertising, remembers their fishing trips in the Adirondack Mountains, near Old Forge, New York. "I think I taught all of Procter & Gamble how to fish," Cummings said. Artzt showed his competitive edge on the riverbanks. The others nicknamed him "the meat fisherman," because he wanted to catch so many fish, and "the bear," because he acted like a tough guy, Cummings said.[19] In bridge and poker games, he played to win. "He frightened the death out of me," said John Thomas, an ex-P&Ger. "The worry was that you'd trump his ace and he'd reach across the table and shoot you in the forehead."[20]

By the mid-sixties, Artzt had ascended to advertising manager in the paper division, another troubled area. CEO Morgens had assembled a team from the soap business to expand distribution of toilet paper, which had failed in seven tries. One of the problems, he said, was the use of a new sales force to introduce a new product. The combination of unfamiliar products and salesmen didn't work. Besides, there were entrenched competitors that sold plenty of good products. Then P&G researchers developed a technology that made a softer tissue, an innovation that helped build the Charmin and Bounty brands, among others.

Another problem of the division was its stepchild status in the personnel department. Recruiters decided that the brightest hires went to soap, the rest to paper. Artzt told the staff recruiters he wouldn't take their picks anymore; he'd do it himself. "That sent a shock through the organization," he recalled. "Everybody thought I was overstepping my bounds." He began a process that has continued every year since the 1960s: personal visits to business schools to recruit new talent. "In Ed's tenure, the paper division went from getting the shakiest personnel to where it was sent the best," said Jack Rue, who worked for Artzt. He also credits Artzt with putting the Charmin name on the cardboard tube inside each roll of tissue to remind consumers of the brand.[21]

As Artzt rose through the ranks, he grew more brazen; "pushy," according to some P&Gers. One piece of company lore describes Artzt at New York's LaGuardia Airport trying to board a Cincinnati-bound plane. He had to get back to headquarters, but all flights were booked. So he slipped past the gate agent and boarded the plane. Once inside he asked the passengers if anyone worked for P&G. When a junior brand person raised his hand, Artzt introduced himself and demanded that he relinquish his seat. Untrue, says Artzt, adding, "I could think of other things I'd do."[22]

In his assignment as vice president of the food and coffee divisions his reputation for toughness grew worse. Agency people feared calling him with bad news about missed deadlines. "People were afraid of him," said Bob Jordan, a former ad agency head.[23] Managers remember an all-night session when the company was preparing a presentation for the Food and Drug Administration. The group had rented two floors at a Rockville, Maryland, hotel where they worked until the early morning hours to get sixty slides ready for the meeting. At about 1 A.M.

Artzt demanded to review the presentation. He questioned each slide until one weary manager finally said, "Mr. Artzt, if you keep asking questions, we'll be here at 9 A.M." (when the FDA meeting was supposed to take place). Artzt turned red and stormed out of the room. [24]

His brusque style didn't seem to hurt his reputation among senior managers. Walter Lingle, then a company executive vice president, remembers hearing the young Artzt talking business in the lunchroom. "I was struck by his intelligence," he said. "I thought, Here's a guy who will go further." [25]

But Artzt's career progress was taking its toll on his family. In 1970 he was asked to go to Kansas City, Missouri, to temporarily take over the recently acquired Folgers division until another manager could be named; the previous manager had been diagnosed with a brain tumor. The Artzts decided that Ruth and the children would remain in Cincinnati while he lived in an apartment in Kansas City. Most weeks he'd come home for weekends. But the estimated five-month assignment turned into nearly a year stay. "After a month or two, you become a guest in your own home," he said. "My kids were mostly teenagers" who would gripe if they had to hang around to see Dad on the weekends. "That's a stress," he said. And Ruth wouldn't bother him during the week with household problems. When he came home, "I'd get all the bad news at once." He said the experience convinced him that managers should always move their families, regardless of the length of the stay.

Artzt doesn't like to discuss his family. He acknowledges that it's been tough to be a good father. "It's hard for a successful father to function or to provide the same nourishment as a loving mother," he reflected. "Ruth does that." The parents' rigidly defined roles are clearly illustrated by two gifts their children gave them for their fortieth wedding anniversary: he received a gold-colored crown; Ruth, a gold-painted toilet brush. [26]

Artzt's experience at Folgers convinced him that every future CEO should work at the acquired company and "deal firsthand with the human and cultural problems" of those employees. In that job, his attention to detail surprised many. Despite his executive role, he still spent hours scanning brand data. Once, during a two-hour meeting, Artzt studied a 200-page binder on the coffee business and picked out flaws in the strategy. For instance, he'd discovered that a competing brand was gaining too much ground in certain West Coast markets. "He just nailed the brand group," said Frank Blod, a former Folgers brand man. [27]

In 1972 he was named a director of P&G's board. A few years later Harness asked Artzt to take charge of the company's European operations. Those who worked with him recall that he had mixed feelings about the assignment. International posts were the equivalent of getting sent to Siberia. "He wasn't sure he wanted international," Bart Cummings said. "It was out of the mainstream." But Artzt said he took the job willingly because he knew that the company's long-term growth would come from distant shores. "Every company that starts with one hundred percent of its business in [its] home country goes through a period when the international business has a stepchild character to it," he said. When he asked Ruth what she thought about moving to Europe, she didn't hesitate: "When do we pack?" The family even took its horses to Brussels, Belgium.

In the new post, Artzt began to see inefficiencies. The different tastes and cultures had given rise to a half-dozen formulas for detergents. More important, the business wasn't prospering because of the oil crisis of the early 1970s. That was a shock to Europe, which during the Marshall Plan years had seen double-digit growth in every country and every business. "People just couldn't believe that the recession that followed the seventy-three oil shock was more than just a temporary aberration," Artzt recalled. Profit margins and consumption were both down. "This was not going to blow over like a rainstorm."

European managers were reluctant to change. Shortly after he arrived, Artzt was asked to approve the annual fancy fete for managers. Instead he canceled the dinner and served cookies and Cokes in the company cafeteria. "Things had to change," he said. "These were troubled times, and we could not afford the big annual dinner of past years." He pledged to bring back the bash if the company returned to its earlier growth. The following year the group was back at the hotel for its dinner meeting. "But the complacency was gone," he said. "It was a different kind of celebration."

One way Artzt cut costs in Europe was to develop a matrix management structure under which managers share responsibility for entire categories, not just brands, and for regions, not just countries. Originally, European subsidiaries were carved into markets protected by tariff barriers. That changed in 1960, when some trade barriers were removed. After that, the P&G operations in each country had to justify their manufacturing sites because a company could ship across country lines. "When I went to Europe, I believe we had nine detergent plants, and each one was primarily servicing its own country, even though there were wide differences in cost," Artzt said. After the tariff walls came down, P&G had to develop a structure that crossed those old lines. It met with resistance because it gutted old fiefdoms. "Country managers were barons," said David Montgomery, a Stanford University business professor who has studied P&G's international operations. "These folks had a lot of power, and they didn't want to give it up."

The new plan gave each manager one-ninth of the responsibility for Europe and 100 percent of the responsibility for the manager's piece of the market. Artzt described this principle of interdependency by comparing it to plumbing. "I've got the key to the toilet but you control the water that flushes it. And that makes us interdependent," he said.

The other goal of the matrix management plan was to eliminate excess layers. Europe was divided into northern and southern halves, so P&G had two separate product development groups. Each worked at the same time on laundry products in different parts of the same technical center. There were different levels of bleach in each country's products, with some containing 31 percent and some 29 percent. Six different perfumes were used for Dash detergents sold in nine countries. Changes were difficult. Artzt's reputation for cutting excesses and poor performers was solidified in Europe. "You ran it right or you were out," Bart Cummings said. [28] "He didn't put up with any nonsense." In the U.K. he cut 13 percent of the workforce. [29]

Artzt's impatience was evident in the restructuring. He considered his management team much "too ponderous" about decisions. He'd complain about the sluggish pace of advances. The company had so many different products and organizations, "it was like getting a bill through Congress," Artzt complained. Harald Einsmann, one of the European managers, coined the word "ponderosity," circled it in red, and drew a red slash through it. He gave it to Artzt and hung copies in all the European offices.

Despite the difficult times in Europe, Artzt considered it the best job in P&G. He was a chief executive, but he didn't have to answer to shareholders, give speeches, or fight with Washington. It was also in Europe that he found young managers such as Harald Einsmann, Durk Jager, and B. Jurgen Hintz, all of whom became his protégés. In 1980 he was named head of all international operations. It was a grueling schedule as he jetted between countries. He made four trips to Europe, three to the Far East, two to Latin America, and one to the Middle East each year—more if P&G was developing business in a new market. At times he was worn out by the pace. He once fell asleep while sending dictation to his office from his Japan hotel room. He woke up a couple hours later to "a very large phone bill," he said.

Japan proved to be his most difficult task. The company had lost $200 million since entering the country in 1972. He tapped Jager to turn around the operations, which have grown into one of P&G's top markets.

Artzt's reputation as the Prince of Darkness worsened as he climbed the corporate ladder. Lou Pritchett, then general manager of P&G's Philippines company, remembers how terrified the troops would be whenever Artzt came for a visit. If someone didn't answer his questions completely, he lost his temper. In one meeting Artzt was unhappy with a product development manager's report. He interrupted the presentation and said, "You're the sorriest excuse for a manager I've ever seen. How did you get your job?" He told Pritchett to fire him, but Pritchett refused. Artzt cooled down, and the manager remained with the company.[30]

Such behavior continues today. No one escapes Artzt's wrath. He's been known to publicly scold his wife. Ethel Hughes, his former secretary, recalled how he snapped at Ruth when she forgot another P&Ger's name. "He could talk nasty to her," Hughes said.[31] Artzt says he never scolds his wife—in public. "Sure, I kick Ruth around, but not in front of people," he said. "And she beats the hell out of me, too. Verbally. She's got a good wit."

Alex Keller, who followed Pritchett as general manager in the Philippines, saw Artzt's dark side as well. The company was making great strides in sales of its Tide Bar, a solid cake of detergent used to scrub clothes. The plants were running at 30 percent above capacity because the product was overtaking the other P&G product, Mr. Clean Bar. In his sales report Keller showed figures on Tide's growth and Mr. Clean's declining share. The combined category, however, was showing strong growth. "Artzt zeroes in on Mr. Clean's volume going down," Keller said. "He just went ballistic."

In a memo from Cincinnati, Artzt ordered Keller to report to headquarters immediately. Keller sent him another memo explaining the changing market. That calmed Artzt. But when Keller attended year-end meetings, friends from Europe told him that Artzt had portrayed his work as shoddy, even though his business was actually growing. "That was petty and petulant," Keller said. At a later meeting Artzt came as close as he ever does to an apology when he conceded, "I guess I overreacted."[32]

Many memos were returned with nasty comments like "Stupid Decision" written in the margins. He uses "goddamn" as a prefix for most words. Some managers whom he doesn't like are simply reassigned to new posts or told to leave the company. Some European sales managers were sent to the United States for training, but Artzt had no intention of letting them return to their jobs. "His idea was out of sight, out of mind," one manager said. [33]

By 1984 Artzt had begun sensing he might have a shot at becoming CEO. He was named vice chairman in charge of international business. Publicly, John Pepper was considered the heir apparent to CEO John Smale; he had been named executive vice president in charge of nearly all P&G's U.S. business and later became president of the company. [34] Other changes were going on domestically, sending mixed signals about the company's future. That same year, P&G cut design engineers' jobs, a move that sent shock waves throughout the company. In the mid-1980s Smale also changed the classic brand management structure to category management, giving managers more responsibilities for the growth of several products, not just one. Older plants were closed and more jobs were cut.

The U.S. business was under siege in the mid-1980s, as competitors such as Kimberly-Clark and Colgate moved faster with diaper and toothpaste innovations. Meanwhile, new product introductions—Duncan Hines cookies, for example—were bombs. P&G began to realize that its real growth would have to come from overseas. [35]

Another turning point for the aggressive Smale came when he was diagnosed with an intestinal tumor. He underwent surgery and missed several weeks of work, but P&G kept it quiet even inside the company. "After he went through that, he realized that life is pretty damn short," said one member of Smale's administrative committee.[36] Smale had built the company in the 1980s, largely through acquisitions such as Richardson-Vicks. The company had products in forty-four categories by the end of the decade, nearly double the number it had when he took over in 1980.[37]

Traditionally, P&G's CEO is groomed years ahead of the public announcement. But the deaths of several key executives changed the succession plans at P&G during the early 1980s. Charles Ferguson, a well-liked group vice president, died in 1981. Artzt considered him "a top-flight guy." In 1986 Sandy Weiner, another group vice president, died at the age of forty-six. Both had been contenders for higher posts. Ferguson's death accelerated Pepper's climb up the ladder. Insiders had hoped that Pepper and Weiner would be the future leaders. "If we'd gotten the tandem of Pepper and Weiner, that would've continued the place that I knew and loved," said Bill Morgan, a P&Ger who left the company after Artzt took over.

Pepper didn't get tapped, for a variety of reasons. For one thing, those who have worked with him say he's too nice. His efforts for consensus makes him waver at times. "He agrees with the last person he talks to," said one manager. In addition, he emphasized the "soft" side of the business, such as career development programs and leadership training seminars. Smale considered these superfluous. But Pepper knew how to rally the troops. "He's the John F. Kennedy of business," praised Kip Knight, a former brand manager at P&G. Doug Hall, another former P&Ger, said Pepper could get employees to do anything. "If John said, 'Doug, I want you to swim the Ohio River,' I'd ask, 'What time would you like me to do that?'" One former manager refers to him as "Jiminy Pepper," the conscience of the company.[38]

Meanwhile, international operations were growing with double-digit returns. P&G would soon find half its sales coming from overseas. Zachary Schiller, a veteran P&G watcher at *Busi-*

ness Week, predicted in an August 1989 article that Artzt's international performance could get him the CEO post. [39]

Two months later Smale shocked insiders and Wall Street alike by announcing at the annual meeting that he was stepping down as CEO and that his successor would be Ed Artzt, not John Pepper. Artzt and Smale reshuffled senior management, sending Pepper to head international operations. Artzt's two favorites from Europe, Jurgen Hintz and Durk Jager, moved into the senior U.S. posts, and a golf buddy from his Folgers days, Gerry Dirvin, became the senior staff person. [40]

A flurry of retirements coincided with Smale's decision to leave. Within a few years most of the senior executives, including Powell McHenry, general counsel, and James Nethercott, chief financial officer, were gone. Artzt surrounded himself with managers who wouldn't question his judgment.

One of his first assignments as CEO was addressing employees at the year-end meetings. He quipped about his reputation as an evil character. His speech elicited only polite applause. When Pepper addressed the same group, he received thunderous applause and a standing ovation. "It was embarassing," Bill Morgan said. [41]

It was clear that Artzt didn't consider Pepper his equal. He has publicly berated him at meetings and reminded employees that he, not Pepper, is still in charge of international. Whenever Pepper talks about people issues at meetings, Artzt rolls his eyes and taps his watch. "He clearly wants Pepper to go away," said one insider. Artzt denies that he has publicly berated Pepper, and said he has "always treated John with a great deal of respect."

Tom Quinn, a former P&G sales manager, saw firsthand how dejected Pepper had become beginning in the mid-1980s. Quinn jokingly started the Expose Your Ass club to counter the tendency to cover ass at P&G. The only requirements for membership were wearing the EYA sticker on your P&G ID badge and a pledge never to CYA. In the elevator one day, Pepper asked Quinn what the EYA sticker stood for. "If you're asking, we're all in trouble," Quinn said. He explained the idea and offered Pepper his own sticker. "I can't," Pepper said. "I have to cover mine ten times a day." [42]

As Artzt settled into the corner office of the CEO, he began putting his imprint on the company. Former CEOs used to talk about the strength of P&G in terms of its people. Brands and buildings could disappear, they'd say, but if the people were left, the company could rebuild. Artzt has taken a different tack. In a 1991 interview he compared firing employees to clearing deadwood. "Sure, I've cleared out deadwood," he said. "Probably some of it was still breathing when it was cleared out." When the line appeared in a first-page story in *The Wall Street Journal*, managers knew that their worst fears had come true. "He figures there's a whole rain forest out there, said one manager. 'If we don't like these employees, we'll just go chop down some more trees.' " [43]

In a company that had long prided itself on a commitment to lifetime employment, Artzt's attitude makes many recoil. "I was told when I was hired that I'd almost have to kill the chairman to get fired," said former public relations manager Marjorie Bradford. Many of those who have left the company are glad they got out before the Artzt years. "I wouldn't go back if they held my children hostage," said David Cullen, a consultant who began his career at P&G. [44]

Headhunters say calls from P&G employees soared after January 1990, when Artzt took office. One said he can tell when Artzt has done a bit of bloodletting, because he gets twice as many calls from Cincinnati. [45]

Artzt pushes for more and more profits. As he sits at his desk, he checks the company's stock price several times an hour on a computer. "We're pumping a little blood," he said to a reporter as he noted the stock price going up. Each uptick adds to his multimillion-dollar fortune. [46] His annual total compensation of $4.71 million allows him to pamper himself with $1,600 hand-tailored suits. [47]

To boost returns even more, he's eyeing unnecessary layers that he can cut. In a 1992 speech to employees shortly before Christmas, he told them that real contributors will keep their jobs. "That really made us feel great," one manager said sarcastically. He is also pushing for individual accountability for profits. "There's a shorter fuse," said one veteran sales manager. "And there's a clear correlation between making a mistake and getting a penalty." At the same time, Artzt wants his managers to step up the pace of new product launches. In the health care division, for instance, a "speed team" was appointed in 1992 to study how to improve the rollouts. "If the team comes back with the right results, Artzt will find out that since he's taken over, everything has slowed down because no one wants to make a decision," said one manager in the division.

Even his protégés have felt his ferocity at times. Artzt lost more of his senior management team than any other CEO in P&G's history. Three of the top company officers left in one year. Hintz was one of three possible successors, but he disagreed too often with the boss, and his business performance in food and beverage disappointed the impatient CEO. At one meeting Artzt made the cutting remark that everyone must have been sitting according to their business results, because Hintz was in the back of the room. [48] Artzt offered Hintz another job, but it was clearly a demotion, so Hintz left in 1991.

In addition, Artzt lost two other senior executives when Dick Nicolosi and Mal Jozoff left the company in 1992. Jozoff, a Pepper supporter, had wanted out ever since Artzt took over. Nicolosi, like Hintz, didn't get along with Artzt. [49]

Those who have remained find that the CEO doesn't allow much room for disagreement or free thinking. Artzt doesn't seem to recall his own disillusioning experience as a twenty-three-year-old, when his creativity was stifled in his Wash Day Sale promotion. One senior researcher remembers meetings where Artzt has told anyone who disagrees to report to his office so he can tell them why he's right. "We're not likely to take him up on that offer," the researcher said. It inhibits creativity because "if he doesn't care what I think, what is he paying me for?" Even senior managers are often told to shut up during meetings. "Nobody is willing to speak up anymore," Lou Pritchett said. "Artzt believes 'I'm the boss and you're not.' " The abuse extends even to managers' wives. At the May 1992 board meeting in Brussels, Artzt invited P&G spouses, along with the directors' wives, to a business presentation. He told the management spouses they couldn't ask questions; only board spouses were allowed to do that. "They were royally pissed off," said one woman familiar with the meeting. [50]

He's also gutted the training programs and anything that doesn't immediately help sell more soap. Programs such as Steve Covey's effective management courses were termed "bullshit" by Artzt. He said that training prior to his tenure "got misdirected" through such "rent-a-programs." "I didn't recognize the things that made Procter & Gamble successful in our training programs," he said. "The focus was not on beating the living daylights out of Unilever or Henkel, which is the way they try to do to us." [51]

Instead he created P&G College, a training program on strategic thinking, technology deployment, advertising, and other basics. It's been nicknamed "Eddie's War College." Some of the "mind-rubbing toughness was eroding a little bit," Artzt said. "When I pounced on the scene, it was a shock to some people. But I'm a product of many, many years of training."

He calls himself the "Johnny Appleseed" of P&G College because he plants the seeds to help employees understand why they're enrolled. He takes the stage for three hours, armed with just three slides, to talk about product strategy. "Never give your consumer a product reason to switch away from your brand," he tells a group of managers. "How many mistakes we would've avoided if we had followed that simple principle."[52]

He wants to recapture the esprit de corps that existed back when he was a junior employee, and senior executives such as Richard Deupree and Howard Morgans would sit in the lunchroom and talk shop. "You were constantly in the presence of your elders, so they could teach you the ways of the hunt and the war and all of that," Artzt said. "But we're not like that anymore. We're not a tribe. We're a huge army. Therefore you have to institutionalize" the training.

His constant use of war terms indicates a changed culture inside P&G. Artzt has referred to himself as a "wrecking crew" and is a big fan of Attila the Hun. He keeps three spare copies of *Leadership Secrets of Attila the Hun* in his office bookcase. "Attila valued loyalty to the cause above all other virtues," Artzt explained. "If you're not loyal to the cause, you didn't stay healthy long with him. I call that commitment to the company. I get a lot of warm feelings out of that one."[53] Like Attila, Artzt seeks out the disloyal and gets rid of them. At one meeting of vice presidents, the CEO stood up, shook his fist, and said he knew someone in the room was leaking information to *The Wall Street Journal.* "When I find you, I'll fire you," he yelled.

When asked why employees describe his management style as "fear and intimidation," Artzt becomes angry. He demands names of those who made the statements. "No one could be successful over a long career at P&G by managing through fear and intimidation," he said. He admits that his greatest weakness is his anger and that "things might get a little hot" when he's trying to make a point with managers. But he "very seldom" ends a meeting on "an angry note." Rather, he believes his team is "uplifted by the whole thing."

Part of Artzt's problems comes from his sense of humor. He

tends to be flip and colorful in his speech. He makes fun of himself occasionally, freely recounting how he was nearly thrown out of a formal dinner honoring him and President Carlos Salinas de Gortari of Mexico. Security guards wouldn't let the CEO into the same room as the Mexican president. Once he got past the guards to attend a press conference, camera crews elbowed him out of the way so they could get a shot of Salinas. "P&G people thought this was good for me," he said.

But often he's just plain rude. In one meeting with sales managers, he referred to P&G's trade customers as thieves. When he walked into a formal dinner for customers in Hawaii, he quipped that the place "looked like a funeral home" and heckled a sales manager who was making a presentation.[54]

Artzt has said that his comments in business meetings have been misunderstood. During a discussion on what to call P&G's two-in-one shampoo-and-conditioner product in Japan, a manager suggested resurrecting the Prell name. "I've been associated with Prell and I'm never going to be associated with Prell again," Artzt said. "You may call it strawberry asshole before you call it Prell." Artzt initially denied that he said that. Then he said it has to be put into context. "It's quite possible that we were having a serious discussion in the meeting, and I said you can call it strawberry asshole, and it comes off sounding serious."[55]

International managers cringe at some of his behavior when visiting foreign dignitaries. At one Japan meeting Artzt ran out of business cards, so he began to give away those he'd collected from the Japanese businessmen. The exchange of cards is an important Japanese custom, so his employees were horrified to discover what the boss was doing. "We shut it down after about twenty minutes," said one manager at the meeting. "After that we put a pretty girl on his arm to keep him occupied and a little distracted."[56]

He didn't score any points with his Middle East managers

when he discussed the prospects of selling cosmetics around the globe. "I don't know of any place that's not a good beauty-care market. Maybe not the Middle East. I haven't peeked under those veils."[57] That prompted angry letters from employees and consumers alike.

Sometimes compassion makes it through the gruffness. Lou Pritchett remembers that Artzt sent him a personal note expressing sympathy when his wife's mother died. Artzt had met her during a visit with the Pritchetts in Manila. "I remember her mother as being a very warm and gentle lady," he wrote. "This has been a difficult month for both of our families. My trip to the Far East was interrupted by news of the death of my mother." Ida Artzt died of a stroke in March 1983 at age eighty-four.[58]

When he learned that retiree Chuck Retrum needed hip surgery, the CEO dashed off a letter to wish him a speedy recovery. Retrum was one of Artzt's early mentors. Artzt also remembers him each year with a Christmas card.[59]

At times he longs for an escape from the pressure of his job. His favorite pastimes are golf, trout fishing in the Snake River near his home in Jackson Hole, Wyoming, and wine collecting. He's built a wine cellar that outranks those of some restaurants in size and quality of vintages.

Artzt works many weekends; he describes his job as "very lonely." He doesn't have many close friends whom he can confide in. There are limits on whom he can talk to inside the company, so he turns to retired CEO John Smale for advice. "I don't automatically say what John says, but every tough situation that faces me, that I've not been through before, I think of John as a sounding board, and he's great."

As of May 1993, it was unclear when Artzt plans to retire. When asked the question in late 1989, Artzt said he didn't accept the position expecting to stay just five years.[60] When asked the same question in recent times, Artzt said his earlier remarks "were the babblings of a foolish youth." Other times he vows to stay at least until he's sixty-five.

He will be remembered for taking the company around the world and for cutting unprofitable brands that Smale and others kept too long. Citrus Hill orange juice, for instance, lost more money than P&G lost in all of Japan, which was at least $200 million.[61] And some of Artzt's toughness was needed. "He's given the company a wake-up call," Pritchett said.[62]

If Artzt sticks to his present plans, either Durk Jager or John Pepper will be the next CEO. The fifty-year-old Jager is considered brilliant. For instance, he speaks seven languages. But his temperament makes Artzt look docile. Jager tells managers to "bust some kneecaps" or do some "gutter fighting" to get results. He cleared out entire departments of managers he didn't like. When he took over the Japanese operations of Richardson-Vicks, forty-eight of the fifty Vicks salesmen were gone within a year, largely because Jager didn't think they knew how to sell goods. "A year later we found out that P&G didn't know how to sell," said one manager who worked for Jager. In the United States, many managers say Jager's arrogant attitude, coupled with Artzt's harshness, chased out those who had been loyal to the company, such as Mal Jozoff. Besides, Jager wants his own team in place, not those who were Pepper loyalists. "Ed knows when he's getting to the point where he's gonna kill somebody," Bill Morgan said. "The shutoff valve comes in and he'll let you live. I don't think Durk has the shutoff valve."

"If the early retirement plan is lucrative and the recession is over, and Jager gets the job, you're gonna see a mass exodus from P&G," Pritchett predicted. "The man isn't user friendly."[63]

Many still hope that John Pepper will get the post. There were rumblings in early 1993 that the board realized that Jager is too harsh and Pepper is the popular choice. Or the board could decide once again to split the chairman and CEO posts between Jager and Pepper. Howard Morgens, the retired CEO, worries about preserving P&G's culture. And so do many inside P&G, who question what Artzt's reign has done to P&G. "Esprit de corps is something that is very fragile," Morgens said. "There has to be a belief that the boss is a pretty good guy and he knows what he's doing and he's looked up to."[64]

3
P&G in Your Shorts

W hen Vic Mills joined Procter & Gamble in the 1920s, plant workers still used kettles to cook Ivory soap. It took nearly two weeks to make a single batch. Like wine, it was aged before the signature blue-and-white labels were wrapped around each bar.

But P&G recognized that the old methods weren't keeping pace with growing public demand. The young chemical engineer had an idea. He figured that soap could be made like ice cream—in a big vat where mechanical paddles could continually stir, scrape, and spin the ingredients. Then the mixture was pumped through a mold to form one long bar that was sliced into small cakes. The new machine made soap in two hours rather than two weeks.

Still, Ivory was a sacred cow. One of the founder's grandsons, William Cooper Procter, used to walk the factory floor to personally inspect the Ivory kettles. Some kettle operators were known to taste the frothy soap to see if it was done. For years, even the slightest change in typeface or design on the label had to be approved by a Procter or Gamble family member. So Mills didn't dare tinker with the process without getting clearance from every manager above him, including Chairman Richard Deupree. He traded his white lab coat for a suit coat and went to the executive offices downtown. He dreaded the meeting at P&G's headquarters; Deupree grew up in the P&G sales force and wasn't much for technical talks. "I knew he'd be bored to tears," Mills recalled. Besides, P&G resisted change.

Mills told him about the cost savings but explained there was one problem that troubled him. "I don't like these new bars," the scientist said. "They come out more soluble than the old ones. It will wash away more rapidly, so the bar won't last as long."

Deupree, still a salesman at heart, jumped up from his desk to congratulate Mills. "It's a great idea!" he gushed. He knew this would save time and sell more soap. Indeed, Mills's soap-making process became one of the most profitable inventions ever discovered at P&G.[1]

For generations, scientists and consumer researchers have built P&G by searching for new ways to sell basic goods at premium prices. The work includes exhaustive testing, from literally splitting hairs and slicing teeth in the labs to conducting research in consumers' bathrooms and grocery stores. They want to observe firsthand how we clean ourselves and feed our families—and how the company can hawk more goods in the process.

The research has led to breakthroughs such as Tide, the first synthetic laundry detergent, introduced in 1946. It has been the leading U.S. detergent ever since, and the cash cow that fueled P&G's growth. Tide and other P&G products are found in about 98 percent of all U.S. households.[2]

Indeed, P&G research was so highly regarded that the U.S. government asked it to build bombs in World War II. P&G built 25 percent of the bombs and shells used by Allied forces in the war. Unknown to most, P&G even helped build nuclear weapons during the Korean War.[3]

Nevertheless, P&G's painstaking research has produced its share of product bombs, such as toothpaste that turned teeth brown and ice cream that tasted like Play-Doh. What's especially troubling for some inside P&G is the lack of a major break-through in recent times—despite spending nearly a half-billion dollars annually for research. The problem is most evident in

P&G's ailing food-and-beverage division, which has become a graveyard of flops. One internal report estimates that P&G wasted $2 billion in capital projects in the 1980s largely for food follies. [4]

Like many U.S. industries, P&G has lost its edge to more agile companies, both in the States and overseas. The push for short-term returns has replaced the traditional long-term view that allowed scientists to work unquestioned for years. Now, scientists say, the push is for quick hits that ultimately never rival a Tide. And when someone does come up with a new idea, it takes years to get it through the layers of management.

"It's scary," said Hoyt Chaloud, a product development scientist who spent forty years in P&G labs. "Where are the breakthroughs going to come from? Everybody is so keyed to the fact that rewards come with short-term successes. I think there's a problem ahead." [5]

That's a far cry from the early days, when P&G was recognized as the leader of inventions. Even Thomas Edison spent time inside P&G. As a Western Union employee in 1865, he rigged up a telegraph line between P&G offices and the soap plant. But he left to invent the light bulb elsewhere. [6]

In those days, P&G had its share of firsts. It was one of the first to conduct formal consumer research. More important, it was one of the first to really listen to its consumers. In 1879 customers wrote to P&G asking for more of its "floating soap," a request that puzzled plant workers. They later discovered that the floating soap came from a batch of its white soap that had been stirred too long. The finished bars had extra air, making them float. Because of the requests, P&G changed the soap so that all the bars would float. [7] The soap was named Ivory. In 1924 Paul Smelser, an economist, began the market research department when looking for more information on Ivory, which became the flagship brand. P&G decided that "wives of the management were no longer representative of all consumers in the United States," according to a company biography, *It Floats.*

So Smelser took samples of different soap perfumes directly to the public.[8]

Smelser spread the word about consumer research and encouraged others in the company to give it a try. One of his early disciples was Howard Morgens, who'd transferred from a sales job in New Mexico to the advertising department in the 1930s. Morgens was a zealot for advertising. But he learned that consumer research among busy housewives was actually more difficult than selling products. "Women would come to the door and obviously be terribly busy and have a baby yelling," the Harvard graduate recalled.[9]

His biggest research assignment was a trip through the South in 1935. P&G wasn't having much luck selling goods there, so he was ordered to find out why. "Even if I took a year, I had to find some answers because the company was losing money in the South," he said.

Outside Augusta, Georgia, Morgens hired an aging insurance salesman to show him the territory. "We'd walk across the plowed fields to cabins," he recalled. "They probably would've shot me if they could have! They thought I was from the sheriff's office. This guy had an uncanny ability with them. He would call out and say, 'We're coming to talk! He's not the sheriff!' "

Inside the homes, they'd sit in the parlors, often on wooden crates. "We'd talk about the weather and hog butchering. Eventually we got around to what kind of soap they were using and where they got it. It took an awful lot of time for them to relax. Then he'd say, 'Go get the soap, will you?' "

Some homemakers brought out a bar of Palmolive soap, a competing brand. But many produced their own. "They only made soap when the moon was right. It was absolutely unbelievable," Morgens said. Why did they watch the moon? "I didn't ask."

After six months, Morgens returned to Cincinnati with his report. He was convinced that P&G couldn't sell in rural markets. People would bring in a half-dozen eggs for a bar of soap at the store. "I told the company to concentrate on the towns, and don't bother with the rural areas." Or use distributors called "jobbers" to sell the soap, he suggested. Morgens's research showed P&G that it should concentrate sales and advertising on the biggest markets and slowly build distribution in rural areas.

His field research convinced P&G to dispatch teams of interviewers across the country on a regular basis. Teams were assigned to different regions, often staying for weeks at a time to visit households and quiz women about its brands. Their presence caught the attention of the news media because no other company went to such lengths to study consumers. A 1953 *Time* magazine article observed: "A staff of 125 P&G girls (not too pretty, lest they attract too many marriage proposals; not too homely, lest they jump at the first offer) travels all over the U.S., talking to half a million women a year, handing out new products for housewives to 'use and compare.' " The women wore white gloves and hats. [10]

The "P&G girls" had to memorize a booklet called "How to Travel Alone and Remain a Lady." The chapter on the "averted eye" warned them not to look into strangers' eyes. Sexism extended beyond the instruction booklet. Women received smaller living allowances than men assigned to do the same research. [11]

David Goodman was one of the few men hired for the interview circuit. "I got a lot of sympathy from women," he said. "They'd look at me and say, 'What does *he* know about laundry?' " He remembers a training session in which instructors gave the class the *Time* magazine article. The story made them feel rather average. "Talk about demoralizing," he said.

At most homes, researchers were invited in for a proper visit. "People would insist you have a cold glass of lemonade," recalled Jack Henry, the head of P&G's market research department for much of his forty years at the company. "Then they'd pour out their life story. There was a lot of loneliness." [12]

Henry and his staff learned that the way questions were phrased was as crucial as the question itself. So even the questions were questioned.[13] The strategy interviewers developed was to appear as informal as possible. They never took notes during the interview. Instead, they memorized answers and wrote their reports in the car. "You wanted it to be a conversation with a friend," Henry explained.

By asking questions, P&G "looks for products that fill a need," he continued. There's a very strong emotional undercurrent involved," especially when asking about babies and teeth. The motto of the department became: "Consumers aren't stupid. They're your spouse."

P&G researchers never used the company name to identify themselves, instead telling housewives they were from the Household Information Bureau. Going door-to-door provided some memorable experiences, especially in small towns. The sheriff in one town arrested some P&G women who were distributing free tampons; he considered tampons obscene materials.

When greeted by a man, the researchers always asked to see the "lady of the house." After making that request, one researcher was escorted to the living room to meet her. The woman was at rest in a casket. "He thought I'd come to view the body," the researcher said. "We had a sort of quota, so I counted it as an interview."

And consumers revealed some odd habits. One woman admitted that she brushed her teeth with Sani-Flush, a toilet bowl cleaner. A farm wife in rural Oklahoma told P&G researchers that she stopped using Joy dishwashing liquid because it killed her favorite sow, Bessie. "We used to pour the dishwater in with Bessie's slop," the woman explained. "After we started to use Joy, old Bessie died."[14]

Often, researchers gave consumers a product and asked if they could watch the family use it. One of the company's more obnoxious exercises was to ask to join consumers in the bathroom. "We'd watch women wash their hair and ask a lot of questions," Henry said. For instance, did she squeeze from the top or bottom of the tube? Sometimes it was much more personal: Did she fold or crumple the toilet paper? One consumer study at P&G broke down bathroom tissue users into categories based on how they used the product: crumpled or flat. "We'd be in the bathroom while they showered or watch them mop floors and change diapers," said Kip Knight, a brand manager in the 1980s. "You pick up subtle things that you'd normally not know."[15]

CEO Ed Artzt recalls how as a paper division manager he used to "humiliate my family by passing out rolls of toilet paper." This was especially embarassing to his teenage daughters, who then had to explain to friends that Dad made toilet paper. "If I wanted to play a prank on them, I'd whip out a roll and ask their friends, 'Have you tried our new Charmin? It's squeezably soft.' "[16]

Another habit of P&Gers—even those outside the market research department—is quizzing friends about their habits. "You were trained when you go to a friend's home, to go to the kitchen and laundry room," former vice president Chuck Jarvie said, "If they had a competing brand, you took it away." "Then you tell them, 'I'll get you a box of Tide Monday. You don't want to use this other stuff.' " Others tell of how P&G dinner guests check their hosts' medicine cabinet to see if they're using Crest toothpaste. It's obvious when the P&Ger has peeked: The host is quizzed if a tube of Colgate is found.[17]

CEO Artzt admits he still does that. "I've been known to rummage through people's cupboards when I'm a houseguest. People frequently tell me that before I come to their house, they do an inventory—change all the soap and toilet paper, hide all the competitive toothpaste, and put the right dishwashing detergent on the counter," he said. "Maybe I don't get invited around as much as I would otherwise."[18]

One manager suggested sorting through consumers' garbage to study what people use in their homes. As a joke, he wrote a memo called GRUMP—Garbage and Rubbish Utilization Measurement Plan—and sent it to his boss. The memo recommended hiring a trash hauling firm to sort trash and prepare reports for Procter. "The boss loved it and sent it on up the line," a manager said. "They didn't realize it was a joke, because it fit the P&G mind-set."

Today one commonly used method of eavesdropping is the focus group. A handful of housewives are gathered to discuss a product while P&Gers sit behind a one-way mirror or watch via video camera from another room. Sometimes they can't find the right accommodations. Knight remembered one Ivory soap focus group that was held in a consumer's kitchen. "We couldn't find another facility, so five P&G guys had to hide in the closet and crack the door so they could listen in," he said.

He also spent a lot of time quizzing consumers in the grocery store. During one session, Knight asked an Omaha woman why she'd picked up a P&G test brand, Brigade toilet bowl cleaner, then returned it to the shelf. "If it's a choice between pot roast and an automatic toilet bowl cleaner, the pot roast wins," she told him bluntly.

"We were paid well enough that we didn't realize people were hurting," Knight conceded. "As you stand there and watch people with coupons, you realize people are on a budget." [19]

P&G gets a great deal of consumer feedback without even probing. Letters pour in from around the world. The company estimates that a consumer writes to P&G every four minutes. [20] Letters sometimes offer advertising suggestions. One writer wanted to ride around the country in a tub of Tide suds, wearing only a hat. Charles Hipps, from Graham, Texas, told how his 200-pound pet lion Blondie, enjoyed bathing in Tide. The lion also liked the taste of the detergent. [21]

One woman disclosed a unique use for Pampers diapers: After the baby used the diaper, she would peel off the back plastic liner and use it to wrap her husband's sandwiches. "We wanted to find that guy and tell him not to eat his lunch," one manager recalled laughingly. Another writer said Scope mouth-wash made a good bath for pet snakes. [22]

Sometimes consumers send in complaints, which P&G politely calls "comments." One woman sent in a spotted dress, blaming Ivory Snow for the marks. Scientists found out the spots came from her antiperspirant. They laundered it and sent it back to her. [23]

Complaints about products go all the way to the top; monthly reports are circulated to brand managers and to the president. "If you get two or three complaints about your brand, you're dog meat," said Matt Ariker, who worked on various brands. [24]

In 1974 P&G began testing a toll-free phone number for consumers to call with questions or complaints. P&G now receives more than 1 million calls a year. Information gathered on the phone forms a huge database on which consumers are using what brands. [25]

The researchers say the best way to truly understand consumers is to use the oldest technique: mingle with them. "I remember Tom Laco [retired vice chairman] had us going to a Laundromat to dispense change and watch women do the wash," recalled one P&Ger. "We even went door-to-door and sold the product. You had little time to sell, so it put the onus on you to focus" on the product.

The research applies even to P&G's promotions, not just its products. Some P&Gers collected old dish and bath towels from consumers to gauge the quality of the free towels offered in P&G's Bonus detergent boxes.

Doug Hall, known inside P&G as a master marketing inventor, spent a lot of time on college campuses to understand the young adult market better. At his alma mater, the University of Maine, he invited seniors for an evening of pizza and beer and asked one question: What do you want out of life? "We talked until two A.M.," he said.

While on the Folgers brand, Hall took a video camera and walked around campus at 5 A.M. asking people if they drank coffee. Often he'd carry a cooler through a park and offer various soft drinks to people to see what was popular.

Some of his research led to new products. After studying shoppers in a grocery store bakery, he helped invent Duncan Hines Pantastic Party Cakes. The cakes are shaped like characters from pop culture such as Miss Piggy and Kermit. "Everyone was buying Cincinnati Bengals cookies, not glazed doughnuts," he said. So he figured character cakes would sell. Initially they did. But P&G had to recall the product later because the kit's cake pan smoldered in hot ovens. The problem was fixed and the cake kit was later reintroduced.

"The old way Procter did research was the right way," Hall contended. "You've got to go out among real people."[26]

Increasingly, time and money constraints have made it more efficient to interview by mail questionnaires or telephone surveys. In the early 1980s P&G hinted that someday its consumers would be able to talk to the company via two-way cable television. The company now buys data gathered in homes where consumers use scanners to register which groceries they purchased. The device, much like those used in grocery checkout lanes, registers the bar codes on packages before the consumer puts them in the cupboard. These homes also have a box on the television to monitor what programs they watch, researchers said. P&G also used hidden video cameras in grocery store parking lots to monitor shoppers' habits.[27]

All the consumer research gathered by P&G marketers gets sent to the company's basic research labs. There scientists try to come up with the next generation of products. P&G was one of the first companies to conduct ongoing basic research, beginning in 1887.[28] Inside the labs, consumer feedback is turned into lab innovations that serve as the backbone of P&G's success. It consistently outspends its competitors in research and development.

In fiscal 1991 P&G spent $786 million, up 13 percent from 1990. [29] "Although Procter & Gamble is generally characterized by the media as a marketing company, in fact, this is importantly a research and development based company," said former CEO John Smale. P&G estimates that its primary competitors, Unilever and Colgate, spend less than 60% of what P&G does, both on a total dollar basis and as a percentage of sales. [30]

All that investment has paid off in other ways too. P&G's expertise was noticed by the U.S. government, which asked the company to build and operate shell-loading plants during World War II. As with gathering information on soap, P&G scientists and engineers studied existing military plants and came up with a better way to build bombs. They applied their packaged-goods technology to develop a continuous manufacturing line to fill shells with explosives. "The government plants weren't doing that yet," explained Howard Morgens, the retired CEO. [31]

P&G built a plant on a forty-square-mile site near Jackson, Tennessee. Each building was surrounded by an earthen barrier so that, if one blew up, the entire complex wouldn't be destroyed. Handling explosives was dangerous work. Before each shift the workers, many of them farmers, would kneel and pray. And they practiced, just to be extra careful. The 140 workers filled shells with brown sugar before using explosives. "They had a better safety record than at our soap plants," Morgens said.

P&G was asked to build a second plant in Mississippi. Eventually, P&G plants produced 25 percent of all the shells and bombs used by the Allies.

After the war, P&G got out of the bomb business, but tne government requested its assistance again during the Korean War. This time P&G Defense Company helped assemble nuclear bombs at an underground facility in Amarillo, Texas. "I was always scared to death that we'd blow up the state of Texas," Morgens confided. Everything was kept quiet, even inside the company. For years Morgens had to file paperwork with the U.S.

government every time he left the country—even for vacations. Everyone feared espionage. To this day, Morgens said, he has never discussed the plant with his wife.[32]

Most of P&G's product development is a bit more mundane. It has built a $30-billion company by making soaps, detergents, toothpastes, and diapers. It excels when scientists invent products that offer a noticeable difference to consumers. Finding those differences takes a lot of nitty-gritty research into obscure aspects of consumer habits and practices.

For instance, P&G has collected washing machines from around the world to study how they work and what kind of detergents should be used. Inside the test labs, a researcher uses a ruler to measure how deep the suds are in a machine. That's important. Many consumers judge a detergent's performance by how much the soap foams, though in reality the level of suds is irrelevant to cleaning. P&G's in-house laundromat does about 50,000 loads of clothes a year. Employees eagerly volunteer for those tests; they get their clothes washed free of charge.

Bar soaps are tested by continual hand washing to see how many rotations are required to make a good lather. The lather is then measured.[33]

P&G once asked its employees to send in soil samples from parks in twenty-two states so scientists could research dirt stains found on children's clothing.[34] One scientist, nicknamed the "stain detective," does little besides analyze grime. The company once dispatched a stain team to a New York apartment complex where residents complained that their laundry had been ruined with yellow stains. They evaluated the stains and discovered three problems: the machine cycles needed to be adjusted, residents were stuffing too many clothes into the machines, and they didn't use enough detergent. Naturally the stain squad recommended that the consumers switch to a P&G detergent.[35]

One researcher spends his days in a climate-controlled room about the size of a closet, measuring static cling. He dries polyester nightgowns and cotton shirts and uses a sort of Geiger counter to register static electricity. A computer records the static levels with and without dryer fabric softener sheets.[36]

Touch testers are trained to determine the softness of towels. An apprentice is first assigned to a trainer to learn the art. Every few months they compare their measurements of towel softness to similar consumer tests, to make sure they haven't lost their touch.[37]

There is an obsession with underwear in P&G labs. P&G recruits consumers to sell their underwear to P&G. P&G issues several pairs to the consumers, who use them for six months and then send them back to the labs. "We once had an auditorium stacked with six hundred pieces of underwear to study detergents," said Hoyt Chaloud, the retired scientist.[38]

Employee underwear is collected, especially for secret tests. Dean Butler, a former brand manager, didn't appreciate how thorough P&G research was until scientists confiscated a pair of his. P&G paper researchers had developed a new lotion-enriched toilet tissue called Certain and wanted to put it to the test. Though employees were told to keep the test a secret, "You knew who was participating in the test, because they'd walk down the hall with their little pouch of toilet paper," said Butler.

Employees were asked to fill out questionnaires about softness and durability. And they were given "an immense supply of underwear." Each pair was numbered. After employees wore the underwear, it was scrutinized to see if the new tissue was, shall we say, effective. "Every week you put it in interoffice mail and shipped it to the labs," he said.[39]

P&G's curiosity can get expensive. It often buys consumers' used toilets and ovens so scientists can really duplicate the home environment. "We magnified bacteria in toilet bowls for an ad," Doug Hall said. "It looked like cauliflower run over by a truck." Despite the test, the New York advertising agency said the bacteria wasn't "tasteful" enough for a commercial.[40]

Most of the testing is done by a cast of Ph.D.s. P&G also

hires medical doctors, dentists, and veterinarians. And the company employs more perfumers than many of the leading perfume manufacturers. One Ph.D. spends his days studying dishpan hands after women soak them in Ivory, Joy, or Dawn dishwashing liquids. Sometimes dishwashing is done by robots. At Ivorydale, a plant and research lab near Cincinnati, a mechanical arm rather than technicians washes dishes. The computer dispenses soil and measures the height of suds. [41]

Aside from the impact of dishwashing detergent, human skin is scrutinized to see how it reacts to other products. When Wondra lotion was being developed, thousands of consumers were given the lotion in unmarked packages for home use. Each person's hands, elbows, and legs were examined under magnifying glasses and graded before and after the test. [42]

Unlike Dial and The Andrew Jergens Co., P&G still does tests on animals. Dogs are shaved and harsh chemicals are applied to the skin for twenty-four to seventy-two hours. Chemicals are poured into the eyes of rabbits. Some are force-fed toxic doses of chemicals to see how they react. One anonymous caller told Cincinnati animal rights groups that P&G has a beagle farm near the city, where dogs are raised for lab tests. Outside suppliers sell beagles for at least $300; bigger dogs fetch $450, according to a price list from Hazleton Research Products in Kalamazoo. In Defense of Animals, an animal rights group based in San Rafael, California, estimates that P&G used about 450,000 animals for tests from 1985 to 1992. The tests are troubling to many because they can be replaced by other means that don't harm animals and still test the products' efficacy and safety for humans. [43]

Besides the usual tests on rabbits and cats, P&G also tests fish at its man-made stream in a Milford, Ohio, lab. Scientists also study how detergent chemicals affect flies and other creatures essential to the life of a stream. "We even studied if fish cough," recalled one manager. [44]

Human tests provide the most useful data in P&G's quest to

rid consumers of bad breath, underarm odor, and other mala-dies. Some of the least desirable jobs in the labs belong to the armpit sniffers and bad breath brigade, who inhale employees' armpits and breath before and after they use P&G's Secret and Sure deodorants and Scope mouthwash. "Trained judges" rate odor from zero (lack of offensive odor) to ten (very strong smell).[45] P&G dentists enlist employees for experiments, offer-ing free checkups for research time in their mouths. P&G has also collected more than 10,000 teeth from dentists around the world. The teeth are stored in boxes stacked floor to ceiling. In one dental experiment, scientists slice teeth to 1/5000th of the thickness of a piece of paper and then magnify the slice with an electron microscope. Visitors are quizzed about their teeth. When the dentist learned that a reporter recently had her wis-dom teeth pulled, he eagerly asked, "What did you do with them? Can we have them?"[46]

Likewise, visitors can test new shampoos and conditioners. Some are asked for a lock or two of hair. It's hard to find much free hair, so P&G buys about 150 pounds for a minimum of $850 a pound from hair brokers around the world. Most of it has to be imported. Hair uncontaminated by perms and dyes is more common in the Far East and Europe. Sleuths inside the labs carefully analyze each batch of hair to make sure the brokers haven't dyed it blond; blond hair commands a higher price than brown hair. "If it's damaged, we send it back," a technician said.[47]

Once they gather the hair, it is put through a battery of tests. In one corner of the lab, a long coil of hair bakes inside a glass oven. The brunet ponytail resembles a sleeping weasel. At nearby sinks, technicians move to the beat of a metronome as they wash and condition switches of hair. There's even a tangling machine that knots and twists hair. A "walking machine" bounces hair, while a humidity machine steams another batch. Scientists muse about inventing a pill that will give women natu-rally curly hair.[48]

While scientists can simulate natural conditions for hair and skin products, nothing seems to work as well as human taste buds when testing food and drinks. So P&G leaves that to trained gourmets. Coffee testers, called "cuppers," sip spoonfuls from up to two hundred cups of Folgers per day. By tasting different brews, they can select better coffee beans. P&G bakers make about 40,000 Duncan Hines cakes a year. Consumer services, which handles the 800 line, sent some of its managers to a daylong baking class to prepare tiered cakes so they could field questions about how to build wedding cakes from Duncan Hines mixes. [49]

The lab work is tedious, but it has led to P&G's biggest breakthroughs. Without question, the company's single best invention was synthetic detergents. Before World War II, P&G had been a small maker of soap and shortening. Those products used more intuition than hard science. Soap making was "entirely empirical," said a 1957 report on Thomas Hedley & Co. P&G acquired Hedley in 1930, and it became the basis for P&G's British operations. "With his tongue, the soap kettle operator tasted the soap, batch by batch," the report said. "Only when it tasted right could he give it his approval." [50]

Consumers were used to soaps made from animal fats for laundry and baths. They were similar to homemade products used for generations. But in the early 1930s, P&G scientist Robert Duncan went to Germany to learn about a new process for making a laundry product from synthetic sources. The first P&G detergent was Dreft. The technology was also used for a shampoo called Drene. [51] "Neither returned huge profits," Hoyt Chaloud recalled. "But it opened our company to thinking that there was something other than soap." [52]

Interest in synthetic detergents grew, especially during the war, when fats were in short supply. Soap companies organized drives to get women to return used cooking fat so it could be used in soap making. A Walt Disney film called *Out of the Frying Pan, Into the Firing Line* helped publicize the campaign. [53] Eventually scientists figured out how to make a heavy-duty synthetic with phosphates for better cleaning. In 1946 the formula was sold under the brand name Tide.[54]

"After the war, everybody did what they could," said Rowell Chase, a retired P&G advertising manager who worked on the Tide project. "Things were tight, and Tide filled a need. It took everyone by storm."[55] Indeed, P&G built an empire around Tide, which was to fuel expansion into other fields. Within two years of its introduction, Tide was the leading detergent brand. By the mid-sixties it provided half of P&G's profits. The country's use of detergents soared to a billion pounds in 1950, up from 275 million pounds in 1946.[56]

Since its introduction, Tide has been improved ninety times. Sometimes the change is minor, such as the slant of the *T* or the dot on the *I*. But the product has also evolved to keep up with consumers' needs. It's now sold in a liquid version, as well as with bleach. Each time it's improved, P&G runs its extensive tests. For instance, more than 30,000 socks were washed as part of the Tide with Bleach research.[57]

"If we hadn't done detergents, we might still be a pretty small company," said James Nethercott, retired chief financial officer. "It gave us a lead over Unilever and Colgate and generated cash to do other things."[58]

Research on soaps and detergents often involved examining calcium in water. That led to research on teeth and another P&G breakthrough that fueled the company's growth: fluoride toothpaste. Scientists were especially interested in how this compound helped slow tooth decay. By 1950 the company had teamed with fluoride researchers at Indiana University.

P&G introduced Crest toothpaste in 1955, but its sales didn't take off until 1960. That year the American Dental Association awarded Crest its seal of approval; the first time the ADA had allowed the use of its name in advertising. By 1962, sales of the brand had tripled, and Crest became the nation's leading toothpaste.

Crest helped finance other projects. It also launched the career of a future CEO: John Smale. The stern Canadian was associate advertising manager on the brand and is credited with winning the ADA approval. That was his ticket to the top of the company.[59]

A third major breakthrough came after P&G decided to expand beyond detergents and toothpastes. In 1957 P&G bought Charmin paper mills in Green Bay, Wisconsin, to experiment with paper goods. Research on pulp and paper led scientist Vic Mills to develop a product for parents to use instead of cloth diapers. He held a couple dozen patents for various projects, among them the Ivory soap-making process. But the diaper work is considered his biggest breakthrough. One reason Mills pushed for this project was purely personal: He was a grandfather. "I had changed diapers," he said. "I didn't like it." At a pilot plant at Miami Valley Labs near P&G headquarters, Mills came up with disposable diapers. Several names, including Tenders, Dri-Dees, Winks, Tads, Solos, and Zephyrs, were considered, but the product was eventually called Pampers. It went into test market in 1961.[60]

Initially, P&G figured disposables would get only a sliver of the diaper market. Disposables accounted for less than 1 percent of diaper changes at the time. One problem was that the first Pampers weren't a great product. And they were too expensive. In Peoria, Illinois, the first test market, P&G offered the diaper for 10 cents each. For the second test market, in Sacramento, California, the cost was lowered to about six cents, making the diaper more popular. By the 1970s P&G had snared 75 percent of the disposable diaper market. Sales of Pampers financed many other projects. And Mills, ninety-five years old in 1992, is still called the grandfather of Pampers.

For years P&G stuck to its core businesses, known as the three Ds: detergents, dentifrices, and diapers. There were many temptations to expand. Given its ability to borrow money cheaply, P&G considered moving into consumer financial services, James Nethercott said. Plans to buy a coal mine were raised and rejected.[61]

Part of P&G's conservative focus stemmed from getting burned on some acquisitions. The Federal Trade Commission forced the corporate giant to divest Clorox Co. after P&G bought it because it feared the sale gave P&G a monopoly. P&G also had to sign a consent decree following its purchase of Folgers, agreeing, among other things, not to acquire any consumer products business for seven years.[62]

Many credit former CEO Morgens, one of the company's earliest consumer researchers, with sticking to basic consumer goods rather than expanding into new fields. "We didn't get tangled up with junk like the auto companies," Nethercott said. "And we didn't become a conglomeration like a lot of companies did in the 1970s. Howard kept us focused on business."[63]

Still, P&G has seen its share of junk as it tries to build its basic businesses. Just ask Fred Cianciolo. He's the owner of a tiny grocery store near the corner of East Seventh and Main streets in Cincinnati. On this particular day, he laments about a box of Tide that has been collecting dust for years.

The grocer reduced the price twice, but this version of P&G's leading detergent, called Tide Sheets, is too pricey. The twenty-eight-count box of detergent-filled pouches is $9.29, twice what a normal box of Tide powder costs. Besides, consumers never really liked the idea of using premeasured packets of detergent to do the wash. So the orange box sits on a bottom shelf, just below the Roach Motels.

Cianciolo's market is the proving ground for P&G successes and flops. Once out of the labs, the products land on his shelves for informal test marketing prior to going into national distribution. Here the decades of lab work meet the ultimate test—the shoppers. "It brings in competitors who want to see what Procter is selling," said Cianciolo, whose grandfather started the business by peddling lemons in a pushcart.[64]

P&Gers have favorite flops, but few were as embarrassing as Teel. A red liquid promoted as a nonabrasive teeth cleaner, the stuff turned teeth brown and was quickly dropped in the late 1940s. In more recent times, P&G has also tried several times to combine a paper towel with soaps or conditioners, only to find consumers don't like them. Fling, a soap-filled paper towel, became "like a wet tissue," said one P&Ger. Abound was a towel with conditioner that consumers wiped on their hair after shampooing. No one quite understood the benefits of a conditioning towel instead of using bottled conditioners. Both innovations failed.

Salvo, a giant tablet of detergent, is one of the more memorable flops. Introduced in 1960, it was a hard tablet of detergent that housewives were supposed to toss in with the clothes. It resembled a hockey puck and performed like one inside the washing machine. The idea behind Salvo, like Tide Sheets, was to offer consumers a premeasured amount of detergent. That way, P&G figured it could combat that nasty habit consumers have of scrimping on how much Tide goes into the wash.

But Salvo's problem was simple: it didn't dissolve. During one focus group, women also complained about the product being too expensive. One woman offered that she stretched the cost over several loads because she thought the tablet was reusable. "She hadn't figured out that her clothes weren't getting clean because the detergent wasn't dissolving," said David Goodman, the former P&G market researcher.[65]

Many of P&G's bombs get defused while still in test market, sparing the company a great deal of expense. But one of its more expensive failures, Encaprin, made it all the way to national markets, where it got clobbered. The biggest problem the coated aspirin capsule faced was a flurry of competition when ibuprofen drugs switched from prescription to over-the-counter sales.

Some insiders predicted the over-the-counter switch of ibuprofen and the rise of products like Advil and Nuprin. They warned the company not to take Encaprin to national markets.

Even experts at P&G's newly acquired Norwich drugs didn't help because "they didn't dare speak up," said one former officer. "It was a Procter idea, so it couldn't be bad. It's technical and marketing arrogance."

"We failed," admitted Geoffrey Place, who headed P&G's research and development efforts. One lesson the company learned, he said, is to "never underestimate what the consumer is looking for in terms of efficacy." In that case, pain relief was more important than stomach safety, the product benefit P&G chose to hype to consumers. Encaprin was pulled from the shelves in August 1986 after only two years on the market.[66]

P&G's source of greatest disappointment by far is its food-and-beverage division. The problems began nearly forty years ago when P&G decided to build a food business out of two brands: Crisco shortening and Duncan Hines cake mixes. "Even then, the first-stringers stayed in soap and the second went into food," said Lou Pritchett, the former vice president of sales. The division has continued to be a stepchild at the company.[67]

One of P&G's problems is the lack of focus on what grocery store aisles it wants to target. For instance, P&G researchers once came up with a product called Cold Snap, an imitation ice cream mix that had the taste of cold Crisco. "It had so much gum and emulsifier in it, it was like Play-Doh," said Thane Pressman, who worked on food projects. To make it worse, it took hours to prepare and had directions similar to a model airplane. "A real bomb," Cianciolo said.[68]

P&G also considered getting into the meat business. Rising meat prices prompted scientists to evaluate products made of soy proteins. "We must have spent fifty million dollars on that project," Pressman said. The dehydrated product was used in a sort of Hamburger Helper mix that, in his words, tasted absolutely "awful."[69]

The fascination with dehydrated foods led to everyone's favorite flop, Pringles potato chips, which has been called the P&G Edsel.[70] The chips were invented because consumers repeatedly complained about stale and broken chips. So the famous inventor Vic Mills and his group devised a way to dehydrate potatoes and reconstitute them into perfect chips. To prevent breakage and preserve freshness, the chips were sold in packages that resembled cans of tennis balls.

Mills thought the chips would be a hit. But it took more than seven years to get them into test market because "the company had so many other things going on," he said. Once it finally introduced the snack in 1968, a confident P&G quickly expanded capacity, installing more of the huge Pringles machines at its factories. Pringles snared 35 percent of its test markets. In one day, Fred Cianciolo sold seventy-five cases. "I had to limit it to two per customer," he said. "But that was more than I sold in the next twenty years."

Despite initial enthusiasm, consumers stopped buying Pringles. First of all, they tasted more like cardboard than potatoes. And, the public's earlier complaints notwithstanding, people really prefer greasy, broken, irregular chips in bags to perfectly shaped discs in cans.

P&G also tried to change the rules of chip delivery. Frito-Lay and others rely on route trucks, where drivers restock grocery shelves. P&G wanted to deliver Pringles along with its other goods to grocers' warehouses to save time and money. The company even designed special racks to hold the Pringles cans in stores. But without the special attention offered by a team of drivers, Pringles were a low priority in stores.

Many P&G managers voted to drop Pringles entirely. "I told John Smale I couldn't fix it," recalled Chuck Jarvie, former vice president of food. Losses on the brand are estimated to be as high as $650 million.

About twenty-five years after the product was launched, P&G insists that Pringles are back from the dead. But one look at the chip aisle at a Pittsburgh Giant Eagle casts doubt on that claim. Pringles still get a tiny portion of the bottom shelf, far from consumers' view.

"Food is more of an art than science. Procter can't invent fluoride for food, so they don't get it," Jarvie said.[71]

Likewise, P&G suffered a similar failure with its ready-to-serve Duncan Hines cookies. Scientists developed a crispy-chewy cookie by combining two different types of dough. "Everybody thought we'd drive dry cookies off the shelf," one manager said.

A test batch was made at a bakery in Chicago. But P&G moved too slowly. By the time it tested the cookies in Kansas City, competitors were rolling out their own home-style cookies. Keebler and Nabisco flooded the shelves with their own brands of soft cookies.[72]

P&G spent about $400 million on a new Jackson, Tennessee, cookie plant, despite internal warnings. Insiders said the company should look for old bakeries and use them until they were sure the brand would succeed. "But the technicians won," a former officer said. "We built an elegant plant that had twelve hundred workers hand-picking and packing cookies. It was just a mess."

P&G later sued Nabisco, Keebler, and Frito-Lay, charging espionage in the test bakery. The suit was settled for $125 million in 1989. But P&G gained little, considering it forfeited the entire market to Nabisco and Keebler. "The huge investment was never recovered," the former officer said.

On the beverage side, results have been equally dismal. To be sure, P&G's Folgers is a leading brand of coffee. But its fortunes vary, depending on the price of green coffee beans. And there are constant promotion wars, with Maxwell House and others, that eat into profits.

As in food, P&G has lacked focus in beverages. It once considered getting into the milk business. "P&G developed an amazingly good soy-based product that tasted like milk," said Dean Butler, the former brand manager who worked on beverage products. And the company's acquisition team has shopped for small beverage companies in every category. One of the stranger offers Butler reviewed was an offer to buy a company that bottled Mexican water.

P&G's puritan ways ruled out buying a liquor or beer business, so the company chose soft drinks. Scientists developed a powdered cola that consumers could mix with water, but it didn't taste very good. P&G also considered buying Royal Crown Cola, Dr Pepper, and 7Up, but deals never worked out. It has even evaluated whether to buy Coke or Pepsi. "We looked at them, but they're as big as we are," said former CFO James Nethercott.

In 1980 P&G got into the business with the $57-million purchase of Crush. Once again, P&G tried to change the rules set by entrenched competitors. It bought a bottling company to learn that end of the business and redo the distribution network. It wanted to rely on its traditional shipment methods through warehouses rather than route trucks used by Coke and Pepsi. But the bottling network proved too powerful, even for P&G. Some bottlers stopped promoting Crush and Hires, P&G's other soft drink, in retaliation.

And there were internal conflicts about what to do to build the brand. "That business was doomed to indecision," said one manager. "We had so many different plans." P&G did develop a low-sugar, high-calcium soft drink, but senior management didn't want to touch a new product until Crush and Hires turned profitable.

In 1989 P&G put the soft-drink business up for sale, and Cadbury-Schweppes bought it for $220 million. "We got in and learned a lot. But not much of it benefited P&G," Nethercott said. [73] Likewise, P&G entered the orange juice business, searching for a big piece of the beverage market. That too has proved elusive.

Researchers came up with a method of freezing orange juice that kept more of its taste and smell. "We had a seventy-five–twenty-five win over other juices in blind tests," Butler said. But management didn't want to spend $4 million for a pilot project until it did more test marketing. Meanwhile, P&G went hunting for an acquisition to get it into the business.

The company settled on Ben Hill Griffin Co., a Florida citrus company, and spent heavily to build a state-of-the-art orange juice–processing plant. Coca Cola's Minute Maid and Beatrice's (now Seagram's) Tropicana relied on older, well-depreciated plants. P&G also dropped contracts to supply juice for private-label brands sold by grocery store chains. P&G needed the orange supplies to make its own big brand, called Citrus Hill. In 1982 Wall Street analysts predicted it could be the biggest thing since Pampers, which at the time produced $1 billion in annual sales. [74]

"We hoped for a thirty share, so we could be in the big three of orange juice," said one P&Ger. Eventually P&G wanted to use the orange juice business to sell nectars and other drinks and, eventually, return to soft drinks. "But we kept ignoring Coke and Tropicana."

Frank Blod, a former P&Ger, was at Minute Maid when P&G introduced Citrus Hill. "Based on what P&G had done in the past on Pringles and Folgers, we knew what their year one and two plans would be. P&G is very predictable. It's template marketing." [75]

The analysis of Citrus Hill's test market showed that the brand was taking market share from private-label brands, not the two market leaders. The brand did well in blind tests, winning sixty–forty over Minute Maid, which had continued to improve its flavor. But when consumers tested products labeled Minute Maid, that brand won because it has a strong trademark recognition among consumers, Blod explained.

Minute Maid also declared war in the grocery stores as Citrus Hill rolled out to new markets. "We loaded the shelves and virtually kept the brand off the shelf" when P&G sent coupons to consumers, Blod said.

Citrus Hill inched to an 11 percent share of the market. But competitors figured it needed at least 15 percent to break even. It lost more share when both Tropicana and Minute Maid launched higher-pulp juices. Steve Dennis, who worked on Citrus Hill, said it was difficult to fight back. "We were losing money so badly, anytime we tried to introduce new products or line extensions, it was going to be tough because the economics on the base business were so bad."

P&G tried to upgrade with Citrus Hill Select in 1985 and sell it at a higher price. "But that didn't stick," Dennis said. B. Jurgen Hintz, then in charge of the beverage division, wanted "us to push for volume and share leadership, or the number two place, and profitability would follow," Dennis said. More gimmicks followed. The brand offered a 96-ounce jug of juice, a resealable cap on cartons, and a calcium-enriched juice. P&G even opened up a toll-free hot line to answer questions about juice and calcium. And Citrus Hill Plus Calcium received the American Medical Women's Association seal. [76]

But all of that was met with a yawn. Many consumers buy whatever juice is on sale. "And everything has calcium in it, even Tums," one manager pointed out. The next change was labeling the juice Citrus Hill Fresh Choice to make consumers believe it was freshly squeezed that very day. That ploy landed P&G in hot water with the Food and Drug Administration. P&G refused to take the word off the label, so the FDA ordered marshals to seize an entire warehouse of Citrus Hill in 1991. P&G quickly agreed to relabel the brand. [77]

Management changes in the division also caused havoc for the troubled brand. Numerous managers have come and gone from the business, including Hintz. As the division's executive vice president, Hintz fought with CEO Artzt on strategy too many times. Insiders say he left partially because of the Citrus Hill mess, most notably the embarrassing battle with the FDA. "Regrettably, the seizure of Citrus Hill could have and should have been avoided," Artzt said in a letter to shareholders. "On one hand, we believe that the FDA acted precipitously. On the other hand, we clearly underestimated the urgency of the FDA's position."[78]

"It's P&G arrogance," Blod observed. "They saw a sleepy, old industry without sophisticated marketing and sales and thought they could revitalize it. But we went to war."

P&G thought technological advancements such as putting calcium in the juice would matter to consumers. "But nobody wants to hear about it," Dennis said. The strategy of delivering whiter socks with better detergents doesn't apply to foods. "In cookies, Pringles, and juice, technology was driving those products, but consumers aren't impressed."[79] P&G finally took the hint: Citrus Hill was abandoned in 1992. P&G couldn't even find a buyer for the troubled brand. It just discontinued it and took a $200 million charge to cover the cost of pulling the plug. After years of trying, Citrus Hill had only 8 percent of the orange juice market.

But P&G hasn't given up on linking science and food. It has been working on a fat substitute called olestra for decades. But this has fallen into the same trap as other food and beverage products and has raised some safety questions as well.

Researchers developed the product sucrose polyester in the 1960s. It looks and tastes like fat but isn't absorbed by the body. There was one major problem, however: it caused diarrhea. Inside P&G the problem was labeled "LSE," for "laxative side effect." P&G contends the problem has been fixed. Internal debates on strategy continued for years. Some wanted P&G to seek approval for olestra as a drug rather than a food so it could be more easily controlled. That might speed up FDA approval. "But the marketing people said, 'How do you sell it?' " Hoyt Chaloud said. So in 1987 P&G submitted olestra for FDA approval as a food, hoping to have it on the market within two years. The original petition asked for use in snacks, commercial and consumer oils, and shortenings. Once again, Wall Street analysts and the press applauded it as a potential billion-dollar business for P&G.

In an era of heightened health consciousness, "there was almost no way we could screw it up," Dennis said.

P&G formed a separate olestra division to create products that would eventually contain the product, such as Crisco Lite. Packaging and advertising campaigns were reviewed. "There was a lot of excitement about whether we could make it another Tide or Pampers," said Frank Weise, former financial adviser in the food division. P&G even broke ground for an olestra plant. "There was a feeling that olestra would be the lead horse for an entire healthy foods business," Dennis said. The team looked at "every product that has fat in it," he said. At Cianciolo's market, the owner said customers "kept coming in and asking for it."

By March of 1988, "it was clear that March of 1989 approval was out of the question. We still felt it might get approved sometime in 1989," Dennis said.

Other problems continued to plague the product. Scientists at the Center for Science in the Public Interest said a review of P&G's own research showed olestra causes cancer in lab rats. [80]

But P&G forged ahead. The FDA required more rodent studies, tacking a couple more years on to the review. P&G maintains the same study cited by CSPI and other research "definitively demonstrate there is no such link" to cancer, tumors, or other health problems. The FDA has reviewed the results of the research and had not announced its findings as of May 1993.

Other companies' products made it to market ahead of olestra. NutraSweet's Simplesse, a combination of milk and egg proteins, was approved faster because it was made from ingredients already found in the food supply. And companies like Kraft's Entenmann's baked goods have found other ways to cut the fat in products without elaborate science.

"Procter was all dressed up with no place to go," said Kip Knight, another marketing manager on the olestra team. "We should've gotten approval and then done the marketing. The only people slower than P&G [are] the federal government."

The olestra division was disbanded in 1990. The petition to

the FDA has been radically scaled back to ask for replacement of fats in salty snacks. P&G has asked Congress to extend its patents, which could expire before it gets FDA approval. Competitors blocked P&G's lobbying efforts to get the special patent protection, but P&G has vowed to try again in the 1993 Congress. [81] "A lot of the bloom will have left that rose when P&G gets to market," said David Williams, partner at New England Consulting.

CEO Ed Artzt and others have blamed the FDA for moving too slowly because olestra is a new addition to the food chain. But those familiar with the project say it's wrong to put the blame on the government. "That's bullshit," said one P&G scientist. "I saw olestra sit at Miami Valley Labs [one of P&G's main research sites] because nobody wanted to touch it. The food division didn't want it because they sold food, not health. People in the health care division said it was a food. We lost years on that project because nobody stepped forward. My blood boils when I see the way olestra was screwed up. It has taken us twenty-five years to get to the point where it's still two years from getting approval from the FDA."

The olestra effort has also set back P&G's efforts to come up with significant breakthroughs. Olestra has been so costly that scientists say they're now told to focus more on short-term projects, not research that takes decades to complete. Recognition for scientific breakthroughs is pegged to quick successes. For instance, P&G created the Vic Mills Society to honor its most prolific inventor. Scientists say it is a hollow reward, however, one that honors only those whose research can be pointed to on store shelves—which helps build profits and the stock price. That doesn't recognize other, long-term research that builds a company over generations rather than fiscal quarters. The result of this change in philosophy has been a plethora of mediocre line extensions of existing brand names, such as a spray version of Comet bathroom cleanser or Duncan Hines microwave cupcakes. "P&G research used to be pseudo-academic," one researcher said. "Now there's a push to make it more relevant, but we're not coming up with anything."

The olestra debacle produced additional fallout as well: It fueled short-term interest in building the company's troubled snack food business, costing P&G even more money that hasn't produced much of a return.

When RJR Nabisco went up for sale in 1988, P&G joined a group of investors to buy the margarine and salted snacks business. Margarine would be a natural for P&G, considering its decades of research on fats and products like Crisco. And if olestra won FDA approval, a fat-free margarine could be a hit. But that bid failed when KKR upped the ante for RJR. "P&G lost its nerve," said one source inside the company. "It was getting out of control. We just wouldn't play at those stakes."

After KKR won RJR, antitrust laws forced it to divest one of its two peanut brands, Planters or Fisher Nuts. KKR owned Fisher from an earlier acquisition. P&G, tempted by the prospect of using olestra in peanut snacks, coveted Planters, which has about 50 percent of the peanut market. KKR wanted $1.2 billion, sources said. P&G offered $800 million.

When KKR couldn't get the higher bid, it offered to sell Fisher Nuts, the number-two brand. P&G prefers market leaders, but it realized that it had to do something to replace growth lost from failures in the labs. Starting more snack food businesses from scratch wasn't realistic. So P&G went on an acquisition binge in food and beverage. The company bought Sundor and Hawaiian Punch, two drink businesses. When Planters wasn't available at its price, P&G went after Fisher. The company moved quickly to evaluate the business before it lost it to other bidders. The review showed some problems. The Fisher brand was supplied by old plants, and the brand name was tired. It was a distant number two behind Planters and was virtually unknown in some parts of the country.

Some on the exploration team figured there was little reason to proceed with the review. It wasn't P&G's kind of business.

"But the team was sent back to look again," one manager said. The management of the food business had convinced senior management that it was a great opportunity. The product was selling for about 20 percent less than Planters, so there was room to increase the price. And the brand could gain share with P&G's typically aggressive advertising and promotion. Besides, some figured it could gain distribution if P&G continued Fisher's practice of distributing the product through food brokers. That would help P&G in the food aisles, where it had previously suffered setbacks.

The plan went to John Pepper, P&G president, who offered to buy Fisher for $145 million. KKR quickly accepted. "We all said uh-oh," the source said. "That's not their reputation. They normally squeeze for more."

P&G soon learned why: A group inside Fisher Nuts was planning a management buyout. Their most aggressive bid was under $90 million. And there were problems beyond the price tag. After the deal closed in late 1989, P&G management didn't allow the group that had evaluated the business to run it. "They're the ones on the hook," one manager said. "They talked you into spending all this money, so make them perform." P&G also ditched the brokers and lost distribution. Once again, the company believed it knew how to fix what was wrong, without any help from the experts. "It was arrogance," said one source. "We were going to show them everything about the nut business."[82]

About the same time as the acquisition, P&G chairman and CEO John Smale stepped down and Ed Artzt took over. In his first month on the job, he attended a review of the Fisher Nuts business. Artzt rebuffed new ideas that required investment, telling the team to build Fisher's market share. He was also discovering what a mess olestra had become and moved fast to do damage control. Even when researchers came up with a low-fat peanut, he didn't want to spend the money. "Can I get my money back?" he said in a 1990 business review.[83]

Since then, losses from food and beverage bombs have been steep. The division earned just $47 million on sales of $3.55 billion in fiscal 1991. [84] Sources say Citrus Hill alone lost nearly half a billion dollars, although P&G puts the loss at just $200 million. In addition, investments in that brand, along with cookies and Pringles, have cost P&G about $2 billion in capital, according to an internal P&G review. "P&G doesn't have critical mass," said Weise, the former controller for food and beverage. [85]

Even its historically successful brands are under siege as consumers change their eating habits. Fewer people use Crisco shortening and Duncan Hines cake mixes as they try to reduce fats in their diets. Other food companies have shifted more quickly to healthier and fresh foods. P&G tried to get into the refrigerated foods business through the purchase of a company that made chilled biscuit dough. But it decided it would stick to dry goods that didn't have to be delivered by refrigerated trucks. "P&G missed the boat on refrigerated foods," said David Williams, the consultant. "Now it would be difficult for P&G to get into it."

Moreover, food companies are selling convenience. "If you really want to be in the food business, you've got to provide the end product," said one former officer. "The world has changed. Is anybody doing any cooking anymore?"

P&G constantly trips when it tries to apply technology-driven ideas of detergents and diapers to the more fickle world of foods. Bill Morgan, who evaluated the food business as one of P&G's controllers, calls the division "a silly waste of resources." He suggests that the business be spun off into a separate company, where it can hire experts who know how to sell foods. "Or they should just sell the damn thing." Some managers suggested a sale could be part of CEO Ed Artzt's restructuring plans in 1993. Frank Blod concurs. "If they were smart," he contends, "they would walk away." [86]

4
Subliminal Sabotage

S usan Dearth's house became their secret meeting place.

    Over coffee in her Inglenook Place living room, women employees of Procter & Gamble gathered each week to plot how they would take a stand against the company. They'd had enough of second-class treatment by their white male bosses. Because of sexist double standards, women weren't making progress at P&G. Many were denied jobs if they admitted they planned to marry or have children, questions that men were never asked. The few women who had been hired for coveted marketing jobs often found themselves trapped in brand assistant positions. And after they left the job each day, the women were reminded of P&G's sexism every time they turned on the television or looked at a magazine, for P&G's advertisements for Tide and Comet portrayed all women as vacuous Suzie Homemakers.

    But it was 1974. The women knew that speaking out could cost them their jobs. They asked Dearth, then thirty-four years old, to lead their campaign. As a P&G stockholder, she could submit a proposal for the company's proxy statement asking other stockholders to pressure P&G into providing more career opportunities for women and revising its advertising campaigns. "I was very irritated and insulted about P&G's ads," said Dearth, later one of the first women to hold a dean's post at the

University of Cincinnati's medical center. "The value of women was wrapped up in how clean the house is and how white the clothes are."[1]

Nearly twenty years have passed since she led the campaign against P&G, and her opinion hasn't changed. "It's very discouraging," said Dearth, "We have moved backward."

P&G, which popularized consumer advertising and daytime soap operas, has built an empire partially by reinforcing stereotypes about women as subservient to men. Its ads all share a theme of condescension toward women and the promotion of consumers' self-consciousness about cleanliness and status. Marcia Grace, who helped create P&G advertising at Wells Rich Greene, said: "P&G is at least twenty years behind the American woman. The problem is throughout the company. Even though it diversified into foods and cosmetics, it started as a soap company and got this fix that a woman's chief delight is a clean dish, clean floor, and clean shirt. The company doesn't seem to be able to step away from that."[2]

One reason P&G's sexist mind-set continually surfaces in its ads is the lack of women inside to challenge P&G's senior management. And the company rarely listens to its agencies. P&G's standing as the country's largest advertiser gives it a stranglehold on Madison Avenue. Armed with a $2.15-billion annual advertising budget, the company blankets the country with messages about Ivory purity, Downy softness, and Scope freshness.[3] Those massive P&G accounts offer steady work in a tumultuous industry, but the soap company controls virtually every aspect of its ad agencies' work. It has tried to block mergers between agencies and moved multimillion-dollar accounts when its wishes weren't obeyed. Even account managers get locked into restrictive P&G agreements that limit where they can work after doing business with the company. Like their counterparts inside P&G, they go along with Procter's ways or they're out. "We're pretty well trapped," lamented the head of one of P&G's major ad agencies.[4]

It is impossible to escape P&G advertising, the budget of which is larger than those of McDonald's, Kellogg, Anheuser Busch, and Coca-Cola combined.[5] Crest toothpaste decorates posters in high school hallways. Tide detergent and Folgers coffee logos are painted on stock cars.[6] P&G's Charmin toilet paper sponsors the women's bathrooms at the Oakland–Alameda County Coliseum, home of the Oakland Athletics baseball team.[7] As soon as a baby is born in most hospitals, its bottom is covered with a Pampers diaper. Free samples are sent home with about 4 million newborns each year.[8] In grocery stores, if a shopper buys Peter Pan (a competitor's peanut butter), a video display reminds her that "choosy mothers choose Jif," the P&G brand. If that hasn't swayed her, at the checkout line the register spits out a 30-cents-off coupon for Jif.[9]

The messages are effective: In polls conducted in 1985, 93 percent of women shoppers could name the familiar bald-headed Mr. Clean, the man who cleans kitchen floors "to the shine," but only 56 percent could identify then Vice President George Bush.[10]

Advertising is the lifeblood of every successful brand. The belief that a message could distinguish one product from another dates back to P&G's early days as a soap and candle maker. Crates of Star candles were marked with a moon-and-stars symbol so buyers could pick out the P&G product from other boxes.[11] The symbol later evolved into the familiar man-in-the-moon symbol that became the company trademark.

The first advertisement to grocers appeared in 1881 in a grocery trade publication. Harley Procter, son of founder William Procter, wanted to build business for Ivory soap.[12] He believed the white bar of Ivory was superior to the yellow soaps of the time. To prove its purity, Procter commissioned a chemist to test Ivory. The scientist showed impurities of only 0.56 percent. Procter subtracted that to come up with the slogan "99$^{44}/_{100}$% pure."[13] A year later P&G ran its first ad in a publication, a national religious weekly called *The Independent*. It recommended Ivory Soap for both laundry and bath, and reminded buyers that Ivory floats. [14]

Procter convinced the company to spend $11,000 on more ads directed at consumers, something other companies weren't doing at the time. From the very beginning, P&G showed a knack for pushing ultracleanliness. Early ads claimed that Ivory would clean everything from babies in the cradle to brass on the car and rid horses of spots and scratches.

One ad, remarkable in retrospect for its blatant racism, declared that Ivory "civilized" native Americans:

> *We once were factious, fierce and wild,*
> *To peaceful arts unreconciled;*
> *Our blankets smeared with grease and stains*
> *From buffalo meat and settlers' veins.*
> *Through summer's dust and heat content,*
> *From moon to moon unwashed we went;*
> *But Ivory Soap came like a ray*
> *Of light across our darkened way.*
> *And now we're civil, kind and good,*
> *And keep the laws as people should.*
> *We wear our linen, lawn and lace,*
> *As well as folks with paler face.*
> *And now I take, where'er we go,*
> *This cake of Ivory Soap to show*
> *What civilized my squaw and me*
> *And made us clean and fair to see.* [15]

To keep readers interested in the brand, P&G would sponsor contests. One in 1911 offered $1,000 for unusual uses for Ivory. More than 50,000 ideas poured in, ranging from massaging sore muscles to polishing jewelry. P&G produced a booklet for new brides, offering hints on how Ivory would scrub floors and remove freckles and tans. (Mix a chopped-up bar of Ivory with the juice of one lemon. A good scrubbing promised to make "the skin white and smooth.") [16]

Perhaps the most enduring Ivory campaign featured Ivory babies. The campaign began in 1887 with—there's no delicate way to put this—a truly ugly baby. P&G's own reports described it as having "a baby's body, but with the face of what seemed to be a middle-aged man." The company later commissioned artists to draw rosy-cheeked infants for Ivory ads. [17]

Another way P&G promoted the brand was to remind consumers of its unique ability to float in water. The "it floats" campaign prompted a famous *New Yorker* cartoon in 1928 captioned "Industrial Crises—The day a cake of soap sank at Procter & Gamble's." It depicted dark-suited executives preparing to dive into a pool to rescue a bar that had sunk to the bottom. [18] When a bar of Ivory (probably from a bad batch of soap) really did sink in 1944, newspapers bannered headlines about the tragedy. [19] Ivory had became as common in homes as the kitchen sink. *Life* magazine called it "a kind of national institution." [20] By its 100th anniversary in 1979, Ivory had sold more than 30 billion bars. [21]

Ivory is a rather bland soap that doesn't offer any special features such as fresh smells or promises of beauty. So its claim of pure cleaning isn't particularly dramatic, considering that all soaps do pretty much the same job. Advertising has sustained the product. "That brand has no right to still be alive," said Milt Gossett, director of Saatchi & Saatchi Worldwide Advertising, which acquired Compton Advertising and the Ivory account in 1982. [22]

The soap received one of its biggest boosts from another P&G innovation: ads based on a continuing saga of a family—all Ivory users, naturally. There were signs of the melodramas even in the earliest ads, which featured "Elizabeth Harding, Bride." They lamented how her new husband might leave her because the house was a mess. [23]

By the 1920s, P&G's newspaper ads featured a fictitious family called the Jollycos. They had three children: Sally, Bobby, and baby Teewee. Other characters included neighbors who helped promote the use of Ivory soap through a story in each Sunday's newspaper. The villain, Mrs. Percival Billington Folderol, used colored and scented soaps. The Jollyco family increased Ivory sales by 25 percent in its first six months in New York markets. [24]

The idea led to radio shows. "The Puddle Family" was introduced in 1932. The following year "Ma Perkins," sponsored by Oxydol, a P&G soap, aired on Cincinnati's WLW in August, then went national on the NBC network four months later. These were among the first soap operas, also known as "washboard weepers" because of the tearjerker plots. [25]

The fifteen-minute show ran five days a week and mentioned Oxydol's name twenty to twenty-five times during each episode. "We knew it would be very irritating to some people and we'd get complaints," recalled Walter Lingle, a P&G marketing executive who helped launch the show. "But the business was bad enough that we decided to try it." P&G received 5,000 letters complaining about "Ma Perkins" within the first week. But after a month, salesmen were calling headquarters to say Oxydol sales were up. By the end of the first year, sales had doubled. [26]

Ma Perkins, played by twenty-three-old Virginia Payne, became America's beloved "mother of the air." Fans wrote asking her advice on their personal lives. Some sent her pot holders. One older woman suggested in a letter that the two could be companions in their "fading days." She asked Ma for directions to her home in "Rushville Center," so she could begin packing her bags. [27]

"Ma Perkins" attracted more listeners than many nighttime shows. To count how many people actually listened, P&G conducted one of its first market research tests on the impact of soap operas. During the show, listeners were offered a package of flower seeds for 10 cents and an Oxydol boxtop. More than a million boxtops flooded P&G headquarters. The show helped sell 3 billion boxes of Oxydol before it was finally cancelled in 1960,[28] with Ms. Payne, by then fifty, still in the title role.

The success of radio led P&G to be one of the first advertisers on television. The company helped sponsor the first TV broadcast of a major league baseball game, the Brooklyn Dodgers versus the Cincinnati Reds, in 1939. Between innings, sports announcer Walter Ranier "Red" Barber pitched Ivory.[29]

In 1941 P&G sponsored the game show "Truth or Consequences" but reached only about 5,000 homes in the New York area. World War II slowed P&G's progress on television. Stations closed and factories made military goods rather than television sets. By the late 1940s, television sets were more common. In 1948 Ivory Snow and Prell shampoo sponsored a series of programs called "Fashions on Parade." The live Friday night show taught P&G the benefits of taping, as actors tripped over props and forgot their lines.[30] The following year Howard Morgens, then vice president of advertising, formed P&G Productions. The subsidiary, run by the future CEO Morgens, was set up to produce or buy television programs and motion pictures.

Television proved to be the most effective way for P&G to reach its consumers. Most women stayed at home raising the children, so P&G tried its soap opera format on television. The first daytime television soap was "The First Hundred Years," launched in 1950.[31] The show lasted only a month, but P&G tried again with "Search for Tomorrow" and a TV version of its radio show, "The Guiding Light."[32] By the mid-fifties it had thirteen different soaps on the air.[33]

The idea of continuing characters influenced P&G advertising as well. Elm City, U.S.A., was the setting for an ad campaign to introduce Comet cleanser. The story line showed homemakers fighting stubborn stains with ease, thanks to Comet. That campaign led to Josephine the plumber, a character played for eleven years by Jane Withers, who got her Hollywood start as a sidekick to Shirley Temple. "Characters like Josephine became part of the American folklore," Saatchi & Saatchi's Milt Gossett said.[34] Other characters included Charley, Dash's washer repairman; actress Nancy Walker's Rosie, the waitress who obsessively mops up spills with Bounty; the annoying Mr. Whipple, who begged shoppers not to squeeze the Charmin; and Mrs. Olsen, a Swedish caterer who insisted that Folgers mountain-grown coffee is the richest tasting. By using familiar characters to make the pitch, P&G struck a resounding chord with consumers. "P&G ads were ubiquitous," said Miner Raymond, who produced about 25,000 P&G ads during his tenure at the company. "The whole family gathered to watch television, and they listened to the commercials."[35]

The company was criticized from the start about the sappy content of its ads and TV shows, but P&G believed it was in the business to sell soap, nothing else. "The problem of improving the literary tastes of the people is the problem of the schools," said CEO Neil McElroy in 1953. P&G consumers "aren't intellectuals—they're ordinary people, good people, who win wars for us, produce our manufactured products, and grow our food." He added, "They use a lot of soap."[36]

P&G products and advertising linked happiness to use of its brands. For instance, many ads are filmed in upscale homes that are beyond most consumers' reach. The original Folgers "Best Part of Wakin' Up" commercial was filmed at a $20-million horse ranch near Ronald Reagan's residence in California. "P&G sets itself up as the gold standard," one advertising manager said.[37]

The strong emotional sells of ads focus on guilt about dandruff and smelly armpits. "Morning breath was a P&G invention," said former P&G brand manager Jack Gordon. To help it sell more Scope mouthwash, the company once hired a Jungian psychologist to conduct focus groups to uncover people's deep-seated fears of having bad breath. The doctor traveled to ten cities to interview consumers. He asked them to lie on the floor and recall their first experience with bad breath. From the sessions, he concluded that bad breath is taboo because it's symbolic of death and decay. [38]

Likewise, the Cascade dishwasher detergent campaigns focus on guilt about spotty dishes or lack of shine on the china. "To imply and demonstrate that people will be concerned about spots on glasses implies such a close microscopic view of a person," said Dr. Carol Moog, a psychologist who has studied P&G's commercials. "It creates so much self-consciousness and distrust of those around you that you won't be accepted for who you are. The sense of being inspected is destructive." [39]

P&G says its advertising mirrors the times and tastes of its consumers. But there's a pattern of destructive messages to women. For instance, in 1949 P&G created a jingle for Prell that featured an animated tube of shampoo called Tallulah singing, "I'm Tallulah the tube of Prell. And I've got a little something to tell. Your hair can be radiant, oh so easy. All you've got to do is take me home and squeeze me." At least one woman was offended by the ad: famed actress Tallulah Bankhead, who sued for $1 million. She later settled for a few thousand dollars. "We didn't mind it," Morgens said. "It was great publicity for both of us." [40]

P&G got more free publicity when it discovered its Ivory Snow mother of the early 1970s, Marilyn Chambers, was also a porn-film star. "She looked like the Virgin Mary," Morgens said. Her sudden notoriety spiked sales temporarily. "A lot of people bought the product just to see her," Morgens acknowledged. [41]

Women inside P&G grew increasingly tired of how the company treated women in the workplace and in the marketplace. Several approached P&G's head of personnel to ask if they could use company office space to organize a women's support group. Management refused, dubbing it "unauthorized." But friends at a local bank offered their office space. In May 1973, about 100 women showed up after work to discuss their problems with

P&G. They called themselves the Womens' Interest Group, or WIG. "It was like water seeking an outlet," said one organizer. "There was so much energy for change." As many as 300 women began attending the monthly meetings.

At first the group focused on educating and networking among themselves, believing they could bring about change in P&G's antiquated views about women, ranging from job discrimination to sexist language in technical manuals. But by 1974 a smaller group within WIG began to push secretly for a public stand against P&G. They went to Susan Dearth to seek her help as the spokeswoman for two proxy proposals that would pressure P&G to change how it treated women inside and outside the company. The first asked for a report on employment of women and minorities. The group reasoned that a company that appeals to a mass market should have women and minorities, not just white males, in decision-making roles. The second requested that P&G advertising depict women in a variety of roles, not just homemaker. At the time, more than 40 percent of women worked outside of the home. [42]

"Advertising in the late sixties and seventies was embarrassing," said a WIG organizer. One ad compared the hands of eighteen- and thirty-four-year-old women to show how Ivory dishwashing liquid preserved youth. The two women in the commercial played tennis, and the older woman was portrayed as a klutz who fumbled a lot on the court. Even the agency discovered the ad was a mistake. "We must've got fifty thousand letters complaining about that," said Bob Jordan, retired vice chairman of Saatchi & Saatchi. "We portrayed age as a negative thing." [43]

WIG found support from a United Presbyterian Church investment group, which fought against investment in South Africa and other issues, and said P&G ads reinforced stereotypes of women and depicted them as housekeepers, mothers, and sex objects. The Rev. Donald R. Purkey, chairperson of the church's Committee on Mission Responsibility through Investment, became convinced of the problem after watching P&G advertising.

Before the annual meeting on October 14, 1975, Rev. Purkey and other leaders of the church met with P&G's senior management to discuss how they could resolve the problem. The thirty-nine-year-old minister admits to having been "a bit naive about the power of Proctor & Gamble," he said. "It's fair to say P&G wasn't pleased by the church's challenge." Although the church held 67,636 shares of stock, P&G didn't take the meeting very seriously. "It was a chilling experience to be ushered into the executive offices and be told that we didn't know what we were talking about," he said. P&G preached to Purkey about the virtues of the company, never acknowledging it had a problem in its ads. "I don't know when I've ever felt so demeaned," he recalled. "I found them monolithic, autocratic, and frightening."

He offered to withdraw a shareholder resolution submitted by the group if P&G would agree to address the concerns about advertising. P&G wouldn't do that, so the resolution went to the shareholders for a vote. Meanwhile, Rev. Purkey met with local leaders of the Presbyterian Church. "That was very ticklish. Many of the leaders of the congregation were corporate officers at P&G. They were rabid," he said. "I felt like Daniel going into the den of lions. They questioned why we were upsetting our churches and said P&G people were good Christians. I guess I understand that. We are all blind when it gets up close."[44]

Dearth's group couldn't meet with senior management out of fear for their jobs. But she did get a visit from Charles M. Barrett, M.D., a director at both P&G and her employer, the University of Cincinnati medical center. He had never visited her before but said the meeting was to discuss her work in continuing education, a topic he'd never shown interest in before. "He was just doing reconnaissance for P&G," Dearth said.

On the day of the shareholders' meeting, dozens of members of the National Organization for Women picketed P&G's headquarters. Forty women pushed babies in strollers and carried signs demanding fair treatment in ads. "WHO PUT THE P&G IN MALE CHAUVINIST PIG?" read several. The demonstrators distributed leaflets that asked, "What woman do you know gets embarrassed and depressed when her french fries are greasy or her hands don't look like a teen-ager's? How many women do you know who secretly squeeze toilet paper in the grocery store?" They said the portrayals of women as "dopey housewives, sex objects and half wits" were as offensive to women as "Aunt Jemimas and shuffling lackeys are to blacks." But P&G's board urged stockholders to vote against the resolutions, stating that the advertising wasn't demeaning. Showing women as homemakers, P&G argued, is natural. [45]

When the meeting began, Rev. Purkey saw his local brethren choose sides. He was chastised by some local preachers, who said he was trying to "destroy the Presbyterian Church, P&G and American industry." Others called his proposal trivial. Women from NOW stood up and countered that the men on the board should start listening to their wives and other women, or they would alienate the largest group of consumers. [46] But P&G's board won the battle: All three shareholder proposals were defeated.

Most of the women who worked with Dearth have left P&G because they felt their careers weren't advancing. Some women inside the company still gather to lament their lack of progress. They have no representation in senior management. Dearth, now a hospice nurse in Washington, is discouraged by the lack of real change. "The ads are still demeaning," she said, and what's worse, some of the messages are more subtle, so people don't always recognize the negative impact they have on consumers.

To quantify the messages of today's advertising, Dr. Moog, who works as an advertising consultant, evaluated various P&G ads, including those ads selected by P&G officials as examples of progressive advertising. But the analysis shows that P&G still believes in Suzie Homemaker advertising. The ads still send disturbing messages to consumers. [47]

One constant theme in these ads is the subservient role of women as sex objects. P&G pulled one ad for Bain de Soleil tanning lotion that showed a girl in a skimpy black bikini seeking the "St. Tropez tan." Offended consumers complained that she was too young to look that sexy. [48]

The message that you're only as good as the whiteness and softness of your laundry is another recurrent theme, which the advertising for Downy fabric softener has consistently deployed. "We called it the Downy guilt campaign," Jack Gordon said. The family notices their clothes are stiff and scratchy, not soft. Mom didn't use Downy. The message is "You're a bad mother and a bad wife," he explained. "It's worked for years."

Another Downy commercial shows two girls stacking towels to compare which are softer. The Downy towels are softer, thus forming a taller stack. The girl piling the towels not rinsed in Downy is miffed because she discovers that her towels aren't as fluffy. She storms out of the room. The Downy girl smiles smugly. The message: You're not a good girl if your towels aren't soft. "I consider that ad reprehensible," said one P&G brand manager. "Ads like that give little girls a confused picture of the way life really is," agreed the president of one ad agency.

P&G runs another guilt campaign for Pampers. A recent television campaign suggests that mothers mistreat their child's skin if they choose cloth diapers over Pampers. Duncan Hines cake mix ads show exuberant children who love their mother more because she made a springy yellow cake. Crisco ads send the same message about baking cookies with that brand of shortening: Your child loves you if use this product.

One of P&G's longest-running and most financially successful campaigns was Folgers' Mrs. Olsen. She always materialized at the back door, bearing a can of Folgers crystals, just in time to salvage a hapless housewife's pot of coffee. Husbands would leave for work angry over having suffered through another breakfast with toxic coffee. The men are abusive and childlike, incapable of fixing their own coffee.

"It was known as the 'there, there' campaign," said Miner Raymond, who helped develop the ads. P&G researched the campaign to see "how ugly and aggressive we could get in the ads," he admitted. Data showed that women "would accept as reasonable all sorts of abuse" in ads because many of them heard it at home. [49]

In a recent Folgers "best part of wakin' up" ad, the husband gets out of bed to make the coffee. But he does it to make up for a fight he and his wife had the night before. One sip of coffee, and they kiss and make up. The message: It's a big sacrifice for a man to do his wife's work, but she's easily placated.

Another problem with P&G advertising is the portrayal of the typical American family. P&G families are mostly white nuclear units. Blacks, Hispanics, and Asians aren't featured in many ads, nor are single-parent households or gays. The National Association of Black-Owned Broadcasters, which represents about 160 radio stations and 15 television stations, has threatened boycotts of P&G because the company doesn't spend much on black media. Similarly, black newspaper owners have complained about the same problem. [50]

When P&G does try to portray modern households, it often bumbles. A TV spot for Dawn dishwashing liquid shows an incompetent boob of a father washing the dishes because Mom is absent. He needs his daughter to coach him on how to properly wash a plate. In Procter ads, girls naturally know how to clean better than boys. "The Dawn ads are considered a cultural breakthrough by P&G," advertising manager Marcia Grace said.

There are amazing double standards in P&G's world. It employs a team of censors to screen television shows, as well as magazines, to make sure P&G ads appear in the appropriate environment. P&G issues a lengthy document outlining what's not appropriate; gratuitous sex, for example. Thus it avoids *Penthouse* and *Playboy*. And P&G doesn't like its ads in magazines or shows that contain any sort of controversial material. One media buyer described it as reaffirming "truth, justice, and the American way."

P&G will pull ads from magazines such as *Sassy*, a teen

publication that deals frankly with questions about sex. Yet it will advertise in *Cosmopolitan* and the *National Enquirer*. Ads for P&G's Cover Girl makeup are sprinkled among articles on Nevada brothels and ads for sexual aids in one issue of *Cosmopolitan*. Crest ads appeared in another issue, in which Irma Kurtz's "Agony" column coached women in great detail on how to perform oral sex, comparing it to eating an ice cream cone.[51] A Noxzema ad appeared next to a story called "Boobs, Boys and High Heels," which featured a photo of a woman in a tight, hot-pink minidress, sitting in a man's lap while two other men ogled her.

The double standard is even more apparent in television programming. P&G produces shows such as "Jesus of Nazareth" and "Marco Polo," a ten-hour miniseries. It also funds "Together," a cable show that features conservative entertainer Pat Boone and his wife, Shirley, chatting about the virtues of marriage as they sip coffee. "We wanted to reinforce Norman Rockwell values," said one former P&G officer.

But P&G's G-rated nature is hypocritical considering its continued sponsorships of the daytime soap operas "Guiding Light," "Another World," and "As the World Turns," which all portray marriage as disposable as diapers. They also patronize women and their roles. Consider "Another World," a long-running NBC soap opera. In a typical episode, women sob about their tortured love lives. Some characters hold jobs, but no one ever seems to do any real work, and it takes an organization chart to understand who's sleeping with whom.

P&G consistently favors plots teeming with sex to attract viewers and build sales. One episode of "Guiding Light" featured Hart and Bridget drinking two bottles of wine, then rolling around lasciviously in a haystack. On "Another World," meanwhile, a hidden video camera behind a mirror secretly films couples' trysts. "Soaps are really the same as the ads," Dr. Moog said. "Women have the same kind of emptiness." P&G censors don't seem to mind.

* * *

P&G's attitudes toward women can't be tempered by advertising agencies. The company is a huge force on Madison Avenue, largely because it's the biggest spender in an industry prone to cutbacks and layoffs. To offend P&G is to lose business. Indeed, the company is such a force that even non-P&G agencies monitor its every move. So do smaller companies. Ogilvy & Mather, which doesn't handle P&G accounts, gives clients a presentation called "What P&G Believes about Advertising."[52] It's difficult to argue with the financial success of P&G products, and many credit continuous advertising campaigns as the driving force in the company's business.

The benefit of having P&G as a client is the steady work with a 15 percent commission. Other clients have tried to cut commissions to 12 percent or lower, but P&G believes in paying top rates to keep the best agencies and is a consistent advertiser, even in tight times. During the Depression, it did not give up on advertising. Advertising agencies grow along with P&G. "This is the account that shaped us," said Milt Gossett at Saatchi & Saatchi. In the early 1990s, the agency opened an office in China to service P&G.[53]

Agencies earn the money because each brand assignment requires a tremendous amount of work before P&G approves a campaign. There are fewer and fewer chances to launch national brands, which is where agencies make the most profits.

P&G accounts require trade-offs. P&G demands loyalty and imposes strict guidelines, much like those forced on its own employees. "It's difficult to distinguish whether you're at an agency or inside P&G," said one account supervisor. P&G describes it as a partnership, "but everybody knows that's phony," said another agency manager. "P&G has the money, and that's all that counts." "Working with P&G is like a marriage," said former Saatchi & Saatchi vice chairman Bob Jordan. "There are moments of exultation and moments of total depression." Even those inside P&G agree. "We have real love-hate relationships," said Steve Dennis, a former P&G brand man.[54] "It's been a tremendously profitable and prestigious piece of business for agencies, but we tend to be arrogant about believing we know what works and what doesn't."

Agency executives and account managers say they forfeit a great deal of control when signing up for P&G jobs. P&G can control even internal business and personnel decisions. "P&G is Jesuitical and a little Japanese," Jordan said.

Any mergers between a P&G agency and another firm must get P&G's blessing, or both firms risk losing their biggest client. P&G had to approve the 1987 merger between N. W. Ayer and Cunningham & Walsh. Executives at Cunningham were told to talk to P&G first or Ayer would be buying an agency but not getting the P&G business that supported it. If P&G didn't like the new owner's ideas, it would threaten to move its accounts elsewhere. If the new owner agreed with P&G's traditional views, it would keep its accounts in place. In this case, P&G blessed the merger but imposed guidelines on what Ayer could and couldn't change. When some Cunningham managers were let go, P&G cut some ad budgets to punish Ayer, according to insiders. "It stunned them," said one Cunningham employee.

Likewise, Saatchi & Saatchi had to get P&G's okay before merging its Saatchi & Saatchi Compton unit with DFS Dorland Worldwide unit in 1987. And the merger between Eurocom and RSCG, two of France's largest agencies, brought a harsh response from P&G, an RSCG client. Eurocom had to drop one of its biggest clients, Henkel, because the German soap and chemical company competes with P&G.[55]

"Procter takes a draconian view of mergers," Jordan said. By October 1986 P&G had reassigned at least $150 million in business after agency mergers of the mid-1980s. Indeed, the company was so upset by mergers that it considered acquiring an agency to do its advertising exclusively in-house.[56] After its mergers Saatchi lost about $85 million in P&G business because it worked on RJR Nabisco's food brands. And it affected other client decisions too. When Ted Bates Worldwide became part of Saatchi, Colgate moved its $100-million account because P&G had such control over Saatchi.[57] "P&G is the Rock of Gibraltar. They're not going to move," Gossett said. "You either sail around it or into it."

Sometimes P&G stretches the definition of conflict to an extreme. Agencies aren't allowed to represent P&G if they conduct business with its archenemies Unilever and Colgate. And P&G bases its conflict policy on broad categories, such as beverages, so it is difficult to attract much business outside of P&G. The advertising firm Wells Rich Greene had to resign the Hills Brothers coffee account if it wanted to work on P&G's Citrus Hill orange juice account. But P&G later took Citrus Hill to another agency anyway. "Procter has a way of causing you to develop dependent relationships with them," said Marjorie Bradford, a former P&Ger. "And then they kill you."[58]

It's getting increasingly more difficult to pass the conflict test because P&G and its competitors are multinationals with multiple brands in each category. For those who do pass, there are other hurdles, such as the regular inspections by P&G's security team. The ex-FBI men come to the agency's offices and check that desks are locked. To pass the security checks, agencies often box up all documents P&G deems confidential and move them to another site. "I felt like a prisoner cleaning his cell before the warden's inspection," said one agency manager.

Agency executives are forbidden to talk to the press about P&G campaigns, even those already on the air, without P&G's prior consent. P&G rarely gives its blessing for any interviews. Each agency also signs a secrecy agreement. The company even discourages agencies from entering P&G ads in national advertising contests. Instead, the company created its own award program to quietly recognize what it considers good advertising.

P&G shares as little information as possible with its agencies. "We would prepare documents with blanks in them for the agencies so they wouldn't see a word about the profitability of our brands," said Bill Morgan, former P&G controller. P&G was one of the first clients to bring its own cost controllers to supervise agency spending.[59]

P&G even controls personnel changes at the agencies, discouraging any reassignment of account executives. "From Procter's point of view, stability and continuity are extremely important," Milt Gossett explained. What's particularly disturbing to agency managers is P&G's control over their future career moves. Those working on P&G accounts are locked out of other P&G agencies for at least a year. Charles Fredericks, former president of Wells Rich Greene, recalled how he moved P&G account executives to another client's business and was later "scolded" by P&G. The company demands such agreements from agencies so they won't rob the best talent from other firms. In the early 1980s it wasn't as restrictive because there were more agencies to choose from. But after the merger mania on Madison Avenue, the Procter policy hurt many careers.

"Many times I was called about jobs, but I couldn't take them," said one longtime creative director. "I consider that restraint of trade because I'm not allowed to advance my career." As one account manager put it, "Who gave P&G the right to run my life?" When Marcia Grace was doing creative work at Saatchi & Saatchi Compton, Wells officials asked her to return to their agency. "We had late-night meetings in hidden places," she said. "It was bizarre." She decided to quit the Saatchi job but had to free-lance for several months before Wells officially announced her hiring. Agencies warn others simply to stay put or they will be blackballed in the business.

If an agency hires someone from one of Unilever's ad agencies, the new hire is banned from P&G work for at least a year. P&G doesn't want any of its ads to look like its archenemy's ads. Besides, P&G tends to fear outsiders, especially those who have worked for its competitors. Anyone deemed unfit by P&G's

management is shut out of jobs. "Agencies think nothing about killing some junior executive to please P&G," said one veteran advertising manager. [60]

The tentacles of P&G wrap especially tight around the necks of creative directors, who basically commit themselves to a lifetime of P&G work. "Other clients look at Procter and think they're androids. You get pigeonholed," said one art director. "It's a death assignment."

That's because P&G has a process for every detail of its ads, and they tend to look for cookie-cutter ads—one pattern makes them all look pretty much alike. Detergent commercials, for instance, always show the dirty garment getting transformed by the end. Downy ads show springy towels that smell good. Coffee ads emphasize smell. Many creatives inside agencies refuse to do P&G work because it's stifling. "I never wanted to work on P&G business," said Bart Cummings, former CEO of Compton Advertising. "I figured I'd have to learn how to use a slide rule." He gave in, however, and spent thirty years on the accounts. [61]

There aren't any slide rules, but there are plenty of three-ring binders full of P&G procedures on how to shoot commercials. There are step-by-step guidelines on how to shoot shower scenes so the water looks good and hair appears beautiful. It can take days to get toothpaste on a brush to look perfect. It has to shine and have a "graceful flip." Blue shirts are worn by actors if they need to show sweat stains; white shirts are used to show dirt. Memos written thirty years ago outlining P&G's staple "slice-of-life" ads—women tackling the stain du jour—still influence ads. Brands have "character statements," an outline of what the product stands for.

A "reel of learning" shows the best historic copy that the agency is supposed to emulate. For instance, Folgers ads tend to show a sleeping man or woman who wakes up, sniffs the aroma of coffee brewing, and smiles. The "good sniff" shot has to feature eyes that are open but not too wide. Too much facial tension connotes a bad smell, so actors are told not to crinkle their faces too much. The best sip shots are called "hero sips" because they show pleasure. "It's very clear up front that P&G managers will be anal and compulsive from the beginning," said one producer of P&G ads. "And they live up to it."

Procter people acknowledge their obsession. They blame it on their business-school training and the tendency to overanalyze everything. "We wanted to see a commercial fulfill a checklist of things," said Charlie Carroll, former vice president of advertising. "Ad agency people tried to teach us that's not how it happens."

But agency managers get sucked into the P&G world. Annual budget meetings are grim times for account executives, just as for their counterparts, the brand managers. Documents as thick as the Chicago phone book must be prepared before the winter meetings. One ad man slipped in a copy of the Gettysburg Address just to see if anyone actually read the entire book. No one at P&G ever mentioned it.

Meetings resemble inquisitions, as agency representatives ranging from the chairman to the account executive face hours of questions by the client. "You stand trial," said Gossett, who remembers spending an entire day defending his plan for Duz. "By the time I got done, I thought it was a complete disaster. But they told me it was wonderful. If that was success, I'm sure I don't want to meet failure."

Once the plan is approved, agencies are on constant call to P&G brand managers. Charles Fredericks received daily calls from three or four brand assistants, along with the brand manager on each product. "They were relentless. They just keep coming at you. They call every day and ask for something." P&G paid careful attention to the agency's project list, which showed every request that the company made. Fredericks had one assistant who did little else but update the twenty-page list. Daylong meetings were held to discuss what was on the list. He received daily faxes from Cincinnati requesting an updated project list. "I'd fax them back saying, 'We're too busy doing projects,' " he said. [62]

After surviving P&G meetings, agencies have to defend why their work should be published or aired. Before P&G agrees on an ad, it directs its own exhaustive tests. Above all else, the product has to be dominant in the ad, and the name has to be repeated often. P&G is so product driven, said Scott Ellsworth, advertising historian at the Smithsonian Institution, "their ads are recognized as a genre on Madison Avenue. The old saying in advertising is sell the sizzle, not the steak. But P&G has traditionally sold the steak." [63]

If a brand manager doesn't like an ad, he will often produce several research reports suggesting why it won't fly with consumers. They don't trust New Yorkers or those in Hollywood to pass judgment for them, either. They test in the Midwest or South to gauge the reaction of housewives. Anything too creative is deemed "too New York" by P&G.

The P&G bureaucracy can slow simple changes for months. Moving a coffee cup in a commercial requires P&G's approval. When P&G planned to redo its Ivory soap wrapper, the company conducted a six-month study to determine the brand's image among consumers. Then the new wrapper was tested for a year. After that P&G conducted another six-month study on the new wrapper's impact. Then P&G's package designer, Don Baker, had to take the new wrapper to Mary Johnston, niece of William Cooper Procter, former chairman, to get her approval. Johnston held a large block of P&G stock, so P&G wanted to please her. She approved, and the package—at last—was changed.

Commercials are often tested four times as they develop from storyboards to finished ads. If consumers balk, the ads are scrapped. One brand that received six complaints prompted a summer-long focus group. Fifteen consumers were given a device that resembles a TV remote control so they could hit various buttons to register their reaction to every second of a commercial. The second-by-second research then produces a graph on how people react to every element of the ad. "I'm not sure why they hire agencies. They think they're so much smarter about advertising," sniffed one account supervisor.

P&G consultants recruit consumers under the guise of testing new sitcoms for TV production companies. They're given a list of products and asked which ones they'd like to take home as a free gift at the end of the session. Test shows, which never air nationally, are then shown to the consumers. The shows contain P&G test ads. At the end of the show, the consumer is asked again which products she'd choose. The test helps measure the influence of the ads in persuading consumers to try P&G brands. It also determines a target score for all other commercials. "If twenty-eight percent remember the commercial, all other ads have to meet that," said one ad manager. "If they don't, you'll never get on the air."

These tests can take years. "If you're always reviewing work in the context of a database, it's hard to innovate," Bob Jordan commented. "There's a tendency to be forced into a mold. It's a little stultifying."

P&G research shows that testimonials and slice-of-life ads build share. For instance, the "Choosy Mothers" Jif campaign propelled the peanut butter to number one, ahead of Peter Pan and Skippy.

The overly analytical nature of P&G leads to some marketplace flops and poor campaigns. Citrus Hill, which struggled for a consistent ad campaign, tried to promote the benefits of vitamin C, a generic claim available to any juice. But P&G wanted to hype the claim that it provided 120 percent of the daily requirement for the vitamin. Consumers didn't care. The campaign was dropped, as was P&G's emphasis on the juice being rich in calcium.

Often P&G's refusal to budge from historic campaigns costs the brand market share. Prell shampoo is best remembered for a 1960s ad that showed a pearl sinking slowly to the bottom of the thick green shampoo. But P&G was equally slow to recognize consumers' interest in cosmetic benefits rather than Prell's cleaning power. The brand has lost share since the sixties and languishes behind numerous other shampoos. "P&G sold it like a floor cleaner," Marcia Grace said. "Now P&G is letting it die of inertia."[64]

Because of failed brands like Prell, the conservative company has tried to loosen up a bit. In 1980 two of every three commercials consisted of traditional slice-of-life themes; in 1990 only one in four. Ross Love, P&G's vice president of advertising, said the shift began in 1984 with ads for Bounce fabric softener and Citrus Hill. Both were different from the typical P&G ad, featuring more music and less copy. By the same token, neither stayed on the air long because it didn't build market share.[65]

Agencies lament that P&G's self-imposed creative boundaries remain firmly entrenched. P&G argued that mergers would hurt the creative process but did little to encourage true creativity. And the agencies, squeezed by cutbacks in spending by many clients, often produce the same old stuff just to save money and please Procter. "You just crank it out," one ad manager confessed. "Quality control amounts to making sure the client is happy, not leading the client."

Sometimes agencies do dare to be different. In the mid-1980s Cheer laundry detergent was losing share to other brands. Its all-temperature copy message wasn't effective. Chicago agency Leo Burnett developed another slice-of-life campaign that P&G liked, as well as a second campaign, featuring opera music and a character who never spoke a word. All he did was demonstrate how Cheer cleaned clothes. P&G officials rejected it, but the agency decided to test it anyway. The ad exceeded all previous scores in consumer tests. Only then did P&G agree to air it. P&G CEO Ed Artzt now deems it "one of the most successful advertising campaigns that Cheer has ever run."[66]

Likewise, a campaign for Always sanitary pads dropped the somber spokeswoman approach for quick shots of women exclaiming, "It's got wings!" There was a lot of nervousness about the ad because it didn't follow the normal testimonial ads. It was too celebratory for P&G. But the commercial tested well with women, who found it less offensive than the other spots. P&G agreed to air the ad after a computerized demonstration was added to hype the science of the more absorbent pad. "Now everybody takes credit for it," said one manager who helped create the campaign.

Most of the really quirky ads never make it on air. A humorous spot for Prell won praise from the New York Ad Club, but P&G still wouldn't put it on TV. In the commercial a baseball pitcher stalls after throwing ball three. The catcher runs out to the mound and yells, "What are you thinking about out here?" The pitcher whips off his cap and says, "I dunno. I just don't think this perm looks natural," to which the catcher replies sympathetically, "You think you've got problems: Take a look at these split ends." The ad drew cheers from the award ceremony crowd, but P&G wasn't amused. Instead it stuck with "Prell: The cleaner the rinse, the fuller your hair."[67]

Likewise, Folgers squandered a golden opportunity to lure more college-age coffee drinkers by nixing a funny campaign called "Jump Start Your Brain." Print ads, tested at Miami University in Ohio, showed Dracula waking up from his coffin, thanks to Folgers. The brand gained a 70 percent trial among students in a test, but P&G backed away from the campaign when it was criticized in the college newspaper for pushing coffee on students. "The coffee market is rapidly gentrifying," said one of the campaign's producers. "Unless the brand appeals to younger drinkers, it will die."

Likewise, P&G will eventually lose market shares in all of its product lines if advertising doesn't move beyond stereotypes and recognize that there's more to life than clean shirts and shiny plates.

5
Guerrilla
Marketing

Pat and Michael Kehm had a good life. The Cedar Rapids, Iowa, couple worked on sketches of their dream house where they could raise their two daughters. [1] The white house would sit on a hill, overlooking a pasture where Pat could ride her horse. [2]

They talked about their plans and dreams at a family outing on Labor Day 1980, when they took the children, Andrea and Katie, to a local park. The Old McDonald's Farm exhibit was a favorite of three-year-old Andrea. "It was a nice quiet day the four of us spent together," Mike Kehm recalled. [3]

But their storybook life began to collapse the next day. Pat had taken her sister Colleen's advice and tried Rely tampons, [4] a popular brand with many women.

Four days after she began using Rely, Pat Kehm was dead at age twenty-five, a victim of toxic shock syndrome. [5] About two weeks after she was buried in Cedar Memorial Cemetery, P&G pulled the tampons from the market. They had been linked to the disease that killed the young mother. [6]

P&G was lauded for taking such a drastic and costly step. [7] It was one of the largest product recalls in U.S. business history, requiring P&G to take a $75-million charge to cover the cost of discontinuing the product. [8] "I am personally proud of the way our people in all concerned departments have behaved under the pressure of real concern for human life," said Edward Harness, then chairman of P&G, in a letter to employees. [9]

But P&G has little reason to be proud. A closer look at the episode and the court cases that followed paint a different picture of P&G: a corporate bully that showed carelessness, indeed recklessness, toward consumer safety. P&G wants to win at any price, and the Rely case shows how far it will go to achieve victory.

The full story of the Rely debacle has never been told because P&G effectively silenced most of its victims and their families through out-of-court and confidential settlements, which imposed on P&G and its insurers as much as $85 million in payments to claimants and defense costs. [10] And it locked up scientific research on toxic shock with millions of dollars in P&G grants. Those who spoke out were offered stipends to keep their research quiet. [11] By the late 1980s more than 1,100 lawsuits and claims had been filed against P&G because of Rely. [12] "P&G lucked out. Had the truth come out back then, they would've been nailed for everything they have," said Dr. Philip Tierno, a New York University microbiologist who has studied toxic shock. "And justifiably so. They didn't do their homework." He calls Rely a "toxin factory." [13]

The Kehm case was one of the few that ever went to trial, providing a glimpse into how far P&G will go to protect its image. "They looked pretty bad in the toxic shock litigation," said Tom Riley, attorney for the Kehm family and about 140 other plaintiffs in toxic shock cases. "They could've saved a lot of lives, including Pat Kehm's. But they're too damn greedy." [14]

The story of Rely began in the early 1960s, when researchers started studying how to make a superabsorbent tampon that would outsell other brands. Once P&G developed the product, it considered names such as Sure, Merit, Certain, Always, and Soft Shape, but chose Rely, [15] which instilled confidence. "Hopes run high in Cincinnati that the tampon named Rely will take a major share of the market from Tampax and Kotex," wrote *Fortune* magazine in July 1974. "Demonstrating the new product, P&G executives plunk Rely and Tampax into separate beakers of water to demonstrate their own product's superiority. They are confident enough about the outcome to make an explicit claim on the package: 'Rely absorbs twice as much as the tampon you're probably using now.' "[16]

Tampons date back to an invention by Dr. Earl Haas, a Denver barber turned physician who got the idea to roll up cotton and sew it together with string. He sold the invention, called Tampax, for about $30,000 in the 1930s.[17] Rely was different. Instead of cotton, it contained superabsorbent synthetic chips of polyester and carboxymethylcellulose, a derivative of wood pulp. It was shaped like a tea bag, with a net to contain the synthetic chips that absorbed menstrual blood.[18] "Rely could absorb an entire menstrual flow in one tampon," Dr. Tierno said.[19]

It was just the breakthrough P&G wanted in order to continue building its paper division. In the late 1970s "it was one success after another," recalls Marjorie Bradford, a former manager in the public relations department. "Some of it was almost embarrassing." The company had the dominant share in the diaper market with Pampers. Indeed, P&G lawyers worried about the Federal Trade Commission crying foul about its near monopoly. Rely was such an immediate hit, P&G figured it would soon lock up another category and boast the country's number-one tampon. "There was a feeling of invincibility," Bradford said.[20]

But women like Judy Braiman, a mother of five and a Rochester, New York, consumer advocate, began to question Rely's safety in 1975. The product was being test marketed in her city when Braiman began to receive complaints from women. The housewife had become an outspoken consumer advocate after her own health crisis in 1966. A severe cough prompted doctors to diagnose her ailment as lung cancer. Tests revealed sixty lesions in each lung but no cancer. Her lungs were covered with boils, which doctors linked to inhaling aerosol hairspray. It changed her life.

Braiman founded a small group called the Empire State Consumer Association. Most days, she and a couple of friends are its only volunteers. The group's checking account balance hovers around $100. When she has a complaint, she prefers press conferences to noisy demonstrations. She appears more like a Junior League member than one of Ralph Nader's Raiders, serving coffee in yellow china cups, with biscotti and linen napkins on the side.

Braiman is anything but demure in her campaigns, however. In 1971 she began what became an annual hunt for unsafe toys at Christmas. That first year she found thirty-nine toys in Rochester stores that were dangerous for children. She began testifying at government hearings about product safety. In 1975 she was asked to serve on the product safety council for the Consumer Product Safety Commission, a watchdog agency. She isn't popular with some. "The day before one hearing, the local sheriff came to the door to say he had a report of a bomb exploding at my house," she said. It proved to be a false alarm.

Rochester women began to call Braiman's home with reports of vomiting and diarrhea after using the free sample of Rely tampons.[21] Then she read a July 1975 local newspaper report that said Rely contained polyurethane, an ingredient that had been linked to cancer.[22]

P&G was aware of the concerns before the newspaper reports. In an internal memo of February 28, 1975, from R. B. Drotman to F. W. Baker, the company outlined "possible areas of attack on Rely." The list said components were cancer-causing agents. It also noted that Rely affected the natural microorganisms and bacteria found in the vagina.[23]

P&G invited Braiman in 1975 to a meeting to discuss her concerns. She had been speaking out about Rely and contacted the company for more information about the product. Braiman had small children at home, so she told P&G officials that she wouldn't be able to leave home for a meeting. Company officials volunteered an employee's spouse to baby-sit her kids while she attended the meeting.

She questioned the use of polyurethane, but P&G assured her the product would be reformulated. She asked to see safety testing results and for an explanation of why women were vomiting when they used the product. But P&G wouldn't provide the data. "They were very condescending," she recalled. Braiman also questioned whether P&G would introduce a deodorant version of Rely. She pointed out that it was unnecessary to put a deodorant in a tampon, because the fluid has no odor as long as it remains in the body. P&G did have plans to introduce a deodorant Rely but did not disclose this in the meeting. "She was right," Bradford admitted. "Even the scientists knew that deodorant tampons were a crazy idea." But P&G also knew they would sell.

Braiman surveyed about fifty women on tampon usage. P&G wanted the names of those who'd suffered adverse reactions. She wouldn't give out the information. P&G "blamed their problems on allergies," she said. The company didn't mention that it had been receiving one hundred complaints per month since June. [24]

Despite these problems, the national rollout proceeded as scheduled. About 60 million sample packages of Rely were sent to 80 percent of U.S. households, at a cost of $10 million. [25] The campaign worked. By mid-1980 Rely had gained about 24 percent of the tampon market and threatened to overtake the leading brand, Tampax, in a very short time. [26]

But Rely's star was already beginning to fade. In the spring of 1980 the Centers for Disease Control, the government agency that tracks disease, issued its *Morbidity and Mortality Weekly Report*, or *MMWR*. It listed fifty-five cases of toxic shock syndrome since October 1979 and noted that the disease was predominant among young, menstruating women. [27] Despite the warning signs, that same spring P&G president John Smale sent chairman Edward Harness a memo requesting approval to move forward with its plans to introduce a deodorant version of Rely.[28]

In early June the CDC contacted P&G's paper division for information on tampon usage for a study of toxic shock. At the time, a doctor from the agency mentioned speculation by a *Los Angeles Times* reporter that tampons might be associated with toxic shock. While P&G continued to assuage consumers' worries, it had been receiving as many as 177 complaints per month since 1975.[29]

The company instructed its sales force not to discuss toxic shock with customers, including doctors. But if asked, the salespeople were given canned answers that denied any link between tampons and toxic shock.[30]

Complaints about the product were deemed routine by P&G. The company always got a lot of calls after introducing new products. Some managers likened the Rely calls to the reports of rashes and other skin irritations that had followed P&G's introduction of Bounce fabric softener in the mid-1970s. They figured it was nothing serious.[31]

But toxic shock *is* serious. Symptoms of the disease, first identified by Dr. James Todd in Denver, include high fever, a sunburnlike rash, vomiting, and low blood pressure. After a while, a victim's skin peels off the hands and feet. Breathing becomes difficult, and the lungs fill with fluid until she suffocates or her heart stops. The name is derived from the severe prolonged shock that accompanies the illness.

Scientists found that the disease begins with *Staphylococcus aureus*, bacteria commonly found in the vaginas of up to 15 percent of all women. Men and nonmenstruating women can get the disease from an abscessed infection where the staph produces the toxin. In menstrual toxic shock, the tampon creates a haven for the bacteria that are present, allowing them to grow and produce deadly toxins.[32]

Superabsorbent synthetics—carboxymethylcellulose, or CMC, and polyester—made Rely especially dangerous. In addition, CMC is partially degradable, which contributed to the bacteria growth. Though CMC is safe enough to be used as an additive in ice cream, P&G didn't test to see how it would react with bacteria. "Rely turned on the production of certain poisons; produced toxins that were absorbed into the blood," Dr. Tierno explained. [33]

When tampon makers were first invited to a meeting with the CDC in late June 1980, they heard a presentation on a toxic shock study, but no particular brand was linked to the disease. P&G sued CDC to get the names and addresses of patients, but the agency refused on the grounds of confidentiality. Instead P&G got some information from doctors and state health departments, while continuing to badger the CDC with requests under the Freedom of Information Act. Company officials were getting increasingly annoyed, especially with a young physician named Dr. Kathryn Shands. She had joined the CDC in July 1979 in the special pathogens department, where researchers tackle unknown pathogens, or disease-producing agents. It was the same group that had dealt with the Legionnaires disease. [34]

Six months into her new job, Shands found herself facing off against P&G's senior management from Cincinnati, whom she described as "fairly intimidating." P&G's attitude was "you guys are freshmen, and you don't know what you're talking about," she recalled. But Shands aggressively fought P&G's request for the names of patients in the studies, citing the obvious invasion of their privacy. In a P&G memo, officials complained that Dr. Shands said she would go public with a statement that this request by P&G "will greatly hinder their work on TSS." [35]

In July P&G distributed 2 million free samples of Rely and planned a high school promotion for late August. [36] That month the company got the news that a woman had died from toxic shock after using Rely. Tom Laco, then executive vice president, called Marjorie Bradford into his office. "Read this," he said tersely, handing her a wire service report tying P&G's product to the victim's death.

"How do you feel about it now?" Laco asked Bradford.

"This changes things," she replied.

"Looking back, Bradford said, For the first time, a company product had been linked to a death. There was no way we [could] get around the public perception of Rely linked to a fatal disease."[37]

That same month P&G considered placing a warning label on the product, as well as sponsoring public service advertisements warning about the symptoms of toxic shock. But according to a P&G memo, company lawyers warned that the ads should be worded so that "we do not leave ourselves open for other tampon manufacturers to make claims against us." The solution: Don't mention tampons in the ads. Another memo that month cautioned against slowing Rely's momentum, declaring "We should continue our planned activity to support this brand and build its share to leadership status."[38] P&G never issued the warning label or ads, despite the growing evidence of problems. "That was corporate murder," Attorney Tom Riley said.[39]

Women continued to complain. Some reported that they were deathly ill each time they used Rely. A July 1980 memo by Owen Carter, a P&G chemistry safety expert, describes how P&G officials met with doctors and county health department workers in Lima, Ohio, to quiet rumors that "mistakenly" linked the tampon to health problems. They heard about a twenty-seven-year-old woman, mother of a six-week-old baby, who fell into a deep shock when she used Rely. Yet P&G officials insisted that Rely was blamed merely because of "unfortunate circumstances of timing involving the sample drop and introductory promotional advertising of the new tampon" and newspaper reports of the disease.[40]

In mid-September the CDC called again to report on a second study, in which 70 percent of the women with TSS reported using Rely. P&G asked the CDC not to mention Rely when it published the results. "It would be realistic to say that P&G would have very much preferred to keep their name out of the study," said Dr. Bruce Dan, then an infectious disease specialist at the CDC.[41]

P&G resisted pulling the product from shelves, believing that such a measure "would've sent the wrong signals," Bradford said. P&G contended that Rely was wrongly linked because so many women had been using free samples, so that when they were asked questions about tampon use, they naturally mentioned Rely. "Rely was one of the biggest ad campaigns that P&G ever had," Bradford said.[42]

In Rochester, consumer advocate Judy Braiman was telling women to stop using Rely. "My phone was flooded with hundreds of calls," she said. Another concern surfaced: The superabsorbent tampon swelled so much that one woman likened it to "trying to remove an open umbrella from her body," Braiman said. When she learned of the deaths, "I was physically ill. I kept thinking, What could I have done to make someone pay attention to me? If someone had listened, some women would still be alive," she said, wiping away tears.[43]

Because the company was making little progress in swaying national regulatory agencies,[44] P&G's Washington office began to lobby for Congressional support to save Rely. Bryce Harlow, a former Nixon aide and P&G lobbyist, was still active in Washington circles. But his Democratic counterpart, Walt Hasty, took the lead to find allies in the Carter administration and Congress who could help override the Food and Drug Administration and CDC.

Ed Harness called top scientists for a scientific advisory group meeting at the Hilton Hotel at Chicago's O'Hare airport on September 21, 1980. From 8:30 A.M. to 7:30 P.M., five doctors from Harvard, the University of Southern California, and other universities debated in room 2027 about whether Rely was the cause. No one could guarantee the chief executive that P&G's product wasn't to blame.[45]

The next day P&G announced it was pulling Rely from the market. Harness wrote the press release himself. "He was just devastated," Bradford said. "I've never seen a man age so quickly."[46]

P&G knew it had to act. The FDA was getting antsy. "The FDA said it would give P&G the opportunity to do something," Bradford said. The message: "If you don't we will," she said. "We knew that meant a recall."

The day after the announcement, P&G met with the FDA, which said the company had yet more work to do. But P&G spent much of the meeting debating whether the action would be called a withdrawal or a recall. P&G disliked "recall" because it seemed to imply safety violations. Exasperated FDA officials finally said, "If you don't want to call it a recall, we'll call it a *banana*." During the meeting, that's exactly how they referred to it. "We just wanted it off the market," said a former FDA official who attended the meetings.[47]

P&G signed a consent agreement in which it didn't admit that Rely was defective or that the company violated any laws. The FDA forced it to undertake a massive ad campaign to notify women to stop using the tampons. In addition, P&G had to buy back the product.[48]

About 3,000 P&G employees were involved in the effort to get Rely off the shelves. Back at company headquarters, managers told of orders to shred documents on Rely. "We were told that all the records shouldn't be kept," said a former top officer of the company. It became known as the "Ides of September." When asked about document shredding, a P&G spokesman expressly denied any order to shred and said the company had an obligation not to dispose of Rely documents during pending litigation. P&G said it retained over one million pages of documents related to Rely.

"My faith was shaken," said one woman manager. "I wanted to know what the company knew and when did it know it." But many got swept up in the accolades of how P&G

had done the right thing, pulling out of a very successful market. [49]

It had been a popular product. Pat Kehm's sister, Colleen, had pestered her during their Monday shopping trips to buy Rely. The two women weren't just sisters; they were best friends. Often their mother and Pat's husband, Mike, would join them for lunch on his noon break from the service department at Bruce McGrath Pontiac. [50]

The day after Labor Day, Pat began to use Rely tampons. By Wednesday, she was sluggish and went to bed early. By Friday, Mike was staying home from work to care for her. She had been vomiting and running a high fever the night before. "I ran up to the store and got her 7Up, but she couldn't keep that down," he said. [51]

When Pat's mother came to pick up the kids for the weekend, she took little Andrea to Pat's bedside to say good-bye. Pat could hardly raise her hand to wave good-bye one last time. [52]

Mike took Pat to the emergency room, but the doctors gave her penicillin and sent her home. Saturday she made an appointment to see her doctor. Her legs were so discolored that she asked Mike to help her put on a pair of his loose-fitting jeans. He had to carry her to the car. [53]

In the doctor's office, the nurse couldn't find her blood pressure. She called an ambulance, even though the hospital was just two blocks away. "That's when I became frightened," Mike said. "I couldn't imagine why—how all of a sudden she became so sick that she had to be taken in an ambulance." [54]

In the hospital, doctors had a hard time finding a vein to start an IV. Her condition grew worse. The nurses asked if Mike wanted to call their priest. "I had never seen Pat like this; she was starting to turn black and blue," he said. [55]

Pat Kehm died around 3:45 Saturday afternoon. The doctor said he suspected it might be toxic shock related to tampons. Mike gave his permission for the physician to perform an autopsy to solve the mystery of his wife's death. He also consented to have her organs donated. But most of her organs had been severely damaged by the disease. Only Pat's eyes could be donated.

Mike went back to the their Bowling Street home. In the bathroom he saw the box of Rely and threw it in the wastebasket. [56] "After she died, Andrea kept asking, 'When is Mommy coming home?' " Kehm recalled. [57]

When the statistics on U.S. deaths were compiled for 1980, the CDC reported that forty-two women died from toxic shock. Seven of the deaths were linked to Rely. Scientists say that because of strict clinical guidelines for what qualifies as toxic shock, those are modest estimates. The real numbers are probably higher. For instance, the CDC labeled another fifteen deaths as "probable toxic shock" because they met four of the five criteria for symptoms. Of those, five were tied to Rely. [58]

Mike Kehm went to Tom Riley's Cedar Rapids law firm in late September to discuss a lawsuit against P&G. Riley, a former Republican state senator, had a reputation for winning tough cases even as a young lawyer in the air force. During the Korean War he had defended enlisted men charged with desertion. None of his clients was convicted, even those who had been AWOL for up to two years and were brought back to the base by the FBI.

Riley had recently left a large firm to open his own firm with his son Peter, who had just graduated from law school. A third lawyer, Todd Becker, Peter's friend from law school, joined the firm. The practice was so new that they spent the first weeks operating out of a mortuary room of a Cedar Rapids cemetery while they waited for office space.

The recall of Rely and the proof that Pat Kehm's illness was linked to the tampon convinced Riley that he had an open-and-shut case. "Like shooting fish in a barrel," he said. Besides, the Riley household had used P&G products for years. "I thought they'd care and accept responsibility." [59]

But he soon realized it would be difficult to tackle the

monolith P&G. The company has the resources to hire a battery of lawyers, in addition to the dozens it already employed in Cincinnati and its local law firm, Dinsmore & Shohl.

What's especially troubling is how P&G used its clout in the scientific community. Riley found it nearly impossible to enlist a doctor to serve as an expert witness, because P&G quickly offered hefty research grants to any doctor researching toxic shock. Through money, P&G can control research. Doctors have testified that the grant applications stipulate that research has to be submitted to P&G twenty-one days prior to submission for publication in a research journal. [60]

P&G financed more than a dozen research projects. Dr. James Todd, the physician who named the syndrome, received a $400,000 grant. [61] Other doctors were invited to seminars in Cincinnati, and wined and dined at P&G expense. Ironically, in a 1976 memo P&G had complained that doctors at Albany Medical College wanted to pay $500 to each woman volunteer who participated in an eight-month study on Rely. [62]

"Researchers are beholden to them," Riley said. "They're entitled to a defense, but this is almost monopolistic. The strategy was to corner the scientific market."

One researcher silenced by P&G was Merlin Bergdoll, a professor of food microbiology and toxicology at the University of Wisconsin. Bergdoll dusted tampons and other materials with a strain of *staphylococcus aureus.* He then grew it overnight in a nourishing solution and found that the staph growing on the tampons produced large amounts of bacterial waste suspected of triggering toxic shock. Tampons containing chemical agents that enhance their absorbency, such as the foam in Rely, had the greatest effect on the production of these wastes.

P&G tried to keep Bergdoll's findings out of court, claiming they were preliminary. Interestingly, when his findings were reported in *The Wall Street Journal,* Bergdoll refuted them the next day in *The New York Times.* It turned out that he'd received several hundred thousand dollars in research grants from

P&G.[63] The prestigious *Journal of the American Medical Association* later criticized Bergdoll and P&G for suppressing the data.

Likewise, Patrick M. Schlievert, another researcher, testified that Rely tampons weren't to blame in toxic shock. He claimed he had tested Rely in the presence of *staphylococcus aureus*, "and the components didn't significantly increase toxin production." He too had received P&G grants.[64]

Riley finally found one expert witness, Dr. Philip Tierno, to testify about his research on toxic shock. His experiments showed that synthetic tampons create a haven for growth of the staphylococcus bacteria. "P&G didn't test what bacteria would do to components of Rely," he explained. Some women have sufficient antibodies to fight it, but others don't.

Tierno wrote to P&G about his study in October 1980, prompting a visit from one of its scientists. He was encouraged to apply for a grant to fund his research. He declined. The weekend before the case went to trial, P&G scientists tried again to bring Tierno into their camp. Again he refused. "They never suggested a certain amount of money," he said. "It was all done very carefully."[65]

Another tactic P&G used was to obfuscate discovery, that part of pretrial preparation in which facts and documents are collected. Riley sent his legal assistant and one of his daughters to Cincinnati to review P&G documents. But the company had hundreds of thousands of papers, and Riley's researchers were allowed to review only one file at a time. Their third day in Cincinnati, they happened to overhear someone mention an index. P&G's attorneys finally gave them access to it after Riley threatened to complain to the judge. "It was like looking for a needle in a haystack," he said.[66]

Frank Woodside, one of P&G's attorneys, bullied plaintiffs such as Mike Kehm in depositions, asking irrelevant questions about their sexual histories and whether they had oral sex. "He asked me if I was sure [Pat] didn't sleep around," Kehm recalled in disgust. "It was downright degrading." The idea was to humiliate and scare him into settling the case before it went to trial. [67]

P&G spared no expense in the Kehm case. The Cincinnati lawyers rented offices at a Cedar Rapids bank building, buying furniture and hiring a team of more than a dozen legal assistants and local lawyers. The company conducted several mock trials in Lincoln, Nebraska, to test its defense strategy. That city was chosen because its demographics matched those of Cedar Rapids, a predominantly white, midwestern town whose citizens were largely of Slavic descent. Juries in each of the mock trials were quizzed about what they liked and disliked in the testimony. Just as it uses focus groups to determine the best way to market toothpaste and detergent, P&G researched how to sell itself in a courtroom. On the third try, its attorneys got the verdict they wanted from the mock jury.

Before the trial commenced in April 1982, the company distributed free product samples throughout Cedar Rapids as a way to drum up good will. During jury selection, P&G employed a psychologist full time to help screen potential jurors. The psychologist stayed throughout the trial to advise the lawyers on how jurors were reacting to the company's case. File cabinets were wheeled in and out for use by the four P&G attorneys. Court reporters were hired to type in fifteen-minute rotations to give attorneys and witnesses continuous updates on testimony.

"It was like the U.S. versus Iraq," Riley recalled. "I had two inexperienced lawyers and one legal assistant." But he did add several homespun touches, such as asking a local television personality, "Dr. Max," to read a deposition from Dr. Earl Haas, the inventor of tampons, who had died before the case got to trial. Haas's deposition explained how he coined the name Tampax by combining the words tampon and pack because women who bled after delivery were tamponed, or packed, with cotton. Dr. Max, a community theater actor, turned the deposition into a dramatic reading. "I told him not to ham it up, but he couldn't resist the script," Riley said. Locals still call Dr. Max's day in court one of his best performances. [68]

But few tactics could have had more impact that Mike Kehm's reading P&G's own memos outlining the company's intentions to go full speed ahead with expansion of Rely just weeks before his wife's death:

"Now Mike," Riley began. "Would you read the date of that memorandum and subject?"

In a calm, steady voice, Kehm read aloud, " 'August 18, 1980. Subject: Rely—toxic shock syndrome—effect on future marketing plans.' "

"Would you read paragraph three?"

" 'Should P&G continue to market Rely with normal advertising and promotion efforts?' "

"And what's the answer or decision they reached three weeks before your wife died?" Riley asked.

" 'Yes,' " Kehm read. " 'If we don't we can expect Rely's share to decline from its current fifteen percent to twenty percent to five percent to ten percent. It would be financially unattractive for Rely to stay in business at this low share level.' " The memo went on to conclude that Procter & Gamble shouldn't issue warnings about toxic shock.

"Now I want you to read the rest of that, but this was three weeks before your wife died," the attorney reiterated. "Would you read the next paragraph, please?"

" 'As a public service,' " Kehm continued, " 'we could communicate the symptoms of toxic shock syndrome so that women would know they should go to the hospital quickly if they have these symptoms. This option should be considered, but it is probably premature to do this at this time.' "

"Was it premature for your wife?" Riley asked pointedly.

"No."

P&G attorneys objected, calling Riley's question argumentative. [69] And during the cross-examination, they quizzed Mike about his income and his wife's IUD. [70]

Despite all the obstacles, the jury ruled in favor of Michael Kehm and awarded him $300,000. Some wanted to award punitive damages in the millions but said they were afraid it would bankrupt the company, considering the hundreds of lawsuits related to Rely that were filed. [71] "I proved a point," Kehm said. "But they got off awfully easy."

Riley later learned one reason why the jury didn't award punitive damages. Gordon Hassing, associate director in charge of product safety at P&G, appears to have misled the jury about discussions on the need to warn consumers. Hassing claimed that Dr. Shands, the toxic shock investigator at the CDC, "who was a young woman herself, indicated very strongly that she was not going to change her tampon habits, and she was going to keep using tampons, and she specifically didn't see the need for a warning." [72]

"That was a real good defense if a top investigator didn't see the need to warn," Riley said.

At the time, Shands couldn't testify because government regulations bar employees from appearing as expert witnesses. So there was no way to refute Hassing's testimony.

"I never said there was no reason to warn consumers," the doctor later said in an interview. While she had told Hassing she wouldn't change her own tampon usage habits, "I'd never used Rely," she explained, "so I didn't see the need to change." Contrary to Hassing's testimony, she did in fact urge distribution of public information to warn that "this disease is dangerous and associated with tampons," she said. The doctor agrees that Hassing's false testimony spared P&G tremendous damages. "It had a powerful effect," she said. "And it's unethical behavior." Shands wasn't aware until after the Kehm trial of Hassing's testimony.

When she left the CDC in the summer of 1982, P&G officials offered her a job. At the time, Dr. Shands was completing a residency in adult and child psychiatry at Atlanta's Grady Hospital. She was asked to join some P&Gers for lunch. "These guys drive up in a big black car, dressed to the hilt, and get me out of the emergency room to take me to lunch," she recalled. The group included some of the same folks who'd belittled her work at the CDC.

During lunch, the officials asked her to work for P&G as an expert witness. They assured her she would be set for life. "We'd like you on our side, and we'll make it worth your while," they told the doctor. They didn't mention a specific figure, but it was "six figures, at least," she believes. At the time, Shands was making just $20,000 a year as a resident in the city hospital. Nevertheless she declined their offer. She also told P&G to stop saying that she hadn't seen a need to warn consumers.

"They were smooth. I knew I could say no, but it was pressured. When they left, I clearly remember this eerie feeling as they drove off in that black car. I had a feeling that they could do me in," said Dr. Shands, now a psychiatrist in Atlanta. "It's kind of like the Mafia showing up at your door." [73]

In a deposition taken for another toxic shock case in Arkansas in June 1983, Hassing changed his story and said that he and Shands "never really discussed" the need for a warning. [74] "The guy was dishonest. He would do anything to win the case," Riley said. He wanted to reopen the case and go after Hassing for perjury but figured it would be too costly to Michael Kehm. "Without that testimony, we had a chance at punitive damages."

P&G harassed Riley even after the case was over. Numerous attorneys in other toxic shock cases contacted him for any documents and the trial transcript for their research. He made arrangements to send the papers for a fee that he would use to pay off Michael Kehm's trial expenses.

P&G was angry because this gave other plaintiffs access to evidence. It sought a court order to seal the documents. Even newspaper clippings were marked confidential in the files. But the court ordered that only two documents were confidential.

They are seemingly innocuous because they pertained to the introduction of a deodorant tampon and other production plans for the now defunct product.

When Riley's assistant was copying the files, she inadvertently included the two confidential papers. P&G sued Riley, claiming trade secrets were being revealed. Riley was cited for contempt because of the protective order. P&G offered to make a bargain. The company would drop the contempt charges if he stopped sending out the documents. Riley refused. "They wanted to keep the plaintiffs' bar from getting together," he said.

The judge ordered Riley to pay $10,000, a quarter of what P&G wanted, for attorneys' fees. "It was a vindictive thing by P&G," Riley said. [75]

Riley continued to fight P&G in other toxic shock cases, and he chronicled the Kehm trial in a book titled *The Price of a Life*. Upon its publication in 1986, he received offers to appear on talk shows, but all bookings were mysteriously canceled at the last minute. As the country's largest advertiser, P&G wields tremendous clout with the media. An appearance by Riley might have cost a program untold dollars in P&G commercials. Apparently no one was willing to take that risk.

Riley ultimately sold about 7,500 books, but many people who followed the toxic shock saga of the early 1980s haven't read it or even seen it in stores. Some suspect P&G bought up copies to keep it out of the public's hands. Riley still gets calls from Iowa City libraries for replacement copies. The book keeps disappearing from the shelves—not surprising, considering P&G has a plant there, Riley says. [76]

Since then, more disturbing evidence has emerged about the case. Patrick M. Schlievert, who testified at the trial that Rely tampons didn't cause toxic shock, later changed his story.

In December 1991 Riley deposed Schlievert for another toxic shock case, *Kathy J. Manning* v. *Tambrands Inc.* The professor of microbiology admitted Rely contributed to toxic shock.

When asked about the contradiction from his statements in the Kehm case, Schlievert had this to say:

> I was giving information based on what we had available at that time. So I don't think I'm being inconsistent at all. I'm just saying we have additional information now that we didn't have back then.
>
> Had the Kehm trial been tried now, I would have been on your side rather than on the Procter & Gamble side. [77]

P&G tried to portray itself as altruistic in its research, saying that it hired scientists to find a cure for toxic shock syndrome, not just as a defensive maneuver to help the company in the lawsuits. But when P&G sued its insurance companies in 1985, the company claimed that the money spent on research was a defense cost, *not* research spending. By doing that, P&G hoped to get its insurance companies to foot the scientists' bills. In the end, P&G and its insurers spent about $85 million in defense and other costs related to the Rely litigation. [78]

In the insurance lawsuits, P&G wanted each Rely lawsuit considered part of one continuing occurrence. Insurers claimed that each lawsuit was a separate occurrence. The difference would affect how much of the expense was covered by insurance. A U.S. district judge in Chicago ruled in favor of the insurance companies, so P&G didn't collect as much as it wanted from the insurers.

Years after the controversy, P&G continues to defend its actions and insists that Rely was unfairly tagged as a culprit. The company said there were no consumer safety concerns "that suggested we shouldn't expand the product nationally." Prior to its introduction, P&G says it conducted "a very thorough safety testing program." Furthermore, the company said "no reliable scientific data then or even now has proven a causal link between Rely and TSS." P&G was so convinced of its position that it purchased the patent for another tampon in 1984.[79] That troubles many, including one of P&G's own senior researchers, who believes his company paid too little attention to the possible dangers of Rely until the crisis struck. "P&G did a lot of questionable things," he admitted. "Memos were overlooked and there were errors in judgment. We got involved over our heads. We didn't know how to handle a product that is inserted into the body and interacts with tissue."[80] Indeed, no women at P&G were involved in the Rely project until after the product was linked with the disease.

Ed Harness, who led P&G in the late 1970s and early 1980s, retired as CEO shortly after Rely was taken off the market. Some say the episode prompted him to leave early. "He figured he didn't have time to overcome the stigma of Rely," Marjorie Bradford speculated.[81] John Smale, who advocated moving ahead with the introduction of a deodorant Rely, was named as his successor.

Since then, the Centers for Disease Control say the occurrence of toxic shock has dropped dramatically. "There's been a striking decrease in the number of cases since 1980," said Dr. Anne Schuchat, medical epidemiologist at the CDC. "The recall of Rely was one factor. It had high absorbency and a high market share." It was the only one with polyester foam and CMC. "We think Rely was a riskier brand," she said. The CDC no longer has any active studies on toxic shock.[82]

It took nearly ten years, but Dr. Philip Tierno was finally vindicated. His research, as outlined in his October 1980 letter to P&G, was published in a 1989 infectious diseases journal. "Other scientists ridiculed me because big money spurred them on," he said. "This made me feel a sense of satisfaction." Dr. Merlin Bergdoll's research, deemed preliminary by P&G, was also duplicated, confirming the impact of synthetic tampons.[83]

P&G settled most of the other Rely suits, in particular those brought by Tom Riley. In some cases, P&G paid $1-million settlements. He is bitter about P&G's deception, especially when he remembers Robin Lynn Spooner. The St. Louis girl was so sick after using Rely that she couldn't attend her sixteenth birthday party in August 1980. She had a temperature of 103 degrees and a rash that looked like severe sunburn. By the end of the month, she had trouble breathing and tried to free herself from the hospital respirator. Doctors had to tranquilize her to keep her calm. In late September she suffered cardiac arrest.

As Riley reads through the Spooner case file, he fights back tears. "If this was the socially responsible company that they pretend they are, this little girl would be alive," the attorney said. Instead, she lived just sixty days beyond her sixteenth birthday and was buried in St. Louis's Oak Grove Cemetery. "With all the power the bastards had to get out the word, they could've saved her life." P&G was pushing Rely at high schools the same month that Spooner "struggled to stay alive," he said. "It was very sad." P&G settled that case out of court; Riley can't reveal the terms.[84]

Mike Kehm is still bitter about P&G and its callous attitude toward women like his wife. "They never displayed any human factor or acknowledged what I was going through. It almost ruined me," he said. "I came close to an emotional breakdown." Time does heal some of the pain, but he still misses Pat. "I can't say that I forgive them. I look at the girls and think she'll never see their confirmations or graduations or other big events," he said.

He has remarried, and his new wife adopted the two girls, Andrea and Katie, who are now both teenagers. Andrea, only three when Pat died, has begun to ask a lot of questions about her mother, so her father gave her Tom Riley's book to read to help her understand. She didn't take it very well, he said. "She feels cheated by what happened to her mother."[85]

P&G has used similar scare tactics to protect another profitable product: disposable diapers. And it pursued another familiar foe—Judy Braiman in Rochester.

After P&G introduced Ultra Pampers in 1986, Braiman once again started getting calls from consumers. This time they complained that the diapers were giving their babies rashes, and that tiny beads of the chemicals used in the superabsorbent diapers were sticking to the children's skin.

The chemicals replaced some of the thick fluff that had been used in traditional, thicker disposable diapers, giving the diapers more power to absorb wetness. The superabsorbent material starts as a dry powder, but once the baby wets, it thickens into a slimy gel. When parents found it on their children, they grew worried. [86]

In 1986 the New York public relations firm Manning, Selvage & Lee placed an ad in Rochester newspapers to address health concerns about the diapers. It quoted Dr. James Todd, the doctor who identified toxic shock, as saying that he would let his own children wear the diapers. The ad neglected to mention his association with the company or that P&G paid for the ad. [87]

Braiman criticized the ad and noted that Dr. Tierno, another toxic shock expert, found that "a very significant potential problem exists because of this diaper's remarkable ability to absorb and hold fluid." He said the skin can shrivel, thus reducing its normal defenses and posing a health risk to the baby. Tierno also found the toxin related to toxic shock in trace quantities in the disposables and said he wanted to pursue more research on that risk.

Braiman wrote more about the diapers for the "Speaking Out" page of the *Rochester Democrat and Chronicle* on July 25, 1987. She informed readers about the hundreds of complaints she'd received regarding skin irritations, oozing blood, fever, vomiting, and staph infections. "After switching their babies to non-chemical diapers, parents report that all symptoms disappear," she wrote.

She quoted Dr. Ruth Lawrence, a University of Rochester pediatrics professor, who in June 1986 complained to the American Academy of Pediatrics about adverse reactions suffered by babies at Strong Memorial Hospital. The hospital discontinued using the product. After P&G learned of Dr. Lawrence's letter, it sent representatives to see her. Braiman learned that P&G now wanted the University of Rochester to conduct a diaper rash study, which the company would sponsor.

"Ironically, history seems to be repeating itself," Braiman wrote. She told of how P&G commissioned Rely research in Rochester but didn't share the safety data. She questioned what the long-term effect would be from the diapers, and she warned the parents participating in the Rochester diaper rash study to be aware of health risks. "We worry about the lack of independent study done on these new chemical diapers," she said. "Maybe it's getting harder to find independent researchers. Isn't there anyone left not receiving some funding from Procter & Gamble?"[88]

Her group petitioned three government agencies to prohibit the sale of synthetic superabsorbent diapers and adult diapers for incontinence and to demand mandatory safety standards for the products. "I didn't want a repeat of Rely," Braiman said. "These are babies."

About a week after her opinion page piece appeared, she received an eighteen-page order from P&G's attorneys. They wanted to depose her in a lawsuit the company had filed a year earlier against three cotton-diaper services and their advertising agency. The lawsuit sought damages of $11 million, alleging that the diaper services and the agency, Pierpoint Group, Inc., spread disinformation to hurt the sales of Ultra Pampers.[89]

"They were getting back at me for Rely," Braiman said. She immediately called attorney Riley, with whom she had talked before about toxic shock and Rely.

P&G knew that Renell Pierpoint, owner of the Cleveland advertising agency, had talked to Braiman about safety testing for the disposable diapers and that both women had attended a government meeting on diaper safety. Based on these facts, P&G alleged that they were conspiring to sabotage Pampers.

In the order, P&G requested all of Braiman's documents

pertaining to conversations and correspondence with various physicians. Company lawyers even demanded any information about her calls or letters to reporter Jolie Solomon, then of *The Wall Street Journal*, who had written on health concerns about P&G's diapers. They also wanted records of any contributions Braiman had received from cloth diaper industry representatives. Braiman said she has never received any. [90]

"It was unbelievable," Braiman said. "P&G was just trying to take away my right to speak out."

Riley was sympathetic, but he couldn't represent her because he wasn't licensed to practice in New York. She turned to Carl Shoolman, an attorney who had worked with Ralph Nader. Shoolman sought a protective order to stop the deposition on the grounds that Braiman was a consumer advocate and that P&G was merely trying to silence her, along with the others. The courts agreed and stopped P&G from deposing her. [91]

In the Pierpoint case, P&G wanted her to stop sending newspaper clippings from the Rochester newspaper, which described how the hospital had stopped using Ultra Pampers because of health worries. P&G even complained that one of Pierpoint's employees had written a letter to the editor of *Time* magazine about disposable diapers. The letter wasn't published, but P&G claimed it was part of the disinformation campaign.

For several years Pierpoint heard about problems from parents who used disposable diapers. She decided to have some testing done when P&G test marketed its new superabsorbent diapers in Wichita, Kansas, in 1984. A client in Rochester referred her to Braiman, who researched the company and its products. Braiman suggested that Delta Labs could analyze the new Pampers. It was the same lab that Braiman had used to study what was in Rely.

The lab tested numerous products, including Pampers and several brands of sanitary napkins. All the products were coded with numbers, not brand names. The testing showed that Pampers contained carboxymethylcellulose as the superabsorbent material. Upon learning the results, Braiman exclaimed, "Oh my God! That's what they used in Rely!" CMC and polyester were the superabsorbent materials found in Rely.

That's when she filed a petition with the Consumer Product Safety Commission, asking for government help in stopping the sale of the diapers. Concerned mothers began returning Ultra Pampers to the stores. P&G sued after the news media began following the story, which the company blamed on Renell Pierpoint. "I was in business, so I was the easiest one to get," she said. "If you have a legitimate question about anything P&G does, they don't tolerate it."

She kept a diary of her battle with P&G. In one January 1987 entry she wrote: "I'm afraid people will lose heart with this legal thing, and I'll be left dangling in the wind with no clients. Just what they want." And P&G did just that. The lawsuit eventually forced Pierpoint to close her agency, which had annual billings of about $750,000.

"Clients didn't want to come on with me because they were afraid I'd be sued," she said. "I lost my reputation." At the same time, she divorced her husband, and her sister Olivia died of a brain tumor. "I felt so alone," Pierpoint said. She took out a second mortgage on her Cleveland house to pay her legal bills, which amounted to approximately $50,000.

Friends at the phone company and in law enforcement checked her phone lines and found evidence of wiretaps. During a six-and-a-half-hour deposition, P&G attorneys asked her questions about private matters "they could've only known from listening to my phone calls," she said. P&G said it has never used, or asked others to use, wiretaps or other methods to eavesdrop on others. Pierpoint was also followed on numerous occasions. P&G attorneys told her lawyer that there could be a job for her in Cincinnati. She also got an anonymous offer to buy her company. The offer was contingent upon her never returning to public relations or advertising. She could never trace the offer, made through a Chicago broker. "They wanted me to sell my soul," she said.

Her Cleveland attorney warned her that the case would ultimately cost her $200,000, which she couldn't afford. Whereas P&G signed settlement agreements with the diaper services, Pierpoint initially refused to settle. "But they beat me to death," she said. A Hamilton County judge dismissed P&G's claims of deceptive trade, unfair competition, and disinformation. The rest of the case was dismissed with prejudice when Pierpoint agreed to sign a settlement agreement. She doesn't regret the fight. "Would I do it again? Absolutely." [92]

Meanwhile, the Consumer Products Safety Commission turned down Braiman's petition to set mandatory safety standards. Neither would the Food and Drug Administration or the New York State Attorney General's office take action on her complaint. P&G reformulated the diapers to replace the carboxymethylcellulose.

But some information still raises questions about disposable diapers and toxic shock. There were several reports of toxic shock syndrome in babies, according to data collected from January 1985 through January 1993 by the National Electronic Injury Surveillance System. The surveillance system collects data on injuries treated in hospital emergency rooms that patients say are related to products. For instance, a thirteen-month-old Missouri boy was diagnosed as suffering from toxic shock in 1989. "The mother alleges that a nurse told her TSS could be caused by the use of disposable diapers," the report said.

Another incident report showed that a thirteen-month-old New York girl "allegedly died from toxic shock syndrome induced by toxins created while wearing a highly absorbent disposable diaper." The pediatrician identified three of the diagnostic criteria established by the CDC to identify TSS. The doctor said that was insufficient to positively identify TSS and the parents would not consent to an autopsy, the report said. [93]

Cloth diaper service owners remain vigilant about such issues, as part of their ongoing efforts to fight giant manufacturers of disposable diapers.

Consider seventy-year-old Nan Scott, who started a diaper service when her husband returned from the air force after World War II. They used a $2,500 loan and his poker winnings, planning to start either a bowling alley or a diaper service. She decided on the latter because "I didn't like washing diapers," she said. But it backfired: Scott ended up washing her own kids' diapers and those of 250 customers.

As their family grew, they packed the five kids into a station wagon, moved from Cumberland, Maryland, to San Francisco, and bought Dy-Dee diaper service. At its peak, Dy-Dee had 4,000 customers. When her husband died in 1971, Nan Scott decided to continue the business by herself. At the time, disposable diapers were beginning to take over the market. "We had been serving every hospital in the Bay Area, but we started to lose accounts," she said. The hospitals liked the service, but P&G offered them free Pampers.

She hired a consultant to direct a market research study. He recommended that she sell Dy-Dee immediately before she lost any more business to disposables. Her customer count was down to about 1,500. She didn't listen.

The business has had its ups and downs, but environment-minded parents continue to use her service as an alternative to disposables. Scott shuns advertising in favor of her own newsletter, which she produces on a typewriter. In each issue she condemns disposable diapers. She's been stepping up her campaign as she watches the cloth diaper industry erode because of more pressure from P&G and other disposable-diaper manufacturers. The company agreed to change some ads that implied disposables were healthier than cloth diapers after the National Association of Diaper Services challenged one of P&G's campaigns. Most of P&G's claims about health and performance come from studies paid for by the company. "We don't have the resources and can't match P&G study for study," said Jack Shiffert, executive director of the cloth diaper service group. [94] Nor can small businesses such as Scott's afford to match P&G's massive advertising budget. "People believe them as if it's gospel," she said.

P&G also has spent millions to battle the green movement that encourages use of cloth instead of single-use products. Roger Noe, a community-college professor and Kentucky state legislator, discovered firsthand P&G's determination to fight back. He introduced a bill to put a penny tax on disposable diapers in an effort to clean up his neighborhood in Harlan, which is littered with diapers and other trash. Indeed, when the Cumberland River floods, diapers hang from tree limbs. Locals call them Pampers trees.

The money collected from the tax would have funded environmental cleanup projects. But the bill never made it out of committee. "A lot of five-hundred-dollar suits showed up" representing P&G and lobbied enough to kill it, he said. "It got more attention than we're used to seeing around here." [95]

P&G has tried to recycle used diapers into typing paper and flower pots, but the project flopped because it was too expensive. The company also commissioned studies to show that cloth diapers do more harm to the environment than disposables. The report was used by lobbyists in California to stop a bill encouraging the use of cloth diapers. [96]

Another tack is to promote the diapers as compostable. Ads showed soil-like substance and copy that read, "ninety days ago, this was a disposable diaper." Some consumers in California and New York were so convinced that diapers were easily composted, they they put their Pampers out with the glass bottles, newspapers, and aluminum cans for a recycling center. [97] New York City charged P&G with misleading advertising for suggesting that disposable diapers were easily composted when in fact composting sites exist in only a few cities. Attorneys general in several states also ordered the company to revise the ads. [98]

But P&G still reaches expectant parents through brochures distributed at childbirth classes and in hospitals. In late 1992 a group of women environmentalists complained to the Federal Trade Commission about P&G's practices, asking for an investigation. [99]

P&G has even engaged in deceptive practices against the other titan of diapers, Kimberly-Clark Corp., which has been eating away at P&G's market share. In 1981 P&G claimed nearly 70 percent of the U.S. disposable diaper market; Kimberly-Clark, about 11 percent. Johnson & Johnson had fallen to about 8 percent from a high of 20 percent and eventually dropped out of the business. By 1985 P&G's combined market share from Pampers and Luvs brands had fallen to 50 percent as Kimberly-Clark's Huggies brand found favor with consumers. [100]

"Kimberly-Clark was kicking our butts," said Bill Morgan, former controller in the paper division. "Everyone was asking what do you do to beat them?"[101] In January 1985 P&G announced it would spend $500 million to upgrade diaper manufacturing plants. [102] No one realized then how far P&G would go to beat Kimberly-Clark.

Until late 1982 both companies believed a thicker diaper was best. Then two P&G inventors, Paul Weisman and Steve Goldman, discovered what they considered a secret for including superabsorbent materials in pulp fluff, which made a thinner yet more absorbent diaper. They filed for a patent and received it in 1986. Meanwhile, P&G tested the thinner diaper in Wichita, Kansas. Its share of the market increased by ten percentage points in about nine months. A national rollout followed into 1986. "It turned the diaper world on its ear," said P&G attorney Allen Gerstein. [103]

Kimberly-Clark also introduced a thinner diaper, Huggies Supertrim. P&G cried foul, suing Kimberly-Clark for alleged patent infringment. [104]

But as Kimberly-Clark discovered, P&G's attorneys and

scientists had misled the U.S. Patent Office. In 1979, before Weisman had his idea, the British patent office published a patent application of an Italian inventor named Gambazzi, whic' had the same basic elements as the Weisman patent. P&G didn't disclose this information when it sought its patent. "Conduct of this type is what patent lawyers call inequitable conduct," said H. Blair White, Kimberly-Clark's attorney. "It used to be called fraud on the patent office." [105]

P&G tried to convince the court that Kimberly-Clark had ripped off its idea during the Wichita test market. But White told the court that the only thing Kimberly-Clark learned from P&G was how *not* to make a thin baby diaper. Besides, he pointed out, P&G wasn't really first with the product; Kao Corp., the leading Japanese consumer products company, was selling one prior to P&G's launch in Kansas. [106]

But Kimberly-Clark saw major problems with both Kao's and P&G's diapers, especially how the pulp fluff was mixed with superabsorbent materials. It worried about the same thing as Judy Braiman: toxic shock syndrome.

In the early 1980s, when Kimberly-Clark began developing its thin diaper, women were worried about toxic shock in the wake of Rely. "That fear affected their attitudes about the kinds of diapers they wanted to put on their babies," White said. Indeed, twelve mothers were asked to examine thin diapers made by Kimberly-Clark. Ten liked them. But then they were told that one of the ingredients inside the diaper was a superabsorbent similar to what had been used in P&G's Rely tampon. "At that point, all twelve mothers expressed serious concern about putting such diapers on their babies," White said. One problem was that the superabsorbent material came out of the diaper onto the baby's skin, leaving a slimy chemical gel. [106]

Kimberly-Clark's solution was to use webbing and bury the superabsorbent deeper within the fluff to keep it farther away from the baby's skin. The same approach had been used in its adult incontinence diapers, Depend. P&G's diapers in Wichita hadn't solved that problem. The very problem that P&G had tried to silence among consumer advocates and cloth diaper services was being discussed by leading diaper scientists three years before P&G sued Renell Pierpoint and others. [108]

After seventeen days of testimony, 1,000 exhibits, and volumes of depositions, a U.S. district court judge in South Carolina ruled in favor of Kimberly-Clark, concluding that P&G had engaged in "inequitable conduct." The Weisman patent was declared unenforceable. [109]

"Clearly the atmosphere at P&G was to hurt the major competitor," attorney White said. "And this misleading declaration is but one manifestation of P&G's attitude." Documents from P&G show that the diaper division analyzed various ways to "financially paralyze" Kimberly-Clark. A handwritten note on one of the documents labeled that conduct as "predatory." [110]

The South Carolina judge also cleared the way for Kimberly-Clark to proceed with its antitrust counterclaim against P&G. The company alleged that such patent infringement suits were without merit and that P&G engaged in predatory pricing. Nearly three years later, P&G settled the suit just three days before it was set to go to trial in Dallas. Insiders say P&G wasn't enthusiastic about the matter becoming public. Kimberly-Clark wanted to recover about $20 million in past legal expenses and unspecified punitive damages. The settlement was believed to exceed that amount. [111] "If the lawyers were successful, P&G could turn back the competitive clock to where it was at the time before Kimberly-Clark became a strong competitor," White said. [112]

P&G has a history of bullying competitors that have gotten too powerful. Sometimes its tricks are crude—such as sabotaging a competitor's test market. In that scenario, P&G salesmen buy up lots of the competitor's new product. That way, the competition believes it has a winner. The flip side is to flood the test market with discount coupons or free samples for the competing P&G brand. Either way, the competitor can't get a clear read on the test results. These maneuvers are frequent because the competition from Colgate and Kimberly-Clark is especially fierce. The tactic is fairly common, according to P&G managers.

At other times, P&G managers say they are encouraged to simply wreck store displays of competing brands; a much cheaper method of destroying other companies' sales. Some managers recall ripping off shelf tags away from competitors' store displays of toothpaste or soap. In some cases they cleared out the whole display and replaced it with P&G products. A store clerk won't reorder the competing merchandise if he can't find tags or evidence of a depleted supply. [113] This strategy can be done fairly easily because many stores still rely on P&G sales personnel to help them restock shelves. The situation has gotten worse as companies fight for better shelf space in an increasingly crowded field of new products. P&G said "sabotaging competitors' test markets and wrecking shelf displays are not practices we use or endorse. Violations of this policy are grounds for dismissal."

But sometimes the competition gets even more aggressive. Consider P&G's efforts against Colgate in 1985, when the toothpaste battles were heating up. Each company was launching a tartar-control formula to build more market share. As P&G planned its launch of tartar-control Crest, the company learned that in February 1985 Colgate had purchased a toothpaste called Darkie from Hawley & Hazel Chemical Co. in Hong Kong. The brand sported a logo of a black-faced caricature, complete with top hat. But press reports on the acquisition didn't appear until April in a Taipei newspaper and in August in the *South China Morning Post* in Hong Kong.

P&G's public relations department showed a box of the toothpaste to the public relations firm Manning, Selvage & Lee, which had been hired to help launch the new Crest in March. P&G wanted the company's advice on how it could use Darkie to portray Colgate as racist. Insiders at Manning say they advised

P&G to tackle it head-on. But P&G said it didn't want the company or Crest brand name associated with a smear campaign.

Some suggest the matter was dropped. "That's just cover-your-ass time," snorted one P&G manager familiar with the campaign. "The reality is that P&G got the news out in a surreptitious manner." Indeed, a senior public relations official went to CEO John Smale with the idea of sending information to various U.S. newspapers and activists. Smale okayed it but said he'd disavow knowledge of it if it ever leaked out. [114]

Eventually, major newspapers, including *The Wall Street Journal,* picked up on the Darkie story. Late that year the Interfaith Center on Corporate Responsibility, a coalition of Catholic and Protestant groups, asked Colgate to drop the name because it promoted an offensive racial stereotype. An American in Thailand had sent the center a sample of the toothpaste. Comedian Eddie Murphy even got in a few jabs during an appearance on "Late Night with David Letterman."

Three Catholic religious orders sponsored a shareholders' resolution to get the name changed, and the Rainbow Coalition demanded that Colgate withdraw the product. In 1989 Colgate announced it was changing the name to Darlie, with a new logo. [115]

A Colgate spokesman said the company was unaware of any involvement by P&G.

P&G has also used its considerable clout in advertising to stifle competitors' advances. In late 1989 Pepsi began a Waterloo, Iowa, test market of a morning soda, Pepsi A.M. The higher-caffeine soft drink was aimed at snaring a piece of the morning beverage market from coffee. Coffee consumption has been declining since 1962, so Pepsi figured it could lure some drinkers who were tired of bitter coffees.

Pepsi convinced some retailers in the test market to stock the soft drink in the coffee aisle by the Folgers and Maxwell House cans. And Pepsi ran ads that asked, "Tired of the same

old grind?" The next page showed cans of Pepsi A.M. surrounded by sunbeams. "Wake up to taste! All Morning . . . It's
cool and refreshing instead of hot and bitter like coffee."[116]

In Cincinnati, P&G's Folgers team was not amused by the
assault. They fought back through a television commercial that
reminded consumers of the sugar content in colas. The ad was a
spoof of a game show, on which a contestant was asked to guess
how many teaspoons of sugar were in a cup of coffee versus each
can of cola. She was informed that cola has eight teaspoons while
coffee has none.

P&G's Mark Upson, vice president of food and beverage,
sent the tape and a letter to Pepsi. Upson said P&G would blan-
ket the airwaves with the ad if Pepsi chose to continue attacking
coffee. He also tried to use the muscle of the entire coffee industry trade group to get Pepsi to back off. It was a clear example of
P&G using its clout and advertising muscle to intimidate competitors into retreating.[117]

To be sure, every company produces ads that attack the
competition. But this was a particularly arrogant gesture on
P&G's part because it went outside the coffee field to eliminate
any brand that looked like a competitor, no matter how small a
threat it really posed. Even P&G insiders said it was an embarrassment because it went beyond what they deemed fair tactics.
In the end, the whole effort by P&G seemed unnecessary, considering the lukewarm response Pepsi A.M. received from consumers, who considered its taste rather flat. By October 1990 Pepsi
had scrapped the project.[118]

It is true that P&G has suffered from its share of competitors' dirty tricks too. In 1984 P&G sued three cookie makers in
U.S. District Court in Wilmington, Delaware, claiming they'd
copied technology for its Duncan Hines cookie. The cookies were
soft on the inside and crispy on the outside, similar to homemade.

The cookie caper included accusations of espionage, such as
P&G's claim that a Frito-Lay agent photographed a Chicago

production line and stole a sample of Duncan Hines cookie dough. P&G also said that a plane from Keebler flew over a cookie plant construction site to learn details of the plant. And in March 1984, when P&G began selling its ready-to-serve cookies, a Frito-Lay employee posed as a P&G customer and attended a confidential P&G sales presentation. [119]

Insiders at P&G also say someone from the competing cookie firms snuck into the company's Cincinnati headquarters and tapped the cookie brand manager's phone. After that was discovered, P&G security made everyone wear ID badges. "Like corporate spies can't figure that out," quipped one manager.

The Duncan Hines cookie had gained a 15 percent market share in a midwestern test market. But when the company took it nationwide, its success crumbled. Within months of P&G's test market, Keebler's Soft Batch, Nabisco's Almost Home, and Frito-Lay's Grandma's Rich & Chewy cookies hit the store shelves. Some say the alleged patent infringement wasn't P&G's only problem. Its cookies didn't taste as good as the competition's. And P&G moved slower than the others.

More details on the espionage were never revealed because P&G received a $125-million settlement from Frito-Lay, Keebler, and Nabisco Brands, Inc., shortly before the case was scheduled to go to trial. The trial promised to have all the trappings of the usual P&G lawsuit: thirty-seven lawyers, 120,000 pages of pretrial testimony, 800 days of depositions, and 10,000 trial exhibits. And most of the court documents were sealed because the companies feared that trade secrets would leak out if they were made public.

The three competitors lost the case but won control of the cookie aisle. P&G took a $435-million after-tax charge for restructuring in the fourth quarter of 1987, including a write-off to close some cookie-production plants. It now sells only three varieties of the cookies, down from a peak of ten flavors in June 1987. [120]

* * *

Perhaps the strangest dirty trick against P&G is the perennial rumor that the conservative bunch in Cincinnati are really closet satanists.

The rumors about P&G's religious beliefs come in several varieties. One, in the early 1980s, suggested a link between the Rev. Sun Myung Moon's Unification Church, the members of which are known as the Moonies. The reason is the century-old P&G symbol, a man in the moon, surrounded by thirteen stars.

A more prevalent rumor is that the thirteen stars are merely a clever disguise for three sixes, a satanic symbol. Some suggest that the curls in the moon's hair are also sixes. Especially irksome to the company is a flier falsely accusing P&G executives of appearing on TV talk shows, pledging a slice of company profits to the Church of Satan. The profit-sharing pact is said to be contingent on Beelzebub first boosting P&G sales, according to the flier.

P&G even removed the moon symbol from its packaging at one point and gave the moon a more contemporary look, straightening out his curly beard, thereby ridding the logo of some of those mystery sixes. [121]

P&G sends "truth packets" to churches, schools, newspapers, and radio stations in states where the rumor crops up. Since 1980 the toll-free hotline has fielded thousands of calls about the rumor. Some P&G salesmen had *666* written on their lawns and their tires slashed. [122] When P&G was building its new twin-tower office building, the architects Kohn Pedersen Fox planned to place logos on the building, but that was nixed because of the rumors. [123]

The logo's thirteen stars actually represent the original thirteen colonies. And the man in the moon was a popular symbol back in the mid-1800s, when the logo was first used. It evolved from P&G's earliest symbol of a plain moon and stars that marked Star candles so customers could identify the product even if they couldn't read. [124]

P&G has filed and settled more than a dozen lawsuits against those who allegedly spread the rumors, including competing Amway distributors, who sell detergents and soaps among other products. It won a $75,000 judgment against two Amway distributors in Kansas.[125]

P&G also sends out its ex-FBI security guards to track down any leads on the rumor and went so far as to enlist the help of Pinkerton and Wackenhut detectives to track down scofflaws. Even the seemingly innocent are harassed if P&G suspects they are rumormongers.[126]

The story seems to flourish in small towns, such as Clymer, Pennsylvania, a coal-mining community with one stoplight and a $3.50 pigs in a blanket dinner special at Luigi's restaurant. Talk of satanism isn't welcome around here. There are four churches within a few blocks of one another, including St. Anthony's Catholic church.

At the church's elementary school, Sister Domitilla Drobnsk was at first reluctant to recall her experience. Though recently recovered from heart surgery, she insisted on showing up for the last day of school—not only of the year but forever. The school was closing its doors because of dwindling population. It was a sad day. She had been principal for eleven of her forty-nine years as a nun.

After the children left, she smoothed her blue-and-white dress and shook her head as she described how she found the flier in her mailbox in 1984. She was concerned and showed it to members of the congregation at St. Anthony's church. She added a note that they should consider not using P&G products if this was true. "I thought I was going to fight for social justice," she said. "I was an innocent victim."

When others told her it wasn't true, she sent a letter apologizing to the congregation and thought that would be the end of it. But shortly after she was quoted in *The Wall Street Journal*'s story on the rumor, Sister Drobnsk received a letter from P&G

threatening her with a lawsuit if she spread the rumor. "I got a call saying they would prosecute me," she said. Others quoted in the story won't even talk about their own ordeals.

P&G complained to her diocese, upsetting her superiors. "The school kids would say, 'Sister, are you going to jail?' " she recalled. Then one night while walking home from school, she heard the clicking of heels behind her. The noise quickened, as if someone were trying to catch up with her. She turned around. It was a woman. She yelled to Sister Drobnsk, "How much are you teaching about satanic cults?" The person wouldn't identify herself. Was it a P&G person? "I'm pretty sure," she said.

Children wearing their St. Anthony's T-shirts were quizzed by strangers about Sister Drobnsk. Mothers who volunteered in the cafeteria were questioned by a man they didn't recognize one day as they prepared lunch. "He had a tape recorder in his pocket," she said. "They spotted it, so they kept still." He wouldn't identify himself.

In the months following the incidents, Sister Drobnsk continued to hear reports of the rumor on talk shows, so she knew she wasn't solely to blame. "I was scared," she said. "And I apologized. But they never apologized to me." [127]

6
Ivory
Snow Job

For fifteen years George Stults worked as a $24,000-a-year technician at Procter & Gamble's testing labs. He spent many weekends on special projects, becoming an expert on Downy fabric softener. While other Cincinnati Bengals fans watched their team in the Super Bowl, Stults was studying a test batch of Downy at P&G's Lima, Ohio, plant.

He didn't mind, though, because the job provided good benefits for his wife, Judy, and their two sons, Adam and Andy. They were able to afford a modest home in Cincinnati's neighborhood of Hyde Park, where the boys could ride their bikes with other kids. They even found a grandmother to "adopt"; an elderly neighbor named Edna Mae.

So the forty-one-year-old technician was troubled when he learned that colleagues were breaking rules at the labs. He reported wrongdoings such as drug use to P&G security, believing he was doing the right thing. But his whistle-blowing cost him his job. And when he looked for another job in Cincinnati, he discovered that P&G's power and money led to loyalty and favoritism throughout the city. [1]

Like Stults, others have suffered because P&G controls Cincinnati. And beyond. The company has tremendous clout that interferes with the government, organized labor, and the news media. Anyone deemed an adversary is squashed. "Every place you look, you'll see the fingerprints of Procter," said one local official. "Trying to describe their influence is like trying to describe the air we breathe," adds another.[2]

To understand P&G's power, you first have to understand Cincinnati. The city began as a small settlement on the river in 1788. Many of the immigrants who built the city hailed from Germany. One neighborhood was dubbed Over-the-Rhine because crossing the Miami & Erie canal reminded many of crossing the Rhine river into Germany.[3]

The 1800s saw Cincinnati's downtown grow as a center for butchering hogs. Visitors noted that it was tricky to maneuver city streets because they were packed with pigs. One woman from Great Britain wrote that Cincinnati in the 1840s was "a city of pigs . . . a monster piggery. . . . Their grunts and squeals meet you at every moment."[4] At one time there were more than fifty butcher shops downtown.[5]

Every part of the pig contributed to some industry. The hair stuffed mattresses. The hooves made glue. The hide made leather shoes.[6] And the fats made soap and candles at the new Procter & Gamble Co.

As the city grew, so did its conservative ways. Mark Twain worked for a time at a Cincinnati printing office and published several of his books there. Historians disagree, but many say he was struck by the growing German conservatism and once said, "If the world would end, I would come to Cincinnati, for everything happens here 10 years later."[7]

Hearty crops of grains helped develop Cincinnati's beer industry. Around the turn of the century, residents consumed fifty-eight gallons per capita, compared to the national average of sixteen gallons.[8] Saloons were as common as the hogs. The Women's Christian Temperance Union and the Anti-Saloon League targeted the city because it was famous for its brew and "boisterous entertainment." Indeed, Carry Nation was so overwhelmed by the number of saloons that she didn't bother to swing her hatchet at a single keg. "I would've dropped from exhaustion before I had gone a block," she said in 1901. When Prohibition passed in 1919, the saloons were shuttered, but local breweries supplied hops and other ingredients to illegal stills around the country. [9]

Cincinnati lost some of its Germanic flavor when World War I broke out. Banks changed their German names to avoid offending patriotic customers. The German National Bank became Lincoln National. German was dropped from the school curriculum. The public library banned all German publications from its shelves. And thirteen streets lost their German names. [10]

But it has never lost its conservative nature. This is the home of antipornography and antiabortion groups such as Right to Life. There are no adult bookstores in the city. In the 1970s, the popular musical *Oh, Calcutta!* was banned from appearing at Cincinnati's Music Hall; a Common Pleas Court judge ruled that a videotape of the production was "pure obscenity." [11] Perhaps the biggest stir in recent times was the attempt by some conservatives to ban Robert Mapplethorpe's controversial homoerotic photos from the Cincinnati Art Museum. That case ended up in court after some wanted to prosecute the museum director for showing the exhibit, which some considered obscene. He won the trial.

Cincinnati's conservatism has many faces, which often contradict each other. James Gamble and other city fathers sponsored the Freedman's Aid Society to provide education and training for former slaves. [12] But blacks were shunned in many circles. The Cincinnati Country Club, the first to have a nine-hole course, had "understood guidelines" that kept it all-white. Black chauffeurs weren't permitted to open the clubhouse doors. [13]

Business leaders like the Procters and Gambles flocked to social clubs such as the University Club and the Queen City Club. But Cincinnati's Jewish businessmen had to establish their own, the Phoenix Club, because they were excluded from other private clubs. [14] Women recall times when they were banned from dining at Cincinnati's poshest restaurant, La Maisonette, if they weren't with a man. (However, unescorted women who said they were from P&G were immediately given a good table.) Women can now dine without men, but the biases still remain elsewhere. Some, like the University Club, are still predominantly white and male.[15]

Over lunches at these clubs, the city fathers developed their plans. P&G CEOs Richard Deupree (1930–48), Howard Morgens (1957–71), and their successors would meet with community leaders to "quietly set the tone of the city," one official remembers. "There was no fuss, no hubbub." The quiet meetings became more formal when P&G CEO Ed Harness and Ralph Lazarus, chairman of Federated Department Stores, founded the Cincinnati Business Committee in 1977. This group of local CEOs wields tremendous power over local politics and policies. Its first executive director was Thomas Collins, a P&G employee given a leave of absence to start the group. And P&G leaders have a lot of clout in the group.[16] When the city decided it needed to redo its infrastructure, it asked P&G CEO John Smale to head the commission. It was dubbed the Smale Commission.[17]

P&G's benevolence over the years led to ironclad loyalty. William Cooper Procter donated $3.1 million to start a children's hospital in the city. He also chaired the Red Cross for sixteen years.[18] P&G has remained one of the largest contributors to the United Way, which funds scores of charities. Employees are required to collect funds from their peers and to give generously to the fund. "You don't have a choice," said one P&Ger. The company's charitable contributions were $32.1 million in fiscal 1990.[19]

Some estimate that P&G has volunteers in 112 of the 115 United Way agencies in Cincinnati.[20] Many times, the P&Gers are the presidents of the groups. "The people running everything are Procter people," said James Nethercott, retired chief financial officer. "It's good, but it's a little overwhelming."[21]

More important, P&G provided jobs even in the Depression and other tough economic times. Ivorydale, its first major plant, has remained open for more than a century, giving the Cincinnati suburb of St. Bernard a steady stream of revenue. About half its tax revenues comes from the earnings tax on Ivorydale's $60-million payroll and from real estate taxes.[22]

P&G's sense of public service shifted, many say, beginning in the early 1980s. It no longer gives without question, and it now tries to publicize its good deeds rather than quietly offer support. "Fifteen years ago you'd ask P&G for a contribution and they'd give it," said one local leader. "But they'd ask you not to tell anybody." Now the company publishes a booklet called "Because We Care" to outline every contribution.

And it has asked for more in return. When P&G wanted to expand the Ivorydale plant, it requested and received a $15-million tax abatement. "They never used to ask for tax breaks. That was part of the contribution to the community," said one former P&Ger. "We'd give money to the schools, but the tax abatement takes it out the back door."[23]

P&G's power gets the company what it wants, when it wants it. In the mid-1980s, the local Board of Health wanted to pass an ordinance to ban smoking in all open areas. Mary Ellen Heintz, a member of P&G's public affairs department, chaired the nine-person board. She and other citizens on the board took oaths to represent the people of Cincinnati, not any political group or corporate interest. But P&G wanted the ordinance stopped. It was considered an inconvenience and would require smokers to leave their desks. Therefore, they'd be less efficient. Insiders say Heintz was summoned to discuss the smoking ban with her boss, Gerald Gendell, who told her to vote against the measure. She refused, saying all she could do was abstain from the vote. The measure passed.

After the vote, Heintz was informed that P&G management didn't want her to stand for reappointment to the board due to a "conflict of interest." Before discussing the matter with her,

P&G officials had already informed the mayor's office that she wouldn't be standing for reappointment. Heintz declined comment on the matter. P&G's resistance seems especially frivolous because it and other companies have since banned smoking in their offices. [24]

Those who challenge P&G on local laws find it can get lonely. Thomas B. Brush, who served on the city council in the early 1980s, pushed for a local ordinance to require labeling of hazardous substances in the workplace. His "Right to Know" ordinance passed in May 1982, despite opposition from P&G, which uses chemicals for its detergents and other products. But he discovered that the company's opposition had lasting effects. "I was amazed at the disdain, the open hostility displayed by P&G employees," he said. Those P&Gers who had previously contributed time and money to his campaign told him they were no longer his supporters. "I have been told that I hit a raw nerve over there," he said. [25]

P&G has used its influence to shape the downtown area. The company has spent heavily to develop the riverfront, including a performance pavilion for outdoor concerts. In addition, P&G entered into a partnership with Federated Department Stores and contributed $2.66 million of a $4-million loan to build the Westin Hotel. [26] But its benevolence ends when its corporate needs outweigh the public good.

When the company built its twin-towers headquarters in the mid-1980s, it wanted the city block adjacent to its Sixth and Sycamore office building. The area included numerous historic sites, such as the Wesley Chapel. The church, built in 1831, was the oldest religious building in the city. The site also included Allen Temple, built in 1852; the Fenwick Club, built in 1918; and the Chapel of the Holy Spirit, built in 1927. There was concern about the demolition, but P&G ultimately got its new building. [27] It quietly bought up the properties before much could be done to block it. Jim Selonick, a real estate consultant who sat on the Cincinnati historic conservation board, recalled, "P&G

dozed those churches overnight." Some of the demolition work did in fact take place after dark.[28]

Selonick is trying to preserve another landmark that P&G has eyed for future expansion. The Taft theater, home to plays and musicals, is likely to become part of P&G's empire after a new arts center is built downtown. P&G has supported the new arts center, to be called the Ohio Center for the Performing Arts, saying it will help attract visitors and new business to Cincinnati. What P&G hasn't been as candid about is its hopes to buy the old Taft theater. Some say P&G's interest is strictly related to its role as patron of the arts, but others say it's driven by the need for more space at its headquarters. When asked, P&G officials told Selonick they "cannot confirm that P&G has no interest in the Taft theater." One official told him that the company was in discussions to acquire the site. When a reporter asked P&G about the Taft theater, a spokesman said the company isn't interested in the site. P&G has met with the property owners, but those discussions have "never led anywhere," the spokesman said.

Those who spoke out against moving performances from historic sites like Taft were told to keep quiet. One leader of a Cincinnati arts group criticized the new center and consequently was harassed by a local bank president. He threatened to stop funding her group if she continued to speak out. Retailers who supported Selonick were scolded by the Chamber of Commerce.

The city leaders decided the issue of whether to build the new center should be put on the ballot. The Cincinnati Business Committee pooled $300,000 from local businesses to lobby voters to vote for the center and against Selonick's group, Advocates of Responsible Theater Spending. So Selonick looked for a local advertising agency to counter the CBC's campaign. "We went to ten ad agencies, and each of them turned us down because of ties to P&G," said Selonick. "How do you run a democratic society under these circumstances?"

Jerry Galvin, a spirited local ad man with no ties to P&G,

took on the assignment. On election day, citizens voted against the center by a 53–47 margin. But plans for the center had progressed so much that the city forged ahead with the construction work in late 1992. *Cincinnati Business Courier*'s editorial page blasted the episode as an example of how "our government does not work."[29] "This is very depressing," Selonick said. The business community, led by P&G, "exercises such a high degree of control over our destiny."

The company controls Cincinnati streets as well. The city wanted to install parking meters on the streets bordering P&G's new headquarters in 1985. The meters would have generated about $39,000 a year in revenue, according to estimates at the time. But P&G thought it would detract from its new Grecian gardens outside the towers. P&G representatives "expressed a very strong desire to keep their frontage free of parking," said Tom Young, then public works supervisor. They said the "aesthetic importance" of P&G's building deserved "special consideration." The solution? The city installed parking meters on just one street, reducing its expected meter revenue from the area to $12,000 a year. Even then, P&G officials complained about the eyesore.[30]

Many Cincinnati residents are tired of P&G's dominance. "There's a problem in this community—the way P&G is treated borders on idolatry," complained Roxanne Qualls, a city council member. "The corporate headquarters might as well be an altar at which you worship."[31]

For others, though, the power of P&G is a source of prestige. George Stults, like other employees, was proud to work for the company.

But he didn't fully appreciate the power of P&G until he started having problems at Sharon Woods labs, one of several assignments he'd held since joining the company in 1974. The job gave him security after a year-long recovery from an auto accident that had forced him to drop out of Ohio State University. Like his father, a career manager at Cincinnati Milacron, he wanted to stay at P&G until retirement. "The impression I got was, 'Get in with a big company and they'll take care of you for the rest of your life,' " he said. [32]

In 1985 he began to notice equipment missing. Once he had to delay a research project because someone stole the metal drums used to mix the test products. More serious was the repeated disappearance of electronic scales valued at $1,000 each. At the same time, he overheard other technicians bragging about all the overtime pay they collected for work they never performed. One technician said he made $90,000, three times his base salary, because he filed for seventeen-hour days, seven days a week for the entire year. Much of the actual work at the lab was handled by temporary workers, called contractors. Some technicians would pay them extra and train them to pick locks and forge lab results. That way the technicians could stay home without getting behind in their work.

Some of those who did report for work were using drugs inside the labs. "I could smell pot coming out of one of the locked rooms in the middle of the day," Stults said. The problems were concentrated in the liquid specialty products division, known as the LSP group. It was so bad the division was nicknamed the LSD group.

One day, as he filled out his lab notebook in the locker room, he overheard other technicians discussing how they would send contract workers to Columbus to pick up "a couple kilos." They were behind some lockers, so they didn't see him come in the room. He knew there would be trouble if they knew he'd overheard their plans. He closed his eyes, stretched out on a bench, and pretended to be asleep until they left.

After he talked to his boss, Stults reported the problems to P&G's security department. Three days later, one of the senior security officials at the lab chastised him for his actions. "Hey

George! Did you report anybody else for drug use?" the security guard asked with a sneer. About thirty other technicians were in the room at the time.

Investigations at the lab turned up other problems beyond employees smoking pot. Drug sales were common in the parking lot. Managers were bringing kilos of cocaine into the lab, measuring it on scales, and reselling it at P&G and elsewhere. Some simply stole the scales to do that work at home.

Managers throughout P&G say there was a prostitution ring that operated unnoticed for months until discovered in 1987. Apparently the lab was quite the bordello. Some people were caught having sex in the "constant temperature" rooms, where technicians test how a product reacts to hot or cold climates.

The prostitution ring was a rather bizarre enterprise. Numerous insiders say women lab assistants, most of them from outside employment agencies, were paid with bogus overtime slips and drugs if they had sex with managers and coworkers in vans in the company parking lots or elsewhere on the premises. Thus P&G was unwittingly footing the bill for prostitutes. A section head manager, a few levels below a vice president, was signing the overtime slips in exchange for sex.

"It was commonly known that people fooled around," Stults said. At the downtown headquarters, P&G managers were told about the escapades at the research labs. "It wasn't one of those official announcements," one manager recalled. "We were just pulled into a conference room and our boss told us what was going on. We couldn't believe these women were prostitutes for minimum wage."[33]

P&G was able to keep the sex and drugs scandal relatively quiet, even though managers were briefed on the problem. Several managers were fired and about twenty outside contract workers were banned from ever returning to temporary work at P&G. Other managers were ordered to quit or the company would file charges with local police. Some estimate a total of five dozen workers were involved in the operation.

The local police in Blue Ash, where the lab is based, have no record of the incident. Lt. Michael Allen, patrol bureau commander, said the department was never involved in any investigation of a drug and prostitution ring. "If there was a report, I would've seen it," he said. But he acknowledges that companies try to keep such matters quiet to protect their corporate image. "We tell them, 'If you want to handle such things in-house, please don't call us in on something that will be a felony. Then we'll have to handle it as a police matter.' "[34]

Stults contends that he offended the wrong people when he reported the drug use to security. Shortly thereafter he was suspended for several days. The charge: sexual harassment. A temporary employee in the LSP division had accused him of harassment because he'd given her an obscene toy for her birthday. He'd previously told her about the toy, which he gave his wife. She thought it was funny, so he gave her one. "She said it was cute," he said.

Management sent Stults home for several days and told him to visit the company psychiatrist. The next time he saw the woman he apologized. She confided that she wasn't really offended. She worked for technicians in the LSP division who were angry that Stults had reported their drug use. They told her to report him "or her job would disappear," Stults said. Upon learning this, he asked personnel to reopen the case. P&G's personnel office refused, insinuating that Stults had bullied her into recanting. "I never meant any harm," he said.

He acknowledges that giving the toy to his female coworker was inappropriate. But the punishment seems extreme, considering how more serious sexual harassment complaints are routinely ignored by P&G management. One woman was nearly raped by her boss, but the division manager refused to take any action because the attacker had been with the company for twenty-five years. "They called him a loyal employee," she said. There were even witnesses who saw the woman being molested. Yet when she complained to another manager in her department, he questioned if she hadn't encouraged the act and re-marked disapprovingly about suggestive body language. Many other women have complained about the man, but he remained on the job until retirement.

Similar stories are told by numerous men and women at P&G. They say some of the worst offenders have been promoted again and again to the highest levels at corporate headquarters. "There's a double standard," said Gordon Canney, a longtime plant worker and union leader from the old Port Ivory plant in New York. "Management looks at it one way and they treat the employees another way." In other words, the higher up in the company you are, the more you can get away with. [35] Many talk about how managers sexually harass junior employees and then use promotions and raises to punish or reward them.

George Stults tried to put the episode behind him. He went to the psychiatrist, who gave him a good report. "People who won't go are no longer with the company," he said. But even after he returned to work, he felt he was being watched. Conversations he had with his wife in bars were repeated to him Monday morning at work. While sitting in a cluster of P&G employees at a Bengals game, he cursed the team's performance. On Monday he was told he could no longer sit in those seats with other employees. "This town has a lot of P&G people in it," he said.

By late 1988 he'd been demoted by lab managers and was working for other technicians, packing products into boxes. In January 1989 he was fired. The reason was vague: Managers thought he harassed fellow employees. After the sexual harassment charge, says Stults, he worked for nearly three years and got along with "90 percent of my coworkers."

Outsiders confirm that Stults has been blacklisted. Shortly after he was fired, a manager at Sun Chemical, another Cincinnati firm, offered him a job in the lab. "I'd worked with George in the early seventies and knew he could do the job," said Larry

Lough, then technical director at one of Sun's plants. George and Judy went out for Chinese food to celebrate.

Two days later, Lough showed up at his front door. "Who did you piss off?" he asked. Lough had been ready to send Stults for the required physical, when Sun's personnel director told him he couldn't hire him. "I was bombarded with questions about George," Lough said. "He was literally blackballed in Cincinnati, and I was up to my knees in hot water for trying to hire him." [36]

Stults believes P&G managers at Sharon Woods resented his whistle-blowing. It's not the P&G way to rock the boat. He sent out more than 200 resumes, often leading to job interviews. Sometimes he was invited back for a second visit, but then the offer would suddenly vanish. The family was living off his savings. While continuing to look for other jobs, Stults sold all of his P&G stock and invested in a toy-store franchise, Hobbytown U.S.A.

The Stultses cut corners by dropping their health insurance. That was a mistake. Judy had a heart attack and required surgery. The medical bills for the thirty-eight-year-old woman came to $75,000. Meanwhile, the store never took off. After less than two years in business, George closed it in July 1991 and declared bankruptcy. Lionel trains, baseball cards, and other toys sit stacked in the living room, waiting for an agent of the bankruptcy court to collect them.

Both Judy and George have found a variety of part-time jobs, such as working at the zoo and the post office. They earn minimum wage and collect food stamps. "At first I didn't file for them," he said. "I didn't want to admit that I was a failure." Edna Mae, the elderly neighbor the Stultses had looked after, fed them for about three months. It was her way of saying thanks for all the winter mornings that George shoveled her sidewalk. She even paid for braces for Andy. "If it weren't for the boys, I'd have given up," he said.

Stults has tried to forget about his former employer. He's thrown out all his P&G T-shirts and everything he ever received from the company. "I'm paranoid they'll barge in here and accuse me of stealing," he said.

Others inside P&G have had similar problems after they were labeled troublemakers at the company. Don Hagler, who worked at P&G's Dallas plant for more than forty years, was accused of being a thief when he tried to take home a $35 telephone from work. Hagler bought the phone to replace those destroyed at his office during a flood. He lost the receipt, so he didn't seek reimbursement from P&G. Instead, he just took home the phone.

Security guards seized the phone, and he was fired in March 1991. Bulletin boards and electronic mail messages told all his coworkers about the episode and labeled him a thief. His former colleagues took copies of the notice and gave it to Hagler, who applied for more than 100 jobs at other companies. But potential employers found out about the incident, and he couldn't get a new job. He filed a defamation suit against P&G. A Dallas jury awarded him about $15 million in April 1993.[37] A P&G spokesman said the company was disappointed by the verdict. No decision has been made on whether P&G will appeal the case, he said.

Throughout Cincinnati, some small businesses fear they will suffer if they do anything to offend P&G. Many won't even discuss their contracts with P&G because they're worried that they'll lose their best customer. One agreed to talk to a reporter only after writing to P&G's CEO for his approval. Then he recorded the conversation.[38] That clout obviously extends to New York. Charlotte Beers, former head of Tatham-Laird & Kudner, a Chicago ad agency that handles P&G accounts, shows remarkable loyalty to her erstwhile client even though she now works as president of Ogilvy & Mather, the agency that handles advertising for archenemy Kimberly-Clark, among others. Beers agreed to an interview for this book but asked that her statements remain off the record because they might offend P&G. What she didn't mention was that she secretly tape recorded the interview and sent a transcript to P&G Chairman Ed Artzt. The chairman confirmed that Beers sent the transcript but insisted she'd done so voluntarily.[39] Beers said she routinely tapes interviews to prevent misquotes and sent Artzt a partial transcript as "a courtesy to a former client."

For Cincinnati advertising agencies and art studios, a piece of P&G business means prestige. Most of the work goes to New York firms, so "they just want the crumbs that fall off the table," said Jerry Galvin, the ad man who doesn't do P&G work. "It allows you to go to smaller firms and say, 'We do P&G work.'"[40]

Don Baker, former head of P&G's art department, estimates that 80 percent of the art studio work in Cincinnati is for P&G. "The company must be one of the biggest art buyers in the world," he said.[41] Indeed, representatives from the studios will sit for hours in the reception area of the eighth floor at P&G's headquarters, waiting for the smallest assignment. John Nixon, vice president of Cincinnati ad agency Galvin Siegel Kemper, and a graphic artist, used to take the morning shift waiting for a P&G art director to call him. "It was truly a zoo," he said. The work was plentiful. P&G would sometimes take a month to design a sunburst for a label that would announce a 10-cents discount or a new fragrance. They were very demanding. "I learned how to get yelled at," Nixon said.[42]

Furthermore, P&G sets tough rules. Vendors are told not to work for competing firms, such as Kao's Jergens unit in Cincinnati. And any P&G assignment is supposed to be completed before devoting time to any other work. "It really makes you mad," said one Cincinnati businesswoman. "They [vendors] drop everything for Procter."[43]

Even market research firms must get P&G's approval before assigning interviewers on a project. They have to be from the "approved list." That means P&G managers will test the interviewer, watch her conduct a session, and grade her performance. "You have to be as close to perfect as possible," said one market researcher. [44]

One of the more egregious examples of P&G flaunting its power was the way it ended its thirty-year relationship with the Cincinnati branch of the American Automobile Association in December 1989. The travel agency, as part of its agreement, had maintained an in-house travel department at P&G's headquarters, along with its other Cincinnati office. [45]

AAA shared commissions with P&G, sometimes giving the company 91 percent of the money. The most AAA received was 50 percent of a commission if a service required extra work beyond normal booking of flights or hotels. In March 1989 P&G asked a number of travel agencies to compete for its business. AAA, in danger of losing the account, submitted two bids in April and August. In November P&G rejected those bids in favor of Lifeco, a competing firm. The original contract had expired in July, but AAA continued to make its revenue-sharing payments to P&G for the next three months. Officials at the agency figured they would "just leave the big giant alone" and continue making the payments, said James Ryan, an AAA executive, in his deposition for the case. [46] But it withheld payments in November and December after learning it had lost the account.

P&G sued in May 1990 for its share of the commissions for those two months, about $385,000 plus interest. "We had already lost a great deal of money handling the P&G account," said one senior AAA official. "I couldn't see sending good money after bad." [47]

AAA's counterclaims sought the money it had given to P&G during the months it continued its revenue sharing despite an expired contract. There were other problems for AAA. As part of its 1987 agreement the agency had agreed to upgrade its computer equipment. The American Airlines SABRE computer system was installed at the P&G branch office and the contract required that AAA maintain a compatible reservation and ticketing system.

The travel agency was wooed by Delta Airlines to change to its computer system. The carrier would have awarded AAA more "override commissions," which are incentives given to get an agency to book on certain airlines. P&G refused to allow AAA to change computer systems until 1993, saying the SABRE system was superior. But P&G never gave the agency any warning that it was planning to look for a new travel agency. AAA figures it lost $1.3 million through 1990 by not switching to the Delta system. [48]

Furthermore, court documents reveal that AAA had to give P&G $1.5 million in "rebates" on international flights, even though AAA contended that practice was illegal. The rebate was money refunded to P&G each time it booked a flight through AAA. Terry Johnson, director of World Wide Travel at AAA from 1982 to 1987, said P&G insisted on the rebates as part of its 1987 contract. "I specifically told the Procter & Gamble people that rebates of commissions for tickets on international flights were illegal under federal law," Johnson said. [49]

The P&G people knew all about the law. Nevertheless they informed him that rebates "would still be a major consideration in any future agreement with worldwide travel," Johnson said. "I felt that worldwide travel would have been in grave danger of losing all Procter & Gamble travel business if we didn't accede to their terms concerning payments of rebates." Reluctantly, AAA agreed to rebate 85 percent to 91 percent of its International Airlines Travel Agent Network commissions to P&G. Lawyers familiar with the case said the law on such rebates isn't strictly enforced, so P&G defended its practice as legitimate. The deposition of Robert J. Reinersman, AAA's vice president and general manager, shows just how far companies will sometimes go when doing business for P&G:

Q: . . . Were you aware that commissions were being shared in connection with Procter & Gamble? . . .

A: Oh, surely. Yeah.

Q: . . . Well, if it is illegal, why did you do it?

A: The best answer I can give you on that is that if Procter & Gamble said, "We want you to do this," we would do it. Short of a punishable-by-jail kind of penalty, we would go ahead and do it. [50]

The two sides reached an out-of-court settlement, and the case was dismissed with prejudice in July 1991.

Often, P&G's clout and demands extend far beyond the banks of the Ohio River. Goldman Sachs, P&G's New York-based investment banking firm, was told to drop Revlon's planned initial public offering in the spring of 1992. P&G objected because the companies compete in the cosmetics business. Such underwriting could bring in about $20 million in fees. Part of the reason for the dispute stemmed from bad feelings over the purchase price P&G paid for Revlon's Max Factor business the previous year. [51]

P&G's influence was strengthened in Washington over the years by former company officials who take government posts. Ex-chairman Richard Deupree was named as head of the army-navy munitions board by President Harry Truman. Neil McElroy, another former CEO, became secretary of defense under President Dwight Eisenhower in 1957. James Reston of *The New York Times* called McElroy "the most attractive new personality to hit Washington in a long time." Just six weeks after he took the job, he was mentioned as a possible presidential candidate for 1960. During his stay at the defense department, NASA was formed, among other highlights. McElroy's political career was brief, however. He returned to Cincinnati to become chairman of the P&G board in 1959. [52]

The company has hired ex-presidential aides to head up its lobbying efforts. Bryce Harlow, for instance, worked for eight years with Eisenhower. He then served as an aide to Richard M. Nixon for two years. He was also director of P&G's government relations department. Between 1956 and 1972 he helped draft nearly every Republican party platform. Many wanted him to take the job as Republican National Chairman, but he turned down the offer. On the infamous Watergate tapes, Nixon can be heard asking asked H. R. Haldeman, his chief of staff, if Harlow could "put a little heat" on then House Speaker Carl Albert to stop a General Accounting Office probe of the White House. Haldeman told the president that Harlow wouldn't do that. "P&G got more than its share of help from Washington because of Harlow," said one former company officer. "He was an extremely influential guy."[53]

Most recently P&G convinced two local congressmen to sponsor a bill to extend its patents on the fat substitute olestra. The company has felt a lot of pressure as competitors have beaten it to market with fake fats while its product languishes in the Food and Drug Administration review. The bill has met considerable opposition by consumer groups and competitors such as Unilever, which has its own fat substitutes and wants to block any special treatment for its archrival.

Michael Jacobson, director of the Center for Science in the Public Interest, has opposed approval of olestra ever since the company first took it to the FDA in 1987. His speaking out prompted an immediate visit from P&G public relations staff and scientists, who tried to convince Jacobson of its safety. P&G maintained the product is safe. But he wasn't swayed.[54]

P&G needs help with the FDA, considering the agency's previous stands on Rely tampons and labels for the company's Citrus Hill orange juice. In the early 1990s, P&G hired former general counsel of the FDA Peter Barton Hutt, along with Stuart Eizenstat, formerly an adviser to the Carter administration, to lobby Congress to vote for the patents-extension bill. "It's worth it to P&G to spend tens of thousands of dollars on lobbying," Jacobsen said. "This product could bring it millions."

To curry favor in the House and Senate, P&G's political action committee forked over contributions to key members, including House Speaker Thomas S. Foley and other key backers of the bill. The House bill extending olestra's patents also included measures that granted Upjohn, Inc. and American Home Products extensions on antiarthritic drugs. The three companies contributed a total of $115,000 to several representatives between 1991 and August 1992, when the bill passed the House with a 278–131 vote. In addition, P&G chairman Ed Artzt had previously given money to Foley, according to campaign records. But the bill died as Congress adjourned in 1992. P&G vowed to push for it again in 1993.

P&G's lobbying certainly helped its cause. The bill was opposed by the Bush White House, yet it gained strong support among Republicans in Congress. The bill also received an assist from ally Foley. The Washington Democrat placed it on a "suspension calendar," which is typically used for noncontroversial legislation. It was debated on a Monday, when many members were still gone for the weekend. [55]

Elsewhere in Washington, P&G wields a great deal of influence in industry trade associations, including the Paper Institute and the Soap and Detergent Association, among others, giving it lobbying power in Congress and at the White House.

Likewise, P&G has used its economic clout to splinter employees' efforts to seek representation from international labor unions. For years it has effectively shut out unions such as the United Steelworkers. One wonders what William Cooper Procter would think of its current practices. Under his leadership in the late 1800s and early 1900s the company strove to strengthen labor-management relations. In 1885 P&G began giving workers Saturday afternoons off. At the time, the Knights of Labor were demonstrating in Cincinnati and demanding better wages and benefits.[56] Procter pushed P&G to start profit-sharing plans and other new benefits that were the models for other U.S. companies. By doing so, P&G avoided union organizers for about a hundred years.

Of its fifty-nine U.S. plants in the mid-1980s, only ten were affiliated with international unions.[57] Some of those came with acquisitions of smaller companies. In some cases P&G simply closed a unionized plant to get rid of the Teamsters and other unions. For example, bleach production was moved to P&G's soap plant from the Kansas City Clorox plant to destroy the union there, according to a former officer. (P&G later had to sell Clorox because of antitrust laws.)

And P&G kept strong international unions out of its other plants by staggering contracts, making them longer than traditional labor pacts and not allowing the plants to affiliate with one another. The company also used one contract, which was negotiated by management in Cincinnati, as the pattern for all of its plants, so there was little real negotiation, union officials said. International labor leaders also note that P&G contracts don't allow for discussions on wages. Instead, P&G undertakes a wage survey of plants and sets the wages. Language in P&G contracts also gives the company the upper hand. Buddy Davis, director of District 34 of the United Steelworkers Union, said the P&G pacts contain clauses that allow the company to change or drop its insurance and pension provisions anytime during the contract.

P&G plant workers did form an amalgamation, a group of unions from different plants. At its peak, it boasted about 3,000 members but now has about half that number, as older soap plants have closed and production at other plants has been curtailed. P&G has also tried to bully union leaders. Walter Donnellon, a veteran P&G worker in Baltimore and leader of the independent union, was continually harassed for his union activities. When he decided to push shareholder resolutions for more workers' rights, P&G management tried to intimidate him. He was told to stay away from the shareholders' meeting, even though he's a shareholder as well as an employee. "I knew my rights," he said. "But they labeled me a troublemaker."

P&G banned union delegates from taking vacation days whenever any plant was negotiating a contract. That way, delegates couldn't assist other plants in their contract talks. When union leaders defied management's orders, they were suspended from work and told they would lose their jobs. The problem was taken to the National Labor Relations Board in 1976, and P&G was found guilty of numerous violations.

Others were encouraged to disband the amalgamation. Gordon Canney, who worked more than three decades at the Port Ivory plant on Staten Island, recalled how P&G management told him they would "make it worth your while" if he dropped out of the group. The union filed charges with the NLRB. P&G hired labor lawyers from around the country to handle the case. "They'd take over entire floors of hotels and spend months on the case," Canney said. "We had one young lawyer taking on this battery of P&G lawyers. He was a Columbo type—his tie was always off to the side. He couldn't find his papers. But he won." P&G had to pay back wages, among other conditions. The case went all the way to the Supreme Court, which refused to hear it.[58]

The independent unions tried to build their clout at smaller P&G plants, not just the big metropolitan soap factories. But that was difficult, especially in areas where a job at P&G was one of the few in town. "You do what they tell you or you don't work there," Canney said. The day before the union vote, P&G managers would distribute newsletters that outlined how a vote for the union could close the plant. "They would really put the fear of God into these people," Canney said.

International unions, such as United Steelworkers, were determined to crack P&G. In 1979 the union began a petition drive to represent Kansas City's soap workers. Officers at the Independent Oil and Chemical Workers, which represented the employees, supported the steelworkers. In less than a year, the union had won with a 308–111 vote.[59]

The union began negotiations with P&G, seeking contracts equivalent to those at other P&G soap plants. The union even said it would accept a contract similar to the one offered to the independent union a year earlier. But P&G resisted. The union accused P&G of punishing workers by withholding wage increases that were given to other P&G workers. In addition, the Kansas City employees had to pay medical insurance premiums that others did not. P&G also shut down entire departments to lay off workers.[60] Employees who attended union meetings say managers discriminated against them for supporting the steelworkers. Wages and benefits were about $400 a month below those at other P&G plants.[61]

During the negotiations, the issue of unsafe working conditions emerged. The union blamed P&G for the January 1981 death of a worker who was ordered to do hazardous work.[62] James Franklin Wilson and another maintenance worker were told to fix a problem with the centralized fire system in a soap storage warehouse. The two men needed to reach an electrical box located about fourteen feet above the floor. They spotted a ladder that would reach the box, but it was chained and padlocked to a support column. No one knew who had the keys. So the men climbed onto a makeshift platform attached to a forklift to reach the electrical box. Once they were elevated, one maintenance man climbed out onto a stack of soap boxes. When he stepped off the platform, Wilson and the platform tumbled off the forklift to the concrete floor. A report by the Occupational Safety and Health Administration (OSHA) said the family didn't want an autopsy performed, but listed the probable cause of death as internal injuries caused when Wilson's head hit the floor.

The OSHA report said that P&G frequently used such makeshift platforms, despite clear regulations against such unstable devices. And there was insufficient instruction on how to safely operate forklifts. Getting P&G to correct these problems wasn't easy, however, because OSHA inspections weren't frequent or thorough, union officials said. "P&G gave OSHA a tough time each time the inspectors tried to get inside the plant," Buddy Davis recalled. Even after a fatality, the punishment wasn't steep. P&G paid a $360 fine following OSHA's investigation of Wilson's death.

P&G fought the steelworkers in contract talks. The negotiating team met fifty-seven times with P&G but couldn't get a new contract. In late 1981 the steelworkers launched a nationwide boycott of P&G products. Bright red "Boycott P&G" stickers and 10 million leaflets were mailed across the country. Union officials asked consumers to sign petitions pledging that they wouldn't use P&G's products. Each list of fifty names was mailed to P&G's headquarters.

The dispute came as P&G was trying to implement a new technician system in the plants. Workers would have to learn how to handle numerous jobs, not just one task. The management made it clear that those plants that resisted were considered obsolete and would be shuttered. [63]

The steelworkers tried other tactics, including a campaign to discredit P&G's environmental practices. At the time, P&G was using NTA, or sodium nitrilotriacetate, in Tide detergent. It replaced phosphates, which had been banned in many states because of their impact on lakes. NTA softens water and helps the detergents clean more effectively. But it had been linked to cancer in laboratory tests and was banned in Germany. In 1970 the U.S. Surgeon General asked manufacturers to remove NTA, and P&G complied. But the Environmental Protection Agency cleared it as "low risk" in 1980.

Steelworkers and others questioned the validity of the EPA clearance because the exposure data used in the agency's report came from P&G. The company asked for numerous changes and managed to get them in the final report. The EPA conceded that collecting independent data was too expensive. Another problem, the union said, was the occupational risks of workers making detergents. The EPA said NTA was a high risk with an estimated cancer risk of one per thousand workers.[64]

The union took its campaign to P&G's headquarters during one of the company's rare meetings with Wall Street analysts. About sixty steelworkers handed out leaflets as the analysts and reporters gathered at the Queen City Club for the meeting.[65]

But the union began to lose ground in 1982. Decertification votes were getting closer, and workers were feeling the pinch of lost wages and benefits. In March 1984 the Kansas City employees voted to return to an independent union. Workers figured they had more security that way. But their colleagues at the Dallas plant found that wasn't the case. They were laid off that same year after having rejected the steelworkers' union in 1980.[66] Other plants on Staten Island and in Chicago have closed. P&G's labor stance earned it a place on the AFL-CIO's dishonor roll.

"It was one of the most frustrating experiences I've ever had," said Buddy Davis, the steelworkers' director who handled the Kansas City campaign. "P&G is a throwback. It's hard to believe that a huge corporation can operate in the 1990s like it did in the 1930s and 1940s."[67]

P&G has shown similar disdain for anyone who criticizes its actions. Even members of the founding Gamble family have turned against the company because of its policies.

Jamie Gamble grew up in Massachusetts, never knowing he was the great-great grandson of the company founder. His parents told him that they were distant relatives. He said P&G brands were not bought for the home, largely because of the premium prices. "My father is a cheapskate," he said. "We didn't grow up with any allegiance to the company."[68]

When he turned eighteen, he learned about a trust fund of $1.5 million, largely from P&G stock. But he soon discovered that his benefactor was a "source of embarrassment" rather than pride. His brother Robbie told him about the human rights abuses in El Salvador after living there for two years and about the influence of big U.S. companies, like P&G, over the country's problems.

P&G buys coffee beans from El Salvador, which was torn apart by civil war for years. Activists believe the death squads that have murdered priests and other civilians are funded by the large coffee growers.

The elder Gamble brother gave away his inheritance. Jamie decided he also wanted to take a stand. He contacted P&G and asked the company to stop buying coffee from the war-torn country. P&G refused. He decided to link up with Neighbor to Neighbor, a San Francisco–based activist group that launched a boycott of coffee from that country after the death squads murdered several Jesuit priests in 1989. Fred Ross, the group's executive director, asked P&G to stop importing Salvadoran beans. The company had been influenced by religious shareholders in the past and had agreed to stop buying coffee from Uganda. P&G met with Ross in late 1989 and showed signs of supporting the boycott. [69]

Things changed in January 1990, however, when the new CEO, Ed Artzt, took over. Some people inside P&G wanted to support the boycott and avoid the controversy. But Artzt consulted State Department and White House advisers to see what the Bush administration wanted P&G to do. Bush wanted U.S. companies to continue doing business with El Salvador. A second meeting with Neighbor to Neighbor was quickly canceled.

The group then targeted Folgers for a consumer boycott. Ross offered to meet with P&G again, but the company refused. The group offered to show the company its plans for a TV commercial promoting the boycott: It showed a bloody cup of Folgers and urged consumers not to buy the coffee that is "brewing misery and death" in El Salvador. The company rebuffed the group's requests for a meeting. So Ross held a press conference in Cincinnati to unveil the ad.

A Boston television station, WHDH, sold the group airtime and aired the commercial six times. P&G reacted strongly, pulling its $1 million worth of advertising for all its brands from the station. [70] "We don't feel we should do business with any television station that is trying to destroy our business," Artzt told reporters. [71]

Jamie Gamble was outraged by the action. "They're trying to be an editorial influence, and that's not their right," he said. He had submitted a shareholder resolution asking P&G to get out of El Salvador. "I asked the company to take a moral stand, not a political one, to say we really support human rights," Gamble said. Only then did P&G want to meet with him. Gerald Gendell, head of public affairs, met with Gamble and his wife. "He really sneered at us," Gamble said. Shaking his finger in Gamble's face, Gendell deemed him a "family embarrassment. He said my grandfather would be turning in his grave."

A Kansas City station had agreed to air the commercial but reversed its decision after seeing what P&G did to the Boston station. Others also refused the ad. "We were angry," Ross said. But the controversy also gained the boycott plenty of publicity. *Business Week, The New York Times,* and other publications wrote about the strong-arm tactics of P&G.

Sen. Edward Kennedy of Massachusetts and other senators and congressmen wrote to CEO Artzt about the company's decision to penalize his constituents at the TV station. "Such economic intimidation comes very close to an effective corporate censorship over advertising content," Kennedy wrote. His letter elicited a terse reply: The ad is a "vicious and misleading attempt to destroy our business." Artzt complained that "Boycott Folgers" stickers were ruining coffee cans in stores around the country. Retailers returned them because they couldn't sell them. [72]

The boycott got some support among retailers. In June Red Apple, a New York supermarket chain, stopped ordering Folgers for sixty days. [73] By October Gamble's shareholder resolution had won attention from other religious stockholders. But it was defeated by a wide margin. Neighbor to Neighbor continued its campaign, producing a video on the problems in El Salvador and distributing it to P&G workers at plants across the country.

Shortly before the 1991 shareholders meeting, at which another resolution was offered, Ross got to meet Artzt for the first time. Rep. Nancy Pelosi of California took Ross to a P&G dinner in Washington. They weaved their way past the tables of Charmin, Tide, and Folgers to find the CEO. He was happy to see Pelosi until she introduced Ross. "I find your tactics reprehensible," Artzt told Ross. He walked away as Ross asked for a meeting to discuss the issues.

The shareholders'·resolution was defeated again, but the boycott received another boost when Pizzeria Uno agreed to drop Folgers from its menu. And Pepsico's Pizza Hut, Kentucky Fried Chicken, and Taco Bell restaurants began demanding a non-Salvadoran blend of Folgers. The restaurants got a letter from P&G, pledging a new brew. [74]

When newspapers publicized P&G's apparent policy change, Artzt got angry, and the company tried to backpedal. The letter, written by food service and lodging manager Richard L. Francis, was deemed unauthorized and inappropriate. Then it was called imprecise and incomplete. Charlotte Otto, head of public relations at the company, called *The Wall Street Journal* seven times in one weekend to try to finesse the company's response to the flap. [75]

A cease fire and peace talks in early 1992 prompted Neighbor to Neighbor to lift the Folgers boycott in March. But it continued to write to P&G to see how the company could work on rebuilding the country. The company had previously said it supported the farmers, so the group figured P&G would want to help. "But they said they didn't want to talk to us," Ross said. "The expressions of sympathy for the poor in El Salvador were strictly a PR defense." As for Boston station WHDH, it later apologized for airing the bloody Folgers cup ad, saying it had improperly singled out that brand.[76]

Others who challenge P&G have seen how difficult it is to get their voices heard. Michael Budkie, national program director of In Defense of Animals, an animals rights group based in San Rafael, California, was arrested when he and others tried attending P&G's shareholders' meeting in 1990. The group's members held proxies, so they had a legal right to attend. But P&G security guards, aided by Cincinnati police, wouldn't allow them to enter the building. When they sat down in the entranceway, the police arrested them. Budkie was charged with attempted trespassing and paid a $33 fine. Another one of the animal rights activists was arrested when she walked on stage during CEO Artzt's presentation. She tried to present the executive with the First Annual Corporate Hypocrisy Award for the company's record of testing products on animals.

When Budkie returned home that evening, a bar of Ivory soap was hanging on his front doorknob. "I took it to say 'we know where you live,'" he said. He figures he's under constant surveillance by the company. One disturbing episode occurred in December 1992. An anonymous caller left lengthy messages at one of the animal rights organization's offices, explaining how far P&G goes to keep tabs on the groups. The caller identified himself as a former P&G security guard. A transcript of the tape-recorded call reveals that the caller knew quite a bit about P&G's security practices, including surveillance of anyone suspected of being sympathetic to animal rights groups. He named several obscure people in P&G's security department, which would otherwise be unknown to outsiders, and he warned the activists to be careful. "The power they have is absolutely incredible," the caller said. "I've seen people followed, harassed. I've seen their personal lives interfered with. You just have no idea." He compared it to the KGB.[77]

Budkie and others are undaunted. Various animal rights

groups continue to push shareholder resolutions to get P&G to stop animal testing. But the fight is difficult, especially for those inside the company. Tina Geronimi, a lift driver at P&G's paper plant in Green Bay, Wisconsin, said she was fired in 1992 after she cosponsored a resolution. "Becoming a cosponsor cost me my job," she said. "But it will not silence me."[78] Budkie's group also has trouble finding newspapers or billboards that will accept his ads about P&G's animal testing.

All too often, P&G does get its way with the media, especially when its ad dollars pay the bills. Those who depend on its ads rarely challenge it. Many women's magazines have an "unwritten rule" to be kind to P&G, said one advertising manager who worked on P&G accounts.[79] Gloria Steinem said that P&G historically has made it clear that it would pull ads from any issue that contained material about "gun control, abortion, the occult, cults, or the disparagement of religion." P&G also withdraws ads from publications it deems antibusiness.[80]

Network officials concede that P&G is powerful. "The network is paying affiliates to carry network commercials, not programs. What we are is a distribution system for Procter & Gamble," said one ABC official.[81]

P&G has a long history of despising the news media. William Cooper Procter, in a letter to his niece Mary Johnston in the early 1900s, lamented that he had to deliver a speech to a press club. "I hate and dread it, no matter how unimportant it is," he wrote.[82]

The company has fought for years to limit the amount of information it discloses. In the 1923 annual report, shareholders who wanted more than the barest details in the four-page report were told to "apply in person" at the company's headquarters.[83] The New York Stock Exchange delisted P&G's stock in 1903 because the company wouldn't disclose enough financial information to the exchange. It was reinstated to the Big Board in 1929. [84]

Even today, Wall Street gets virtually no information on P&G. Many companies have quarterly meetings with stock analysts, but P&G has held such meetings only four times in the past two decades. When CEO John Smale announced he would meet with analysts in 1982, newspapers hailed it as big news. Stories on the event snared prime space in *The New York Times* and other papers, even though he said virtually nothing newsworthy. Indeed, the *Times* story was accompanied by a cartoon showing a man at a podium pointing to a blank brick wall. [85] "One analyst told me I gave new meaning to 'stonewall,' " said James Nethercott, the retired chief financial officer. "I was always very proud of that." [86]

There is one exception to P&G's silence: new product launches. When Liquid Tide was introduced, P&G held a press conference at a New York disco. A two-story inflatable bottle of Tide and a jazz band helped unveil the product. [87]

On real news, however, P&G's public relations department is trained to say nothing. One of the big problems, insiders note, is the number of former advertising managers who land in the PR department. They are known as "beached whales" among those managers who were trained in communications before joining P&G. "They've washed up on the shore and can't make their way back to the advertising waters," said Marjorie Bradford, a former company spokeswoman. Unfortunately, she says, the company promotes the former ad people to the senior posts, "which doesn't make the professional PR people feel too good." The latest vice president of public affairs, Bob Wehling, came up through the advertising ranks. [88]

The advertising mentality—buy the coverage you want—has shaped the company's policies on how to deal with the news media. For instance, Bradford recalled that she was told simply to hang up on reporters if she didn't like their questions. They'd explain it as phone trouble if the reporter ever succeeded in getting someone back on the phone. "Advertising people didn't understand because they couldn't control the news media," Bradford said.

News releases resemble Swiss cheese. The company-authorized biography, *Eyes on Tomorrow*, offers little of substance. The book ignores Rely, which had been on the market for several years. Nor does it mention the toxic shock crisis. Oscar Schisgall, a biographer, was hired to write the book, but it was drastically rewritten by the company's public relations department and senior management. P&G's idea of good journalism is the company magazine *Moonbeams*, an always cheerful look at new products, promotions, and other propaganda. One retired officer compares it to *Pravda* in the 1960s. "It's like something the Communist party would write," he said. "I didn't realize what I was a part of."[89]

The similarities to the KGB go further. Pat Hayes, another former PR man, remembers the company keeping files on reporters. Outside public-relations firms such as Hill & Knowlton were asked to investigate new reporters assigned to cover P&G. "We'd get copies of other stories they'd written and try to gauge whether they were antibusiness," Hayes said. They'd also gather as much information as possible on a reporter's personal history.

Helping a reporter on a story didn't score points with senior management, he said. PR is considered "a necessary evil." And PR managers are encouraged always to criticize reporters' coverage, even when they thought a story was fair and accurate. "The process wasn't healthy," Hayes said. "P&G considered itself the keeper to the vault of truths. They have the keys and you don't."[90]

But the P&G beat is important, especially in business publications and advertising trade magazines. "When P&G sneezes, everyone reaches for a Puffs," said one advertising reporter. "No matter what they do, it will have ramifications throughout the marketing and advertising worlds."[91]

Despite the strong interest, P&G fights reporters on nearly every story. One veteran P&G watcher offered her favorite joke about the company: "If you ask a P&G PR person, 'How's the weather in Cincinnati?' he'd say, 'I'll have to get back to you after I get a statement approved.'"

She dreaded every visit to P&G's PR department because "I'd get pulled aside for a talking-to on what I'd written." Gerald Gendell used to regularly remind reporters that he was actually allergic to their publications. He said he wore gloves to read *The Wall Street Journal.* When Bob Goldstein was vice president of advertising, he would spend part of each Monday ripping apart *Advertising Age.* He would circle the articles he deemed offensive, send them with a nasty note to P&G's agencies, and scold them for talking to the press.

Local reporters have an especially tough time covering P&G because of its clout in Cincinnati. "People think of P&G as the church," said one reporter who followed P&G for several years. "It is the source of all good things, so you don't question it much or challenge it." Some reporters grow weary of the special treatment P&G news receives. Even the smallest product news gets played on the business pages. And senior management of the newspapers are friends with P&G officials. Sometimes it was an unspoken agreement; sometimes it was overt. "I felt pressured to be good to P&G," said one former business editor. "There was no real commitment to business coverage." The editor resigned because "I couldn't stand the hypocrisy."

Others disagree and say some reporters have simply grown weary of trying to crack the Kremlin walls. Dick Rawe, a fifty-year veteran of the *Cincinnati Post,* watched P&G for much of his career. As a stringer for *Time* and *Fortune,* he would regularly submit questions to P&G for magazine stories. A week later the list would be returned with "N/A" written after most of his questions. It either meant no answer or nonapplicable, he said. John Smale, who ran P&G during the 1980s, was the first CEO Rawe ever interviewed. "And it wasn't because I didn't ask," he said. "I could get access to any other CEO in town, but not them."

Other reporters tell of submitting requests for interviews and getting a response eight months later. "That's how they wear people down," said one reporter. And they'll respond only if it's a topic deemed palatable, such as P&G's commitment to total quality. But they don't like to talk about satanism rumors, Salvadoran coffee, advertising, or departing executives. And P&G PR people can be surprisingly smooth when they lie. "I've never seen any major corporation that lies and obfuscates with such confidence and calm," said one former Cincinnati business writer. "It is very effective."

P&G doesn't even like to discuss sports. David Wecker, columnist for the *Cincinnati Post,* was asked by editors to do a feature on Bengals-mania when the football team was headed for the Super Bowl in 1988. Someone had heard that "even the starched and staid offices in certain corners of P&G were decorated in orange and black" in support of the team, he said.

So Wecker, unfamiliar with the usual bureaucratic channels of P&G's PR department, simply showed up at the company's offices and asked to see the Bengals regalia. The receptionist made a couple of calls, and Wecker was soon given an ID badge and shown to some cubicles where young brand assistants were wearing orange and black. He was almost finished with the interviews when three security guards, dressed in matching blazers, hurried down the hall toward him. "They explained that I was done and that I should accompany them to another part of the building," he said. They took him to a conference room and quizzed him about who he worked for. "I'd already identified myself, but they wanted proof," he said. He showed them a *Cincinnati Post* ID badge, which, he notes, "looks like it was manufactured in somebody's basement."

Then the guards demanded to read his notes. "I let them see them because it didn't seem like a big deal," Wecker said. "I was kind of amused. But they didn't seem happy with me." After further questioning, he was escorted out of the building. "I got the distinct impression that someone was going to suffer. It was all very Big Brotherish." He compares it to going through customs at an airport, only worse. "What a bunch of Nazis," he said. "I was just doing a fluff piece."

Often, P&G won't even confirm that a product is on the market. One reporter had spotted a new spray cleaner, Cinch, in a Kansas City test market. She called to ask about it, and the PR department denied that it existed. "Are you sure you're not seeing things?" he asked the reporter. After several calls, P&G changed its answer and confirmed that the product was for sale.

It doesn't like to discuss history, either. The Smithsonian Institution, as part of its advertising history collection, had collected interviews with the founders of Noxell Corp., makers of Cover Girl makeup. P&G had acquired the company in 1989 and tried to stop the project, which was near completion by the Smithsonian's staff. "They said it would give proprietary information to competitors," recalled one staff member. "That's ridiculous. It's history." The project was completed, despite P&G's objections. [92]

Likewise, it will go to great lengths to kill a story that isn't favorable to its brands. Two company officials, along with a Chicago attorney, visited a television reporter who inquired about short-sheeted rolls of Charmin. "Three of us sat there and counted sheets of toilet paper," Pat Hayes said. "It was ridiculous, but we could have lost considerable share of the market" if that story had been aired. It became known as the Great Toilet Paper Caper. The count showed those rolls of Charmin weren't missing any sheets after all.

In other cases, P&G simply wants to discourage any discussion of the downside of some products. Bounce dryer sheets had a problem because they caught fire in some dryers. P&G sent a team of women to convince news editors that the product was safe. The team visited towns in advance of the product's introduction to that market. When asked about those visits, P&G's

PR department denies they happened, even though they were widely reported at the time of the product's introduction. And insiders at the department remember going to see editors. [93]

P&G's battles with *The Wall Street Journal* are constant, even though CEO Artzt tried to loosen up the company after he was named to the post. He shocked the media by holding a press conference the day after his appointment was announced. He spoke to a public affairs department dinner to remind the group that they served "one of the most important functions in this company." He challenged them to be "the best in the business." [94]

But he doesn't seem to trust his PR advisers. Artzt rewrites even basic news releases and must approve everything before it goes out. He did make changes in senior management of the public affairs group, placing different advertising managers in the top jobs to replace Gerald Gendell, who clashed with the new CEO on how to handle the media. Gendell encouraged Artzt to cut off any contact with the *Journal* after it published a story about bypassed heirs apparent and how they reacted to losing the CEO post to a rival. The story featured P&G president John Pepper, who was expected to succeed John Smale as CEO but lost the post to Artzt. It also noted that Pepper had been approached about other jobs, including the top spot at Campbell Soup. [95]

Pepper refused to be interviewed for the story, but Gendell sent threatening letters to the *Journal* prior to publication, trying to quash the piece. [96] When the story was published, Gendell urged Artzt to sever ties with the *Journal*. "We cannot let these instances of irresponsibility go by with impunity," he wrote in a memo to the CEO. Artzt told him to move forward with a "proactive PR policy" with the *Journal*. Still, Gendell told his subordinates to disregard the boss's orders. We shouldn't "go out of our way to help" the *Journal*, he said. [97]

P&G's definition of a proactive PR policy provides insight on how it believes it can manage the news. At one point, P&G

paid $15,000 to have Hill & Knowlton consultants review a stack of *Journal* stories. P&G's PR department was cetain the coverage was too negative. The Hill & Knowlton advisers concluded that P&G had been treated fairly. Still, a February 1991 memo—the WSJ Media Relations Development Plan—outlines how the company would try to place "good" stories with the paper. It tells how PR people would "selectively place" marketing stories and get desired stories on happy subjects—composting and quality, for example.

The memo lists P&G's objectives as favorable coverage with "strong influence on the stock price," and news and features that reinforce P&G as a "top marketing company and an excellent place to work." [98] Because P&G has been so successful in hiding behind its "99 44/100% pure" facade, too often people believe that.

7
Fear on the Fenholloway

Joy Towles Cummings comes from a long line of hell-raisers and outlaws. Her uncle Bill, once sheriff of Taylor County, Florida, was charged with murder. Her grandfather Martin Towles, who helped get his son elected sheriff, later asked the governor to impeach him. Grandpa was hardly the model citizen either: He sold bootleg booze to Al Capone and his Chicago mob during Prohibition.

Even as a child, Joy learned the way to survive in Florida's rough cracker country, where her family has tended cattle for six generations on an 8,000-acre ranch. By age five she was practicing her gunslinging by shooting blackbirds with a .22 rifle. Grandpa paid her a nickel per crow. [1]

The forty-five-year-old rancher still carries a gun in her purse, but for different reasons these days. She's leading a fight against Procter & Gamble and its Buckeye pulp mill, Taylor County's biggest employer for more than forty years. The mill, located near the Fenholloway River and the town of Perry, in the northwestern part of the state, is the source of one of Florida's worst environmental disasters. [2] And women who have fought to clean up the Fenholloway have been terrorized simply because they oppose P&G. [3]

Perry is a company town seemingly out of the 1800s, not the 1990s. Here P&G shapes the local landscape and influences all aspects of life. Paternalism has gone so far that some refer to P&G's Buckeye mill as "Uncle Buck." The story of the mill sounds "like a bad movie," says one local woman. "But it's not."[4]

The Fenholloway used to be a fishing paradise. Mullet and redfish were plentiful. Oysters and crabs, gathered where the river empties into the Gulf, graced dinner tables throughout the United States. Natural mineral springs that feed the Fenholloway were thought to be therapeutic treatments for the weary and were bottled under the Fenholloway Sulphur Water label. James Jackson, a longtime Taylor County resident, remembers how his family sold the water throughout the South as a cure for arthritis and kidney problems.[5] Nearby Hampton Springs and its sumptuous hotel attracted Hollywood stars for holidays under the palms.

The river inspired a song by Norman Hendry, who with his wife, Janette, would cut swamp cabbage and catch fish from the river for Fourth of July picnics. His "The Old Fenholloway" tells of the river's happier days:

> *I know you've heard of*
> *the Shannon*
> *And the sleepy Rio Grande*
> *But there's a better river*
> *Down in Dixie land*
>
> *A stream flows from*
> *San Pedro Bay*
> *And westward winds its way*
> *Now you should know about*
> *The Old Fenholloway*
>
> *Fed by the springs along*
> *the way*

God's gift to ailing man
And those who drink its waters
Praise our sunshine land

The nearest thing to the
Fountain of Youth
That God has given man
These springs that give men life
and hope
In Dixie land. [6]

But the Fenholloway's days were numbered in the late 1940s, when P&G began to scout around for a location for its Buckeye Cellulose division's pulp mill so it could expand beyond soap and detergents into paper goods. [7] Local residents and P&G leaders convinced the state legislature in 1947 that Taylor County would have better luck attracting P&G if the Fenholloway was classified as an "industrial river." Rivers are ranked in classes one to five, with the highest number belonging to industrial rivers. The state legislature bowed to P&G, giving it the class-five rating, which allowed the company to dump anything into the Fenholloway. No other plant in the southeastern United States is allowed to dump as much toxic waste into a river. The law says the plant can "deposit sewage, industrial and chemical wastes and effluents, or any of them, into the waters of the Fenholloway River and the Gulf of Mexico." [8]

P&G purchased the property and began producing pulp at the Buckeye Cellulose mill in 1954. The process converts pine logs into cellulose, which P&G uses in its disposable diapers, Pampers and Luvs. It also sells the cellulose for use in plastics, rayons, explosives, film; even sausage casings. [9]

One of the immediate environmental problems residents noticed was the clear-cutting of large tracts of trees. Hardwoods, such as oaks draped with Spanish moss, were replaced with pines, destroying the groves where animals and birds nested.

The bigger problem was the river. In order to plant more pines, P&G drained areas that fed water into the river's source. [10] That cut down on the amount of natural water in the river, which was replaced with 50 million gallons per day of the plant's discharge. [11]

Shortly after it opened, Buckeye had a major spill of untreated effluent. Thousands of gallons of black water filled the Fenholloway. Residents remember the hundreds of dead fish that washed ashore. [12] Since then, conditions have deteriorated even further. The river is as black as motor oil and is laced with dangerous chemicals from the pulp mill. Studies in 1990 by the Environmental Protection Agency showed that residents who regularly eat fish from the Fenholloway River increased their chances of developing cancer because of dioxin.

"As far as river quality, I can't think of anything worse in Florida," said Jim Harrison, a U.S. EPA scientist. [13] At the time of that study, the Fenholloway had dioxin levels 1,900 times higher than what the agency considers an acceptable risk. Some of the other chemicals found in the water are so complex that scientists haven't been able to identify them. While EPA scientists say the mill has reduced its dioxin discharge, it remains the worst river in the entire Southeast and one of the worst in the country. "It's an industrial sewer," said Marshall Hyatt, a toxics specialist at the EPA. [14] Similar environmental problems have been found at other P&G plants, such as another pulp mill in Grande Prairie, Alberta. P&G closed that mill for several days in early 1992 because of pollution problems in the Wapiti River. Alberta has banned residents from eating Rocky Mountain whitefish caught in the Wapiti and Smoky rivers because they contain too many dioxins and furans, two cancer-causing agents. When the plant was closed, P&G pledged to spend $10 million for pollution-control equipment, but a couple of months later, it sold that plant to Weyerhaeuser. [15]

In Taylor County, the Towles family had relied on clean spring and river water to nourish cattle and wild hogs, which roamed the open range between the Fenholloway and Stein-hatchee rivers. Martin and Julia Towles bought the farm in the 1920s and raised 20,000 head of cattle. The couple also raised their granddaughter, Joy, after her father, James X. Towles, was killed in a tractor accident and her mother, Ruby Beach Towles, died of a heart attack. After Joy graduated from Perry High School in 1965, she went to Florida State University but dropped out after marrying and having a son, Trey, two years later.

Later divorced, she worked days as a secretary and attended night classes in agricultural business. She took a job in Alabama selling chemicals to cotton farmers. There she learned more about the effect of chemicals, especially as birds dropped dead after eating pesticide granules. One day she found a farmer unconscious in his field. His hands were stained with chemicals, which had seeped into an open cut and rendered him unconscious. She picked him up and took him to the emergency room, where he was revived. "That really made me question all these chemicals," she said.

Grandmother Towles was getting old and asked Joy to return to the family farm in 1981. So Joy took over half of the farm, with the other half going to her brother James. She married Red Cummings, who helps her run the farm and a hunting camp on the property. Joy quickly noticed how bad the water had become. Trey challenged his mother to do something about the river, which he deemed "disgusting and black. I guess he was the original environmentalist," she said.

She began her research on the pulp mill when she first locked horns with P&G in 1989. The company held a timber lease with the family but disputed who should maintain the fences. Towles Cummings said the company was responsible, but P&G didn't do it. When P&G loggers showed up to cut timber, Towles Cummings chased them away. P&G told her she'd have to sue the company to solve it. So she did.

In the lawsuit, she also challenged the contamination at another property she owns about three miles from the Fenholloway. Towles Cummings suspected the mill was to blame. During the deposition on the fence, P&G lawyers were clearly interested in what she knew about the contamination. "We didn't have all our facts then, so we didn't pursue that," she said. She eventually filed for personal bankruptcy to force a judge to settle the lease issue. P&G later canceled the lease, and she sold the timber to another company.

With that issue resolved, Towles Cummings began devoting her time to investigating the polluted river. Inside her grandparents' 1916 farmhouse, she began to unravel the mystery of the polluted river. Her experience in chemical sales helped her deal with P&G. "I've seen this from a big company side," she said. "I know the lies they tell people."

She began talking to people who lived near the Buckeye mill and discovered that P&G had been scurrying to keep the water problems quiet. Many landowners who complained about contaminated wells were given offers to swap land with P&G. Others had new wells drilled, courtesy of P&G. When employees complained about the bad taste of the tap water inside the plant, P&G managers told some to add powdered drink mixes to the water to make it more palatable. [16]

Towles Cummings visited area springs, where she used to swim as a teenager, which bubbled up some fresh water, but much of the water had turned the color of the dirty river that the springs fed. A putrid stench far worse than rotting trash makes visitors to the Fenholloway gag. "Have you ever seen anything that black?" asked Towles Cummings as she stood on the bank. "I can't tolerate much of this." Little fish swim from the spring water and dart back when they reach the murky black Fenholloway. Despite the smell, some kids still wade in the spring or dangle from the rope swing suspended from a tall oak. "I wouldn't want mine in there," she said.

The long-term impact of the mill's pollution on children is scary, when you consider what it does to fish. Female fish have developed male characteristics because pollution causes hormonal changes in fish. Will Davis, an EPA scientist, calls them "bearded ladies." Scientists believe the hormonal change is linked to the breakdown of pine oils from processed trees at the mill. [17] It has been difficult to get accurate cancer statistics on the area because most of the terminally ill patients from Taylor County go to Tallahassee for treatment and are recorded in another county's statistics.

A network of insiders began to feed Towles Cummings information about the plant. She learned that sinkholes beneath P&G's wastewater ponds allowed untreated discharge to flow freely into the river. P&G's own documents reveal a sinkhole problem at the plant. [18] An unlined dump, used to ditch tons of garbage and untreated pulp waste, leaches into the water table. "Every department's waste goes out there," said former bulldozer operator Maria Kyler, who pushed the waste into the pit at the mill. She also dumped ashes from the powerhouse. "The most toxic substances are out there." [19]

Large containers of hydraulic oil were discarded in the river. There's even a pipe that workers say bypasses the treatment ponds so it can run directly into the river when the mill has a big spill.

By the spring of 1991, Towles Cummings had amassed reams of information. She placed an ad in the Perry newspaper asking those with water problems to call her with their stories. About the same time, Julie Hauserman, an award-winning environmental writer at the Tallahassee *Democrat*, began investigating the Fenholloway's problems. She wrote a powerful series exposing the situation. The paper called it Florida's Forgotten River. [20] Towles Cummings never talked to the reporter until after the series appeared, but residents who saw the story began responding to her ad. "My phone rang off the hook for days," said the activist, estimating she fielded 400 calls in two weeks. Other residents, including Janice Blair-Jackson, Linda Rowland, Stephanie McGuire, and Maria Kyler, joined the cause. Many were former P&G millworkers who could provide firsthand accounts of what goes on inside the plant.

She and other women began to get threats from neighbors who accused them of stirring up trouble. They were followed, harassed, and threatened on a daily basis. One anonymous caller told several women he would cut out their tongues if they didn't hush. That's when Towles Cummings began carrying her .38 pistol in its rattlesnake holster. She prefers Red's .44 pistol but laments that it's too big for her purse.

P&G supporters launched a smear campaign against Towles Cummings. The Defenders of Taylor County, a group of local business leaders who support P&G, sent state environmental regulators a letter questioning her group as a "pseudo-environmental cult." They also distributed a copy of court documents related to the settlement of her grandmother's estate, a family spat that is completely unrelated to the river. "They will go to great lengths to discredit people and hurt you," she said.[21] When she had her well water tested, she read the results in the local paper under a page-one headline: TOWLES' WELL COMES CLEAN.[22] The water has not passed inspection for all chemicals, and she suspects the results were leaked to the paper by the testing agency or by P&G, which has strong ties throughout the community.

But the bullying only increased her determination. Towles Cummings took six-packs of bottles filled with the toxic river and well water to environmental meetings. Each one had a blazing orange label with skulls and crossbones and warnings that the unfit water came from P&G, or "Profit & Greed." "P&G put T-bones on our table, but we've been washing it down with polluted iced tea," said Blair-Jackson, a former P&G worker.[23]

One especially important meeting took place in June 1991 in Orlando, Florida. The Environmental Regulation Commission, a state agency that develops state policies to enforce EPA laws, was holding a public hearing on dioxin limits in water. The meetings are attended by concerned residents and state regulators who enforce EPA regulations. Towles Cummings and Blair-Jackson decided to show the officials what it's like at a Taylor County dinner table. The women rose in the early morning hours to cook mullet, hush puppies, and swamp cabbage. They made two dinners: one plate had mullet caught in the Fenholloway, the other had a fish from the Steinhatchee. "We could tell the difference when we fried them because one smelled real bad," Towles Cummings said. "But when they were on the plate, you couldn't tell the difference."

As the meeting began, the two women sat in the back with the dinner platters. Clifford Henry, a P&G official, spotted the food and remarked, "I guess they're gonna meet through lunch, because they've brought in meals." The women just smiled and listened to the crowd of paper lobbyists plead for more lenient dioxin laws. By 2 P.M., Henry walked by the dinners again, lamenting that good food was being wasted. "I wanted to say, 'Here Clifford, have one,' " Towles Cummings said.

By evening, the women finally got their turn to speak. Towles Cummings stood up and explained the problems of the Fenholloway and the need for stricter limits on dioxin. To reinforce her speech, she passed out the plates of fish and jugs of river water. She told them they were getting two sets of fish, but only one was contaminated with dioxin, like the ones that Taylor County residents have eaten for years. She invited the commissioners to dig in.

"Which is which?" asked Commissioner Kenneth Wright of Orlando. [24] "You folks have a choice. Y'all don't have to eat that fish," Towles Cummings said. Blair-Jackson chimed in a bit of advice that her mother used to offer her fourteen children at the dinner table: "Say your blessing and eat your fish." They declined to eat the meal.

Their pitch had an impact. The commission delayed its decision on changing dioxin standards, pending further review. "At least we didn't get the standards set by the paper industry," Towles Cummings said.

The commission eventually used EPA regulations because it was confronted with so much conflicting information on dioxin. That didn't satisfy the activists, considering the Bush administration's track record of favoring big business over the environment. Furthermore, the EPA has been influenced by lobbyists from the American Paper Institute and the Chlorine Institute. Both groups have been promoting dioxin as less dangerous than previously thought. [25] P&G is a key member of the paper institute. And as in studies on toxic shock syndrome, P&G-sponsored scientists have helped develop the scientific studies to defend the company's actions in the dioxin debate.

Shortly after the Orlando meeting, the activists got more proof: Tests showed that the Buckeye mill was to blame for groundwater pollution. The mill water has killed most fish and contaminated the groundwater that supplies residents' backyard wells. The danger extends well beyond Taylor County, for fish and crabs caught in the gulf are contaminated by the dirty river water and sold around the country.

Residents living near the river were told not to drink their water. Even as P&G disputed scientific evidence, the company was recommending its own managers drink bottled water. And the company eventually began giving away free bottled water to residents. [26] Each visitor to Towles Cummings' ranch now gets a gallon jug of distilled water for drinking and brushing their teeth. They still shower in the water, but it leaves a film on the skin.

Many residents who grew up drinking the tap or well water aren't healthy. They complain of arthritislike symptoms, short-term memory loss, and skin and respiratory problems.

With proof of the connection between the mill and the polluted water, Towles Cummings decided it was time to send a message to P&G Chairman and Chief Executive Ed Artzt at company headquarters in Cincinnati. In October 1991 she sent a jug of the river water to animal rights activist Michael Budkie, who offered to deliver it to the executive's house the day before the company's annual shareholders' meeting. [27] When questioned about the river at the meeting, Artzt didn't exhibit much concern. "They showed me a couple of fish yesterday, and they looked pretty good," he said. He also offered to drink the water and eat a Fenholloway fish. [28]

His cavalier attitude toward the pollution isn't hard to understand, considering P&G's virtual stranglehold over Taylor County. The company's financial clout is huge, especially in a county that had the highest unemployment rate in Florida. The company has a $40-million payroll and pays half the property taxes in the town of Perry. [29]

And this is not a place where many people challenge the establishment. In many ways, it's stuck in a time warp. Locals commonly refer to blacks as "niggers," and segregation still exists at restaurants and bars. Some still talk about Dixie "rising again." Men joke about using whips to turn women into "good housewives." Disputes are often settled with guns. [30] Ken Carson, a Perry resident, yanks up the left leg of his shorts to reveal proof of his gunfights. A 12-gauge shotgun blast left a scar resembling a billiard table pocket in his thigh. [31]

"Here you've got to turn your watch back about forty years," said Maria Kyler, the former millworker. (Thanks to P&G's benevolence, Taylor Country residents can get the correct time: The company funded a time and temperature line that allows people to dial a number and get current figures.) [32]

The company gets preferential treatment from local politicians and law enforcement officials. Janice Blair-Jackson, who worked at the mill, recalled that she once wanted a judge to write an order to get her son into a drug rehabilitation program. When the judge refused, a P&G manager escorted her to the courthouse and persuaded him to change his mind. [33]

Local residents, including law enforcement officers, often work part-time at P&G. [34] The county commission helps P&G too. It issued $7.5 million in industrial revenue bonds for construction of additional pollution-control facilities at Buckeye. [35]

Industrial revenue bonds provide cheaper funds than bank loans and are typically provided for start-up companies in need of cash. Some county residents criticized the use of government-backed bonds for a prosperous company such as P&G. The commission's action is not surprising, considering that numerous members of the group have been P&G employees. In 1992 two of the five county commissioners worked for P&G; previously, *four* members of the group were on the company payroll. Townspeople joke that if P&G leaves, there won't be anyone to run the government. P&G even got a "resolution of encouragement" following media coverage of the Fenholloway; a sort of three cheers for P&G in its time of crisis. Irvin Hill and Vance Howell, the two current commissioners who work at P&G, voted for the resolution. They said their votes did not constitute a conflict of interest. "Nothing gets approved by the commission unless the mill approves first," said Mike Zawada, a local resident and P&G employee. [36]

Part of P&G's clout comes from intense lobbying. Because P&G objected, the Florida Department of Environmental Regulation softened a letter warning residents not to drink their well water. Even after environmental tests showed the P&G mill was to blame, the company countered that the contamination could "possibly occur naturally," and that the letter was too harsh to P&G. [37]

Other businesses in the area, dependent on P&G, do their part to help too. The Perry-Taylor Chamber of Commerce, another group full of P&G supporters, suggested marketing the area as "The Nature Coast"—a bizarre pitch, given the county's environmental problems. But it's not surprising, considering that Jim Hunt, then chamber of commerce president, runs the Hard Hat Cafe, a restaurant inside the mill. [38]

P&G has friends scattered throughout the community who can feed company managers information on the activists' plans. "One woman comes by regularly just to pick up any information," said Towles Cummings. "And it goes right back to P&G." She decided to test her theory. She made up a story about radical environmentalists who planned to show up at the mill during the town's forest festival parade and chain a boat to railroad tracks so railcars couldn't enter the mill. "There were security guards everywhere the day of the parade," Towles Cummings said. "Now whenever I want them to know something, I just tell her."

She also suspects that her phone line has been tapped. In various conversations, she offers information about false plans, invariably bringing a response from P&G. She doesn't have much faith in local law enforcement officials. Sheriff John Wesley Walker is "being used by P&G," she claimed. "People in the department do exactly what they're told by P&G." Walker said he tries to stay neutral in the battle. [39]

Besides the Tallahassee paper, no local reporters keep close tabs on what's really going on in Taylor County. The local television station, W69-AX, is a P&G cheerleader. It's a low-budget shop, with the owner and his family running cameras, hosting shows, and taping commercials. P&G pays the station to tape the county commission meetings twice a month. The normal charge for such services is $100 per hour, but the station gives P&G the cut rate of $50, regardless of how long the meeting lasts. That is the same price offered to churches. [40]

C. D. Reams, a Baptist preacher, met Hudson Randall, owner of the station, in October of 1991, when his family moved back to Taylor County. A Ph.D. in philosophy, religion, and theology, Reams works several odd jobs and agreed to host a Sunday morning show, "Search the Scripture," and another called "Taylor Talk in Focus." Although he was not paid for his work, he had been a journalist in the navy and enjoyed hosting the programs. Viewers responded to the call-in talk show, where topics ranged from hospital care to AIDS.

Reams invited Towles Cummings to discuss her battle with P&G. He asked her questions about the lawsuit, but they also touched on other environmental matters such as acid rain and the ozone layer. Randall praised the show afterward.

But just two days later the *Perry News-Herald* reported that Reams was no longer affiliated with the television station. Randall had not bothered to notify him of his dismissal. [41] The owner had been pressured by one of his biggest advertisers, South House furniture store, which is owned by a retired P&G public relations official, Jim Southerland. The store owner said he received threats to burn down his store because his ads appeared in the program featuring Towles Cummings. The show was "the worst form of yellow-tabloid journalism," Southerland huffed to the Perry newspaper. And W69-AX's owner told Reams that he'd gotten calls threatening to burn down the TV station if the talk-show host wasn't taken off the air.

In addition to booting Reams, Randall gave Southerland forty minutes to talk about P&G's efforts in the community. He hosted the show and apologized repeatedly to viewers for allowing Reams to interview Towles Cummings. "If we lose Buckeye, I'll go bankrupt," Southerland said on the show. "We have faith in P&G." He pointed to his burly son Mark as proof that Taylor County isn't dangerous to their health. "My son was born here. He didn't turn out too wimpy or small." But even Southerland had to admit the Fenholloway stunk, remarking, "When you passed over the Fenholloway, you'd tell your wife to get that baby out of the car and change him." [42]

Reams doesn't mind losing the job at the station, but he is livid about the lack of free speech. "The Bible has ten commandments," he said. "We have an extra one here: Thou shalt not say anything against P&G." [43] He does not personally support all of Towles Cummings' efforts. "But I really do believe in the Constitution and First Amendment rights," said the Vietnam veteran. "And everyone in Taylor County has an inherent right to breathe clean air and drink clean water."

As for the local papers, the *Taco Times* and the *Perry News-*

Herald, Reams suggests "wrapping mullet in them." The papers devote considerable space to soft features such as ninety-year-old J. L. Gibson and his sixty-three-pound watermelon. P&G plant managers are regularly featured in photos extolling the company's latest donation to the hospital or local boys and girls clubs. News stories on the P&G controversy favor the company. [44] The June 24, 1992, issue of the *Taco Times* refers to "alleged contamination of drinking water," even though environmental experts had confirmed a year earlier that the water was polluted because of the mill. [45]

Julie Hauserman, the Tallahassee environmental reporter who exposed the Fenholloway's problems, was harassed by county officials and local residents after her series appeared. Anytime she visited Taylor County, she would be rebuked by P&G supporters. She got plenty of angry letters. And the Defenders of Taylor County bought a full-page ad in the *Taco Times* to condemn her coverage. They also accused Knight Ridder, the parent company of the *Democrat,* of emitting dioxin at its newsprint mill in Georgia. [46] Officials at the newsprint facility say tests have shown no measurable dioxin from the plant. The plant uses hydrogen peroxide instead of chlorine to bleach newsprint, officials said.

Mike Evans, a Taylor County economic developer, wrote a scathing column in the Perry newspaper expressing his outrage at Hauserman's coverage. The Tallahassee media have been "bombing our county like Hitler's Germany," he wrote. [47]

When *Democrat* executive editor Lou Heldman addressed the Perry Kiwanis Club, he was scolded for his newspaper's stories on the river. "I knew this wasn't going to follow the normal pattern when Kiwanis President Charlton Knowles said they'd be skipping the weekly song to leave more time for questions," said Heldman. "At the end of my speech, there was no applause, which is probably a service-club first." [48] At the end of 1992 Hauserman left the newspaper to write a book on Florida's environment.

P&G has locals trained to report back if they spot any out-of-town newspaper or television reporters. Towles Cummings gives all reporters the grand tour of the area, including a stop to pick up her bottled water from a roadside shed near downtown Perry. The contractor P&G hired to hand out jugs of water demands that a reporter put away her camera, or Towles Cummings won't get her water.[49] He said he was told to refer all reporters to P&G's PR man Dan Simmons. The company got particularly antsy after she showed up with a film crew from "60 Minutes." During a brief appearance in a segment on terrorism against environmentalists, Towles Cummings offered CBS reporter Lesley Stahl a glass of water inside her home.

"It's kind of yellowy-browny," Stahl said with a grimace. "That came out of the tap?"

"Would you drink it?" Towles Cummings asked.

"No. I don't want to drink it," Stahl said.[50]

One of the dangers of talking about P&G's pollution is the retaliation that often follows. Linda Rowland and Stephanie McGuire, cousins who ran the Fenholloway Fish Camp, got involved in Towles Cummings's group after seeing how the pollution affected fish. Rowland, the more outspoken of the two, spent fifteen years at Buckeye and knew what was causing the problems. "I dumped chemicals in those landfills at the mill," she explained.[51]

The cousins started receiving anonymous calls in May 1991. One day, after a trip to get their hair cut, a man called and in an ominous voice asked McGuire, "Are you getting pretty for me or for getting laid in a casket?"

The calls came four, five times a day. They had a tracer put on the phone, and the calls stopped. Then tragedy struck Towles Cummings: Her twenty-three-year-old son, Trey, was killed when the driver of a truck in which he was riding lost control of the vehicle. Shortly after the accident, Rowland and McGuire started getting more calls. "You know how accidents happen. They can happen to you," the man told McGuire.

Boats docked at the fish camp were cut loose. Pheasants caged near the house were poisoned. And the phone calls continued. The two women never traveled alone or without a gun. At about 5 P.M. on April 7, 1992, McGuire's son, Shawn, asked if he could go to the store to buy a Gameboy with money he'd saved. Rowland offered to take him; she had to run some errands in town. McGuire stayed home because one fishing boat was still out in the Gulf and hadn't checked back into the camp. Rowland and the boy left to do their shopping. "I was washing dishes in the cook shed when they left," McGuire recalled. "And I heard a boat come in." She assumed it was the last fishing boat and went outside.

McGuire spotted a man in a camouflage outfit walking toward the house. "Who owns the cows up the road?" he asked. "I think I might've shot one." She felt uneasy; he looked familiar. McGuire turned to go back into the house when two other men came out of the wooded area near the house. One struck her on the head with a rock and tossed it in the river as she fell to the ground. She struggled to her feet and punched him in the mouth, knocking loose one of his teeth. He reached underneath the camouflage mask he wore and put the tooth in his pocket.

Her assailants knocked her back to the ground and stomped her hand. Then they burned her skin with a cigar and slashed her face with a razor. One poured river water in her open wounds and growled, "*Now* you have something to sue us about." They told her to stop battling P&G. The third man, the one from the boat, didn't wear a mask because he said he "intended to leave me dead," McGuire said.

"This is the last face you'll see," he told her. Two of the men then raped her. Her life may have been saved by one of her terriers, Boo-boo. The dog bit one man in the face, hanging onto his cheek. He flung the dog into the river as blood gushed from the wound.

The men retreated to the boat and one reached for a shotgun. "I thought, 'Oh God, they're fixing to shoot me,'" McGuire recalled. But the boat's driver revved the engine, making the other two lose their balance. They sped off down the river toward the gulf.

McGuire crawled back into the house and called a neighbor who lived about five miles down the road. She also dialed 911 for an ambulance, although she doesn't remember making that call. When Rowland and Shawn returned home about six o'clock, neighbors met them in the driveway and told her what had happened. The ambulance arrived, and the driver called the sheriff. "She didn't want to go to the local hospital because it's a Band-aid station," Rowland said. So they went to a Tallahassee hospital.

In the emergency room, Rowland learned that McGuire had recognized one of the men. They had seen him at a local restaurant, the Brass Lantern, where the environmentalists had met with a woman from Greenpeace. But Rowland couldn't remember many details about his description. McGuire recalls that they didn't dress like local hunters, who typically wear beat-up camouflage and knives on their belts. And they didn't have the southern accent of locals. "I think this was a professional hit," Rowland said.

The sheriff's department remains skeptical. "They didn't believe she was raped," Rowland said. "And they tried to blame me, saying we had a 'lovers' quarrel.' " Others said it was self-inflicted, but possible further proof of her story came six weeks after the assault, when McGuire said she suffered a miscarriage.

The women moved to another Florida county to escape the harassment. As McGuire recalls the episode, she cracks her knuckles and wipes away tears. She cuddles Boo-boo, who was rewarded with a steak dinner for biting the attacker. She lives in fear, never leaving the house alone or without a gun. She and Rowland keep shotguns and pistols throughout the house and in their cars. Her son, Shawn, looks scared as he listens to his mother talk. When the rottweilers in the yard begin to bark, she quickly peers out the window to see if someone has broken into the locked fence. "Somebody is going to pay for this," she said. "If I catch somebody inside the fence, I'll shoot him."

Only Towles Cummings knew where they'd moved. The two women drove to her ranch to give her the new phone and address, suspecting that her phone was tapped. Towles Cummings accidently mentioned the number during a phone conversation with another friend. The harassing calls then started again. They also mentioned to one friend over the phone that a private investigator had videotaped McGuire to document her injuries. Shortly after that call, the sheriff called to say he knew about the videotape. "That's when I knew the phone was tapped," Rowland said.

The local newspaper published a story saying where the women had moved.[52] Months after the attack, they were still being stalked. One of their rottweilers, Keala, died after someone dumped table scraps laced with antifreeze inside the fence. During a trip to a Tallahassee store, the man who had been unmasked in the attack came up behind McGuire. She was so stunned that she couldn't move. Before she could yell for help, he darted out the door.

To make matters worse, the sheriff's department took the unusual step of seeking criminal perjury charges against her. An affidavit filed by the department said she was making up the story about getting pregnant after the attack. The sheriff's department made the affidavit public, another rare move, considering that no arrest was made. McGuire wasn't told about the complaint and learned about it by reading the Perry newspaper. She said it is part of the ongoing attempt to discredit her and the whole group. "If I go to jail, it'll make P&G look good, like it was all lies," she said. "I wish I was lying about this. It would be easier to deal with."[53]

The case was turned over to Jerry Blair, state attorney for the Third Judicial Circuit, which includes Taylor County. Sources familiar with the investigation said that Blair, an elected official, was pressured by Taylor County officials and P&G to seek criminal charges. Blair received two phone calls from Jim Hunt, the Chamber of Commerce president and owner of the mill's café, and Dan Simmons, the mill's public affairs manager. Blair declined to press charges against McGuire. "They wanted to vindicate the honor of P&G," said one insider. "It is in the best interest of the community and P&G that the attack didn't happen and she be discredited."[54]

Initially, P&G disputed that the attack had any link to the river controversy and the company. John Sipple, director of P&G Cellulose's Florida operations, said, "I think there's no connection." But P&G later offered a $5,000 reward for any information on the incident.[55] The police have closed the case. Nevertheless the two cousins continue to help Towles Cummings in her fight. And they've joined the class-action suit against P&G. "They thought we'd be quiet," Rowland said. "But all this did was piss us off royally."

As a former millworker at Buckeye, Rowland knew that anyone who challenges P&G gets trouble. She was once reprimanded by her manager because she dated a man who was separated from his wife. "I was called into the office and told to stop dating him," she said. "I told them, 'What I do on the job is your business. What I do outside is mine.'" Even managers are told not to date Taylor County women, she said.

That was only part of the harassment Rowland endured while at the mill. The forty-one-year-old woman lost her front teeth when a a high-pressure water hose she was using to clean the plant knocked her over. There were few safety precautions to prevent such accidents, she said. Sometimes the vats overflow, covering the mill floor with soggy, thick pulp. She was trying to clean up such a mess when she slipped and fell into a drain, permanently injuring her back. She complained about the working conditions. Her manager, told other plant workers, "Let's see how long she lasts at the end of a shovel!" She was assigned to clean-up duty in the woodyard. She quit in 1987 and is seeking back wages through a workers' compensation complaint.

Rowland's stories are similar to those of other workers. These accounts are difficult to dismiss because some who still work there confirm the unhealthy conditions. They endure the hard work because P&G offers better wages and benefits than the minimum-wage jobs available elsewhere. So they tolerate abuse and even constant surveillance by undercover spies who mingle with workers to nab the disloyal. Some work eighty or more hours a week, including sixteen-hour days with few breaks. "We the good mothers of Taylor County, to ensure our kids could wear Reeboks and have perms in their hair, worked as many hours as we could," said one woman who worked at the plant. "I signed a power of attorney at the local hospital in case one of my kids needed surgery. If I left the mill to be with a kid, my pay would be docked." A rate of only 2 percent absenteeism guarantees a stern reprimand from the bosses for anyone having to miss a day of work. Some women, including Janice Blair-Jackson, are suing P&G for back wages, among other things.[56]

For some P&G workers, the mill job in Taylor County was their only choice if they wanted to keep a job when P&G closed other plants around the country. Some, like Michael Zawada, were transferred to the Florida plant with promises of golden years in the sun. In the 1980s Zawada was out of work after P&G consolidated food and soap plants in the north.[57] He'd spent the bulk of his career with the company, beginning as a cleanup man before working his way up the Duncan Hines line at the Port Ivory plant in New York. He remembers his job anniversary date as quickly as he recalls his wedding day. His father retired from Port Ivory as a machinist; several aunts and uncles were longtime P&Gers too. "I tried for nine years after high school to get hired there," said the forty-seven-year-old Staten Island native.

He held production records for his work on the cake and muffin lines, but he still had to reapply when he wanted another P&G job. The opening came at the Buckeye plant, where wages are based on what other Florida paper mills pay, not what other P&G plants offer. The Florida job offered a salary of about $12 an hour, down from the $17 he'd been paid at Port Ivory. And he wouldn't receive major medical insurance as he had at the other plant. Still, Zawada wanted to stay with the company. "I figured once I worked for P&G, I'd always work for P&G," Zawada said. So in 1989 he moved his wife, Linda, and their daughter, Lisa, to Perry for the new job.

They bought a house and began to settle into the new community. They were ostracized as outsiders because of their New York accents. A month after they arrived, Linda learned that the water was unfit to drink because of the mill. "This is not the P&G we used to know," she said. She pulls out her copy of the company's official biography, *Eyes on Tomorrow*, and highlights the statements about value and character.

In 1990 Michael Zawada was diagnosed as a diabetic and missed a lot of work. He began receiving disability payments. P&G managers questioned his illness and wouldn't accept the doctor's word regarding his condition. The company tried to get his medical records. Managers called his house to harass him about returning to work. Zawada received psychiatric care for two weeks because of stress from his mill job. While P&G is quick to send employees to its company psychiatrists, his managers questioned why he was seeking such help. "My doctor recommended that we move to another town," he said.

After Zawada returned to work in September 1991, he learned that P&G was planning to sell the Buckeye plant because management decided it was more cost-effective to buy its pulp from other suppliers. P&G's pulp and chemicals group earned $74 million pretax in fiscal 1992, down from $222 million in 1991 and $307 million in 1990.[58] Zawada feels betrayed. "My loyalty and trust for the company has left me," he said. "I wanted to stay with P&G, not whoever buys it. If I wanted to do that, I would've stayed in New York and worked for Macy's."

As the plant waited for news about the sale, his department held a "last supper" featuring sirloin tips—paid for by P&G. But Zawada chose to skip it. Instead he took the day off so the family could go to Orlando. "I feel bad for Lisa and Linda," he said. "They didn't deserve this." His wife agrees. "This is very hard for us to deal with again," Linda said, chain-smoking Marlboros and sipping bottled water.

Their daughter is wiser than she should be at age ten. A writer of poetry, Lisa describes life at the local schools, which shut down and rearrange football game schedules to match plant shifts: "If you're not a manager's kid, you're nothing," she said. Even in school, the children are taught to praise P&G. "We can't speak out. It's like there's no Constitution down here." She laments that her father's possible job loss will hurt the family. "I hate to see my parents go through this pain," she said. "My father's face is so gray." She has coined a new phrase to mark the sale. Instead of P&G Cellulose, she figures it should be called P&G Sell-U-Lose. "We should make it into a bumper sticker," she tells her mother. "Smart kid," answers Linda.

The Zawadas have another mantra to help soothe their hurt:

When I was young
and full of hope,
I washed myself
with Ivory soap.
Now I'm old
and have no hope.
I wash myself
with any old soap.

To complicate matters, they discovered that the house they purchased was part of a complicated financial swindle on a local savings and loan. They received a letter from bankers saying they didn't really own the house because the contractor took their money but failed to pay off the bank loan. They were given a choice of either buying the house again or paying rent.

They wish they'd accepted a buyout package instead of moving to Florida when the New York plant closed, but they have become committed to helping other locals fight back. "We're a lost cause, but the people who lived here are plumb out of luck," he said. "This was their home."

A union representing about 500 of the plant's 700 hourly workers doesn't help much. "P&G owns it," Zawada explained. "That's why P&G doesn't want plants in the Northeast anymore." His boss told him he would get more money if he wasn't in the union.

After P&G announced the sale of most of its pulp mills to Weyerhaeuser, Zawada and others waited for news of who would buy the Florida plant. Other workers, including some managers, were told in late 1992 that they had no future at P&G. Some who were home on disability leaves were told to either return to work or quit. Otherwise they would be fired. During a three-week maintenance shutdown, he and others had to work ten-hour days with only one day off.

Over lunch at the local Denny's, the Zawadas met Maria Kyler, the former P&G millworker who quit after years of fighting about pollution and harassment at the mill. While working in finishing, she'd noticed that a spray chemical solution irritated workers' skin and caused paper cuts to become infected. The chemical was sprayed on the sheets of pulp to make it more absorbent. She reported the health problems on numerous occasions, but no one did anything. "We were told that nothing in the chemical can hurt you," she said.

Kyler tracked down the barrels that were used to ship the chemical to the plant. The labels were removed, so she didn't know what was in the solution. Another clue came, however, when she discovered that scraps from this line couldn't be recycled into other pulp mixtures because of the spray.

The spray system was changed to an overhead sprinkler system, and she had to walk under the spray as she worked. She wore dust masks to cut down on the amount she inhaled, but it didn't help much. She got throat infections frequently. As a member of the plant's safety team, Kyler decided to investigate. She convinced one manager to help her find out more. The manager gave her the keys to the safety department's filing cabinet. Inside she found reference to the chemical: it was listed as a carcinogen. She found out why the cellulose couldn't be repulped: The Food and Drug Administration didn't want it used in foods, such as sausage casings and potato chips.

She found a phone number for another P&G plant that shipped the chemical to Buckeye. The manager said she would call and find out more about it. "Don't call from your home phone," Kyler warned her. "You know how secretive they are." The next time she saw the manager, the woman refused to discuss the matter. "They caught me," she whispered. Within weeks, the manager had left her job. Kyler doesn't know where she went. Soon thereafter Kyler was transferred out of finishing, despite a freeze on transfers. She also lost her spot on the plant's safety team.[59] P&G said no chemicals used in the pulp-making process put employees at risk for cancer. "Our workplaces are completely safe for our employees," P&G said.

Kyler's new assignment was driving a bulldozer. In some ways, she welcomed the move away from the chemicals, but she saw other environmental and health problems outside. She discovered the thirty-year-old landfill when her bulldozer got stuck in the pit. The hole was at least twenty feet across and she couldn't see the bottom. Part of the initiation in the woodyard is to let the newcomers accidently find the pit. "To good ol' boys, this is fun," she said.

Besides scrap pine wood and pulp, thousands of gallons of

hydraulic oil were spilled on the ground or pushed into the dump. "It was hideous," she said.

Kyler was questioned about obscure matters, such as her hair. In the summer she would braid it and tuck it under a scarf and hard hat. Managers considered that unsafe. Another time, when she questioned a manager about the filthy rest rooms, which were infested with fire ants, she was told to spray the toilets.

Many workers were harassed during a drug sweep at Buckeye. Undercover security guards placed throughout the plant listened for clues about people who used drugs. Workers were told they were selected at random for questioning by management about drug use. Kyler was notified that she was in the group but said she didn't want to go. "Your job depends on it," the manager told her. Asked if she knew anyone who sold drugs in the plant, she didn't offer names. Many were nabbed simply because they frequent local bars. Some employees who were fired had to be rehired with back pay after the dispute went to union arbitration. Union officials at other P&G plants confirm that similar tactics are used at their locations. [60]

"To work here, you have to do what you're told and not ask questions," Kyler said. "So we're good little mushrooms—kept in the dark and fed bullshit." She quit in 1989 and sold her P&G stock. "Is there life after P&G?" Zawada asked Kyler. "Oh, yeah," she said. "I'm on food stamps, but my life is still better than when I worked out there."

A growing number of Taylor County residents joined Joy Towles Cummings's group when they realized P&G had turned its back on the decades of environmental problems—and, not coincidentally, after the company announced its intentions to unload the Buckeye plant. She took her fight to P&G's hometown in October 1992. The day before the annual shareholders' meeting, Towles Cummings and a TV news crew went door-to-door in

CEO Artzt's Indian Hill neighborhood. She brazenly rang the doorbell at his house and asked his wife, Ruth, to help her arrange a meeting with the executive. Mrs. Artzt said she couldn't help them. Someone called the Indian Hill Rangers, the community police, who threatened to arrest Towles Cummings for trespassing.

On the morning of the meeting, two Indian Hill Rangers' cars and officers blocked Artzt's driveway, just in case she returned. [61] But Towles Cummings and others from Greenpeace were at company headquarters, hoping to address the shareholders and meet with Artzt. She had a cooked Fenholloway fish and a jug of her well water for the CEO. Security guards asked her why the jug had a skull and crossbones on the label. "Because you poisoned it," she said. The guards confiscated the fish and water, but four friends had more fish and water stashed in their pockets as they entered the meeting.

Towles Cummings sat quietly through the entire meeting as Artzt fielded questions on his salary, Salvadoran coffee, and animal testing. Security guards in navy suits kept a watchful eye over her and other activists. By the end of the meeting, Towles Cummings got her chance to speak.

"Last year at the shareholders' meeting you said you'd be the first to drink the water and eat the fish," she told the CEO. Gail Martin of Greenpeace walked to the front of the auditorium to hand the executive the fish and water. One of Artzt's security guards stopped her before she reached the stage. "I'm waiting for you to eat your fish," Towles Cummings chided. She described the problems of Taylor County to the audience of several hundred shareholders. But Artzt disputed the problem, noting that P&G was doing its share by giving out free bottled water to residents. She tried to interrupt him to refute his remarks about the river, but Artzt ordered a P&G guard to take away her microphone.

After the meeting, Towles Cummings waited in the lobby for a chance to talk to Artzt. She waited again the next day, but he wouldn't meet with her. Greenpeace issued a news release with the headline "Desperately seeking Edwin."[62]

In Taylor County the fight continued. More people stepped forward to share their stories. Louis Parker sat at the Holmes Grill with Towles Cummings and described his relatives' arthritis and respiratory problems. Dust from the mill fell on his cars and house, eating away the paint. "The light fixture on the carport fell off," he said. "The chemicals just ate the metal." Parker figures the family will be healthier if they move to Tennessee, where he owns some property. "It's bad to be born here and have to leave."[63] At the Winn-Dixie, business is brisk in the aspirin aisle. "Everyone knows the best sinus and arthritis medications," Blair-Jackson said.

Many residents remain afraid to challenge P&G's reign and its abuse of the river, out of fear that they will lose the county's biggest employer. They worried that no one would buy the environmentally troubled site from P&G. After a lengthy search, in late 1992 the company sold only half its interest in the mill, to an investor group led by a former P&G executive. Many here still fear the plant will have to close because of the environmental problems, leaving residents without either jobs or a clean river.

But Towles Cummings and dozens of others have sued to make P&G pay for its damages. Their lawyer is John Deakle, who won more than $4 million against Georgia-Pacific, the paper company, in two pollution cases at its mills.[64] "Our cases up here in Mississippi are not nearly as egregious as those cases down there," Deakle said. "I personally cannot believe that in 1992 a river like the Fenholloway can exist."[65]

In a class-action suit, the group of residents has also charged that P&G conspired to hide the dioxin information as early as 1985. They are seeking unspecified damages. About 120 people have joined the lawsuit. "Even if we have to form a posse, we're gonna make them clean it up," Towles Cummings said. "That river doesn't belong to them."

By late 1992 Towles Cummings was introducing at least a

dozen new people to attorney Deakle each week, and she has a team of scouts who sign up new plaintiffs. Bertie Branch, a sixty-year-old Perry native, had signed up fifty people for the lawsuit after just ten days on the job. Branch and her friend Vera Peskan live in what used to be their beauty salon. The shop had to close because of water problems. A cosmetologist since 1968, Peskan had owned a salon in Tallahassee for ten years before moving to Perry. "I couldn't get a perm to stay in after I moved here," she said. "I thought I'd lost my touch, but then I discovered it was the water."

Branch suspected the water was the culprit in the health problems she saw while working at a Perry medical clinic. A former X-ray technician, she collected names at the clinic, waiting for the day when she had enough evidence to sue P&G. In eighteen months she gathered over 200 names of people who shared similar symptoms. "Three of five cases we saw had the same symptoms," she said. Branch plans to devote "the rest of my life" to fighting P&G. "They're gonna clean up this place."

Towles Cummings continues to spend her evenings on the telephone or sitting with neighbors who discover that their water is polluted by the mill. One evening at the ranch, Buddy Odom tells Towles Cummings about the test results from his well water. He has just learned that the water is contaminated. "I didn't want to hear this today," says the white-haired Odom, a retiree who spent fifteen years at the Buckeye plant.[66] He just built a $20,000 barn on his twenty-eight-acre farm, located six miles north of the mill. "If the water is so bad, who will buy it? That's what I got to leave my kids." She asks him to stay for a dinner of pork chops, okra, butter beans, and cracklin' corn bread so they can discuss his problem.

"Don't worry, Buddy," she says. "Uncle Buck will pay."

8
Supermarket
Showdown

As a junior Procter & Gamble salesman, Lou Pritchett learned how to fight with grocers. The P&G sales force was nicknamed "Push & Grunt" because of its bully tactics. Salespeople used rulers to measure shelf space and ads to make sure Tide and Crest got prime display areas. [1] At one retailer's office, P&Gers were so disliked that they were greeted with a sign that said, "PLEASE CHECK IN WITH THE MORGUE." [2] One time an owner aimed a pistol at Pritchett and chased him out of the store.

Complaints about P&G's methods didn't faze senior management. Sales grew every quarter, so the company saw no need to change. But after he became vice president of sales, Pritchett worried about the growing rebellion—and shrinking market shares in the 1980s. So he decided P&G had to build alliances. The tough part was finding a retail partner that would let him in the front door long enough to talk.

He was rebuffed by K mart. The Tennessee native then turned his attention to the backwaters of retailing: Bentonville, Arkansas, where Sam Walton had built his Wal-Mart empire. The fast-growing chain had won over consumers with rock-bottom prices on everything from pistachios to Ping-Pong tables.

But getting Walton's attention wouldn't be easy. P&G hadn't been particularly friendly to the retailer. Wal-Mart executives once called P&G CEO John Smale when his company was selected as Wal-Mart's vendor of the year. The call was routed through various secretaries; the CEO never returned the call. Many Wal-Mart phone messages were ignored because P&G thought it was "some wallpaper company in Arkansas," one P&G manager said.[3]

"P&G was one of the more dictatorial and difficult companies to do business with," said David Glass, a Walton protégé and current Wal-Mart CEO. "It was an aggravating relationship that wasn't profitable."[4]

So Pritchett called a friend from his days as a Boy Scout, George Billingsley, who lived in Arkansas and knew Walton. "I've got to find a big customer to dance with," Pritchett told him. "How well do you know Sam?"

"You'll never get to Sam through the front door," Billingsley explained. The homespun Walton hated corporate suits, especially those who worked for Procter. So they arranged an unconventional meeting. They invited Walton on a canoe trip on the south fork of the Spring River in Hardy, Arkansas, in July 1987. Pritchett and Billingsley had first met there in the late 1940s as summer camp counselors. "I'll get him there," Billingsley pledged.[5]

Pritchett and his wife, Barbara, went in style. He signed out one of P&G's Gulfstream jets, the one that CEO Smale took on trips to Japan. The plane was too big to land at the tiny Hardy airstrip, so the pilot took them to nearby Walnut Ridge. Billingsley and other boyhood friends had gathered at a lodge for dinner, but there was no sign of Walton. Pritchett fidgeted, checking his watch. The hours passed. Walton was three hours late. Pritchett began to worry. How would he explain to the boss why he took the Gulfstream to Arkansas for a canoe trip? "I was sweating bullets," he said.

Then he heard a knock at the door. A lanky man with white hair and a yellow legal pad under his arm walked in. "Sam! Where have you been?" Billingsley yelled. The multimillionaire had trouble navigating his secondhand plane; the Hardy airstrip didn't have any lights.

The next morning the group ate a breakfast of ham, eggs, and grits before climbing into their canoes for the twenty-five-mile trip. Walton paddled alongside the Pritchetts' canoe. "Tell me a little bit about what you do," Walton asked Pritchett. The salesman apologized for his company's boorish behavior over the years. None of P&G's senior management had bothered to call on Wal-Mart. Instead, the company had sent scores of greenhorn salespeople. Walton complained that the high cost of something as basic as shipping and selling soap hurt U.S. manufacturers' chances against foreign competitors. "We can't continue to pass the costs through to consumer," he lectured Pritchett. "This is going to cripple America."

The crew took a midmorning snack break at a riverside gas station. Walton, wearing only swimming trunks, didn't have his wallet. So Pritchett sprang for Walton's choice in snacks: a 90-cent banana flip. Back on the river, Walton grilled Pritchett, breaking occasionally for a swim. They talked nonstop during the weekend. Walton would scribble notes on the yellow pad. "Do you like my stores?" he asked Pritchett. "Do you have a good feeling when you walk inside?"

By the end of the trip, the two had agreed to assemble their top officers for a meeting. "Are you sure you can pull it off? Will they really listen?" Walton asked.

Pritchett did more than get his bosses to listen. The river trip evolved into a model for manufacturer-retailer partnerships. Wal-Mart now sells more than $1.5 billion in P&G goods, up from $500 million in 1989.[6] It has direct linkups with P&G factories, speeding up reorders and delivery of goods. And it has seventy P&G managers at its beck and call near its Arkansas headquarters. In a letter to Pritchett, Walton praised his work: "I think back on our first canoe trip and how we evolved our partnership process with P&G. It was one of the best things that ever happened to our company."[7]

But the rosy days of P&G's improved retail relations were short lived. Retailers, wholesalers, and P&G's own sales management say the company's strong-arm tactics today are worse than ever. Even the Wal-Mart relationship is strained because senior management now wants to shift the control back to its marketing and advertising strategy, not alliances with retailers. Giving up power to the retailers "just scares them to death," Pritchett said. "So it's not a priority anymore."[8]

P&G has reason to be nervous. U.S. market shares in key categories are in decline. The company lacks real product breakthroughs, and private labels, along with competing national brands, are taking over more shelf space. Recession-weary shoppers are finicky and less brand loyal. So P&G has become even more aggressive in its fight for control of the nation's grocery shelves.

P&G managers say the company has resorted to deal making not permitted under Robinson-Patman when spending promotion and allowance money to move its goods.[9] P&G maintains that its programs comply with the Robinson-Patman law. Inside P&G, the sales department is chaotic. Senior and middle managers depart each time the company shifts its policies. In recent times, more than 1,000 sales jobs have been cut—more than a quarter of the U.S. force. In addition, P&G has replaced many full-time salespeople with part-time workers.[10] Even Pritchett, the architect of the successful Wal-Mart partnership, quit because ultimately he couldn't convince P&G's senior management to change its ways.

P&G has long resented the retail trade's place in the supply chain. The company considers stores a necessary evil; a place to park its products temporarily while it bombards consumers with television advertising. The commercials have prompted generations of shoppers to look for P&G brands in the stores. The company figures the retailers should be grateful that it has helped

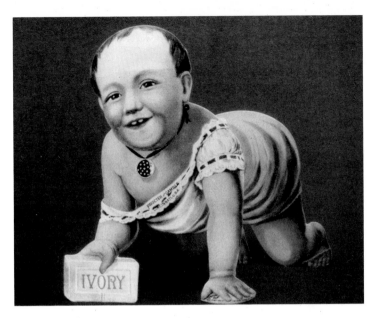

Ivory babies have sold a lot of soap for Procter & Gamble. The first Ivory baby debuted on store countertops as part of the company's early advertising pitches for the "99 44/100% pure" soap.

During World War II, the U.S. government hired P&G to operate a shell-loading plant in Tennessee. P&G produced 25 percent of the bombs used by Allied troops. Workers practiced filling shells with sugar before using the real explosives. ROYCE MOORE

John Smale (*left*) was P&G CEO in the 1980s, a time of rapid growth and change at the company. After retiring from P&G, he later became chairman of General Motors. Ed Artzt (*right*), current CEO, earned his stripes by expanding P&G's international operations. His temper earned him the nickname "The Prince of Darkness."

John Pepper (*left*), president of P&G, and Durk Jager (*right*), executive vice president. Insiders predict one of these two will be the next CEO.

Tom Riley is one of the few people to take on P&G—and win. The Cedar Rapids lawyer has filed scores of lawsuits on behalf of victims of toxic shock syndrome who contracted the disease after using P&G's Rely brand tampons. His research exposed how the company sold the product for years, despite consumer warnings about its dangers.

Judy Braiman, a Rochester, New York, consumer advocate, warned P&G about illness in women who had used Rely, to no avail. When she spoke out about the possible dangers of Ultra Pampers, P&G's new superabsorbent disposable diapers, she found herself facing deposition in an $11-million lawsuit brought about by the company.

Renell Pierpoint questioned the safety of disposable diapers, prompting P&G to sue her. She lost her advertising agency and spent thousands of dollars defending herself against lawsuits.

George Stults once supported his family as a technician at P&G's research labs. After he was fired by P&G, he had trouble finding another job in Cincinnati. At times the family has relied on food stamps to get by.

Steelworkers set up picket lines at the Kansas City plant to protest stalled talks with P&G. THE UNITED STEELWORKERS OF AMERICA

The United Steelworkers launched a national boycott of P&G products after the company thwarted the union's efforts to win a contract at its Kansas City plant. P&G has kept most big unions out of its production plants. THE UNITED STEELWORKERS OF AMERICA

WASHDAY BLUES: BROUGHT TO YOU BY PROCTER & GAMBLE COMPANY

Recently on the Merv Griffin television talk-show a group of cults were brought to the attention of the public. Among these appeared the owner of the Proctor and Gamble Corporation. He said that as long as the gays and the cults have come out of the closet, he was going to do it too. He said that he had told Satan that if he would help him prosper, he would give him his heart and soul when he died. And he gives Satan all the credit for the riches he possesses.

So would you please take copies of this letter and the list of his products and pass them along so that Christians will not give him any more business or money. Use what you have, but buy no more.

All these products have a satanic insignia on them: it is a quarter-moon shape and has the three 6's (666) and ram's horns, which are the antichrist symbology.

Some of Proctor and Gamble's products are:

Deodorant - Sure and Secret
Shampoos - Prell, Head & Shoulders, Pert
Toothpaste - Crest
Lotion - Wondra
Mouthwash - Scope
Permanents - Lilt
Paper products - Charmin, Bounty
Washing products - Bounce, Downey, Biz, Comet, Mr. Clean, Joy, Dawn, Ivory, Camay, Bold, Tide, Zest
Also, among other products - Crisco Shortening, and Folger's Coffee

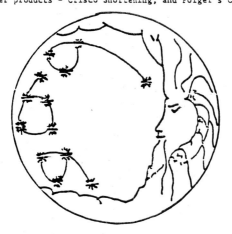

An examination with a magnifying glass of this symbol on any Proctor and Gamble product will show the constellation star pattern forming the "666" the head of Satan, and the rams' horns.

False rumors linking P&G's man-in-the-moon logo to satanism have been a persistent source of irritation to the company. This memo claims that the "satanic" insignia of three sixes can be seen in the logo's stars. P&G has sued those it finds spreading rumors.

P&G quietly helped spread the word about Colgate's acquisition of Darkie toothpaste, hoping to stir up negative publicity about its competitor.

In Taylor County, Florida, Joy Towles Cummings carries jugs of dirty water from local wells and the polluted Fenholloway River, where P&G operates a pulp mill. Her brand name for the water: P&G—Profit & Greed.

Stephanie McGuire (*left*) and Linda Rowland, cousins who ran a fish camp on the banks of the Fenholloway River, say they have been terrorized ever since they spoke out against P&G's pulp mill and pollution of the river. Stephanie was beaten, burned, and raped by three men who told her the attack was her punishment for talking too much. P&G disputed that the attack had any link to the river controversy and the company, and later offered a $5,000 reward for any information regarding the incident.

Lou Pritchett (*at far left*), retired vice president of P&G sales, forged a partnership with legendary retailer Sam Walton (*at far right*) during a canoe trip down the Spring River in Arkansas. His efforts saved P&G millions. But since then, the company has made little progress in its relationships with retailers.

When word spread that P&G had convinced Cincinnati police and prosecutors to track news leaks from inside sources, the company was roundly castigated in the media for invasion of privacy.

create traffic in the stores. Manufacturers such as P&G spent time and money to research consumers' habits across the country, but grocers historically understood only their neighborhoods, so it was easy for P&G to become arrogant and treat retailers like pests instead of partners. In addition, the corporate mentality inside P&G has always placed a higher premium on marketing and advertising functions, not the actual selling of goods.

So P&G has continually looked for ways to cut down on the number of steps between its factories and consumers' kitchen cabinets. In 1919 William Cooper Procter decided to eliminate the use of wholesalers, or jobbers. Wholesalers watched the volatile prices of fats and oils, which were used to make Ivory soap and Crisco shortening. Like any smart buyer, they would stock up on P&G brands when raw material prices were low and stop buying when prices soared. The inventory could then be resold to small shopkeepers at a profit, regardless of P&G's pricing. That buying schedule made for erratic production at P&G plants. Procter believed that workers valued job security more than anything, so he instituted even production instead of manufacturing goods to fit wholesaler's orders. [11] The sales force was increased to 600 men from 150. It was a risky move, considering that wholesalers and the independent grocer network accounted for 95 percent of the market. [12]

P&G informed small retailers that it would ship five-case loads only, so the mom and pop shops could no longer order one case at a time. Storekeepers were angry and cancelled orders. Wholesale publications lashed out at the company:

"We have known for a long time that Procter & Gamble were as rotten as their soap grease, but we couldn't figure out whether they were dead or a living pile of pollution walking around to save funeral expenses," wholesalers wrote in a grocery publication. "We hope the retailers will resent this dastardly act on the part of P&G to confiscate their business. We know every grocer with guts will resent it. The man who doesn't strike back in defense of his business is a lousy cur, unfit to call himself a merchant and unworthy to wear the name of man." [13]

Some wholesalers refused to sell to stores that bought products directly from P&G. "The greetings I got were terrible," recalled ninety-six-year-old A. M. Wood, a salesman who worked at P&G from 1921 until 1961. He was chased out of some stores. Howard Morgens, the retired CEO, said retailers were returning more goods than they sold. "The company almost went broke," he said. [14]

P&G endured the boycotts to smooth out its own production schedules, but a national recession aggravated the battle with wholesalers. Manufacturers like P&G had built up production after World War I. However, due to decreased demand during the recession and high prices of raw materials, P&G ended up writing off a loss of $30 million. [15] Shopkeepers referred to P&G as "Passed & Gone." [16] In 1923 P&G announced its pledge of guaranteed employment, but it didn't close out all wholesalers. In the rural southern and western states, it was impossible for P&G salesmen to go to all the tiny shops that ordered fewer than five cases. In those areas, wholesalers were used once again to distribute the goods. [17]

By the 1950s, the sales force was recruiting young college graduates who could learn how to manage angry retailers. Pritchett got his start in P&G sales after hearing about the company from his father, Joe Pritchett, who worked as a belt repairman at P&G's cellulose mill in Memphis. After the younger Pritchett graduated from Memphis State University, he went to the mill to apply for a job. Instead he took the manager's advice to go into sales for the parent company. His first job was selling soap in Tupelo, Mississippi. Sporting a crew cut, maroon sport coat, and blue suede shoes, Pritchett boarded a bus for Tupelo. He got a company Chevrolet emblazoned with the moon-and-stars decal on the door. He carried a thick leather binder, the bible of the P&G salesman. "You slept with the damn thing," he said. "It told you everything about P&G products. But we were taught nothing about the customers." The only training he received was a rehearsal of the sales call. The key was to tell, not ask, the shopkeeper what he wanted to order. And salesmen also breezed into the back room to check stock. "We never gave them a chance to say no," he said. [18]

He'd fight for space for his P&G posters in the window and stack boxes of P&G brands in the front aisles. He rearranged shelves to move competing brands from prime display. Some salesmen took it a step further, stashing competing brands in the back room.

Shelf management was important because it was the last chance to influence the consumer's purchase. Sales reps were rewarded on a quota for sales of goods in each district. Pressure was intense to meet individual goals because the whole district would lose the bonus—equivalent to three months' salary—if quotas weren't met.

Most days Pritchett made at least fifteen sales calls. The universal rule at Procter was to "call on every store that has a door." The other rule was to unload as much product as possible at each store. Salesmen were considered a failure if they didn't sell every size in every brand. A common motto among the sales force: A loaded customer is a loyal customer. The push was extra hard toward the end of the fiscal year, June 30, when P&G wanted to make its yearly volume goals. If a customer didn't want the fourth size of the same brand, P&G salesmen would canvass the neighborhood around the store and distribute "buy one, get one free" coupons for that fourth size. That way consumers would come in and demand that size. As a manager, Pritchett lectured his junior salesmen on how to sell any reluctant store owner. "We would arm the sales guy with a bigger hammer and a one-way plane ticket," he said. "And we'd tell them to go back and beat the SOB into submission." Being tough with the trade "was a judge of your manhood," said Allan Schoenberger, a former P&G salesman. [19]

P&G enjoyed two advantages throughout the 1950s and 1960s. One, its products were better than competitors' brands. Big brands such as Tide detergent dominated the shelves. The emphasis on advertising, especially with the advent of television, made it impossible for retailers to ignore P&G brands. House-wives listened to radio and television soap operas. When they wrote their shopping lists, they wrote Tide and Crisco, not just "detergent" and "shortening."

The second advantage was the lack of information available to retailers. They didn't keep close tabs on what was selling, but P&G monitored it. P&G would tell the retailers which brands to promote to attract the most customers.

At the time, the system worked. The focus was only on transferring products from P&G factories to stores. But the 1970s brought new problems. P&G's competitors starting developing products to challenge the giant. And retailers, now moving to the suburbs with supermarkets, realized the importance of information. They installed scanners to track who was buying what brands and began to understand more than just their own neighborhoods. Private-label products began to attract interest from budget-minded shoppers.

One of the biggest problems was created by P&G's own pricing decisions. During the price controls of the Nixon admin-istration, P&G raised its list prices so the company wouldn't be caught short if the government froze prices. Then the company used temporary price reductions in the form of promotions to get the prices down. "Dealing backward" through promotions and giving allowances for shelf space became common practices. No one understood what was the real price and what was promo-tional money. Chaos reigned as P&G doled out the promotion money based on confusing and capricious formulas. The man-ager at a midwestern supermarket chain recalled that P&G once told him he would get his promotion money only if he ran a two-column-inch newspaper ad for Tide. The P&G salesman came in, measured the ad, and discovered it was only 1.9 inches. The store manager didn't get his money. [20]

By the late 1970s and early 1980s, P&G's lack of technological breakthroughs had forced the company to introduce line extensions—different sizes, scents, or flavors—to big brands such as Ivory and Tide. That gave P&G more shelf space and built up sales volume. "We went crazy," Pritchett said. "It increased the retailers' costs, but we didn't pay a lot of attention to that." Indeed, any store that challenged the amount of space P&G wanted suddenly found the company salesperson threatening to cut back the store's shipment on special deals or big brands like Tide. [21]

Retailers, meanwhile, stocked up on special deals to avoid paying full price when P&G ended a promotion. This "forward buying" allowed stores to stockpile a warehouse full of discounted goods and then sell them to consumers at the full price. An entire industry grew out of the practice of diverting goods bought on special deals in one region for resale in another. Big chain stores began ordering products from central buying offices, telling P&G and other manufacturers to stop calling on individual stores. [22]

Pritchett, an energetic and effective salesman, focused on these problems when he became national sales manager for P&G's paper division in the mid-1970s. To lessen tensions with the retail trade, he told his sales managers to adopt personal accounts. The mission was to get closer to the customer and do more than fill orders and give away promotion money. "We just had managers managing other managers," he said. "No one was dealing with the customers." The Winn-Dixie supermarket chain was his account. "That was unheard of," he said. Up till then "one of the perks of being promoted was not dealing with the goddamned customers anymore."

For several years, he made annual presentations and

worked on Winn-Dixie's problems. But senior management asked him to go to the Philippines in 1981 to turn around one of P&G's worst markets. The company there was bankrupt, and its brands a distant third behind Unilever and Colgate.

The financial crisis stemmed from the short-term focus of general managers assigned to such posts. They tended to stay for three or four years before returning to the United States and pushed volume growth to inflate their results. That meant using the U.S. style of loading up the retail trade with little concern for their needs.

Overstocked grocers led to an even bigger problem in the Philippines: Consumers weren't making repeat purchases of P&G brands. Market shares for Camay and Safeguard were only 12 percent, even though consumer satisfaction tests showed the soaps received preference scores of 70 versus 30 over competing brands. That's when Pritchett discovered that consumers were buying thirty-week-old bars in the stores. Storage temperatures were well over 100 degrees, so the soap resembled a slimy rock by the time consumers bought it.

So Pritchett took his first step in revamping the P&G sales system by doing the unthinkable: P&G stopped selling products. Inventories had to be trimmed to four weeks from thirty. He sent a telex to Ed Artzt, then president of international operations, declaring the moratorium. "If you don't agree," Pritchett said, "get yourself another boy out here." Artzt agreed.

P&G also worked with the customers to introduce the bar code system, which computerized the inventory and kept track of what consumers were buying.

Pritchett's success in the Philippines attracted attention back in Cincinnati. At annual meetings in Hawaii, both John Smale and Artzt noted that he'd made a lot of progress "for a sales guy," Pritchett said, showing their bias against those who didn't come up through the brand marketing and advertising ranks.

His reward was the sales vice presidency. Pritchett, then

fifty-three, was thrilled. Finally he could make changes in P&G's stodgy ways. Soon after returning to headquarters in 1984, Pritchett began to shake up the eleventh-floor executive suite. He shunned the austere decorating policy and filled his office with Oriental rugs and other artifacts from his Far East assignment. He'd often skip lunch in the executive dining room so he could mingle with the troops in the employee cafeteria.

His first step in tackling P&G's sales strategy was to write his vision for the organization. In the statement, he said the sales force should be challenged, rather than "inspected, audited and controlled" by senior management. He advocated working with the trade customers rather than fighting with them. He criticized P&G as being too stiff. The company has a "high intolerance for anything out of place," he wrote.[23]

The response was fairly chilly. "Smale thought I was loony tunes," Pritchett said. But P&G president John Pepper and vice chairman Tom Laco wanted to know more. Some suspected he was launching a palace coup, because sales VPs were supposed to be low-key. "Sales vice presidents worry about the kind of cars we drive, salary stuctures, whether we put AM/FM radios in the cars," he said. "I was supposed to keep the waters flat."

But his research into the sales organization proved it needed help. During one trip to P&G's Baltimore, Charlotte, and New Orleans districts, Pritchett met with forty-one district and field managers in three days. He discovered a slew of problems. There was little cooperation between P&G's sales and marketing managers. Fewer than 10 percent of the sales managers surveyed could name one marketing manager assigned to the same brand. Too often, it was Procter versus Procter. One retailing executive said P&G account managers would try to bump competing P&G brands from the store's newspaper ads just to snare more advertising space for their brand. Another said the private-label business at his store wouldn't exist if P&G had focused more on the customer in the mid-1970s.[24]

The sales force also felt stifled. Their monthly letters outlining their business were either rewritten or destroyed if they contained any complaints from retailers or anything remotely controversial. They were told to follow the rules because of the company's strong reliance on "conformance over performance."

Radical changes had to be made. Pritchett proposed restructuring the sales force to eliminate the separate sales teams for each division. These had become virtual fiefdoms for their general managers—and a nuisance for the supermarket trade. "Customers didn't want nine guys calling on their stores," he explained.

Smale was typically reluctant. He often resisted modest changes. Even in the mid-1980s he questioned why P&G needed so many computers in managers' offices. But Pepper and Laco supported Pritchett's ideas. More important, the new VP of sales proved to be a pied piper with the sales force. At the 1985 annual sales meetings, Laco told him to tone down his planned speech because it was considered too radical. He'd invited an outside speaker to address the group, which is heresy in the P&G culture. The event featured hundreds of sales managers singing "We are the ones" to the tune of "We Are the World."

Before the evening presentation, hundreds of sales managers rode a riverboat up the Ohio River for a cocktail hour. (Heavy rains turned the fifty-minute ride into a three-hour journey.) The group of drunken managers chanted "Lou-ie! Lou-ie!" in response to Pritchett's dinner speech. After midnight they set off fireworks from the boat to surprise him for his birthday. "We woke up a lot of people in those little towns along the river," Pritchett recalled. Brad Butler, company chairman, later scolded Pritchett for his un-Procterlike behavior. "He thought I was setting up a personality cult," Pritchett said. "I called it leadership." Indeed, scores of sales managers wrote to him after the meeting to praise his work. "You have rekindled a flame that was flickering and nearly out of fuel," gushed one California manager. A St. Louis manager wrote that in his dozen years at P&G, he'd never felt as motivated.[25]

Pritchett pushed to break down the walls between retailers and the soap company. For the first time, sales officials called on Sears, then the nation's largest retailer, to see if they could get Tide and other P&G brands in its stores. Not only would the household goods be a logical fit, but P&G could offer Sears its research on washing machines, which it had developed from research on Tide. Sears tested selling P&G brands in about twenty stores, but it never grew into a substantial business.

Pritchett then began to work with Zayre, a Massachusetts-based discount chain that until the mid-1980s had seven different P&G sales representatives calling on its stores. Instead, Pritchett advocated a team approach. For one meeting, he called in P&G's ad agencies to help Zayre develop pitches for its Hispanic and African-American markets. The store and manufacturer worked out a twelve-month plan of events tied to special promotions.

P&G sent trailerloads of Charmin and Bounty to Zayre warehouses to keep the products in stock during special promotions. When other customers canceled orders, Zayre got the extra goods, allowing it to forward buy at a good price.

Pritchett also invited senior Zayre officials to a Special Olympics meeting at the Kennedy family compound in Hyannis Port, Massachusetts. They attended Boston Celtics games together. P&G space-management experts analyzed Zayre shelves and suggested cutting out some of the company's own products if competing brands were more popular. For instance, Colgate toothpaste is more popular in Hispanic markets, so they suggested giving it more space than Crest. "That's when P&G showed us it was really a partnership," said one former top Zayre official. P&G production managers called Zayre after a plant fire to assure the store that its supply of Tide detergent wouldn't be interrupted.

At its peak, Zayre was a $3.5-billion company. Sales of P&G goods tripled in two years. But a problem arose: Zayre officials were draining the store's resources in favor of other ventures. "Everyone knew Zayre was teetering on the edge of bankruptcy," Pritchett said. "We were perfecting this system with someone who was going out of business." Zayre eventually did sell to Ames, another discount chain, in 1988. [26]

When Pritchett saw what was happening, he began to look for another partner. It had to be a big-name store that would have clout at P&G's home office. Joseph Antonini, chairman and CEO of K mart, said no thanks. Like others, he'd had his share of battles with P&G. At one point the chain had dropped some P&G brands from its shelves.

That was when Pritchett convinced his boyhood friend George Billingsley to set up a date with Wal-Mart founder and CEO Sam Walton. During the canoe trip, he learned that Walton's biggest concerns were the high costs and lack of cooperation between manufacturers and his company. "We realized that our two very sophisticated companies were communicating with each other by slipping notes under the door," Pritchett said.

Typical meetings between a P&G seller and a Wal-Mart buyer were adversarial. "The protocol was to sit down and see if everybody can walk out with more flesh than they came in with," said Bob Martin, executive vice president at Wal-Mart. [27]

When he returned from the canoe trip to his P&G office Monday morning, Pritchett bounded into Laco's office with the news about Walton. He and Laco immediately asked Pepper if they could both go to Arkansas to meet Walton. "When do you want to go?" Pepper replied.

Eventually two dozen managers from P&G and Wal-Mart met to start working out the details of simplifying the business of selling soap. Instead of just buyers and sellers, they would bring systems, finance, legal, and marketing managers as well. For two days in Bentonville, both sides discussed how to work together. During their meetings, they gained some insight into Walton: they met on October 19, 1987—Black Monday—the day of a massive stock market crash that saw the Dow Jones Average plunge a record 508 points. Walton lost about half a billion dollars. Upon learning the news, he responded, "It's only paper."[28]

The folksy Walton preferred to keep life simple. P&G secretaries have bigger offices than the Wal-Mart CEO's office in Bentonville. The Arkansas headquarters is plain brick and decorated with inexpensive paneling, plastic chairs, and worn carpeting. During a trip to P&G's headquarters, Walton and his associates were amazed at the executive suite, a museumlike floor with expensive oil paintings and silver coffee urns. "Boy, you can see who's making all the money in the soap business!" quipped one Wal-Mart official.

The first Cincinnati meeting with Walton was hosted by CEO Smale. He'd met Walton a few years earlier to atone for the Great Snub. Smale had flown to Arkansas only after the local sales team begged him to appease Walton. They remember it as the time "Smale had to genuflect to a bunch of hillbillies. He went screaming and kicking," one manager recalled.

Uncomfortable with the notion of partnerships, Smale began the Cincinnati meeting with his traditional marketing pitch about P&G brands. Walton asked him why P&G needed to make so many sizes of the same detergent. He told Smale that Wal-Mart could do without most of them—the equivalent of a parishioner suggesting the preacher dispose of the Old Testament. "Talk about dropping a clod in the churn," Pritchett said.[29]

Walton wanted P&G to help Wal-Mart drive out excess costs so U.S. manufacturers could be more competitive with foreign goods. As Walton described it, P&G should ship soap and Wal-Mart would ship the money. The teams began to analyze the process from beginning to end. They discovered that Wal-Mart stores typically ran out of stock on Pampers so often that one-third of consumers couldn't find the brand when they needed diapers. Sloppy delivery systems were to blame. So they hooked up Wal-Mart stores to P&G's diaper plants via computer. That way the stores got prompt delivery of Pampers whenever they needed it. The replenishment process once took six weeks. It's now instantaneous. P&G shipments match Wal-Mart orders 75 percent of the time, whereas industrywide P&G delivered only 52 percent of its shipments on time and without error, according to its 1990–91 estimates.[30] Inside the company, CEO Ed Artzt has groused that the sloppy rate is costing P&G millions of dollars. He wants the fulfillment rate to climb to 90 percent by 1994.

Because of the computer hookup, P&G can find out how every one of its products is selling in every Wal-Mart store on a daily basis. That helps test market new products and give immediate results.

After prodding by Billingsley and Pritchett, Walton invited Smale and his wife, Phyllis, to Bentonville for dinner and a trip to a Saturday morning meeting at Wal-Mart. The raucous gathering came as a surprise to the staid Smale. In typical P&G fashion, Smale asked to review an agenda prior to the meeting. Walton replied, "What agenda?"

When the Smales returned the invitation to have the Waltons visit them in Cincinnati, Pritchett sensed problems. He was excluded from the dinner. "That's when I knew I was in deep shit," he said. He had been pushing for too much change too fast. "Lou was too charismatic," said one former associate. "So they shot him down."

Smale didn't agree with Pritchett's emphasis on people rather than the process. Nor did he see a need to change the reward systems that emphasized increased volume at the expense of customer satisfaction. With Wal-Mart, the CEO wasn't thrilled with the notion of assigning a full-time team to service one account, and initially he balked at the idea of sending the team to live in Arkansas to be closer to the customer. "This was a bargain at any price," Pritchett still insists.

The tension and stress of being a change agent in a conservative company finally got to him. One morning his wife found him unconscious in the bathroom. Pritchett had lost four pints of blood from a bleeding ulcer. He was hospitalized and missed three months of work. "I had been killing myself," he said.

When Pritchett returned to the job, senior management suggested he become president of P&G's Canadian operations. He refused because there was too much work to be done in sales. This angered Ed Artzt, who had respected his work in the Philippines. Meanwhile, Smale wanted him out of the top sales job; he'd offended too many other vice presidents. In February 1988 he was named vice president of customer development efforts. "Boat rockers, mavericks, change agents, and plain old employees who try to tell management what they don't want to hear are rarely welcome within the corporate bosom," said Pritchett, who retired sixteen months later. "I was burned out trying to break traditions."

Colleagues, as well as leading retail executives, say the company's efforts to work with customers has regressed since Pritchett left P&G. Both Smale and his successor, Artzt, groom general managers from the advertising ranks, so the sales force doesn't carry much clout. "Lou was the only guy who had the guts to stand up and say the emperor had no clothes," said one fellow P&G sales manager. "For that, he was executed." His allies, Laco and Pepper, lost their influence too. Laco retired, and Pepper was bypassed for the CEO job. "No one on the eleventh floor gets out anymore," said one former officer. "When they do, they don't want to hear complaints." One leading wholesaler said, "I stopped being a Procter basher for a few years. Not anymore."[31]

Pritchett now lectures to other manufacturers who see the impact of a retailer backlash against P&G. More than ever, P&G is beating up customers, which it blames for the mayhem in the marketplace. Retailers have their own problems, exacerbated by

P&G's stubborn policies. Grocers' profit margins are less than 5 percent. Buyouts and mergers of the 1980s left many deep in debt. So promotion money from manufacturers has helped ease short-term money crunches. Some estimates note that forward buying accounted for half of the total goods in distribution. [32]

P&G doesn't like wild price swings from promotions because they erode brand loyalty. Consumers have a set of several brands that they will buy, depending on what is on sale in a given week. One P&G estimate showed that 33 percent of every promotional dollar goes to the consumer, 33 percent goes to retail profits, and the rest is lost to inefficiency. "That scares us," said Dean Skadberg, director of industry affairs at P&G. [33]

Diverting of goods really aggravates P&G. One major midwestern wholesaler discovered a $100,000 shipment of Folgers coffee that came back into the warehouse after it had been sold six months earlier. It had changed hands about ten times, with the price marked up a bit more at each stop, before being returned to its original buyer. P&G sold one buyer millions of dollars' worth of health and beauty care products for export to Russia. P&G offered a good price to the buyer, figuring that it would help establish its brands in that new market. But the company began to notice that U.S. sales volume in that category was slipping. When the problem was investigated, the company discovered that the goods were being sold to U.S. stores instead. [34]

To stop some of the pricing games, P&G decided in late 1991 to use an everyday low price on some brands. The decision was inspired by the success of Wal-Mart stores, which follow the low-price strategy. The idea has some merit, but retailers and wholesalers say P&G never considered how they would adjust to the drastic cutbacks in promotional spending. "P&G's attitude is retailers will have to make their profits in a different manner," said one company sales manager.

One retailing CEO compares P&G's tactics on pricing change to another surprise attack. "There was zero warning," he said. "Now I know how the Hawaiians must've felt when Pearl

Harbor was bombed." His company, one of the largest in the grocery business, cut back on P&G products by 10 percent following P&G's announcement. His orders from Unilever are up 12 percent. At Vons' supermarkets, about thirteen items were cut, and the store suspended its merchandising of other P&G brands for several months. Safeway and other supermarkets also bumped P&G brands from the shelves. "We can't get rid of Tide, but we've done away with a lot of the different sizes" and slower-moving products, said a wholesaler who supplies more than 300 stores. Competitors such as Kimberly-Clark are ready with promotions to get space that normally went to P&G brands.

Upscale grocers, which feature delis, florist shops, and other services, are especially pinched because their costs are higher than those of discount stores. Smaller stores, such as Big Y Foods, a Springfield, Massachusetts, grocery chain, try to tailor promotions and shelf offerings to individual markets. But P&G is becoming more rigid about its product offerings. For instance, some of the chain's stores sell more liquid detergents than powders, depending on the hardness of the local water. But P&G is militant about sticking to its canned programs. "P&G's response is take it or leave it," said Claire D'Amour, vice president at Big Y. "P&G wants to control our shelves." In 1992 the thirty-store chain cut some P&G brands, including detergents, in favor of competing brands and private-label goods.[35] Other grocers have followed the lead, and the long-term threat to P&G's dominance is real.

What's especially irritating to retailers is P&G's indecision about the pricing plan. The company had agreements with some customers to ease the plan in slowly. But the company backed out of those deals, causing a huge uproar in the industry. "They lost credibility and trust and reversed what they did a few years ago," said one industry executive. Besides, grocers note that P&G was the one that created this monster in the first place. "They told us what to put on sale and offered promotions to do it," D'Amour said. Buyers predict that P&G will change its sales rules again, simply because the company can't figure out how to deal with retailers effectively. "We get on their bandwagon, then they switch it," D'Amour said.

Even senior sales managers inside P&G concede that the company is losing clout. "The trade is now powerful enough to make us fail," said one veteran sales manager. "It's a myth that P&G is indestructible."[36] Lewis G. Schaeneman, chairman and CEO of the grocery chain Stop & Shop, was more direct in his remarks about P&G's tactics: "We think dictators will end up where most dictators end up—in trouble."[37] P&G salesmen refer to his chain as "Stop & Rob."

Inside the company, sales managers weren't briefed on how to deal with questions from retailers. "We ended up doing a lot of damage control," one salesman said. Durk Jager, executive vice president in charge of the U.S. business, told the sales force that he could hire people at half their salaries and get them to sell plenty if they didn't like the new strategy. "We are the whipping boys," said one sales manager.

P&G is back to the advertising-driven strategy. Jager and CEO Artzt believe anyone can sell goods with $10-per-case promotions and allowances. "They want to rely more on new products and advertising instead of sales," said one salesman. Sales reps say they try to keep the peace on the front lines. But customers like Safeway aren't easily appeased. During 1992, Peter Magowan, then CEO of Safeway, wouldn't "even return calls from Jager," said one salesman.[38]

P&G hasn't completely abandoned its deal making to enhance volume, especially in the tight U.S. economy. In some cases, P&G sales representatives gave preferential deals to some retailers, which violates federal laws on equal treatment for competing customers. An audit of P&G's paper division, conducted in early 1992, showed that the sales force routinely gave special allowances to customers to help build volume. A common deal was to add a "drop ship" allowance to an order. That allowance is given to those customers who take delivery directly at the store instead of the warehouse. The advantage for P&G is that those shipments come in a minimum of 100 cases, guaranteeing that it gets more of its product in the store. But the audit showed that some customers received drop ships on the bulk of their orders, even though most of the goods were going to warehouses, according to insiders familiar with the audit. "People with volume problems broke the rules," said one sales manager. P&G wrote off about $250,000 for just one customer with such deals. That wasn't even the biggest one, and insiders said the total write-offs amounted to "tens of millions of dollars." In some cases P&G sales reps got kickbacks from retailers who took the deals.

P&G officials ignored the problem until it got out of hand, and the audit showed how serious the deal making had become. Several dozen sales representatives were fired. But the front-line sales force is angry that the head sales officials weren't punished. "When they started hunting scalps, they hunted the Indians and the midlevel chiefs," said one veteran sales manager. "But the commanders are responsible."

Senior sales officials considered asking the retail customers for some of the money back, even though "they did exactly what we told them to do," said one sales official. "We were one hundred percent at fault."[39] A P&G spokesman said the company's programs with retailers "are structured carefully to ensure they are in compliance with all laws, including the Robinson-Patman Act."

Many retailers and wholesalers are suspicious that P&G's deal making is widespread and that it gives Wal-Mart preferential treatment whenever possible. "We get around the Robinson Patman laws by calling everything a test," said one ex-sales manager. "Half of Procter's business is from these tests. And the lawyers look the other way. Customers like Wal-Mart have more tests than Carter has pills."[40] He recalled writing off $2 million in deductions on the Wal-Mart account, which had accumulated from giving the discount chain a break on prices to correct "mistakes" on invoices. "We made presentations about how this old Yankee company treated customers fairly," he said. "But P&G cheats and helps Wal-Mart at every corner." At times, the incestuous relationship extends beyond the sale of soap. One manager recalled that his boss at P&G suggested he apply to Sam Walton's bank for a "preferential mortgage" on a house in Arkansas. "This is a billion-dollar customer, and they want me to be beholden to him for a mortgage?" he asked incredulously. Others have questioned the deals Wal-Mart receives, but P&G officials defend them, saying Wal-Mart gets breaks because of efficiencies in the delivery system.

P&G and Wal-Mart do need each other, especially as the discounter expands into more club stores and groceries. Pritchett figures Wal-Mart will hit $100 billion in sales by the turn of the century. The chain is growing in new states, as well as Puerto Rico and Mexico. Wal-Mart plans to build thirty warehouse clubs and combination grocery and discount stores in Mexico by the end of 1993.[41]

If measured by sales, Procter will be less than half of Wal-Mart's size by the year 2000. "Wal-Mart will have the power to market whatever the hell they want to," Pritchett said. And other retailers will continue to consolidate. P&G used to do half its business with approximately two hundred accounts. Now fewer than a dozen control 85 percent of the business.

Chains like Wal-Mart are getting more information more quickly because of improved technology. In some stores, consumers' movements are tracked with special devices on the shopping carts. That tells Wal-Mart a great deal about shopping habits. In the future that information could help the retailer tailor a sales pitch to each consumer as he or she walks through a store. "The technology payday has just started," said Wal-Mart CEO Glass.

Wal-Mart has a growing customer base that relies more on information from the retailer and less from television ads. Shoppers aren't watching network television as much as they used to or shopping solely for brand names advertised by companies like P&G. This fact can become a powerful tool, especially as Wal-Mart expands into its own Sam's American Choice product lines to compete with national brands. The company was confident enough to replace six-packs of Coke and Pepsi with Sam's cola, and it is eliminating other products based on scanner data that show which brands aren't moving. Other retailers are doing the same. Some categories—canned fruits and vegetables, for example—are now largely private label. Inside the Wal-Mart in State College, Pennsylvania, Sam's coffee creamer sells for $1.38, as opposed to $1.97 for Coffee-mate. "It's the value-driven consumer who is not going to be as brand loyal as she was in the past," Glass said. "When I was a young man starting in the retailing business, it was tremendously important where you bought an item. But attitudes have changed. Now it is socially acceptable to talk about what you paid for a product, not where you bought it."

Wal-Mart's brands are selling well and will be expanded whenever "we feel like national brands have become very difficult to work with or they don't represent a value anymore," Glass said. But he quips that Wal-Mart is still learning: "We don't know enough about marketing to wad a shotgun." [42] The numbers suggest otherwise. Its operating costs as a percentage of sales are about 15 percent to 17 percent, compared to 28 percent at K mart and 32 percent at Sears. [43]

P&G insiders are bracing for the time when Wal-Mart begins to bump even the big brands from its shelves. Some suggest that P&G will have to start making private-label goods to supply the likes of Wal-Mart if it wants to keep up with the trend.

The growing power of the chain is one reason that senior management has gutted the partnership programs, merely maintaining the bare bones to keep it alive. "P&G gets three dollars of results for every dollar it invests, but we still have to beg for the next dollar to invest," said one insider familiar with the Wal-Mart team. He compares it to asking the research department to develop revolutionary products while at the same time chastising scientists for "how many test tubes they broke each week."[44]

The reason is fear about the future. "P&G is beginning to see the long-term implications of what they've done," said Carl Steidtmann, chief economist at Management Horizons, a division of Price Waterhouse. "It's like Dr. Frankenstein. They've created a retailing monster."

The P&Gers who helped build the team have either quit the company or have seen their careers derailed. Throughout sales, management continually changes course. "We've cut the heart out of the sales organization," said one senior company official. Despite the high volume and profits generated by the Wal-Mart team, its leader, Tom Muccio, wasn't among the scores named vice presidents, even though he runs the company's biggest single account. "The culture of the company doesn't recognize them," said one manager. That's because the two leaders of the company, Artzt and Jager, consider it "just another little sales program." Insiders figure they've got about two years to make fundamental changes in the relations with retailers, or the company will be at a competitive disadvantage to companies like Unilever.

Meanwhile, P&G is repeating its mistakes of the 1970s and 1980s. Since the company is lagging in breakthrough products, it focuses on repackaging products or changing flavors and scents to build volume. Senior management tells retailers that P&G is scaling down on the number of offerings that clutter shelves, but its practices suggest otherwise. Consider Cheer laundry detergent, available in unscented, concentrated, and other varieties, even though it's a second-tier detergent behind Tide and competing Unilever brands.

Some chains are fighting back. Publix in Florida reduced the number of paper suppliers it uses for its entire aisle of napkins, towels, and tissue. That way, Publix figures it can compete more with the growing number of club and warehouse stores, which are growing despite the limited variety they offer.[45] "Retailers are waking up," said Claire D'Amour of Big Y. "We don't have to put up with this anymore."[46]

9
Pampering
the World

In Seoul's Apkujong neighborhood, the sparkling Galleria department store has replaced *pojangmacha*, the traditional street vendors. Locals call this South Korea's version of Beverly Hills' Rodeo Drive. Gucci handbags, Chanel perfumes, and Tiffany jewelry are de rigueur.

Inside the Galleria, women search the shelves for everything from squid to shoes. "Merchandising ladies" stand at each grocery aisle offering mothers a 10-percent discount to try Huggies Baby Steps, the newest diapers by Yuhan-Kimberly, a Korean pharmaceutical company's joint venture with Kimberly-Clark. The aisles are well stocked with other Yuhan-Kimberly goods: Kleenex facial tissues, paper towels, and Kotex feminine pads.

Oho Kyung Sook picks up packages of Huggies and Pampers, Procter & Gamble's brand, for her infant son and tosses them into the cart with bananas and potato chips. She is constantly looking for a better diaper because "my baby is important." She is likely to stop buying Pampers because she prefers Yuhan-Kimberly's products. "They have been in the market a long time," she explains. "They are famous to me."

Other shoppers share her interest. The paper goods aisle doesn't give much space to P&G. A handful of its products are stashed beside the Purina Cat Chow. Yuhan-Kimberly sales in the store are 20 million *won* a month, about double the 1991 monthly sales, thanks to more new products. [1]

Winning a diaper sale in South Korea is important. The country's 44 million consumers are hungry for disposable goods such as diapers. Sales of the product exploded to $163 million in 1992, from $22 million in 1987. And that's with just 25 percent market penetration, so more growth is certain as more parents switch from cloth diapers. Yuhan-Kimberly, a twenty-year-old joint venture, owns 50 percent of the market. P&G's Pampers ranks a distant third with just 11 percent. The pattern is similar in feminine pads: Yuhan-Kimberly has 42 percent versus P&G's 18 percent share. [2]

Part of P&G's problems stem from a failed joint venture with its Korean partner, STC, a diversified conglomerate. The experiment seemed as disposable as its goods. It lasted only three years and racked up losses estimated at 34 billion *won* ($44.2 million) and debt of $62 million. [3] "I never got the impression that P&G was interested in working with joint venture partners," said one Korean executive. "They use them and discard them." Other joint ventures around the world have collapsed because P&G "is way too strict," said a twenty-year veteran of the paper business. "It's their way or no way." Now P&G is investing in its own paper mill to make diapers in Korea, but its competitors aren't likely to forfeit much of this market. [4]

In the race to globalize, it's clear that P&G is repeating the tactics that helped it capture U.S. cupboards forty years ago. While it teaches the world to diaper its babies, wash its laundry, and brush its teeth, it is also imposing the rigid Cincinnati culture and pervasive ways on households from Cairo to Caracas. The company's bully tactics with consumers, suppliers, retailers, and unions are helping it crack even the toughest markets, such as China. P&G's staple advertising, built on guilt about whiteness of shirts and freshness of breath, manipulates Third World consumers, who are often illiterate. Such tactics are often more overt in countries where there is little concern for truth in advertising. [5]

P&G's global strategy is also shaped by the bloodbath it

suffered in Japan, where it was clobbered by archrival Kao Corporation and others. The twenty-year history in that country shows how far P&G will go to succeed. After vicious price wars, union clashes, and more than $200 million in losses, P&G is now making money in Japan. It even parlayed its loss into tax breaks back home, giving it one of the largest tax breaks in U.S. history. [6]

Succeeding in the Far East and other new markets is crucial because Kao and other companies are moving into U.S. and additional key markets. Moreover, what happens in Korea and other new frontiers will make or break P&G because its traditional strongholds in detergents and diapers are under siege by Kimberly-Clark and others. Breakthrough products are scarce and most of P&G's new growth has come from acquisitions and international expansion, which mask problems at its core. P&G market shares have dropped in all its key categories since the mid-1980s. [7]

It's been hard for P&G to adjust to the new reality that comes with tougher competition. This was a company built on products that weren't easily matched by competitors. Tide detergent has been called "the stud horse" that paid for many other P&G brands. Pampers disposable diapers enjoyed similar success until the early 1980s. Both products built up a war chest with which P&G could then acquire drug and cosmetic companies such as Richardson-Vicks and Noxell to make up for its own shortcomings. But as the U.S. markets have grown more competitive, P&G also had to diversify into new areas around the globe. Vicks and other acquired companies gave it access to foreign markets, but if it stumbles in foreign markets, there aren't many ways left to cover up P&G's problems.

P&G's international business took decades to develop. Its first venture outside the States was a plant in Canada in 1915 and the purchase of a small English soap company in 1930. Five years later P&G bought a company in the Philippines, a source of raw materials for its oil business. After World War II it moved into Mexico, Venezuela, France, and Belgium, among other countries. [8]

Walter Lingle was the company's first international manager, in 1945. By 1969 international sales accounted for only 1 percent of the company's total business. "We didn't commit our best people to the international business," Lingle said. "In fact, there was a general belief that anybody sent to international couldn't make it in the U.S. That's one reason I was hesitant to go."

P&G had its share of problems as it tried to understand foreign governments. In Cuba P&G couldn't fire anyone without the permission of the Minister of Labor. When a salesman was suspected of falsifying his daily reports, P&G collected affidavits from retailers to prove he was cheating the company, but the government encouraged shopkeepers to recant. After four months in court, P&G was allowed to fire the man. But when Fidel Castro seized power in 1959, his new labor minister ordered P&G to rehire the salesman with seven years of back wages. "We had to do it," Lingle said. In 1961 Castro expropriated the P&G plant in Cuba. P&G estimates it lost $4 billion on the plant, Lingle said. [9]

The importance of international markets grew in the late 1970s and 1980s as U.S. markets began to stall. In 1985 P&G saw earnings plunge nearly 30 percent, the biggest decline in thirty-seven years, because competitors such as Colgate and Kimberly-Clark moved faster in launching new products. P&G managers had defected to other companies, taking their marketing expertise with them. [10]

The company has never really recovered. P&G spends 3 percent of sales on research, but there isn't much coming from the investment. Much of its gains in the 1980s came from pricing, as managers tried to earn bonuses based on net profits. In addition, private-label goods won more share as consumers opted for lower-priced products. [11]

P&G has lost its edge in numerous key markets. Lever 2000 bar soap helped Lever Bros. capture 31.5 percent of the $1.6 billion market, while P&G's share has fallen to a historic low of 30.5 percent for Ivory, Camay, and Safeguard. Those three used to control more than half the category. "It's an indication that Procter can be beaten—and we beat them," said Greg Creed, a Lever manager. P&G insiders say the division was sacrificed to fuel other projects. "Now we're scrambling to protect what's left," said one sales manager. That's especially troubling to veteran P&Gers because P&G is often dubbed "the house that Ivory built," and Camay launched the successful brand-management plan. [12]

The toothpaste wars have intensified as Colgate CEO Reuben Mark pushed for more global sales. Worldwide sales of the brand are about 43 percent of the market, up from 29 percent a decade ago. Unlike P&G, Colgate was pressured to fix its problems after a takeover scare by Sir James Goldsmith. The British financier was buying up companies he considered poorly run. Mark, a Harvard graduate who turned down a job at P&G, moved faster than P&G, with innovations such as toothpaste in a pump. [13]

In diapers, Kimberly-Clark snuck up on P&G with a contoured, refastenable diaper called Huggies. P&G's once dominant 70 percent share with Pampers and Luvs has eroded, and Kimberly-Clark's sole brand now claims more than 30 percent. Supermarkets often give preference to Huggies rather than the two P&G brands to save on space. Kimberly-Clark also edged out P&G with disposable training pants. Its Huggies Pull Ups grew into a $300-million market just months after they were launched in 1990. "Huggies gave our company a whole lot of confidence," said Tom Newby, who has worked at both P&G and Kimberly-Clark. "It showed us we could run with the big boys. It shocked them." [14]

Elsewhere, P&G has stalled as smaller companies such as

Helene Curtis have nibbled away at shampoo sales. A great deal of its its food-and-beverage business research has been gutted because olestra, the fat substitute, received so much attention in the effort to garner government approval to take it to market. [15]

The marketplace is beginning to reflect the lack of success in the labs. One internal estimate said only two of eighteen recent test markets of products were successful. "We're not producing products that provide meaningful benefits to consumers," said one senior researcher. "The marketing people take anything and make a euphoric introduction, and two years later it flops. That's what killed us. And we're not out of the woods yet." [16]

A sluggish U.S. economy only compounds these problems. P&G CEO Artzt cautioned shareholders at the fall 1992 meeting that the company was feeling the squeeze. In the early 1980s the economy was weak, just as in the early 1990s. But, said Artzt, the "big difference in the U.S. then versus now was that things were getting better. We're not seeing that here yet. The same is true in our major international markets." [17]

Skepticism abounds over P&G's acquisitions of cosmetics, because the company isn't agile when it tries to sell imagery rather than product performance. "There's more sizzle than steak," said Morgan Hunter, a retired P&G officer. "They're in way over their heads. It will be a shocker to see Procter become successful in the cosmetics business without a material change." What's more, Kao and other competitors have devoted more research money to cosmetics, which offer higher profit margins than detergents or diapers. "We're not afraid of P&G," said Yoshio Maruta, Kao's chairman. "We just ignore them." [18] In the late 1980s, Kao bought the Andrew Jergens Company, based in P&G's hometown of Cincinnati, and opened a research center to broaden its product line. Shiseido, another Japanese powerhouse, invested $29 million to form an Institute for Advanced Skin Research and gave another $85 million to support Harvard's Research Center for Skin Biology. [19]

* * *

P&G has reason to worry about the likes of Kao and Shisedo, given its twenty-year battle to start a business in Japan. A look at its history there provides a glimpse at what the future may hold around the globe. Indeed, Harvard Business School offers a case study of P&G's Japan debacle as a lesson for future business leaders on the pitfalls of globalization. [20]

Japan is the second largest consumer market in the world. Consumers are well educated and have money to spend. In many product categories, including diapers, feminine napkins, and hair care, the Japanese use twice as many products as Americans and Europeans. Getting into Japan wasn't easy. In the early 1970s, when Howard Morgens was CEO, many of the company's senior management scoffed at the idea of entering the market. Even Chairman Neil McElroy was skeptical. "He remembered going there in the 1950s and not having a pleasant experience," said Ed Shutt, a retired P&G vice president. But Morgens disagreed. "We're gonna fight the Japanese all over the world, so we just better get in there," he said. He was a board member at General Motors and saw what the Japanese were doing to U.S. auto makers. He feared the same would eventually happen to P&G. [21]

P&G wanted as much equity as possible in any joint venture. Executives talked to officials at Kao and Lion, among other Japanese companies, but they didn't want to do business with P&G. After meetings with the prime minister and other officials, P&G agreed in 1972 to form a joint venture with Nippon Sunhome, a group of soap companies that hadn't been successful against Kao and Lion. Initially, the Japanese business community was extremely apprehensive about P&G. [22]

P&G's first products were Camay and Cheer, and there were problems from the start. Cheer didn't produce many suds if fabric softener was added to the water. [23]

Once that glitch was resolved, the company began to build the business. Its 1977 annual report noted that Cheer was a market leader. Kao and Lion began to compete more aggressively. P&G responded by cutting retail prices in half, a tactic that drew criticism from Kao's president. According to the Harvard case study, in August 1978 two boxes of Cheer sold for 555 yen, as compared to 800 to 850 yen suggested retail price for one box. The detergent volume helped P&G break even in fiscal 1978–79.

Lion countered with Top detergent, which contained cleaning enzymes. It quickly gained more than 19 percent of the market, bumping Cheer from its dominant share. Kao's new Wonderful brand grabbed about 9 percent of the market. P&G cut prices again, even though a second oil shortage pushed raw material costs higher. Kao and Lion didn't lower prices. Eventually P&G had to raise its prices, but the competition didn't budge. There were no price increases in detergents for several years.[24]

Meanwhile, P&G decided to launch Pampers diapers in the market. Free samples were delivered to maternity wards. P&G hired drivers to distribute diapers in apartment buildings; mothers could get Pampers by tying a cloth diaper to their balcony. The disposables market grew to 10 percent of diaper changes, up from just 2 percent. But at about $50 a month, they were too pricey for most mothers.

Pampers were also too thick and bulky. Japanese mothers tend to change their baby's diapers about fourteen times a day, more than twice as often as Americans.[25] They wanted a thinner diaper that was easier to store and use. Uni-Charm, another Japanese manufacturer, responded with a superabsorbent thin diaper called Moony. It gained 23 percent of the market, taking sales away from Pampers, even though Moony was 40 percent more expensive.[26] "It was clear that we were out of the ball game," said Ed Artzt, then president of P&G International.[27]

Inside the company, there were problems between P&G and its Japanese partners. Sunhome couldn't afford to spend as much as P&G. To end the dispute, P&G bought out the joint venture. P&G was accused of taking advantage of the Japanese company. [28] Dumping Sunhome didn't endear P&G to the retail trade. With a small sales force of 150 people to handle 400 primary and 2,000 secondary wholesalers, P&G products had trouble gaining wide distribution. Wholesalers are important because they cover 65 percent of all retailers. And Japanese companies such as Kao enjoyed better relations with the trade, in part because Kao sold through its own 125 direct sales units. It also developed an automated distribution center that reduced the time needed to fill orders. [29]

Another problem was pricing. P&G's strength in the United States was moving goods with promotions. This didn't work in Japan because they cut into wholesalers' profits. "We had to learn different selling methods," Ed Shutt said. P&G tried to focus on a handful of wholesalers and build better relations with the large supermarket chains. [30]

Advertising presented yet another dilemma. Traditional side-by-side product demonstration of whiter shirts and socks don't appeal to the Japanese, who prefer harmony and polite business dealings. P&G also fumbled because it didn't understand basic habits and values of the Japanese. For instance, the ad campaign for all-temperature Cheer assumed that Japanese women, like Americans, wash clothes in different temperatures. The pitch was irrelevant, for Japanese women do the laundry in tap water or leftover bathwater.

P&G foolhardily recycled U.S. and European advertising strategies. A Camay campaign pitched the soap as making women more attractive to men, a common theme in P&G advertising. The ad showed a Japanese man walking into the bathroom while his wife sat in the tub. Japanese women were offended by the ad because it is "bad manners for a husband to impose on his wife's privacy while she is bathing," explained Mia Ishiguro, who worked on Camay in Japan. "Our consumers resented the breach of good manners and the overt chauvinism of the situation." The campaign was later changed to show European women in a Western-style bath, but P&G never changed the ad's chauvinistic overtones. [31]

With all its troubles in pricing, distribution, and marketing, P&G was getting hammered by Kao and Lion. By 1983 the company had $250 million in operating losses on annual sales of $120 million. Cheer ranked number four in the market behind Japanese brands. One problem was the shift to no-phosphate detergents, which Japanese companies had introduced before P&G. Retailers bumped Cheer from the shelves. Pampers, too, lost its edge to Moony and other contoured, superabsorbent diapers. "You might say we were dead, but we didn't know it," Artzt said. [32]

Artzt changed the management of the Japanese business. He recruited Durk Jager to be advertising manager and work for Russell Marsden, the country manager. Employee morale was low, especially among Japanese managers. In addition to poor sales, P&G's brand-management system conflicted with the Japanese tradition of earning jobs by seniority and age. Harvard's case study said Japanese managers in their twenties were put in brand-management jobs, so they were treated as "semi*gaijins*" (semiforeigners) by other Japanese at P&G. [33]

Shortly after Artzt took over the international post, he began to clean house. The old Japanese company was liquidated and P&G Far East was formed, a move that also yielded a sizable tax break back home. Normally, when a company invests in a subsidiary, it's like buying stock in another company. If the company is profitable, dividends are paid, but if it goes out of business, the investor suffers a loss. P&G argued that the losses were financed by the U.S. operation, so the Internal Revenue Service allowed it to take about $240 million in tax deductions. "It was a huge tax scam," said Bill Morgan, who ran the finance department in Japan for several years. "It was all hush-hush." He said it was the largest tax deduction ever for a U.S. business. The IRS won't comment, citing confidentiality rules on disclosing taxpayer information. [34]

In Cincinnati, P&G senior management was divided on what to do about Japan. The U.S. business was spending heavily to expand into new categories, and some didn't want to pour any more money into Japan. But the board decided P&G should stay. P&G stepped up efforts to improve its detergent and diapers. In 1984 the unfitted Pampers had been replaced with a tailored, superabsorbent product. The brand's share had dropped to 22 percent from 45 percent a year earlier, while Japanese brands continued to move ahead of Pampers. Despite this refinement, by early 1985 P&G's business in Japan was smaller than in 1973. The company's diaper market share dropped as low as 6 percent in 1985. Artzt describes the experience as humiliating, especially when Japanese executives would insult and taunt P&G as if "we were a bunch of meatballs. . . . There was a sense that the great Procter & Gamble Company wasn't so great when it got into Japan," he said. [35]

P&G faced yet another problem when Marsden had a stroke and had to take early retirement. Artzt considered running the business himself but instead appointed Jager as general manager of the country. He met with Jager each quarter and reported to the board monthly on the Japanese problems.

Jager, determined to stabilize P&G's listing Japanese operation, studied Japanese at night school. He was the opposite of the quiet Marsden. Jager was known as "crazy man Durk" because he was the antithesis of the typically diplomatic Japanese managers. [36] "He was the first person at Procter I was afraid of," said Morgan, the finance manager. He and others found their careers derailed because Jager surrounded himself with only a handful of confidants. Everyone else was shunned. Morgan discovered that he was being replaced when a new organizational chart was passed around the table at the company's annual meeting in Hawaii. "Needless to say, I hadn't been consulted," he said. A couple of weeks passed before he was officially told that it was time to return to the States. The reason was that Jager wanted to promote someone else into his key finance job, even though Morgan's performance reviews were always excellent. The company shuttled him between various positions for several years before he accepted a buyout package. "I was told I made an enemy of Jager," he said, although no one ever explained why. [37]

To turn around the business, Jager and Artzt came up with an aggressive new business plan they called *Ichidai Hiyaku*, or "great leap forward." [38] P & G eavesdropped on consumers to learn more about their habits. Researchers videotaped women changing diapers and discovered the need for smaller diapers, which convinced the company to upgrade its diaper plants around the world to produce thinner, superabsorbent diapers. It spent $500 million to introduce Ultra Pampers, the first superabsorbent diaper in the United States.

Market research also showed that it had to launch a public relations campaign to get the P&G name linked with its brands, an unheard-of practice at P&G. Traditionally, each brand stands on its own without the company name. That way, if consumers grow disenchanted with one product, they don't automatically drop other P&G brands. But according to Japanese research, up to 20 percent of consumers purchased a product based on the company name, not just the brand name. So the letters *P&G* began appearing on packages and in ads. The normally secretive company even held press conferences and open houses. P&G stock was added to the Tokyo stock exchange, and Jager offered regular updates to the media.

New problems arose for the growing company. Jager cut 1,500 wholesalers and concentrated P&G's business with fifty wholesalers. Plant management was cut. Harvard's case study said: "Only one-third of the managers held the same job they had had at the beginning of *Ichidai Hiyaku*." And P&G incurred the wrath of organized labor when it retrenched at certain plants. [39] One incident involved P&G's plans to close an old Richardson-Vicks plant in Suzuka, about 180 miles south of Tokyo. The plant made Clearasil Face Wash, Vicks cough syrup, and cough drops. P&G decided it would instead make the products offshore or license production to other Japanese firms. The company wanted to sell the plant and use the proceeds to purchase land for its new technical center.

A local union filed a lawsuit demanding reinstatement for the plant's sixty-five workers. The union considered the shutdown and offer of job transfers unfair labor practices. Shinji Watanabe, a lawyer who represented the union, said, "The decision, which ignored advice from the public authorities and badly cornered the employees, goes against prevailing labor-management practices in Japan." The union was accused of having Communist ties and plots to sabotage P&G. Angry workers picketed P&G's office building.

Some inside P&G were troubled by the closing because P&G had vowed that it wouldn't disrupt Vicks when it purchased the company in 1985. For more than two decades, the Suzuka plant had been the livelihood of many rural residents, and Vicks had pledged lifetime employment to those workers who had been displaced from their farms when the plant was built. The battle further soiled P&G's reputation among the Japanese. And it took P&G until 1992 to close the plant.

Others inside the old Vicks company were forced out of jobs. Nearly all of the fifty salespeople in Vicks's Japanese operations left the company. Some had been assigned to remote outposts because P&Gers from Cincinnati figured they knew more about selling than their Japanese counterparts. Sales of the Vicks line suffered. Similarly, P&G cut many of the Max Factor's Japanese employees after that product line was acquired in 1991.[40]

Most estimate Japan will surpass Germany as P&G's largest international market. But P&G continues to struggle there. Management turnover continues to be a problem. And Kao and others are aggressive in new product development. One strong challenge came when Kao developed the technology for a superconcentrated detergent called Attack. Within six months of its spring 1987 launch, Kao cornered 17 percent of the market with the compact brand. P&G responded with its own superconcentrates around the world, beating Kao in many markets. Likewise, P&G's introduction of its two-in-one shampoo and conditioner, Rejoy, was followed within four months by Kao and Lion. By comparison, the same product in the United States, called Pert Plus, didn't face serious competition for four years. [41]

Despite what it learned in Japan, P&G seems to be making some of the same blunders as it expands into the rest of the Far East. This is evident in South Korea, the second largest Asian consumer market.

In many ways South Korea is reminiscent of the United States in the 1950s and 1960s. Households are expanding and consumers are buying more disposable goods. New apartment villages are sprouting up throughout the capital of Seoul and surrounding towns. The smell of asphalt reminds visitors of progress, while peddlers of tripe stew offer a taste of simpler times. A Kodak forty-five-minute photo-processing lab stands next to a woman selling bananas from her canvas mat on the sidewalk. Ceramic pots of a spicy dish called *kimchi* dot the balconies of modern buildings. Tractor-trailers travel alongside *sonsoola*, or pushcarts, and women balancing parcels on their heads and carrying babies on their backs. [42]

This is a country that was repressed by military regimes and dictators for decades, so its markets and citizens are now eager for the liberalization democracy brings. Average urban household income is about $12,400, and the number of two-income families is rising. Disposable income has climbed 141 percent since 1986. [43]

The market is also seen as a springboard into China and the eastern portion of the former Soviet Union. Here U.S. companies have the rare chance to get a jump on their Japanese counterparts. Koreans still harbor deep resentment toward the Japanese, who occupied their country from 1910 to 1945. During World War II Koreans were drafted to fight in Japan's army. Nearly fifty years later, many Japanese goods are banned from the market. "Koreans don't want the Japanese buying the peninsula like a condo. U.S. companies should take advantage of this," said one U.S. consultant in Seoul. "There is no other place around the globe like this." [44]

P&G tried to take advantage of the market's growth by forming a a joint venture with STC in 1989 to sell diapers, soap, and toothpaste imports. Its diaper archenemy Kimberly-Clark enjoyed a significant head start, having formed a joint venture with Yuhan in 1970. In a virtual replay of its Japanese experience, P&G's venture was troubled from the start, and it eventually bought out STC's 40 percent stake. [45] Artzt attributed the breakup to the partner's lack of money to expand the business. Others say P&G's ventures fail because it doesn't listen to its local partner, a shortcoming of many U.S. companies. [46]

Now P&G is trying to build the market on its own. It recently received approval to build its own diaper manufacturing plant, but it is struggling to learn this market. Yuhan-Kimberly is considered one of the top ten companies in Korea, with sales of $285 million in 1992. Its success shows how a once sleepy paper company can take on a giant even in the toughest of world markets. [47]

The venture was formed when J. D. Lee, who had worked in paper manufacturing since 1954, saw the need for U.S. technology in the Korean paper market. He brought Kimberly-Clark and Yuhan Pharmaceutical together and runs the company. Their combined investment was $250,000, with the majority ownership going to Kimberly-Clark. Despite its majority interest, the U.S. company put the Yuhan name first in the joint venture company, giving it instant recognition with Korean consumers. P&G, also the majority partner in its venture, put its name first in P&G-STC.

One problem Lee faced was the lack of materials for manufacturing. The venture's first paper machine was made with old gun barrels he'd salvaged after the Korean war. The machine is still in use at the company's original plant in Anyang. [48]

There the company began production with Kotex feminine pads and Kleenex facial tissues. Those two brands became generic words in Korean. Popee bathroom tissue, priced lower than traditional U.S. brands, was added in 1974 and became the national leader in Korea. It's not as soft as most U.S. products, but it was key to developing a market where people used newspapers in the bathroom for more than reading. Even now, only 68 percent of the market uses tissues. But sales are growing. By 1992 the market stood at nearly $300 million, up from $175 million five years earlier.

Yuhan-Kimberly used a similar approach to develop the disposable diaper market. Between 600,000 and 700,000 babies are born each year in Korea. Mothers used cloth diapers until the company introduced its first diaper, Kleen Bebe, in 1980. The diaper is a basic rectangular pad of pulp fluff with a plastic backing. Rubber bands or plastic pants are used to hold the diaper in place rather than tape fasteners. It sells for about 12 cents each. In 1983 the company introduced its panty-shaped diapers, Huggies, to keep up with more affluent consumers willing to spend about 29 cents per diaper. At the time, no one competed for the market, as Huggies was the first superabsorbent product in Korea.

The company still saw a need for an intermediate product for parents who didn't want to spend as much for Huggies but wanted something better than the plain pad. The solution was Kimbies, a contoured diaper that has all the features of Huggies except the plastic tapes. Instead, a reusable belt holds the diaper in place, which reduces the price to about 19 cents per diaper. It's also sold in the Philippines.

Yuhan-Kimberly has held about 50 percent of the diaper market with its three brands, despite new competition from nine other local and foreign companies that have entered the market in the last ten years. Ssangyong is the second largest seller with its Ultra Cutie and Cutie Slim brands, followed by Pampers.

One of P&G's problems, local managers say, is its lack of

products for various segments of the market. P&G's strategy is to focus on the premium end of the market, but that makes the products too pricey for many shoppers. "In the Philippines, Thailand, Indonesia, and other countries, you really have to have products in both segments," said one competitor. "It's tougher to get market share because the prices are so high."

As the foreign markets develop, Kimberly-Clark exports its better products; for example, Huggies Baby Steps, a series of five diaper sizes tailored for different stages of a baby's life. Likewise, observers expect Kimberly-Clark to introduce its disposable training pants to Asian markets as it pushes for more simultaneous launches of its brands around the world.

The company also upgraded its Kotex and Freedom napkin products to beat P&G's launch of Whisper, the Korean version of the U.S. brand Always. But it still sells budget brands because almost half of Korean women use those products, and Yuhan-Kimberly still leads that market with about 42 percent share.

Besides paper goods, Kimberly-Clark has relied on its Korean partner to test new technologies that can be sold around the world. Its disposable fabrics are often tested in Korea before they are sold in the U.S. Locally, the materials are used for everything from suitcases to roofs in ginseng gardens.

The venture is expanding as it prepares for even more competition from P&G and others. A third paper plant in Taejon will add capacity for various products, an important step because the Korean government continues to liberalize the market. Japanese companies are already forming joint ventures with local firms. Uni-Charm, a Japanese diaper maker, has a partnership with Ssangyong to produce the Ultra Cutie diaper. Shiseido, the cosmetics maker, had a counter in Seoul's Lotte department store just weeks after the Korean government opened the market to foreign cosmetics. Business was brisk despite the expensive price tags: a pink lipstick sells for $20.

U.S. investment in Korea is rising, with $242 million worth of investment from January to September of 1992, up slightly from the same period one year earlier.[49] But companies aren't moving as fast as they should. "The Japanese put both elbows in and are prying it open," said a consultant to U.S. firms. "They're not afraid to spill a few dollars."

P&G isn't breaking into the detergent market yet, largely because of strong local competition from giant Korean conglomerates, or *chaebols*. Lucky-Goldstar Group, for instance, makes everything from detergents to escalators. Ssangyong, besides making diapers, refines oil, builds trucks, and mixes cement. The revenue of the top five *chaebols* (the others are Samsung, Hyundai, and Daewoo), equals 61 percent of Korea's gross national product.[50]

Some of P&G's U.S. competitors are moving in despite the heavy competition. Amway Corp. began detergent sales in Korea in 1991. The company built a plant one hour from Seoul, in Eumsung, to make five different types of detergents. It will soon expand to include food and cosmetics. One reason Amway can compete against local giants is its unique network method of selling through individuals rather than retailers. Its door-to-door sales technique has been a hit in Korea: the company sold more than 30,000 starter kits shortly after it entered the market.[51]

Distribution for companies such as Kimberly-Clark and P&G isn't that easy. Tiny mom-and-pop stores are still the source of goods for many families. But more convenience stores and giant supermarkets are being built alongside new high-rise apartment buildings. Convenience stores, like the family shops, offer little shelf space to manufacturers. At one 7-Eleven in Seoul, only one bag of Pampers is offered for sale on a bottom shelf. Deliveries to the small stores are often made by bicycle, with the rider balancing a six-foot stack of cartons as he weaves through Seoul's congested streets. In some areas of downtown, there are ten lanes of traffic, making it a dangerous ride for the delivery men. Other shops are supplied by a fleet of wholesaler trucks. About 40 percent of deliveries are now direct from manufacturers.

Once the goods are on the shelves, Yuhan-Kimberly has several hundred women employees who walk the store aisles promoting their goods. The company has another advantage over P&G because its products are made locally, not imported. At a Hyundai department store, manager Shin Toski complains that he is often out of Pampers because they are shipped from Canada. "Yuhan-Kimberly is quick to reorder products," he said. "That's a big difference." And the service shows in the shelf space. Huggies commands twice as much space in the paper goods aisle as Pampers. "P&G isn't all that popular with the trade," said one local manager. Yoo Tong Yul, owner of a closet-sized store that stocks everything from champagne to batteries, sells about $1,300 worth of Yuhan-Kimberly products a month. He shuns Pampers because they're imported. [52]

Until 1991 P&G imported its diapers from Japan because those Pampers provided a better fit for Korean babies. But the Korean government stopped P&G's shipments: Japanese diapers are on its list of forbidden products. "Instead of being sensitive to the situation, P&G sent a Cincinnati delegation to Washington to put pressure on the Korean government," said one official familiar with P&G. "These guys will resort to anything."

The U.S. government didn't intercede. "It wasn't in the best interest of other American companies," explained a U.S. government official in Seoul. P&G's Korean branch tried to import its U.S.-made Pampers, but Korean mothers didn't like the product as much. P&G lost share. Now P&G's Canadian manufacturing makes diapers for Korea until local production can supply the market. [53]

A major problem for U.S. firms is Korea's thriving black market, the source of most foreign goods. Every neighborhood has its *tokebi shijangs*, or goblin markets: small stores stocked with products diverted from U.S. military commissaries in Seoul. The military store sells goods for about 25 percent less than prices at U.S. supermarkets. About one-third of what's sold at

U.S. bases ends up on the black market. It's illegal but nearly impossible to stop.[54]

At one downtown shop a dealer offers Ivory Snow, Tide, and Dreft. A box of imported Kleenex facial tissues, made in Neenah, Wisconsin, sells for 3,000 *won,* or $3.90, for a box of 250 tissues. That's three times what a nearby store charges for a 280-count, locally made box of Kleenex. The only other difference is the plastic wrapper around the imported box. In some ways the black market has helped give Koreans a taste of Americana. Pringles potato chips, one of P&G's famous flops, became a Korean favorite thanks in part to the black market. Sales of the brand were so brisk that Korean P&G now imports them. The chips get enormous end-of-aisle displays in supermarkets. Even street vendors sell them.[55]

P&G has had to contend with Korean advertising practices such as plagiarism. Coke ads have been copied practically verbatim by local shampoo and yogurt makers. Package designs are also copied. A unit of Lucky-Goldstar makes *Tie* detergent and packages it in an orange box that looks remarkably similar to P&G's Tide brand. Dong San sells Bory soap, which looks like Ivory, as does Lucky-Goldstar's White soap.[56]

P&G wants to target Korean women, who share some similarities with U.S. women of the 1950s and 1960s in that many are stay-at-home mothers. But advertisers here have a trickier time trying to reach them. The Korean government has a censorship board to monitor advertising. While it doesn't stop plagiarism, it does limit what goes on the air or into print. David Healy, who worked in Seoul as president of McCann-Erickson, Inc., said the censors can be quite subjective. Government censors balked at one of his beverage ads that showed two bare-chested men, a construction worker and a tennis player, drinking the product to cool off. The censors told him to remove the tennis player because they considered his exposed nipples offensive. Healy argued that boxing matches revealed bare-chested men. The censors contended that it was suitable for television programs but not advertising. The agency reshot the ad to cover up the tennis player's chest but left the laborer shirtless. The ad got on the air without further problems. Later, Healy asked why only one of the men had to be covered. The censors said the worker wasn't offensive because he was on the job, not having fun. "I guess *working* nipples are allowed," Healy joked.

The censors are extremely fussy on the subject of women in ads. One ad revealing a woman's shins was banned because censors feared it exposed too much. A side view of a woman running up a staircase was scrapped even though it revealed nothing; censors argued that someone sitting under the stairs would be able to see up her dress.

Once the censors clear the copy, getting airtime can be nearly impossible. One reason is that television stations show test patterns during much of the day. TV shows are shown only from 6:30 A.M. to 10 A.M. and in the evenings. The Korean Broadcasting Advertising Corporation brokers the airtime that's available. When companies sign up, they are given time slots for perpetuity. That's a problem now that the market has liberalized somewhat and more companies want to advertise. "This is the most difficult market outside of mainland China," Healy said. He estimated that only 15 percent to 25 percent of total airtime is available to newcomers. Furthermore, all ads are grouped in six-minute blocks at the end of the shows, creating an incredible clutter of fifteen-second spots. Companies can get airtime through only one agency, so it doesn't benefit P&G to use numerous agencies as it does in the U.S. "You can't plan in any sophisticated way," Healy said. "You might get some airtime, but it might be during the Saturday morning cartoons."[57] Occasionally companies get lucky and get invited to appear on talk shows, where they can talk about their brands. One of Yuhan-Kimberly's mill managers appeared on a KBS talk show to answer consumer questions about diapers.

Creativity in advertising is inhibited because of the restrictions, so about 70 percent of the ads consist of talking heads holding the product. P&G has used its U.S. formula of the presenter demonstrating a product or offering comparisons to other brands. Whisper ads, for instance, compared the product's absorbency to Yuhan-Kimberly's Kotex brand. But the comparison used an outdated product, so it wasn't accurate. P&G has run similar campaigns in the Philippines to disparage the Kimbies diaper, which is meant to compete with cloth diapers, not disposables. That women also switched from Pampers to Kimbies because Kimbies sold for about half as much as P&G's brand and still worked certainly fueled P&G's strong reaction. Once again the company misfired, as mothers were offended by its advertising. "If you're a Filipino, you've been through earthquakes, typhoons, and the Marcos regime. You've finally got a disposable diaper that you can afford, so you don't appreciate ads telling you that you're using rubbish," said one consumer products executive.

Yuhan-Kimberly has tried to tap into the local culture in its ads for Huggies Baby Steps. Diaper ads in Korea cannot show a baby alone, and babies cannot talk, as they frequently do in U.S. ads. Korean mothers are less practical in their diaper purchases, worrying instead about subjective aspects such as her perception of the baby's comfort. To appeal to mothers, ads to launch Baby Steps featured Korean expressions that mark the stages of a baby's life. *Saegeun-saegeun*, which means quiet breathing, was the key phrase in the newborn diaper ads, while *unggeum-unggeum*, or crawling slowly, was the phrase for size three, or medium diapers. Diaper makers have also learned that it's important always to sell a white unisex diaper, despite the industry-wide shift to pink diapers for girls and blue for boys. The reason: women have to admit they have a daughter every time they reach for the pink package. "That's important in countries like China where there's only one child per family," said one marketing manager and where sons are vastly preferred. The chauvinism shows when some Koreans use baseball terms to refer to describe their families: daughters are strikes and sons are balls.

As in markets everywhere, Korean women also rely on recommendations from family and friends when buying diapers. Their opinions are influenced by ads in women's magazines, which they swap among their friends. Korean magazines are as thick as the Philadelphia phone book and feature 120 pages of ads at the front. It is estimated that six women read each copy of a magazine sold. "Consumers are uncynical about ads," Healy said. "They get information from them."

But few advertising executives trust Korean newspapers. No agency audits newspaper circulation figures, which influence advertising rates, so advertisers have little proof to verify a paper's distribution claims. What's more, editors bully companies into placing an equal number of ads in all papers. If they refuse, the editors publish nasty stories about their products. Indeed, Korean companies are expected to pay local reporters *chonji*—gifts or cash bribes—to ensure good coverage. "Newspapers here are arrogant and bad," said Healy, who has been threatened by various newspaper editors. "The power and influence they have is immoral."

All of these pressures mean it's going to be difficult for P&G to truly crack the Korean market. And the heat is on because more Japanese competitors will work their way into the markets, just as Shiseido and Uni-Charm did. Unlike P&G, they understand the importance of local help in their ventures. "The problem P&G will face is timing," said Jerry Wind, a marketing professor at the Wharton School. "Japanese companies are investing heavily in the rest of Asia. There's a real risk long term that they won't be able to catch up."[58]

P&G has tapped another market where little Japanese competition exists: Latin America. There P&G has often taken a beating, but it remains long after others have left. "There's not as much pressure of time because it's primarily local competitors in those markets," Wind said. The area is increasingly important as the U.S. relaxes its trade agreements with Mexico. P&G's Vallejo facility in Mexico is already the world's largest detergent plant, producing about 40 percent more than any other P&G site. The plant already ships Ariel detergent into southwestern states for sale in Hispanic communities. [59]

The demographics of the region fit P&G's profile: young consumers who are trying to improve their standard of living. About 38 percent of the population is under age fourteen, compared to the United States, where about 21 percent is under fourteen. "We see the characteristics we saw in the States in the 1950s," said Kip Knight, a former P&Ger who now works in Latin America for KFC, the fast-food giant. [60] "Everyone wants to be in the good-old middle class."

But P&G has a long way to go. Poverty is extreme. Few markets have recovered from years of military dictatorships. Peru is one example of a market where P&G has stayed despite incredible obstacles. The company began to produce detergents there in the 1950s but faced years of military regimes that nearly destroyed the company's business. P&G had to forfeit 10 percent of its business per year to the employees until they owned 51 percent of the company. As the government changed, P&G was able to buy back the shares and build the business.

In contrast to its practice in the Far East, P&G has allowed some local managers, not expatriates, run its Latin American operations. Peru's country manager is Susana Elesperu de Freitas, the daughter of a Lima cotton broker, who graduated magna cum laude from Dartmouth College. Trained as a geologist, she had worked in the Pyrenees Mountains of Spain and France but wanted to return to Peru. Since her first day on the job at P&G, she has confronted one crisis after another. Inflation has been 2000 percent to 3000 percent in some years. It is tracked weekly because it fluctuates so much. At times, managers line up outside her office to submit their resignations and flee the country. She is escorted everywhere by two armed bodyguards because terrorists have kidnapped or killed managers from U.S. companies. "You have to keep a low profile," she said. That can be tricky for one of the few woman managers in a very chauvinistic country—and company.

Security precautions have been taken. In Venezuela local managers spread the word that the P&G plant property is full of land mines, just to keep intruders away. Bunkers of concrete and steel surround the plants. One former officer said that according to P&G tests, it would take a terrorist forty-five minutes to break through the plant. Microphones are planted near the entrance to eavesdrop on delivery truck drivers' conversations. If guards hear something suspicious, they order the driver to leave. [61]

To survive tight financial times, local managers cut out long-distance calls, magazine subscriptions, and business meals. At one point Peru's managers even stopped calling Cincinnati. Even when there is money to spend, it can be hard to get basic goods and services. Electricity is typically shut off 20 percent of the time in offices and plants as the government tries to conserve energy. Spare parts for machines are scarce. Some plant machinery runs on pistons from a used Volvo, the engine block from a Toyota, and Nissan valves. "Sometimes I don't know how we do it," Elesperu de Freitas said.

Despite all its problems, P&G officials said volume in the Peruvian business doubled from 1970 to 1980. Then it fluctuated until 1985. By 1990 it was off by one-third. P&G said it lost money only in 1988, when a number of other companies pulled out of the country. Despite some improvements, it remains a difficult market. Selling basic goods takes time. Half the population has little income, and its habits are extremely old-fashioned.

Most consumers live on a small daily budget and shop each day for what they need. In Mexico local detergent makers sold their product in small cones rolled from used newspapers to undercut P&G's prices. So P&G developed a tiny plastic bag of detergent that gives consumers enough for about one load of laundry. Sachets of shampoo for two washings are the most popular size in Latin America. Colgate, the leading toothpaste in the region, sells tubes containing enough for four brushings. In the early 1980s P&G sold packages of six Pampers, but tariffs on the imported brand became too steep and it was discontinued. It would be extremely difficult to manufacture the product locally because there's no source of pulp and imports are too expensive.

Distribution is another problem because it's difficult to reach the *bodegas,* stores about the size of a garage. In Caracas salesmen lose cars to hit-and-run accidents. The locals say that traffic lights here are taken as mere suggestions. Instead, drivers simply wave out the window to signal they're taking their turn to speed through the intersection.

P&G uses a fleet of Volkswagen trucks to deliver small orders in some markets. Sometimes wholesalers distribute the goods. But it's difficult to keep products in supply. At one Caracas store, Mas por Menos, the manager says he has been out of Crest for a week. "That's bad," replies a P&G salesman. Like their counterparts around the world, many retailers simply don't like P&G. The reputation has been that "we're too strict," said Raphael Henao, P&G's manager in Venezuela.

P&G has to contend with a retailing network that has a long way to go before it catches up to those of more developed regions. At Automercado Orinoco in Caracas, bags of detergent are ripped and leaking on the shelves and floor. The meat department smells as if something died there. Bugs swarm to rotten fruit. A crying baby sits alone in a shopping cart, reaching up her chubby arms and yelling, "Mama!"

In Lima's La Victoria district, one of the city's poorest neighborhoods, salesmen are told not to carry cash because of thieves. The mud streets are full of merchants selling their goods. A woman guts a large silver fish, while another slits a chicken's throat and plucks its feathers. Fire eaters and auto parts salesmen line the streets hoping to earn some money from motorists stuck in traffic jams.

Marketing in these countries is challenging, especially when many residents are illiterate. In Peru P&G relies on radio commercials in Spanish and various local dialects. The company can command a great deal of airtime because it will pay cash in advance to lock up time slots. Due to the lack of education, consumers tend to be easily influenced by P&G's persuasion. Rather than just mention the brand name, ads remind consumers to buy the red bag of detergent because many can't read package labels. P&G influences more than buying habits. Television ads for Camay in Peru featured an actress wearing a white strapless dress. Teenage girls flocked to stores looking for the same dress for their proms. "We set a new fashion trend in the city," Elesperu de Freitas said.

The guilt theme of its U.S. ads are used in Latin America too. Ariel campaigns show a mother lamenting that she won't be able to clean her child's dirty clothes. When she does get them clean, she is a hero to her kids simply because she does the laundry. [62] And P&G ads use authority figures to preach about their brands. Dentists hawk Crest, which received the Peruvian equivalent of the American Dental Association seal from a local school of dentistry. Safeguard uses nurses as spokespeople to talk about the germ-killing ability of the product.

Sometimes P&G gets away with ads that would be considered ridiculous in the U.S. It sells a Pantene hair tonic in Peru that claims to help the roots of men's hair. It's targeted at balding men who fear more hair loss. Sales tripled when P&G advertised it as a good Christmas present for fathers. [63]

To help get products to consumers, P&G sends teams of women into neighborhoods to distribute products and ask housewives questions. It's difficult to get a straight answer. "The Latin mentality is that you have to be nice to people," Henao said. "When you ask questions about products, consumers just say it's 'muy bueno [very good].' " Going into homes, however, often reveals that is not the case. In Mexico P&G discovered that its Ace detergent, a low-suds product designed for use in washing machines, wasn't popular with women. The product didn't produce many suds, which many consumers use to judge cleaning performance. In addition, many Mexican women still wash garments by hand in the sink even if they own a washing machine.

P&G researchers don't identify themselves when they visit the homes. "We just say we're a research company investigating laundry," said Patricia Foster, a market researcher in Lima. "We leave the Procter badges at the office." At the home of eighty-two-year-old Hilda Dunn de Lambert, a handful of P&Gers watch her scrub the collar of her burgundy blouse in her tiled sink. She receives a box of detergent wrapped in plain brown paper as her gift for allowing them to watch her do the laundry. They pick up some unusual tips: one woman uses margarine to remove a grease stain. Another uses lemon and salt.

The researchers focus on certain neighborhoods and avoid the poorest areas. A P&G salesman points to rows of *ranchitos* on the hill and confides, "You can't send a woman up there because she would disappear." But extreme poverty exists everywhere. Marisabel Alzamore, who lives in Lima's Miraflores neighborhood, is doing her daily wash. She is also watching her nephew Jonathan, who wears cloth diapers underneath an old plastic grocery bag tied around his bottom. When she hears the plastic rustle, she looks up to check on the toddler. The woman uses a 225-gram bag of P&G detergent for two loads of laundry. About fifteen families share one stone sink in the common area at the center of their hovels. Watching this scene reveals that women tend to switch brands when one of the elder women tries something new. Alzamore complains about the high price of the detergents as she scrubs a cream-colored jacket.

Even those who can afford a city apartment try to save on basic goods. Mercedes Benitez, one of five adults sharing a small apartment in Caracas, uses Ace dishwashing detergent and Safeguard soap. But she switches to other brands if they are on sale. Some who have tried the convenience of disposable diapers, however, won't give them up. Isabel Osuna, a grandmother sharing an apartment with five adults and five children, keeps a stack of fifteen bags of diapers in the hallway. "They may not have enough to eat, but they will have their disposable diapers," said Eva de Mizrahi, a P&G researcher.

It can be difficult to convince some women to give up the local brands. Maria Moreno, a Caracas mother of three, lives in a clay *ranchito* where only worn sheets separate the living quarters for six adults and six children. Here in Barrio Zamora barefooted youngsters run through streets littered with rotting garbage. Moreno is scrubbing a cloth diaper with Las Llaves, a locally made bar of soap. She rinses the cloth with rainwater gathered in a metal barrel. She also uses the soap to scrub her dishes and floors, brush her teeth, and disinfect her children's cuts. The reason: "It's a cheap soap."

The Latin American experience provides perhaps the most valuable lesson for P&G as it moves into undeveloped regions such as Eastern Europe, China, and the former Soviet Union. Consumers in those countries are similar in that they have little income. And the distribution network and retailing outlets aren't advanced. "It's gonna be tough," CEO Ed Artzt acknowledged. [64]

P&G has once again selected joint-venture partners to enter Russia, Hungary, Poland, and Nigeria. Many consumer products companies are eyeing Vietnam, hoping to enter the market once trade restrictions are lifted by the U.S. government. In Czechoslovakia P&G was allowed to purchase a former state-run detergent and cleaning product company called Rakona. As part of the deal, P&G is teaching employees about capitalism: each received five shares of P&G stock. [65]

To pry open Poland, P&G invested heavily in advertising and distribution of free samples of its Vidal Sassoon Wash & Go shampoo. Some consumers were so happy to receive something free without waiting in lines, they cried. One postal employee sent P&G roses to express his thanks. [66]

But P&G found its marketing efforts can backfire. Thieves

ransacked mailboxes to get the free samples, so P&G had to repair a lot of mailboxes.[67] Other consumers spread rumors that the shampoo made you lose your hair. P&G told them there was no evidence to support the rumors, but locals were skeptical because they grew up believing that everything is propaganda. Some described it as inverse logic: the more something is advertised, the worse it must be.

P&G also discovered that consumers appreciate foreigners' efforts to adapt to the local language and customs—to a point. Research showed that the detergent labels should be written in imperfect Polish to demonstrate that foreign companies were trying to fit in but weren't quick enough to know the language.[68] In other countries—the Czech Republic, for example—consumers want labels in English or German because they associate local dialects with poor quality.[69]

In China the biggest problem was converting profits into dollars. P&G found help from Hutchison China Trade Company, owned by Li Ka-shing, the richest man in Hong Kong. Artzt said P&G delayed entry into China by about five years because it was looking for the right way to convert the currency. "We got in later than some, but we're doing a lot better" because we waited, he said.[70]

Even though families are limited to having one child, marketers expect it to be a good market for disposable goods such as diapers. "It's the golden baby syndrome," said one U.S. official seeking joint ventures in China. "Couples will spend up to a week's wages to buy infant formula. They only have one, so they want to give him the best."

The exact size of P&G's Chinese business is a mystery. Company officials told the Chinese press that 1990 sales were $50 million, three times those of a year earlier. It sells Head & Shoulders and Rejoice shampoos, Whisper pads, and Oil of Ulan, the local version of Oil of Olay skin cream. Pampers will be the next product sold there. Little else is known because, as James McGregor wrote in *The Wall Street Journal,* "The company may be the only organization in China that is more secretive than the Communist party."[71] Competitors joke that P&G still hasn't caught on to the importance of fitting in with the locals. Its Guangzhou plant is adorned with Roman columns.[72]

P&G is buying up all the advertising time it can find to send its messages to new consumers in these markets. In Russia P&G produced a twelve-minute infomercial to tie in with cellist Mstislav Rostropovich's first performance in his homeland since he was exiled in 1974. He appeared at the end of the commercial for Pampers, Tide, and other brands. The spot had a potential audience of 118 million.[73] In addition, P&G is creating its own television programs, just as it did in the U.S. In Europe it sponsors a sort of televised bingo game called SAT.1 Bingo, which airs six days a week.

P&G has also sent these new markets one of its oldest U.S. products: the soap operas "Search for Tomorrow" and "Guiding Light."[74]

10
The Dark Side
of the Moon

I nvestigator Gary Armstrong, a burly veteran of Cincinnati's Fraud Squad, sat at the table in the dingy fifth-
floor interrogation room. Just before 10 A.M. on August
8, 1991, he switched on his tape recorder.[1]

"This is Gary Armstrong. Also present is . . . a former employee of Procter & Gamble Co. who came in voluntarily at my
request to answer some questions in regards to an investigation.
. . . I instructed him that he has the right to get up and leave at
anytime that he wishes."

The man was informed that P&G, where he'd worked for
more than two decades, had complained to the Cincinnati police
about trade secrets leaking out of the company. "Do I need a
lawyer? Are you accusing me of something?" he asked Armstrong.

"No, I just want to talk," the detective replied.[2]

However, it wasn't merely a simple chat, but a search for
traitors. P&G enlisted the police department to comb through
millions of business and home phone records to identify sources
of the leaks. Those who dared to call me at *The Wall Street Journal* or at home were being questioned at the police station.

What happened in the months that followed sparked a huge
outcry against P&G and ultimately put Artzt's job on the line.
New York Times columnist William Safire blasted P&G, comparing the phone escapade to Watergate. "The maker of Tide and

Ivory can only come clean by showing its publics, and tomorrow's business leaders, that it understands that abuse of power and invasion of privacy are no mere errors in judgment, regrettably inappropriate—but are unethical, bad, improper, wrong."[3]

P&G had begun hunting for leaks two months earlier, after I learned in early June 1991 some news that Artzt wasn't ready to release: B. Jurgen Hintz, executive vice president and an heir to the CEO post, was being forced out of the company. I tracked down Artzt by telephone one Saturday as he was playing golf in Pebble Beach, California, where the board of directors was gathered for its monthly meeting.

I'd left two phone messages and faxed Artzt a brief letter explaining that the *Journal* planned a story on news of senior management changes and would like to include his comments. I also talked to his wife, Ruth, who assured me she'd give her husband the message to call me when she saw him at lunch.[4]

After stowing his 30-year-old Arnold Palmer putter, Artzt returned the call on his mobile phone.[5]

"How did you find me?" he groused.

"It's easy. You register under your own name,"

"What's the story?"

"I hear Hintz is leaving the company."

"Who have you been talking to?" Artzt demanded.

I wouldn't offer names.

"Fine. Then I won't have any problem telling you nothing."

I asked if he would at least discuss background, so we could get the story straight. He refused again. "I don't know anything about it. Why don't you ask Hintz?" he said.

"I'd love to, but I can't seem to find him. Maybe you can help me. He's not registered at the hotel. Shouldn't he be there, considering he's a director?"

Artzt was silent.

I rephrased the question. "Will we look foolish printing this? We just want to get it straight."

"You're gonna look real foolish. It's a big stinkeroo," he

yelled. He mumbled that I was "breaking every ethical rule in the book." Then he hung up.

My sources were excellent, but I couldn't ignore a vehement denial from a CEO. Besides, Artzt had been straight with me in the past. I waited to run the story until I could locate Hintz, who wasn't answering calls at his Cincinnati home.

I continued to check with P&G's PR department Sunday to see if there would be any news releases that weekend. During three phone calls, P&G spokesman Don Tassone continued to deny that Hintz was leaving. Late Sunday, a friend called to say, "P&G is really trying to screw you this time." The caller said that the PR department, following Artzt's orders, had called *The New York Times* and the Cincinnati papers to announce Hintz's departure and other executive changes. I called Tassone one more time to see if he had a news release for the *Journal*. He still insisted there wasn't any news.

Artzt had deliberately lied and tried to sabotage the *Journal*. Luckily, the tip came early enough to get a story in about half of the *Journal*'s 2 million newspapers Monday morning. By 10 P.M. Sunday, the early edition of the *Times* was on the streets in Manhattan. It carried the Hintz story, complete with Artzt's quotes in the news release.

The next day I called more sources and dug up further proof of problems that led to Hintz's "resignation." His departure was linked, in large part, to the deep troubles in P&G's food-and-beverage business. In addition, Hintz wasn't getting along with the boss who'd hand-picked him to overhaul the mess. Artzt had asked financial advisers to evaluate whether to sell some brands. In recent weeks he'd complained to insiders that it was the "worst managed" part of the company. [6]

So Tuesday's *Journal* carried a long story on the division's woes. [7] The piece helped explain Hintz's departure, but it was hardly a bulletin. *Business Week*, the *Cincinnati Enquirer*, the *Journal*, and others had covered the subject before. Still, it brought another round of fire from Artzt.

That afternoon, he took the extreme step of issuing a news release to deny the story. He accused the *Journal* of sensationalizing the news to promote readership. He acknowledged that the food-and-beverage business "has its problems" and never ruled out the basic premise of the story: that pieces could be sold.[8] How could he? He had told insiders again and again that he would get rid of brands that didn't perform.

Immediately after the stories were published, Artzt ordered an internal search of the company's phone records to be led by James Jessee, the ex-FBI agent who heads P&G's security department. Jessee searched in-house phone logs from March through June 1991 looking for suspects. At P&G, the phone system identifies all incoming calls by phone number. It also tracks and times each employee's calls.[9]

At least six insiders were interrogated after their office numbers appeared on Jessee's list, according to an internal memo. The results were hardly startling. Four of them were in public affairs.[10] Patrick Hayes, then associate director of public affairs, was asked why he talked so much to the *Journal.* "I'm in PR!" Hayes retorted. Artzt demanded more. He quizzed his advisers about how to nab me. "Is she paying people for information?" he wanted to know, hoping that would make it a crime.

Others suggested that P&G hire someone to follow me when I was in Cincinnati that summer as a way to spot anyone leaking information. P&G denied that it had me followed. "It's been a real witch-hunt around here," said one longtime manager who sat in on the meetings. "Artzt wants to find out who talked and tar and feather them." It's unclear how long I was followed.[11]

Previous CEOs in the company's more than 150-year history were equally powerful, but none had resorted to such severe tactics. But there are few checks and balances in the Artzt regime. Other CEOs were surrounded by senior advisers who were trusted for advice. Now that circle is virtually powerless. Jim Johnson was relatively new in the job as general counsel, so he wouldn't challenge the boss. And many of the previous CEO's senior advisers had retired. Veteran PR staffers weren't consulted.

The search remained private until three days after the Hintz story appeared in the *Journal*. Jessee instructed staffer Ed Casey to call the Hamilton County prosecutor's office. Bruce Garry, assistant county prosecutor, referred P&G to Armstrong at the Fraud Squad. [12]

A complaint from P&G was enough to prompt the Hamilton County prosecutor's office to open a grand jury investigation. The county prosecutor, Arthur Ney, now a local judge, was quick to help. He has received campaign contributions from senior P&G management, including former general counsel Powell McHenry. [13]

At Cincinnati Bell, there was no delay in turning over the phone records. Bell Chairman Dwight Hibbard is a friend of Ed Artzt, and both serve as directors on the board of Teradyne, a Boston company. [14]

When a grand jury subpoena was issued to track phone calls from March 17 to June 17, Cincinnati Bell promptly complied. [15] Additional subpoenas were issued to get records of calls from the northern Kentucky region served by the phone company to the *Journal* office and my Pittsburgh home. [16] To answer the subpoenas, Cincinnati Bell scoured about 35 million toll calls from about 800,000 homes and offices in the greater Cincinnati area. [17]

Meanwhile, P&G tried to keep its investigation quiet. I continued to encounter stonewalling when I tried to write about P&G during July and early August. When I sought comments from Artzt about some international joint ventures, I learned that he was still angry about the Hintz stories. "Tell Swasy she's lucky if I piss on the best part of her," he told his PR staff. I asked P&G spokesman Bill Dobson for basic information about a Russian joint venture. "Surely a snooping reporter like you can find out that information," he sneered. "Why don't you call some of your famous sources?" Artzt sent his top PR people to see *Journal* managing editor Paul Steiger to complain that I'd talked to insiders for my stories, a common practice at all newspapers. The PR people even hinted that they were researching whether any state laws had been broken by the disclosure of the news, but they never let on how far this search had gone. Only a few people close to Artzt knew about the police probe. That would change when a manager with more than twenty years at P&G was summoned to the Fraud Squad interrogation room in early August.

Here is a sampling of the questions: [18]

Armstrong: Have you had any contacts with Alecia Swasy, the reporter assigned to cover P&G, since you left the Procter & Gamble Company?

Suspect: I met Alecia at a reunion of P&G people in Chicago literally the week after I left P&G. . . .

Armstrong: You have had phone contact?

Suspect: Sure.

Armstrong: Uh, during this phone contact have you divulged any information to them in regards to Fisher Nuts? . . .

Suspect: Absolutely not. . . .

Armstrong: Have you ever called her at her house?

Suspect: Yeah.

Armstrong: Why would you call her at her house?

Suspect: Because I couldn't get her at work. . . .

Armstrong: Oh, I understand that.

The ex-manager was asked whether he still talked to others inside the company and if he recognized other names on Armstrong's list. Some were familiar, the man said. Then he asked the detective, "Is there a law against talking to reporters?"

"No, that's not against the law," Armstrong admitted.

"Then show me what's got people so concerned." Armstrong went through his file but couldn't pinpoint any trade secrets that had been divulged. [19]

A few hours after his interrogation, the former P&G manager returned to his home. He dialed the *Journal*'s Pittsburgh bureau to warn me about the search. "I just spent the morning at the police station because of my calls to you," he said. "The cops want to know what I told you about P&G."

He was nervous that P&G would retaliate. He wanted to remain loyal to his former employer, but he couldn't believe P&G had gone this far. "I was stunned that the police hadn't called you," he said. "I agonized about being the one to break the news, but not for too long." He was especially disturbed that the police had pages of his long-distance records, not just his calls to my home or office.

I alerted the *Journal*'s Pittsburgh bureau chief, Carol Hymowitz. She called Paul Steiger, the managing editor. We all realized this was no longer just a dispute about coverage; this was a story of a company's abuse of power. Steiger told us to hire a private detective to check the *Journal*'s telephones for bugs. The detective said they were clean.

Journal attorney Dick Tofel asked me if I had any friends in the Cincinnati area who might have been harassed by the police, making this an even greater invasion of my privacy. I told him of a few people whose phone records could have been searched. I called some friends and sources to see who else had been invited to the police station for a chat. One retired senior executive, whose name appeared on Armstrong's list, laughed loudly when asked whether he'd been called by the police. But he became quite somber when I explained that the investigation was serious. Another insider called his attorney when he heard the news. Most were angry to learn that their phone records had been seized. If the list was complete, the police should've had CEO Artzt's phone records. He routinely returned calls to my office and home numbers. Sometimes, he'd call just to yell at me. During one call in February 1991, he cursed and screamed about a story on P&G's spending cuts. "It's a good thing you're not here right now," he yelled.

Shortly after hearing about the investigation, Tofel faxed a letter to Cincinnati Bell demanding that the newspaper have a chance to quash the subpoenas in court.[20] But he learned that it was too late; the phone records had been turned over to the police.

By Friday, August 9, Jim Hirsch, a colleague in the Pittsburgh bureau, had confirmed my source's story with Armstrong of the Fraud Squad. That same morning, the ex-P&Ger was summoned again to discuss his phone calls. This time the request came from Jessee, P&G's head of security. He'd gotten a full report from the police, and decided to follow up.

"Could you come in and see us?" Jessee asked the former manager. "Are you kidding?" he replied. "I'm offended by this call."[21]

"You're our number one lead," Jessee continued. "Well, Jim, being the number one lead in a felony investigation, I'm gonna take that to mean I'm your number one suspect. I have no interest in talking to you."

"This sounds like a pissing contest between P&G and *The*

Wall Street Journal," the ex-manager told Jessee. "As a friend of the company, let me give you some advice: This is extremely ill advised. You'll lose this one."

Jessee countered that he wouldn't drop it because "Swasy broke the law."

Meanwhile, the *Journal*'s New York editors decided the phone call investigation deserved a lot of attention; a story about it would run on page one Monday morning.

Sunday afternoon P&G had a prepared statement ready when reporter Hirsch called for comment about the investigation. "They knew the call was coming," said Hirsch, who surmised that the police notified P&G about his questions concerning the investigation. P&G said it had no prior knowledge of the *Journal*'s story plans. In one conversation, P&G general counsel Jim Johnson expressed surprise that the *Journal* considered this newsworthy. "I didn't tell him that it was going on page one, but I said the *Journal* did take very seriously the idea of P&G getting subpoenas for phone records," Hirsch recalled.

Arthur Ney, the county prosecutor who obtained the subpoenas, proved elusive. When Hirsch called his Cincinnati home for comment Sunday morning, Mrs. Ney said he was asleep but would be awake and leaving for church at 11 A.M. At about 10:45 A.M., Hirsch called back. This time his wife said he was out on the golf course. "What happened to church?" Hirsch asked.

On Monday, August 12, column four on the *Journal*'s front page carried a story under the headline PROCTER & GAMBLE CALLS IN THE LAW TO TRACK NEWS LEAK. [22] Scores of newspapers, magazines, and television stations followed with their own coverage. Several outside law firms called the *Journal* that morning to volunteer their services if we wanted to file lawsuits to challenge the trade secrets law or the invasion of privacy.

Editorial pages lashed out at P&G's tactics. The *Journal* offered the first round the next day under the headline WHAT

POSSESSED P&G? "We understand that P&G swings a big stick in Cincinnati, of course, and maybe the local law can, like Pampers, be stretched to cover the leak. It is not funny, though, to the folks being hassled by the cops." It went on to call P&G's actions "sinister."[23]

The *Washington Post* editorial read: "In this affair P&G has suffered a certain loss of dignity as well as abrasions to its reputation for common sense."[24] Even the usually friendly *Cincinnati Post* editorial page blasted P&G: "After years of working to improve its reputation as a corporate bully and impenetrable fortress, this incident paints that picture all over again."[25]

And cartoonists lampooned P&G's abuse of power. For *The Dayton Daily News*, Mike Peters drew a lone cleaning woman in the KGB office telling a caller, "Sorry Comrade . . . the agents are gone. They all went to work for Procter and Gamble."[26] At the *Cincinnati Post*, Jeff Stahler's cartoon showed P&G's famous man-in-the-moon logo with a gag over the moon's mouth.[27]

"The phone investigation shows the same kind of judgment that was made in the Mapplethorpe case," said David Goldberger, Ohio State professor of law. "It was a case of 'we don't like this sort of expression. It offends the rules of our little preserve.' The people who govern Cincinnati treat the town like a plantation. Local officials protect the good old boys. And P&G is a good old boy."[28] Arthur Ney, the county prosecutor who aided P&G's investigation, was the same prosecutor who'd led the fight against the local art museum and its director for displaying Robert Mapplethorpe's photographs.

In Cincinnati, the local chapter of the Society of Professional Journalists wrote to Artzt demanding that he drop the investigation. "The misguided action Procter & Gamble is taking threatens to trample the First Amendment and obviously reflects more concern in identifying a possible leak within the company rather than protecting any trade secrets. . . . Your complaint has prompted a prosecutorial and police fishing expedition that amounts to censorship before the fact and could lead to further abuse of the First Amendment by other companies also disgruntled by news media coverage."[29]

P&G initially defended its actions, citing Ohio's 1967 statute that bars anyone from giving away "articles representing trade secrets," which is a felony.[30] But after the *Journal*'s story appeared, P&G began citing a separate law, a statute that makes it illegal for an employee to discuss business secrets with outsiders, which is a misdemeanor.[31] Either defense was a stretch, legal experts say, because the *Journal* was publishing routine business stories, not the formula for Tide. Furthermore, the man Armstrong interrogated was a former P&G employee and not subject to those laws. "Anyone with a first-year law school education would know there's trouble with this one," said David Goldberger.

"It was simply outrageous," added Kevin O'Neill, Ohio legal director for the American Civil Liberties Union. "P&G has law enforcement at its beck and call. It's an ugly story."[32]

Even Cincinnatians used to P&G's dominance in the city began to ask questions. Councilman Tyrone Yates asked for a full report on the investigation. He also asked whether anyone connected with the police investigation had ties to P&G. "This didn't have the right taste," he said.[33]

His question forced P&G and the police to disclose another fact embarrassing for P&G: Gary Armstrong, the lead investigator from the Fraud Squad, was also a part-time security officer for the company.[34] Artzt learned of the connection and issued another statement: "There is no impropriety here but I am concerned about the appearance. . . . I want to be clear we have not influenced this investigation in any way."[35]

For his part, Chief of Police Lawrence Whalen thinks his department handled the case with great deftness. Armstrong, he said, is one of the force's finest. He saw no conflict in Armstrong's ties to P&G. "We have police officers by the hundreds who work for private employers daily," he said.

Even Whalen has been a P&G security guard. He recalls

one assignment as a guard for an employee party at a Disney on Ice show at the Cincinnati Garden. During 1991, thirty Cincinnati police officers performed part-time work for P&G. [36]

When Councilman Yates began to question the ethics of the investigation, he was visited by lobbyists from P&G. "There was no compelling case made by the corporation," Yates said. "Laws were stretched too far. We've been attempting to regain some of our cosmopolitan and national luster. Incidents like this make us look like a small town." [37]

Inside P&G, employees were embarrassed and angered that Artzt resorted to such Big Brother tactics. An internal survey conducted by P&G shortly after the first stories appeared asked employees how they felt. [38] Overwhelmingly, they were outraged by P&G's behavior. One letter from a P&G employee said, "I am appalled by the gestapo tactics used by P&G." [39]

Some suggested that this would bring down the CEO. William Safire's September 5, 1991, column, "At P&G: It Sinks," turned up the heat on the P&G board. "Obsessed by leaks, a powerful Chief Executive directs eager-to-please law officers to find out which of his aides have been using the telephone to call reporters. When caught out abusing his power by causing the invasion of privacy, the leak-plugger insists he broke no law, belatedly admitting only an 'error in judgment.' "

In the column, Artzt began backpedaling. "I've had a lot of time to think about this while I was fishing," he said. "We made an error in judgment. We regret it. We thought we were doing the right thing, and frankly, we were just plain wrong."

Safire quizzed him on the ethics of the phone search, but Artzt said it wasn't unethical or improper, to which Safire responded, "He still doesn't get it. His fishing-boat epiphany is limited to acknowledgment of a public-relations blunder."

Artzt pledged that he would give "the whole story" on how he was trying to counter espionage to his board, which was to meet the following Tuesday. Safire said outside directors had an obligation to commission an independent report in time for the

October 8 annual meeting "and not to turn a morally blind eye to a corporate culture that confuses doing stupidly with doing wrong. Take it from an old Nixon hand: Full disclosure now will save P&G headaches later." [40]

The Safire column hit hard at headquarters. Insiders said former CEO John Smale and other directors were angry about the entire episode. "John didn't unclench his jaw for about the first week," said one manager. [41]

The same day Safire's column appeared, employees received a letter from Artzt, who now called the phone investigation "an embarrassing experience for the company and a difficult time for our employees. We made an error in judgment. . . . We created a problem that was larger than the one we were trying to solve. We regret that."

He went on to explain that the company "had a series of serious breaches of security. The problem surfaced last February, and involved disclosures to both the media and at least one competitor. It included very confidential business information, such as our capital spending figures." [42]

Directors offered little public comment, except a brief statement after their meeting: P&G "acted in good faith and responsibly" when it asked law authorities to trace news leaks. The eighteen-member board "carefully considered both the legal and ethical issues involved" and concurs with management "in considering the matter closed." [43] Insiders say Artzt was forced to write his mea culpa letter after being pressured by Smale. But the company never offered further explanation of those alleged leaks to competitors.

In a letter to Dow Jones attorney Tofel, P&G's general counsel said the company regretted the conflict but had "no choice but to turn this matter over to the authorities." [44]

P&G tried to distance itself from the phone search. "As you know, the subpoenas were sought by the authorities, not us," P&G said in a letter to the *Journal*. "I want to assure you again that all our actions were directed solely at trying to deal with and solve our internal problems with these disclosures of business plans and strategies." In early September the *Journal*'s top editors and I met with Artzt and three of his handlers to discuss coverage. The New York meeting had been planned prior to the phone caper. Artzt acted subdued. His handlers carped about my coverage. As Safire said in his column, they still didn't get it.

The leaks-to-competitors explanation came late in the game, when P&G desperately needed something more to explain its way out of this massive invasion of privacy. It was rather hollow, considering P&G made my phones the target of the investigation. If there were leaks to competitors, why not track calls made to Colgate, Unilever, and Kimberly-Clark, not just the *Journal*? P&G belatedly tried to say that I wasn't a target. The public relations department tried to sugarcoat it. "You were a data collection point," said Charlotte Otto, vice president of PR. Meanwhile, P&G's top security officer was labeling me a criminal, telling people that I'd broken the law.

After discrediting the *Journal*'s coverage of the troubled food-and-beverage division, Artzt did the inevitable. He announced in late 1992 that P&G was getting out of the orange juice business. Citrus Hill was such a troubled brand that P&G couldn't find a buyer; it simply discontinued the brand at a cost of $200 million. The stories that he once labeled inaccurate and sensational—and his excuse for calling in the cops—were now confirmed by the CEO himself.

P&G has never figured out who inside has been talking. The ex-manager interrogated by the Fraud Squad wasn't the source. The case was labeled inactive by August 1991.[45] But Armstrong, the detective and P&G security guard, still called to question me, even though the case was supposed to be closed. Tofel, the Dow Jones attorney, called the police chief and told him to stop Armstrong from harassing me. Since then, Armstrong has retired from the Cincinnati police department. He now works full-time at P&G.

The media coverage continued long after Artzt recanted.

Fortune magazine dubbed the phone search one of the Ten Biggest Business Goofs of 1991. [46] Some shareholders were miffed by the stunt. "People at the top of big companies get out of touch sometimes," said Frederic F. Brace, Jr., a stockholder and Chicago attorney. "They have so many people kissing their ass, they don't know right from wrong." [47]

Epilogue

In the fall of 1992, General Motors called on former Procter & Gamble chairman John Smale to rescue the world's largest company. Smale, a longtime GM director, pulled off a boardroom coup, giving chairman Robert Stempel the boot and shaking up the rest of senior management.[1]

Now Smale runs the GM empire from a corner office just down the hall from his old executive suite inside P&G's Cincinnati headquarters. Some days the eleventh floor resembles a branch office of GM. Nervous vice presidents fly in from Detroit, pacing the green-carpeted floors before meeting with Smale. He's even called on P&G sales teams to coach GM's troubled management on how to save the faltering auto maker.

In another corner office, John Pepper, president of P&G, fields offers from New York executive search firms. The rumor mill routinely pins his name to high-powered vacancies, such as the presidency of Yale University or the CEO's post at American Express. Still, he waits in hope that he will get tapped to be the next CEO of P&G. A few doors down, Durk Jager works on rebuilding P&G's beleaguered U.S. markets, where shares of detergents, diapers, and toothpastes have slid since the 1980s. He waits for word of CEO Ed Artzt's retirement, hoping that he will get the nod instead of Pepper. As of early 1993, Artzt vowed that he would stay at least two more years. When he does retire, the

CEO has said he wants to fix a faltering company, as his friend Smale is doing at GM. [2]

The idea of ex-Procter executives fixing anything is a chilling one. P&G has manipulated and abused its own employees, consumers, and competitors and gotten away with it for years. What's more, these are not change agents who practice enlightened management techniques that are essential for survival in the 1990s. Smale refused to attend W. Edwards Deming's quality seminars at P&G, saying that he only needed to listen to P&G managers, not outsiders. Consultant Deming taught the Japanese how to rebuild after World War II. As a GM director, Smale should have listened to Deming; the Japanese auto industry sure did. Instead he ruminated about trivia such as the color of the lid for instant Folgers coffee. He also helped eviscerate P&G's traditional reward systems, in both factory and management jobs, pushing short-term goals rather than long-term growth. [3]

More disturbing is Smale's role in the Rely episode. He wrote a memo to P&G chairman Ed Harness, arguing for expansion of Rely, despite years of consumer warnings about the product. [4] As he pushed for market share and profits, at least forty-two women died in 1980 from toxic shock syndrome, many of them after using Rely. [5] A P&G spokesman said Mr. Smale and other executives at the time acted responsibly, citing the lack of reliable scientific data then or even now that proves a link between Rely and TSS. In a 1987 speech, Smale said that a "corporation has a responsibility to society at large" and management is a "moral undertaking." [6] Explain that to teenager Andrea Kehm, who grew up without her mother, one of the women who died after using Rely. [7]

Meanwhile, hypocrisy continues to reign inside P&G. As CEO Artzt tried to silence Joy Towles Cummings and others who live near the polluted Fenholloway River, he accepted the Appeal of Conscience Foundation Award for his company's environmental record. Even many of his own employees thought it was a joke. At the $10,000-per-table banquet, Artzt told the audience that "conscience is a wonderful thing. It can change the world. It can do what no laws, no rules, no threat of punishment or penalty can ever do; because it is an enduring, self-regulating positive force."[8] Yet his lieutenants bully Florida's state attorney to press for criminal charges against a woman who apparently was beaten and raped merely for criticizing P&G's environmental record.[9] Hardly an act of conscience.

P&G's actions continue to receive little scrutiny as long as the financial returns are solid. *Fortune* magazine listed the company as the sixth most admired corporation in its 1993 ranking, up from number nine in 1992. The reason: P&G is one of the "financial paragons" that has rewarded its shareholders. "Financial consistency is more important than it gets credit for, in terms of reputation," Artzt told the magazine.[10]

The myth of P&G continues to be passed on to young business school graduates who eagerly enlist for a brand-management post. P&G is listed in the 1993 book *The 100 Best Companies to Work For in America.* It was praised for "openness/fairness" and "camaraderie/friendliness."[11] As employees read how wonderful P&G was to them, they braced for a restructuring planned for fall of 1993. P&G said it would cut 13,000 jobs, sending many employees to headhunters for new jobs. Others lamented that P&G isn't the place they thought it would be. As one young brand assistant wrote in an employee opinion survey: "This organization has a tendency to resist the truth."[12]

It's time to heed the warnings from inside P&G. Those who embrace P&G because of its financial strength need to rethink the steep price of that success. As one senior officer put it, "It is entirely possible for a strong corporation like P&G to rot from within, just like GM or IBM." As pressure on P&G builds, especially in weaker U.S. markets, everyone suffers the consequences. The company takes more drastic measures against competitors such as the tiny cloth diaper services, and steps up lobbying efforts from state houses to Washington to secure regulatory approvals on products and practices. And it pushes into Third World countries and other new markets, where few checks and balances exist to prevent P&G from repeating what it's done in the United States—or worse.

P&G and other companies should be held accountable for more than their quarterly dividends-and-profit report. For starters, independent science—free from P&G's grants—should substantiate the company's claims on products, such as its fat substitute.

As of May 1993, P&G said it remained confident that the Food and Drug Administration will approve olestra for public consumption. Consumer advocates have warned that the substance caused tumors and other health problems in some laboratory animals. P&G maintains that the substance has been tested extensively and does not cause health problems. If it's safe, let P&G prove it. The FDA shouldn't rush into this one. And olestra is just one product that will require approval. P&G is pushing ahead into the pharmaceutical business, where profit margins are greater than in detergents and diapers, and so is the impact on consumers' lives.

Likewise, state and local governments need to reconsider how much of P&G's power and influence a free society should tolerate. The Environmental Protection Agency and state regulators need to keep closer tabs on what's coming out of P&G's plants. Those who work and live near those sites have a right to know exactly what's been spewed into their air and water. It's not enough to measure effluent and test fish for dioxin—study the long-term health of men, women, and children too.

And the Ohio legislature needs to rethink the laws that permit P&G to invade the privacy of thousands of its citizens. Those "trade secrets" provisions are dangerous devices that go well beyond any need to protect competitive information. Rather, P&G has used them to try muzzling employees and the press.

Regardless of what anyone thinks of the news media, no one should be subjected to police interrogations or record searches simply for exercising First Amendment rights.

Little changes unless people question corporate giants like P&G. That can be daunting, considering its enormous financial and political clout. P&G's army of attorneys can overpower many of its competitors and adversaries. But even some inside P&G say it's time for a change. They risked their jobs to tell their stories. And others, such as the environmentalists of Taylor County, Florida, risked much more in order to make their voices heard. They refuse to buy the Ivory-pure image so carefully cultivated by P&G's years of marketing. We should all do the same.

Notes

Prologue

1. Information on stock appreciation and dividends found in P&G CEO Ed Artzt's speech to shareholders, Oct. 13, 1992.
2. Figure on U.S. households with P&G goods is a company estimate.
3. Information on the influence of P&G's management practices gathered in interviews with current and former P&G employees.
4. Details about the P&G and police investigations into phone records were gathered from police documents and interviews with people familiar with the search.
5. Information about P&G's treatment of employees comes from hundreds of interviews with current and former employees.
6. Specific documentation on P&G's tactics against competitors, its research, the Florida river, and other issues can be found in endnotes for each chapter.

1 Proctoids

1. John D. Williams, Michael Waldholz, and Jolie Solomon. "Vicks Board Accepts Friendly Bid From P&G Totaling $1.24 billion," *The Wall Street Journal*, Oct. 2, 1985.
2. James B. Stewart and Michael Waldholz, "How Richardson-Vicks Fell Prey to Takeover Despite Family's Grip," *The Wall Street Journal*, Oct. 30, 1985.
3. Interview with Mary Jaensch.
4. Interview with David Cullen.
5. Description of culture is based on scores of interviews with various P&G managers.
6. Oscar Schisgall, *Eyes on Tomorrow: The Evolution of Procter & Gamble* (Chicago: J. G. Ferguson, 1981). An authorized biography of P&G, which was edited by the company's public relations department.
7. Reference to Porkopolis found in *The Pride and the Promise: A Chronicle of*

Cincinnati Business: 1788–1988, a bicentennial collection of photographs and short stories produced by Deloitte Haskins & Sells and the Greater Cincinnati Bicentenniel Commission, 1988, p. 15.

8. Schisgall, p. 17.
9. Ibid., p. 26.
10. Speech to employees by John G. Smale, P&G CEO, at year-end company meeting, Nov. 7, 1986, p. 10.
11. Smale speech, p. 10
12. Interview with Hoyt Chaloud.
13. *You and Procter & Gamble,* an employee booklet, p. 11.
14. Company-provided information on first life insurance plan.
15. Schisgall, p. 97.
16. Interview with Dan Ransohoff.
17. Schisgall, introduction, p. ix.
18. Ibid., p. 77.
19. Interview with Lou Pritchett.
20. Interview with Gordon Wade.
21. Information about cafeteria food found on P&G menu from May 20, 1985 shows Jif and jelly and Jif and bananas sandwiches were offered to patrons for 50 cents and 75 cents.
22. Interview with Henry Wilson.
23. Interviews with various business school professors.
24. Salary data collected from interviews with P&Gers who hire new managers, based on 1991 information. Information on recruiting from Harvard gathered in interview with James Nethercott.
25. Interview with Howard Morgens.
26. Alecia Swasy, "Slow and Steady: In a Fast-Paced World, Procter & Gamble Sets Its Store in Old Values," *The Wall Street Journal,* Sept. 21, 1989, p. 1.
27. Interview with Susana Elesperu de Freitas.
28. Interview with Doug Hall.
29. Wilson interview.
30. Interview with Kip Knight.
31. Information on personality tests gathered in interviews with managers who recruited for P&G.
32. The number of Ph.D.s provided in P&G's written responses to author's questions, April 15, 1992.
33. P&G said brand management dates back to the late 1920s. Neil McElroy refined the system in a May 13, 1931, memo.
34. Information on brand manager turnover is based on interviews with various P&G managers.
35. Interview with Patrick Hayes.
36. Hall interview.
37. Information in this chapter on brand managers' work is based on interviews with various P&Gers.

38. Information on EEOC suit found in Bob Weston, "P&G Cheats Women on Seniority, Suit Says," *Cincinnati Enquirer,* May 8, 1979. Information on settlement found in interview with EEOC official.
39. Information on the University Club from interview with Mark Ross.
40. Information on Dallas plant desegregation found in *The Wall Street Journal,* April 1977.
41. Interview with Marjorie Bradford.
42. Interview with Floyd Dickens, Jr.
43. Internal P&G memo on Dick Nicolosi remarks.
44. Interview with Artzt.
45. Information on white male culture gathered from interviews with current and former P&Gers, both men and women, as well as outside consultants hired by P&G.
46. Information on dress code gathered from interviews and company memos. Information on culture found in interview with Thane Pressman and numerous others.
47. The "avoid showing skin" remark is found in Stan Sulkes, "Up the Organization," *Cincinnati Magazine,* October 1989.
48. Interview with Walter Lingle.
49. Dan Shingler, "At P&G, the Right Corporate Image Extends All the Way to the Cafeteria," *Cincinnati Business Courier,* Nov. 6–12, 1989.
50. From booklet, *You and Procter & Gamble,* distributed to employees. Information about rules on drinking at lunch gathered from interviews with both P&Gers and ad agency executives.
51. Interviews with Wade and Chuck Jarvie.
52. Decorating rules, office size, and efficiency gathered from interviews.
53. Testimony on no-smoking ordinance by L. V. Powell before Cincinnati Board of Health, Oct. 1, 1985.
54. Information on urinals, salad bar traffic, and walking based on interviews.
55. Cynthia Browne, "Jest for Success," *Moonbeams,* Aug. 1989.
56. Interview with Elinor Artman.
57. Information on wives found in various *Moonbeams* articles and from interviews.
58. Information on politics based on interviews with P&G managers, including Robert Beeby.
59. Information on P&G memos was gathered from interviews with scores of managers.
60. Interview with Jack Gordon.
61. Information on memos from speech: "If I Were a Brand Manager Today . . ." by Tom Laco to consumer advertising departments, April and May, 1981.
62. Interview with Matt Ariker.
63. Information on rewrites, memorization, and quizzes based on interviews with David Williams and numerous others.
64. Interview with Rowell Chase.

65. Artzt interview.
66. Information gathered in various interviews.
67. Tom Laco's farewell speech to P&G's operations committee, June 12, 1989, p. 2.
68. *Moonbeams*, Feb. 1989.
69. Cullen interview.
70. Information on the Crest budget book collected in interviews.
71. P&G security department's guidelines on travel, *Travel Smart*, Jan. 1988.
72. P&G employees report various warnings about security violations.
73. Alfred Lief, *It Floats: The Story of Procter & Gamble* (New York: Rinehart and Co., 1958). The company authorized this book after Mr. Lief was hired to write a pamphlet for the company's use, according to P&G's archivist.
74. Security measures were discussed by numerous retired officers, as well as current management.
75. The typewriter episode, relayed by a high-ranking P&G manager, fits with a pattern of P&G security measures.
76. Scores of P&G managers confirm the rigorous security measures, including interrogation and review of personal records. P&G said that it can check its phone records for security problems and confirms that it does ask employees to report substance abusers.
77. The Procter & Gamble 1975 stock option plan, as amended effective May 1991, Article G, conditions of options.
78. Hayes interview.
79. Pritchett, Jarvie, and other senior officers provided details on administrative and operations committee meetings.
80. Laco farewell speech, p. 2.
81. Laco brand manager speech, p. 21.
82. Information on incentives and other factors affecting the climate at P&G provided in numerous interviews, including Bill Morgan.
83. Information on bonus cutbacks from Donnellon and others at plants and in management.
84. Interview with Morgan Hunter.
85. Interview with Ethel Hughes.
86. Interviews with consultants.
87. Interview with Dean Butler.
88. Hall interview.
89. Information on P&G alumni provided in interviews with John Thomas and Ted Stanley. Information on lawyers contacting ex-P&Gers found in numerous interviews, including William Willis, head of executive search firm in Greenwich, Conn.
90. Numerous insiders talk about being blackballed from other Cincinnati companies.
91. Information on P&G lawsuit against Douglas Cowan gathered from the following court documents: *Procter & Gamble Co.* v. *Drackett Co., Bristol Myers*

Canada Inc., Douglas G. Cowan. Filed July 8, 1983, Hamilton County Court of Common Pleas. The complaint was dismissed without prejudice Oct. 24, 1983.

92. Information on harassment of former P&G employees was gathered in interviews with numerous current and former managers.

93. Jaensch interview.

2 Prince of Darkness

1. CEO Ed Artzt's trek cross-country with his family was described by him.

2. Nickname "Prince of Darkness" coined by others inside P&G. Artzt contends it comes from his penchant for long hours, especially at night. Others say it stems from his temper and harsh treatment of employees.

3. Artzt referred to Middle Eastern men as guys with towels on their heads several times, even in sessions with reporters.

4. Artzt's search of phone records described at length in chapter 10.

5. Artzt's admiration for Attila the Hun came out in February and March 1991 interviews for a page-one profile in *The Wall Street Journal*, March 5, 1991.

6. Artzt's micromanaging was confirmed by numerous employees throughout P&G.

7. P&G's predominantly white-male culture is apparent on many fronts, including a review of its upper-management ranks and board of directors. In addition, numerous P&G managers, plant workers, and others confirm that the company doesn't embrace diversity of any kind.

8. Interview with Alex Keller, retired P&Ger who worked for Artzt.

9. The comments listed about Artzt and Jager reflect those made by numerous P&G managers.

10. Artzt's comments about "help you fail" were made in his "How to Become a Winning Manager" speech, delivered March 2, 1988, to students at the Wharton Graduate Business School's Lauder Institute of International Management, University of Pennsylvania, Philadelphia.

11. Information about Artzt's biography provided in various interviews with him.

12. Reference to Artzt practicing basketball until 2 A.M. comes from company profile published in *Moonbeams*, March 1981. Other information taken from interviews.

13. Artzt's record in game against San Bernardino found in Beverly Hills High School yearbooks, provided by school library.

14. Description of Artzt's early journalism work taken from interview with Romaine Pauley, now retired in Beverly Hills, Calif.

15. Information about his social life gathered in interviews with classmates and fraternity brothers, including Larry Black.

16. Information on P&G's WASPy culture and Artzt's decision to shun Judaism found in chapter 1.

17. Interview with Morgan Hunter confirmed origin of nickname "Prince of Dark-

ness," which is widely known throughout the company. Artzt disputes the nickname, saying it comes from working long hours. No one denies that he does put in long hours.

18. Comments attributed to Ruth Artzt come from interviews with Ed Artzt. He refused to allow any family members, including his brother and wife, to be interviewed for the book.

19. Interview with Bart Cummings.

20. Interview with John Thomas.

21. Interview with Jack Rue.

22. The episode at LaGuardia typifies the stories told about Artzt's demeanor with his subordinates. He disputes the story, along with most others that convey his darker side.

23. Interview with Bob Jordan.

24. The FDA meeting was recalled by insiders who have worked for Artzt.

25. Interview with Walter Lingle.

26. Artzt showed the gifts during an interview at his home.

27. Interview with Frank Blod.

28. Cummings interview.

29. Brian Dumaine, "P&G Rewrites the Marketing Rules," *Fortune*, Nov. 6, 1989, p. 38.

30. Episode in the Philippines confirmed by Lou Pritchett, retired vice president of P&G.

31. Interview with Ethel Hughes, former P&G secretary who worked for Artzt.

32. The incident, as told by Keller, is typical of those involving Artzt and his subordinates, according to numerous people inside the company.

33. Information about Artzt's management style and response to memos was gathered in various interviews.

34. Damon Darlin, *The Wall Street Journal*, April 13, 1984.

35. Information about change to category management, plant closings, and other changes in 1980s was gathered from *Wall Street Journal* coverage and various interviews.

36. Smale's operation was kept quiet, but members of his senior management group confirm that he underwent surgery and missed several weeks of work.

37. Information on number of categories based on P&G data.

38. Information on succession inside P&G was gathered in various interviews with current and former P&G executives.

39. Zachary Schiller, *Business Week*, Aug. 28, 1989.

40. Alecia Swasy, *The Wall Street Journal*, Oct. 11, 1989, p. B1.

41. Information about Artzt's speech gathered from interviews, including Bill Morgan and others.

42. Information about Artzt's treatment of Pepper, along with Pepper's remarks to others, gathered in various interviews.

43. Alecia Swasy, *The Wall Street Journal*, March 5, 1991, p. 1, and information from interviews.
44. Interviews with Marjorie Bradford and David Cullen, both former P&G managers.
45. Interviews with headhunters who recruit at P&G.
46. Artzt's comments made during intervew.
47. Pay figures are from "P&G Chairman Gets Raise Following Lackluster Year," *The Wall Street Journal*, Sept. 10, 1992. Cost of Artzt's suits comes from interview when he pulled out a notecard covered with fabric swatches and price list for hand-tailored suits. He also showed it to others.
48. Zachary Schiller, *Business Week*, Feb. 3, 1992.
49. Information on Jozoff and Nicolosi departures gathered in interviews with those familiar with the reasons for their resignations.
50. Anecdotes about Artzt's treatment of managers, spouses, and others gathered in various interviews.
51. Artzt acknowledged that he didn't respect the Covey program.
52. Comments from P&G College provided in an edited version of a session in 1992.
53. Remarks about Attila the Hun were made in interview for March 1991 *Wall Street Journal* profile.
54. Information about Artzt's behavior was gathered from managers who attended the Hawaii meeting.
55. Artzt refuted the strawberry asshole comment, but then explained that it might have been taken out of context, making it sound serious. Those who attended the meeting say he was serious.
56. Artzt's behavior with Japanese customers was described by associates present at the meeting.
57. Alecia Swasy, *The Wall Street Journal*, March 1991 profile.
58. Pritchett provided the letter from Artzt.
59. Interview with Chuck Retrum.
60. Interview with Swasy, October 1989.
61. Valerie Reitman, *The Wall Street Journal*, Sept. 18, 1992, p. A3.
62. Pritchett interview.
63. Anecdotes about Jager gathered from several interviews with those who have worked with him, including Pritchett, Morgan, and many others.
64. Morgens interview.

3 P&G in Your Shorts

1. Interview with Vic Mills.
2. Estimates on P&G's presence in U.S. households are company figures.

3. Bomb information found in Oscar Schisgall, *Eyes on Tomorrow: The Evolution of Procter & Gamble* (Chicago: J. G. Ferguson, 1981), pp. 143–50, and interview with Howard Morgens.

4. Estimates on P&G's wasted spending come from insiders familiar with the report.

5. Interview with Hoyt Chaloud.

6. Thomas Edison information provided in company responses to questions.

7. History of the floating soap later named Ivory is found in "Ivory Soap, Celebrating 100 Years as America's Favorite," a special edition of *Moonbeams*, 1979, p. 3.

8. Information about Ivory research found in Alfred Lief, *It Floats: The Story of Procter & Gamble* (New York: Rinehart & Co., 1958), p. 154.

9. Interview with Howard Morgens.

10. Research teams described in *Time*, Oct. 5, 1953.

11. Field stories found in "P&G MRD Directory of Ex-Field 'girls' and 'boys.'" The directory was compiled by former market researchers in 1985.

12. Interviews with David Goodman and Jack Henry.

13. Information on questioning found in interviews with current and former market researchers at P&G.

14. Interviews with field researchers and anecdote book, pp. 211, 220.

15. Interview with Kip Knight.

16. Interview with Ed Artzt.

17. Interviews with Chuck Jarvie and others.

18. Artzt interview.

19. Knight interview.

20. Information on letters from P&G booklet, *The Story of P&G.*

21. Letters to P&G found in *Moonbeams*, Oct. 1955.

22. Consumer comments gathered in interviews with various brand managers.

23. Ivory Snow anecdote found in P&G brochure "Your Questions, Please," printed in 1980.

24. Interview with Matt Ariker.

25. Interviews and information from P&G brochure "Your Questions, Please."

26. Interview with Doug Hall.

27. Information on research from devices like in-home scanners from sources at P&G.

28. First lab mentioned in P&G's 1982 annual report.

29. Research figures found in P&G's 1991 annual report.

30. Smale's comments on R&D found in speech at research and development dinner, 1983. Figures on P&G spending versus competitors found in same speech. P&G confirmed figures.

31. Morgens interview.

32. Bomb-building details found in Lief, p. 214, and from Morgens interview.

33. Washing information gathered in interviews and tour of lab.

34. Soil sample anecdote found in Ronald G. Shafer, "Company Data on Soap and

Detergent Ads Given to FTC Is Thorough, Contradictory," *The Wall Street Journal*, Aug. 20, 1973.

35. Stain research found in *Moonbeams*, Nov. 1988, p. 11.
36. Static cling information gathered on tour of labs.
37. Softness training found in Joy Kraft, "When Every Day Is Laundry Day," *Cincinnati Post*, May 12, 1987.
38. Interview with Hoyt Chaloud.
39. Interview with Dean Butler.
40. Hall interview.
41. Dishwashing detergent information gathered on tour and from *Moonbeams*, Nov. 1984, p. 19.
42. Wondra research described in P&G's 1979 annual report.
43. Information gathered from In Defense of Animals.
44. Stream research described in *Columbus Dispatch*, Sept. 23, 1990.
45. Ron Shafer, *The Wall Street Journal*, Aug. 20, 1973.
46. Dental and armpit research information gathered during tour of labs and questions to P&G.
47. Hair research information gathered during tour of lab.
48. Walking machine and scientists work on pill to make curly hair found in Harriet Stix, Herald Tribune News Service, published in the *Cincinnati Enquirer*, July 22, 1960. "Secretaries get waves on P&G company time."
49. Cake work is described in *Moonbeams*, March 1981. Cupper described in P&G brochure, "People and Products."
50. Testing soap information found in 1957 Thomas Hedley & Co. report. The company became part of P&G in 1930.
51. Duncan's work with detergents described by Schisgall, pp. 138–39.
52. Chaloud interview.
53. Disney film found in Lief, *It Floats*, p. 220.
54. Discovery of first synthetic detergent described in Lief, p. 244.
55. Impact of Tide described in interview with Rowell Chase.
56. Growth of Tide found in Lief, p. 246.
57. Information on how Tide has changed gathered from interviews and *Moonbeams*, Jan. 1989.
58. Interview with James Nethercott.
59. Crest information gathered from Schisgall, pp. 204–9, and from P&G annual reports and interviews.
60. Pampers history found in Schisgall, pp. 216–20, interview with Mills, and other sources.
61. Ideas of expansion found in Nethercott interview and Lief, p. 168.
62. Morgens and others described the FTC actions and the impact on P&G.
63. Nethercott interview.
64. Interview with Fred Cianciolo.
65. Information on Teel, Abound, Salvo, and other bombs gathered in interviews with P&Gers.

66. Encaprin described in various interviews, including Geoff Place and other senior researchers.
67. Interview with Lou Pritchett.
68. Cold Snap described by Thane Pressman, Cianciolo, and others.
69. Pressman interview.
70. Reference to Pringles as the Edsel found in numerous interviews.
71. Saga of Pringles described in numerous interviews including Cianciolo, Kip Knight, Chuck Jarvie, and others.
72. Cookie fiasco described by various managers familiar with the project and by Alecia Swasy, *The Wall Street Journal*, Sept. 11 and 13, 1989.
73. Beverage problems outlined by Dean Butler, James Nethercott, and numerous other managers.
74. Wall Street analyst Hercules Segales was quoted in Bill Abrams and Paul Ingrasia, "P&G Plotting Big Move into Orange Juice," *The Wall Street Journal*, Oct. 8, 1982.
75. Interview with Frank Blod.
76. Interview with Steve Dennis.
77. Bruce Ingersoll and Alecia Swasy, *The Wall Street Journal*, April 25, 1991, p. B1.
78. P&G CEO Edwin L. Artzt letter to shareholders, April 30, 1991.
79. Blod and Dennis interviews.
80. Information on olestra found in correspondence to FDA from Center for Science in the Public Interest and in analysis of olestra toxicology by Dr. Melvin Dwaine Reuber for CSPI, Dec. 1, 1987.
81. Olestra information gathered from interviews with Chaloud, Dennis, Knight, Frank Weise, David Williams, and others. Also includes information from Swasy articles in *The Wall Street Journal.*
82. Information about Fisher Nuts acquisition gathered in numerous interviews with P&G sources.
83. Alecia Swasy, *The Wall Street Journal*, March 5, 1991, p. 1.
84. Financial data on food and beverage division found in P&G annual report for fiscal 1991.
85. Information about $2-billion costs gathered in interviews with insiders.
86. Comments about P&G's failures in food and beverage taken from various interviews, including those named in the text and other insiders. They reflect scores of others who agreed that P&G should abandon the cause.

4 Subliminal Sabotage

1. Information collected in interviews with women inside P&G and Susan Dearth.
2. Interview with Marcia Grace.
3. Budget figures from "100 Leading National Advertisers," *Advertising Age*, Sept. 23, 1992, p. 1.

4. Information on relationships with P&G gathered from scores of interviews with current and former ad agency executives, account managers, creatives, artists, producers, and copywriters, as well as brand-management officials inside P&G.

5. Based on "100 Leading National Advertisers."

6. Alecia Swasy, *The Wall Street Journal*, Nov. 25, 1988, p. B1.

7. Carrie Dolan, *The Wall Street Journal*, May 31, 1989, p. B1.

8. Industry estimates on number of free Pampers distributed at hospitals.

9. Judann Dagnoli, "P&G Helps Develop Promotion Scanner," *Advertising Age*, May 5, 1987.

10. Poll information from questions and answers in P&G information kit on the "Search for a Few Bald Men" to become the new Mr. Clean spokesman, Oct. 2, 1985.

11. Alfred Lief, *It Floats: The Story of Procter & Gamble* (New York, Rinehart & Co., 1958), pp. 23–24.

12. Oscar Shisgall, *Eyes on Tomorrow: The Evolution of Procter & Gamble* (Chicago: J. G. Ferguson, 1981), p. 29.

13. Ibid., pp. 32–33.

14. Ibid., p. 34.

15. Ad copy from booklet "What a Cake of Soap Will Do" published by P&G in late 1800s. Provided by Smithsonian Institution's advertising archives.

16. Lief, p. 115, and ads from Smithsonian archives.

17. *Moonbeams*, June 1979, p. 21.

18. Ibid., p. 35. Cartoon originally published in *The New Yorker*, Aug. 18, 1928.

19. *Moonbeams*, June 1979, p. 35.

20. Lief, p. 297.

21. *Moonbeams*, June 1979, p. 35.

22. Interview with Milt Gossett.

23. Ads from Smithsonian archives.

24. Lief, pp. 149–50.

25. *The House that Ivory Built*, by the editors of *Advertising Age* (Lincolnwood, Ill.: NTC Business Books), p. 185. *Tune In Yesterday: The Ultimate Encyclopedia of Old-Time Radio, 1925–1976* by John Dunning (Englewood Cliffs, N.J.: Prentice-Hall, 1976), pp. 383–85.

26. Interview with Walter Lingle.

27. Lief, p. 179, *Cincinnati Post*, Jan. 3, 1950, and Dunning, pp. 383–85.

28. Lief, pp. 177 and 276.

29. Ibid., p. 235.

30. Schisgall, p. 189.

31. Ibid., p. 192.

32. Ibid.

33. P&G brochure, Lief p. 272, and interview with Neil McElroy, *Time*, Oct. 5, 1953.

34. Gossett interview.

35. Interview with Miner Raymond.
36. *Time*, Oct. 5, 1953.
37. Interview with advertising agency officials.
38. Interviews with Jack Gordon and other P&Gers who worked on Scope brand.
39. From analysis by Dr. Moog.
40. Information about Bankhead found in *Cincinnati Times-Star*, Sept. 8, 1950, *Cincinnati Post*, March 16, 1949, and from Morgens interview.
41. Morgens interview.
42. Information on Womens' Interest Group gathered in various interviews with P&G women and Dearth.
43. Interview with Bob Jordan.
44. Interview with Donald Purkey.
45. P&G Notice of Annual Meeting and Proxy Statement for meeting Oct. 14, 1975, p. 12.
46. Dennis Doherty, *Cincinnati Enquirer*, Oct. 15, 1975.
47. Analysis based on tape provided to *The Wall Street Journal* by P&G. It contained what P&G management deemed its most progressive work. Analysis also included a second tape of ads shown to new recruits in training videos.
48. *The Wall Street Journal*, May 7, 1990.
49. Raymond interview.
50. *The Wall Street Journal*, March 23, 1988, and Valerie Reitman, "Black Newspaper Group Threatens a Boycott of P&G," *The Wall Street Journal*, June 15, 1992.
51. *Cosmopolitan*, Feb. and March 1992 issues.
52. Faye Rice, *Fortune*, Aug. 4, 1986, p. 130.
53. Information on P&G's treatment of ad agencies, compensation, mergers, and other issues was collected in scores of interviews with current and former ad agency executives, including Gossett, Jordan, and others. Also reflects information provided by P&G insiders.
54. Interview with Steve Dennis.
55. Joanne Lipman, "Saatchi Is Closer to Pact on Merging Units, Sources Say," June 1, 1987, and E. S. Browning, Nov. 29, 1991, "Eurocom-RSCG Merger Stirs Up Aides, Clients and Rumor Mills," *The Wall Street Journal*.
56. Laurie Freeman, "P&G Weighs Possibility of Agency Buy," *Advertising Age*, Oct. 20, 1986.
57. *Advertising Age*, Sept. 29, 1986, p. 3, and Sept. 15, 1986.
58. Interviews with ad agency officials, Marjorie Bradford, and others.
59. Morgan interview.
60. Information on P&G's personnel practices with agencies gathered from a variety of interviews.
61. Interview with Bart Cummings.
62. Information on P&G strict ad guidelines and meetings gathered in interviews.

63. Alecia Swasy, *The Wall Street Journal*, May 7, 1990, p. B1.

64. Information on Jif, Citrus Hill, Prell, Folgers, Always ads gathered in interviews.

65. Interview with Ross Love for *Wall Street Journal* story, May 7, 1990.

66. Speech by Ed Artzt, "Grooming the Next Generation of Management," Association of National Advertisers, Oct. 28, 1991, p. 16.

67. *The Wall Street Journal*, May 7, 1990.

5 Guerrilla Marketing

1. Testimony of Rebecca Spore, childhood friend of Patricia Kehm, in *Michael L. Kehm, Administrator of the Estate of Patricia Ann Kehm, Deceased* v. *Procter & Gamble Manufacturing Co., Procter & Gamble Distributing Co., Procter & Gamble Paper Products Co., and Procter & Gamble Co.*, U.S. District Court for the Northern District of Iowa, Cedar Rapids Division. Trial held in April 1982. References to the Kehms' life are found on page 1,127 of trial transcript.

2. Ibid., testimony of Colleen Jones, p. 1,079.

3. Testimony of Michael Kehm in 1982 trial, p. 1,408 of transcript.

4. Kehm trial transcript, testimony of Jones, p. 1,077.

5. Kehm trial transcript, p. 1,439.

6. Testimony by Dr. Bruce Dan, CDC researcher on toxic shock, pp. 199–200.

7. Speech by Jere E. Goyan, commissioner of Food and Drug Administration, before the Health Industry Manufacturers Association, Washington, D.C., Oct. 2, 1980.

8. Jane Brazes, *Cincinnati Post*, Sept. 23, 1980.

9. Ed Harness letter to P&G employees, Sept. 24, 1980.

10. William Gruber, *Chicago Tribune*, March 27, 1989, and Paul Souhrada, *Cincinnati Business Courier*, March 27–April 2, 1989.

11. Interviews with Dr. Philip M. Tierno and others.

12. Paul Souhrada, *Cincinnati Business Courier*, March 27–April 2, 1989, p. 1.

13. Tierno interview.

14. Interview with Tom Riley, attorney who handled the Kehm case and about 140 other toxic shock cases.

15. Reference to other tampon trademarks found in "Marketing: What's Next for P&G?" *The Wall Street Journal*, Oct. 2, 1980.

16. Peter Vanderwicken, *Fortune*, "P&G's Secret Ingredient," July 1974.

17. Tom Riley's opening statement, Kehm trial transcript, p. 69.

18. Kehm trial transcript, pp. 71 and 66.

19. Tierno interview.

20. Interview with Marjorie Bradford.

21. Interview with Judy Braiman.

22. Armand Lione and Jon Kapecki, *Rochester Patriot*, July 23–Aug. 5, 1973, p. 1.
23. P&G memo by R. B. Drotman to F. W. Baker, "Possible Areas of Attack on Rely," Feb. 28, 1975.
24. Information on the number of consumer complaints about Rely found in Kehm trial transcript, Martin Cannon testimony, p. 2,361.
25. *The Wall Street Journal*, Sept. 19, 1980.
26. Market share information found in Dean Rotbart and John Prestbo, "Killing a Product, Taking Rely off Market Cost Procter & Gamble a Week of Agonizing," *The Wall Street Journal*, Nov. 3, 1980.
27. P&G memo on chronology of key events on toxic shock and Rely.
28. Smale memo to Harness about introduction of Rely deodorant, May 14, 1980.
29. P&G memo from G. T. Davis to M. G. Leman, Feb. 22, 1980, about consumer comments.
30. P&G memo to sales personnel, June 27, 1980.
31. Interviews with P&G managers familiar with the calls.
32. Description of toxic shock syndrome comes from Kehm trial transcript, opening statement by Tom Riley, pp. 62–67.
33. Interview with Tierno and pp. 71–72 of opening statements of Kehm trial.
34. Information on P&G's meetings with the Centers for Disease Control gathered from memos and interviews with Dr. Kathryn Shands and Tom Riley.
35. Interview with Shands.
36. Kehm trial transcript, pp. 61–62.
37. Bradford interview.
38. P&G August file memo by P. F. Wieting on warning statement and Wieting memo about expansion of Rely Moderate.
39. Riley interview.
40. Owen Carter file memo, July 25, 1980.
41. Information on study and Dr. Bruce Dan quote from "P&G's Rely Tampon Found Implicated in Rare Disease by U.S. Disease Center," *The Wall Street Journal*, Sept. 18, 1980.
42. Bradford interview.
43. Braiman interview.
44. Interviews with various P&Gers and Shands.
45. Information on the Chicago airport hotel meeting gathered in interviews and from the following *Wall Street Journal* story: Dean Rotbart and John A. Prestbo, Nov. 3, 1980, p. 1.
46. Bradford interview.
47. *The Wall Street Journal*, Nov. 3, 1980, p. 1.
48. Ibid.
49. Interviews with numerous P&G officials, including retired officers who were on the administrative committee at time of crisis.
50. Kehm trial transcript, p. 1,079.
51. Ibid., Mike Kehm testimony, p. 1,412.
52. Ibid., p. 1,433.

53. Ibid., p. 1,428.
54. Ibid., pp. 1,430–31.
55. Ibid., p. 1,437.
56. Ibid., pp. 1,440–41.
57. Interview with Mike Kehm.
58. Information on deaths provided by CDC.
59. Interview with Riley.
60. Tom Riley, *The Price of a Life: One Woman's Death From Toxic Shock* (Bethesda, Md.: Adler & Adler, 1986), p. 67.
61. Ibid., p. 73.
62. Ibid., p. 39.
63. Ibid., p. 264.
64. Kehm trial transcript, p. 2,489.
65. Tierno interview.
66. Riley interview.
67. Interview with Mike Kehm.
68. Riley interview.
69. Kehm trial transcript, pp. 1,464–66.
70. Ibid., pp. 1,469–71.
71. United Press International wire report, published in *Chicago Tribune*, April 23, 1982.
72. Kehm trial transcript, Hassing testimony, p. 1,894.
73. Interview with Dr. Shands.
74. Hassing deposition, June 23, 1983, p. 31.
75. Riley interview.
76. Interview with Riley and sources at P&G.
77. Schlievert deposition in *Manning* v. *Tambrands Inc.*, Dec. 1991, p. 144.
78. Souhrada, *Cincinnati Business Courier*, March 27–April 2, 1989, p. 1, and Gruber, *Chicago Tribune*, March 27, 1989.
79. Liz Armstrong and Adrienne Scott, *Whitewash, Exposing the Health and Environmental Dangers of Women's Sanitary Products and Disposable Diapers— What You Can Do About It* (Toronto: HarperPerennial, 1992), p. 115. P&G's response found in written answers to author's questions.
80. Interview with senior researcher at P&G.
81. Bradford interview.
82. Interview with Dr. Anne Schuchat.
83. Dr. Tierno interview.
84. Riley interview.
85. Interview with Michael Kehm.
86. Braiman interview.
87. *The Wall Street Journal*, Nov. 21, 1986, p. B1.
88. Judy Braiman-Lipson, "Speaking Out," *Rochester Democrat and Chronicle*, July 26, 1987, p. 17A.
89. Braiman interview and court documents from *P&G* v. *General Health Care*

Corp., Sketchley Diaper Services Inc., West End Diaper Service Co., and Renell Pierpoint and Pierpoint Group Inc.

90. Order to take depositions of Judith Braiman-Lipson and Harvey Tucker from Kramer, Levin, Messen, Kamin & Frankel, Aug. 4, 1987.

91. Braiman interview.

92. Pierpoint interview and court documents from *P&G* v. *Pierpoint Group.*

93. Information about toxic shock found in *Epidemiologic Investigation Reports,* Nov. 5, 1986, and March 16, 1989. Reports found in data collected by the National Electronic Injury Surveillance System.

94. Interview with Nan Scott and other cloth diaper advocates and *The Wall Street Journal,* "Procter & Gamble Co. Disposable Diaper Ads to Be Altered by Firm," Dec. 30, 1992.

95. Interview with Roger Noe for the *Wall Street Journal* story, Aug. 26, 1991.

96. Interviews with industry officials.

97. Alecia Swasy, *The Wall Street Journal,* Aug. 26, 1991, p. B1.

98. *The Wall Street Journal,* Sept. 20, 1991, and complaint to Federal Trade Commission by The Women's Environmental Network—U.S.A., Nov. 10, 1992, p. 2.

99. Women's Environmental Network complaint to FTC, Nov. 1992.

100. Disposable diaper market shares based on industry estimates.

101. Interview with Bill Morgan.

102. *Moonbeams,* Feb. 1985, about $500-million upgrade for diaper manufacturing.

103. Information on diaper improvements from *P&G* v. *Kimberly-Clark Corp., U.S. District Court for the District of South Carolina, Charleston Division,* vol. 1 of trial transcript, opening arguments, p. 17. Statement by Allen Gerstein, lawyer for plaintiff, April 10, 1989.

104. Ibid., p. 5.

105. Ibid., pp. 39 and 47.

106. Ibid., p. 53.

107. Ibid., pp. 53–54.

108. Ibid., pp. 56–57.

109. Brief for appellee Kimberly-Clark Corp, U.S. Court of Appeals by H. Blair White, Sidley & Austin, p. 1, statement of case.

110. *P&G* v. *K-C,* trial transcript, p. 50.

111. Information gathered from interviews with sources familiar with the cases.

112. *P&G* v. *K-C,* trial transcript, p. 33.

113. Information on P&G tactics gathered from numerous interviews with current and former P&G employees.

114. Information on Darkie was gathered from sources familiar with P&G's campaign to discredit Colgate. Sequence of events on news coverage found in memos provided by sources familiar with Darkie.

115. *The Wall Street Journal,* Jan. 30, 1989.
116. Michael J. McCarthy, *The Wall Street Journal,* articles from Sept. 28, 1989, p. B1, and March 30, 1990, p. B1.
117. Information on P&G's campaign against Pepsi A.M. was gathered in numerous interviews with sources familiar with the project.
118. *The Wall Street Journal,* Oct. 15, 1990.
119. Alecia Swasy, *The Wall Street Journal,* Sept. 11, 1989, p. B8.
120. Alecia Swasy, *The Wall Street Journal,* Sept. 13, 1989, p. B8.
121. Patricia Gallagher, "New Logos Will Eclipse P&G Moon," *Cincinnati Enquirer,* July 10, 1991.
122. Interviews with sales managers at P&G.
123. Jolie Solomon, *The Wall Street Journal,* June 10, 1985.
124. Alecia Swasy, *The Wall Street Journal,* March 26, 1990.
125. *The Wall Street Journal,* March 20, 1991.
126. Jolie Solomon, *The Wall Street Journal,* Nov. 8, 1984, p. 1.
127. Information on Sister Drobnsk's experiences was gathered in an interview with her.

6 Ivory Snow Job

1. Information about George Stults from interviews.
2. Comments on P&G's clout from sources in Cincinnati and within P&G.
3. Geoffrey J. Giglierano, Debora A. Overmyer, with Frederic L. Propas, *The Bicentennial Guide to Greater Cincinnati: A Portrait of Two Hundred Years* (Cincinnati: The Cincinnati Historical Society, 1988), p. 83.
4. Iola Silberstein, *Cincinnati Then and Now* (Cincinnati: League of Women Voters of the Cincinnati Area), 1982, p. 35.
5. Giglierano, p. 45.
6. Silberstein, p. 37.
7. Ibid., p. 61.
8. Giglierano, p. 90.
9. Silberstein, p. 49.
10. Giglierano, p. 84.
11. Jerry Stein, *Cincinnati Post,* April 9, 1977.
12. Silberstein, p. 42.
13. Giglierano, p. 358.
14. Ibid., p. 80.
15. Information on separate dining rooms at University Club found in Giglierano, p. 60, and from interview with Mark Ross, general manager of the club.
16. Carol Sanger, "Public Profile Shines During Harness Years," *Cincinnati Enquirer,* p. 8, reprint of stories on P&G: Profile of a Corporate Citizen.

17. Smale Commission information from interviews in Cincinnati.

18. Silberstein, p. 41.

19. Information on P&G's demands that employees collect and donate money to United Way comes from scores of interviews with insiders. Dollar amount of P&G's charitable contributions provided by P&G.

20. P&G said it couldn't count how many agencies its employees participated in. Insiders estimated the 112 figure.

21. Interview with James Nethercott.

22. Information on St. Bernard tax money from Ivorydale found in Giglierano, p. 465.

23. Information on Ivorydale tax break gathered in interviews.

24. Information on P&G's efforts to block the smoking ordinance came from interviews with sources inside the company and the Board of Health.

25. Sanger, *Cincinnati Enquirer* reprint of P&G profile, p. 7.

26. Ibid., p. 9.

27. Giglierano, p. 62.

28. Interview with Jim Selonick.

29. *Cincinnati Business Courier*, Nov. 16–22, 1992.

30. Parking meter information from *Cincinnati Post*, Feb. 7, 1985, and *Cincinnati Enquirer*, Feb. 7, 1985.

31. Interview with Roxanne Qualls.

32. Information on Stults's experience taken from interviews.

33. Information on prostitution and drugs confirmed in various interviews with managers at P&G and others in neighborhood around Sharon Woods labs.

34. Information from interview with Michael Allen of Blue Ash police.

35. Interviews with Gordon Canney and other men and women at P&G.

36. Information on Stults's job search came from interviews with Stults. Larry Lough confirmed the episode at Sun Chemical.

37. Jessica Seigel, "Called Thief on Bulletin Boards, Fired Worker Wins Millions," *Chicago Tribune*, Apr. 28, 1993.

38. Information on P&G officials monitoring interviews for this book comes from various insiders, as well as some former P&Gers. In addition, various retirees, including former P&G chairman and CEO Howard Morgens, confirm that they were warned not to talk to the author. Neither Morgens nor the author told P&G about his interview; P&G wouldn't reveal how it found out about it.

39. The tape recording by Beers was confirmed by CEO Artzt when he revealed a thick transcript of the interview during a meeting with the author.

40. Information on local firms from interview with Jerry Galvin.

41. Interview with Don Baker, former head of P&G's art department.

42. Interview with John Nixon, graphic artist who has worked for P&G.

43. Information on P&G's clout with local vendors provided in numerous interviews with Cincinnati business leaders.

44. Information on market research firms provided by insiders at P&G, as well as outside firms.

45. Information on the dispute between P&G and the Cincinnati Automobile Club was gathered from court documents filed in Court of Common Pleas, Hamilton County, Ohio, Case No. A9004496, *The Procter & Gamble Co.* v. *Cincinnati Automobile Club.*

46. "Let's just leave the big giant . . ." quote taken from p. 108, deposition of James P. Ryan for *P&G* v. *Cincinnati Auto Club.*

47. Quotes taken from court documents, *P&G* v. *Cincinnati Auto Club.*

48. Estimates of lost revenue found in affidavit of Dan Dietrich, Cincinnati Auto Club, in *P&G* v. *Cincinnati Auto Club* court documents.

49. Information on rebates on commissions found in March 6, 1991, affidavit by Terry Johnson, director of World Wide Travel at Cincinnati Auto Club from 1982–87. Document part of court record in *P&G* v. *Cincinnati Auto Club.*

50. Deposition of Robert J. Reinersman, Feb. 25, 1991, pp. 39–41, in *P&G* v. *Cincinnati Auto Club.*

51. Randall Smith, *The Wall Street Journal*, May 1, 1992.

52. Oliver M. Gale, "They Shaped Our City" (Cincinnati: Oral History Foundation, 1990), pp. 1–8.

53. Information on Bryce Harlow found in "Bryce Harlow to Return to Nixon Staff as Adviser," *The Wall Street Journal*, June 15, 1973, and Polk Laffoon IV, "Bryce Harlow—Not Just P&G's Man on the Hill," *Cincinnati Post*, April 9, 1977, as well as interviews with former P&Gers who knew Harlow.

54. Information on P&G's lobbying efforts on olestra gathered in interviews with Michael Jacobson, competitors, and other Washington sources.

55. Gary Lee, "House Favors Patent Extensions for 3 Firms; Consumer Advocates Call Measure a Payoff to Special Interests," *The Washington Post*, Aug. 5, 1992. Information on contributions found in campaign finance records.

56. Silberstein, p. 41.

57. Thomas M. Rohan, *Industry Week*, Oct. 15, 1984, p. 68. Also gathered in interviews with union officials at P&G plants.

58. Information on amalgamation, NLRB dispute, and other union matters gathered from interviews with Walter Donnellon, Gordon Canney, and others.

59. Information on steelworkers' organizing drive found in *IRRC*, vol. ix, no. 7, July–Aug., 1982. Also from interviews with steelworkers' union officials.

60. Information on P&G's tactics found in various union documents, including the following: *Labor & Investments of AFL-CIO*, vol. 2, March 1982, p. 1; letter from steelworkers, June, 11, 1982; *IRRC*, p. 135.

61. Wage and benefit information from Rohan, *Industry Week*, p. 68.

62. Information on deaths of workers at P&G plants found in *IRRC*, p. 135, union documents, and the OSHA reports on James Franklin Wilson's accident.

63. Information on boycott gathered from interviews, steelworkers' documents, and Rohan, *Industry Week*, p. 68.

64. Information on NTA found in *IRRC*, pp. 138–40.

65. Margaret Josten, "P&G Has No Surprises for Nation's Analysts," *Cincinnati Enquirer*, Feb. 19, 1982, p. C-9.

66. Information on layoffs and decertification votes found in Rohan, *Industry Week*, pp. 68–69.
67. Interview with Buddy Davis, director of District 34, United Steelworkers Union.
68. Interview with Jamie Gamble, great-great grandson of P&G founder.
69. Information on Neighbor to Neighbor gathered in interview with Fred Ross, executive director of the group.
70. *The History of the Salvadoran Coffee Boycott*, chronology provided by Neighbor to Neighbor, p. 17.
71. Comments by CEO Ed Artzt about pulling ads were made at press luncheon on May 21, 1990.
72. Letter from Sen. Edward Kennedy to P&G CEO Ed Artzt cited in Neighbor to Neighbor chronology. Artzt replied to Kennedy in May 23, 1990, letter.
73. "Red Apple Stops Buying Folgers," *The Wall Street Journal*, June 19, 1990, p. B1.
74. Gabriella Stern, "P&G, Pressured by Boycott, to Market Coffee Blend Without Salvadoran Beans," *The Wall Street Journal*, Nov. 15, 1991.
75. Information on P&G's response to articles gathered in interviews with Ross, *The Wall Street Journal* reporters, and Gabriella Stern, "P&G Backpedals on Plan to Cut Use of Salvadoran Coffee," *The Wall Street Journal*, Nov. 18, 1991.
76. Ronald K. L. Collins, *Dictating Content: How Advertising Pressures Corrupt a Free Press* (Washington, D.C.: Center for the Study of Commercialism, 1992), p. 52.
77. Information on Michael Budkie's battle with P&G gathered in interview.
78. Tina Geronimi described her experience at P&G's shareholders' meeting in October 1992.
79. Information on unwritten rules about P&G coverage in certain magazines was gathered in numerous interviews with current and former ad agency executives, as well as P&Gers.
80. Collins, p. 27, based on Gloria Steinem's essay "Sex, Lies & Advertising."
81. Collins, p. 13.
82. William Cooper Procter's sentiments about speaking to the news media were found in an April 25, 1817, letter to his niece Mary E. Johnston, found in *Letters of William Cooper Procter* (Cincinnati: The McDonald Printing Co. Inc., 1957), p. 85.
83. Procter & Gamble Co. 1923 annual report from P&G archives.
84. Oscar Schisgall, *Eyes on Tomorrow: The Evolution of Procter & Gamble* (Chicago: S. G. Ferguson 1981), p. 57.
85. Sandra Salmans, "P&G Woos the Analysts," *The New York Times*, Feb. 20, 1982.
86. Interview with Nethercott.
87. *The Wall Street Journal*, Dec. 13, 1984.
88. Information on P&G public relations department based on interviews with

numerous insiders and former PR managers, including Marjorie Bradford and Patrick Hayes.

89. Interviews with retired senior executives confirm the sanitizing of company information, like *Moonbeams.*
90. Information on P&G's investigation of reporters comes from interviews with Hayes and others in the department.
91. Information on P&G's tactics with the news media gathered from numerous reporters at local and national news organizations who have followed the company.
92. Interview with official at Smithsonian Institution.
93. Bounce information found in *The Wall Street Journal,* Sept. 25, 1975.
94. CEO Artzt's speech to P&G's public affairs department was reprinted in *Moonbeams,* Jan. 1991, p. 9.
95. Alecia Swasy, *The Wall Street Journal,* July 10, 1990, p. B1.
96. Letter from Gerald Gendell to Swasy, July 3, 1990.
97. Gendell memo to Artzt, Aug. 24, 1990. Artzt's responses and Gendell's orders to his staff were scribbled in the margins and circulated to the PR department.
98. P&G media relations memo written by Charlotte Otto, Feb. 26, 1991.

7 Fear on the Fenholloway

1. Information about Joy Towles Cummings and her ancestors was gathered in interviews and visits to Taylor County.
2. Information about the condition of the Fenholloway River was gathered from EPA reports, the Legal Environmental Assistance Foundation in Tallahassee, and a series of stories in the Tallahassee *Democrat* by environmental reporter Julie Hauserman. Specific references to reports and newspaper articles are outlined below.
3. Information about harassment of women was gathered in interviews with numerous Taylor County residents.
4. The "like a bad movie" quote came from a resident of Taylor County.
5. Julie Hauserman, Tallahassee *Democrat,* Aug. 25, 1991.
6. "The Old Fenholloway," written by Norman Hendry. Information on Hendry's picnics found in Hauserman, Tallahassee *Democrat,* Aug. 25, 1991.
7. Interviews with residents.
8. Information on law about river classification found in Laws of Florida, chapter 24952–no. 1338, House Bill no. 242, 1947.
9. Julie Hauserman, Tallahassee *Democrat,* March 17, 1991.
10. Buckeye brochure for twenty-fifth-anniversary celebration of plant, May 5, 1979.
11. State of Florida, Department of Environmental Regulation, Division of Waste Management, Bureau of Waste Cleanup, Ground Water Investigation Report #91-05, Dec. 1991, p. vi.

12. Local residents supplied information on spill into river.

13. Julie Hauserman, Tallahassee *Democrat*, March 17, 1991.

14. EPA figures on dioxin risk and information on complexity of chemicals are found in Julie Hauserman, Tallahassee *Democrat*, March 17, 1991, and from interview with Marshall Hyatt of the EPA.

15. Erin Ellis, *The Edmonton Journal*, Feb 6, 1992, and Feb. 13, 1992.

16. Information on land swaps, new wells, and managers drinking bottled water gathered in interviews with plant workers and neighbors surrounding plant site.

17. Julie Hauserman, Tallahassee *Democrat*, March 17, 1991.

18. Buckeye twenty-fifth anniversary brochure.

19. Interview with Maria Kyler, among others, confirmed use of pits for garbage disposal.

20. Julie Hauserman's series published March 17, 24, and 31, 1991, in the Tallahassee *Democrat*.

21. Letter from Randall Poppell, chairman, Defenders of Taylor County, to Stephen Humphrey, Environmental Regulation Commission, given to Towles Cummings.

22. *Perry News-Herald*, May 17–18, 1991.

23. Interview with Janice Blair-Jackson.

24. Julie Hauserman, Tallahassee *Democrat*, June 7, 1991, p. 1A, and interviews with Towles Cummings and Blair-Jackson.

25. Jeff Bailey, *The Wall Street Journal*, Feb. 20, 1992, p. 1.

26. Julie Hauserman, Tallahassee *Democrat*, July 21, 1991 and June 20, 1992.

27. Interview with Michael Budkie.

28. CEO Ed Artzt's comments found in transcript of Oct. 8, 1991, annual meeting of shareholders, p. 153.

29. Julie Hauserman, Tallahassee *Democrat*, March 24, 1991.

30. Information on segregation, racism, and sexism gathered in numerous interviews during visit to Taylor County.

31. Interview with Ken Carson.

32. Buckeye twenty-fifth-anniversary brochure.

33. Interview with Blair-Jackson.

34. Interviews with sources in Taylor County.

35. Buckeye twenty-fifth-anniversary brochure.

36. Information on P&G's clout with county commission gathered in interviews, as well as news clippings in local papers, such as *Perry News Herald*, May 10–11, 1991, p. A1.

37. Julie Hauserman, Tallahassee *Democrat*, Nov. 8, 1991.

38. Julie Hauserman, Tallahassee *Democrat*, Feb. 5, 1992

39. Interview with John Wesley Walker.

40. Information about local television station's treatment of P&G was gathered from interview with C. D. Reams, former talk show host, and from tapes of shows.

41. *Perry News-Herald*, June 19–20, 1992, p. 1.
42. Southerland appearance on "Taylor Talk in Focus."
43. Information about television and newspaper coverage was gathered from local programs, months of articles in the *Taco Times* and *Perry News-Herald*, and interview with C. D. Reams.
44. Reference to soft features from review of papers. Review of several months' coverage shows bias towards P&G and its managers. A sample: *Taco Times*, Sept. 11, 1992, p. A8, shows Florida Sheriffs Youth Ranches receiving check from P&G employees. Page-one coverage July 15 and July 29, 1992 show more P&G good deeds, like checks for boys and girls club in Taylor County.
45. *Taco Times*, June 24, 1992, and Tallahassee *Democrat*, July 21, 1991.
46. Full-page ad in *Taco Times*, July 31, 1991, p. A8, from Defenders of Taylor County.
47. Reference to Hitler made by Mike Evans, Taylor County economic developer, in *Taco Times*, Feb. 26, 1991, p. A3.
48. Lou Heldman, Tallahassee *Democrat*, July 28, 1991.
49. Information about P&G's orders to refer all questions to the PR department came from the author's visit to Taylor County.
50. Comments by Lesley Stahl came from "Clean Water, Clean Air," CBS News "60 Minutes," Sept. 20, 1992.
51. Information about McGuire and Rowland came from interviews.
52. Interviews with McGuire and Rowland.
53. Julie Hauserman, Tallahassee *Democrat*, Sept. 11, 1992.
54. Information on pressure from P&G and chamber president gathered in interviews with sources familiar with the case.
55. Julie Hauserman, Tallahassee *Democrat*, April 9, 1992.
56. Information on working conditions gathered in interviews with numerous plant workers at Buckeye mill.
57. Information about Michael Zawada, Jr., gathered in interviews with the Zawada family. Others in Port Ivory plant confirm promises made to workers who transferred.
58. P&G fiscal 1992 annual report, p. 25.
59. Information on Kyler's investigation of the chemical gathered in interviews.
60. Information on P&G surveillance gathered in numerous interviews with P&Gers at various plant sites, including Baltimore, Port Ivory and the Buckeye plant.
61. Information on Towles Cummings's visit to Cincinnati gathered from interviews.
62. Greenpeace news release, Oct. 15, 1992.
63. Interview with Louis Parker.
64. *The Sun Herald*, Feb. 1, 1992, p. 1.
65. Julie Hauserman, Tallahassee *Democrat*, June 12, 1992, p. 2C.
66. Interviews with Bertie Branch, Vera Peskan, and Buddy Odom.

8 Supermarket Showdown

1. Sales tactics gathered from interviews with numerous P&G sales managers, along with retired senior management.
2. Morgue sign reference found in Lynn Donham, *Emory Business Magazine*, Fall 1991.
3. Information on P&G's treatment of Wal-Mart gathered from interviews with current and former P&G sales managers, along with Wal-Mart officials in Bentonville, Ark.
4. Interview with David Glass, Wal-Mart CEO.
5. The canoe trip story was provided during interviews with Lou Pritchett, retired vice president of P&G. Information about the beginning of the P&G–Wal-Mart partnership was also confirmed by numerous sources, including George Billingsley and others close to the late Sam Walton. The information was also confirmed with letters written by Walton to Pritchett.
6. Sales figures on P&G's business at Wall-Mart were obtained from sources familiar with the companies.
7. Sam Walton letter to Lou Pritchett, Jan. 16, 1991.
8. Information on P&G's problems with retailers was gathered in scores of interviews with the company's sales force, former sales executives, retailers, wholesalers, and competitors.
9. Information on deal making gathered from sources inside P&G.
10. Estimates of job cuts in sales confirmed with numerous managers inside P&G's sales organization.
11. Interview with Morgens.
12. Oscar Shisgall, *Eyes on Tomorrow: The Evolution of Procter & Gamble* (Chicago: J. G. Ferguson, 1981), pp. 88–93.
13. Ibid., p. 93.
14. Interviews with A. M. Wood and Howard Morgens, now retired.
15. Losses noted in Shisgall, p. 96.
16. Passed & Gone reference found in Shisgall, p. 94
17. Use of wholesalers in rural areas mentioned in Shisgall, p. 97.
18. Information about sales training gathered from numerous interviews with P&G sales force. Pritchett interviews provided material about his career.
19. Interview with Allan Schoenberger.
20. Information about P&G sales rep measuring ads comes from *Fortune* magazine, Nov. 6, 1989, p. 40.
21. P&G's strong-arm tactics were revealed in numerous interviews with insiders and retailers.
22. Information on forward buying comes from various interviews and *The Economist*, July 25, 1992, p. 61.
23. Lou Pritchett's memo "A Vision for P&G Sales," Oct. 9, 1984.
24. Pritchett field trip memo, June 30, 1986.

25. The meeting events were confirmed by various sales managers and in letters from sales personnel around the world.

26. Information about P&G's dealings with Zayre comes from Pritchett interviews. It was also confirmed by retailing sources.

27. Interview with Bob Martin, executive vice president, Wal-Mart.

28. Walton remarks supplied by Pritchett and others.

29. Information about Smale's comments provided by Pritchett and others familiar with the meetings.

30. Estimates of on-time, error-free deliveries by P&G to customers found in *Moonbeams*, Winter 1992 issue, p. 11. Wal-Mart figures from sources familiar with the business.

31. Information about P&G's recent relations with retailers was gathered from interviews with customers, as well as insiders.

32. *The New York Times*, April 26, 1992, p. 5, citing *The Harvard Business Review* study from 1990. Information about retailers' profits comes from *The Economist*, July 25, 1992.

33. Interview with Dean Skadberg in Fred Pfaff, *Food & Beverage Marketing*, May 1991.

34. Information on diverting P&G goods provided by various industry sources.

35. Information on Big Y Foods from interview with Claire D'Amour, a vice president of the chain.

36. The comment about the trade being powerful enough to make P&G fail reflects the information gathered from numerous sales managers inside the company.

37. Lewis G. Schaeneman, quoted in *Supermarket News*, June 1, 1992, p. 1.

38. Comments from P&G sales managers are representative of scores interviewed on the subject of the company's dealings with retailers.

39. Information about P&G's deal making was gathered from interviews with sales personnel and others familiar with the paper division audit.

40. Numerous retailers and other industry sources talked about special treatment for Wal-Mart. Sales officials familiar with the company confirm it got breaks like the special deductions far greater than other retailers.

41. *The Wall Street Journal*, June 1, 1992, p. B3.

42. Glass interview.

43. Estimates on operating costs as percentage of sales provided in interview with Carl Steidtmann.

44. Interviews with sources familiar with P&G–Wal-Mart partnership.

45. Elliott Zwiebach, *Supermarket News*, July 27, 1992.

46. D'Amour interview.

9 Pampering the World

1. Information about Oho Kyung Sook and other consumers gathered during visit to Seoul.
2. Market share and diaper sales figures provided by various industry sources in Korea.
3. *The Wall Street Journal*, May 15, 1992.
4. Comments from insiders familiar with the P&G-STC joint venture reflect those made during numerous interviews.
5. Details on P&G's tactics with consumers, retailers, and unions provided in notes throughout this chapter.
6. Information on tax break was provided by Bill Morgan, the finance expert who worked on the tax case while assigned to P&G's Japanese subsidiary.
7. Market share figures provided by various sources.
8. Early expansion described in P&G annual report for 1980, p. 11.
9. Cuban experience described by Walter Lingle.
10. Drop of 1985 described by *Fortune*, Aug. 4, 1986, p. 130.
11. Description of impact of private-label goods and other market conditions gathered from various interviews with current and former P&Gers.
12. Valerie Reitman, *The Wall Street Journal*, March 19, 1992.
13. Colgate market shares from Wall Street estimates. Description of Reuben Mark found in *Fortune*, May 11, 1987.
14. Diaper market information gathered from interviews with various Kimberly-Clark officials, including Tom Newby, in 1991.
15. Shampoo market information described by Timothy Schellhardt, *The Wall Street Journal*, Nov. 19, 1992. Olestra information gathered in interviews.
16. Test market failure rate described by senior management to employees in 1992 speech. Information provided by insiders who attended the session.
17. Ed Artzt's speech to shareholders, Oct. 13, 1992.
18. Interviews with Morgan Hunter and Yoshio Maruta.
19. Figures on Shiseido's investment found in 1992 Artzt speech to the Cosmetics Executive Women, a trade association.
20. Details on P&G's problems in Japan come from a variety of sources, including interviews with the CEO and other senior managers who worked in the country. The Harvard case studies used are cited in other endnotes.
21. The events that shaped Howard Morgens's decision were described by Ed Artzt, Ed Shutt, Morgens, and others.
22. The apprehension is described in Harvard case study, Procter & Gamble Japan (A), p. 1.
23. Cheer's problems were described in 1988 interview with Ed Artzt for story by Alecia Swasy, *The Wall Street Journal*, Feb. 6, 1989, p. B1.
24. Detergent and diaper information found in Harvard case study A, pp. 8–9.
25. *The Wall Street Journal*, Feb. 6, 1989.

26. Moony diaper information found in Harvard case study A, p. 10.
27. Artzt interviews.
28. Criticism of P&G by Japanese press cited in Harvard case study A, p. 8.
29. Distribution information found in *Business Quarterly*, Winter 1989, p. 15. Additional information found in Harvard case study A, p. 6.
30. Pricing problems described by Shutt.
31. Advertising blunders described by Alecia Swasy, *The Wall Street Journal*, Feb. 6, 1989. Ishiguro remarks found in P&G speech "Winning in Japan," which is delivered by Artzt and others.
32. Kao and Lion beating P&G cited in Harvard case study A, pp. 1, 10 and 11. Artzt's "dead" quote from story by Patricia Gallagher, *USA Today*, Nov. 9, 1989.
33. Management problems found in Harvard case study A, p. 11.
34. Tax information described by Bill Morgan, who was responsible for the finance department at P&G's Japanese subsidiary.
35. Information on P&G share declines found in Harvard case study B, p. 2 and case C, p. 3. Artzt comments from interviews.
36. Description of Jager as "crazy man Durk" found in Harvard case study C, p. 2.
37. Morgan described his experience with Jager in interviews.
38. Artzt's remarks found in *Moonbeams*, Dec. 1989, p. 4.
39. P&G's research, efforts with public, and cuts found in Harvard case study C, pp. 5–9.
40. Information about Suzuka plant gathered in interviews with various managers who worked in Japan. Other details in Yumiko Ono, *The Wall Street Journal*, April 3, 1991.
41. Information on recent introductions by Japanese competitors found in Harvard case study C, p. 9, and from interviews.
42. Description of Korea comes from visit to Seoul.
43. Damon Darlin, *The Wall Street Journal*, June 15, 1992, p. B1.
44. Information on Korea gathered from interviews with various Seoul consultants and business executives.
45. *The Wall Street Journal*, May 15, 1992.
46. Artzt's comments found in his interviews. Others familiar with the joint venture say P&G wanted too much control, so it failed.
47. Information on Yuhan-Kimberly provided by industry sources.
48. Information about Yuhan-Kimberly's history found in Kimberly-Clark annual report for 1990 and from industry interviews.
49. Estimates of U.S. investment provided by South Korean government officials.
50. Information on Korea's *chaebols* found in Damon Darlin, "Tougher Times: Korea's Goldstar Faces A Harsh New World Under Democracy," *The Wall Street Journal*, Nov. 8, 1989.
51. Amway information found in Amway press release from 1991.

52. Interviews with various consumers and shopkeepers conducted in Seoul in late 1992.

53. Information on P&G's efforts to import diapers gathered in interviews with numerous officials in the U.S. and Korea.

54. Damon Darlin, *The Wall Street Journal*, July 19, 1991, p. B1.

55. Market information gathered in Seoul.

56. Copycat packages described by Damon Darlin, *The Wall Street Journal*, Dec. 5, 1989, p. B1.

57. Advertising information from interview with David Healy.

58. Interview with Jerry Wind.

59. Information about P&G in Mexico, Venezuela, and Peru was gathered during a two-week visit to those countries and P&G operations. Some of the material cited in the chapter was first published by Alecia Swasy in *The Wall Street Journal*, June 15, 1990. Additional information came from interviews with current and former P&Gers.

60. Interview with Kip Knight.

61. Information on P&G surveillance provided by former company officers.

62. Ad for laundry detergent in Mexico cited in *Moonbeams*, Spring 1992, p. 9.

63. Pantene product described in interviews with company officials.

64. Artzt comments from interviews.

65. Alecia Swasy, *The Wall Street Journal*, June 20, 1991.

66. Jennifer Lawrence, *Advertising Age*, Sept. 30, 1991.

67. E. S. Browning, *The Wall Street Journal*, July 30, 1992.

68. Stephen Engelberg, *The New York Times*, May 26, 1992.

69. E. S. Browning, *The Wall Street Journal*, July 30, 1992.

70. James McGregor, *The Wall Street Journal*, April 3, 1992, p. B1. Artzt comment from interviews.

71. McGregor, ibid.

72. Photo and information about P&G plant in China provided by sources in China.

73. Rostropovich performance and P&G's commercial described by Laurie Freeman and Laurel Wentz, *Advertising Age*, Feb. 12, 1990.

74. European programming described by *Advertising Age*, Feb. 4, 1991, p. 25.

10 The Dark Side of the Moon

1. Statement of former P&G manager to Cincinnati police specialist Gary Armstrong, Aug. 8, 1991. Interrogation transcript obtained from Cincinnati city attorney following a Freedom of Information Act request. The name of the former manager, along with others listed from the phone record search, were deleted before the attorney released the document.

2. Ex-manager's question about needing a lawyer was part of his phone conversation with Armstrong prior to his visit to the police station. The information was gathered in interviews.

3. Essay by William Safire, "At P&G: It Sinks," *The New York Times*, Sept. 5, 1991, p. A19.

4. Conversation with Ruth Artzt, June 8, 1991.

5. Conversation with Ed Artzt, June 8, 1991. He returned the call to my home after receiving a couple of phone messages and a faxed letter at his hotel.

6. Description of events leading to Hintz's departure found in Alecia Swasy, *The Wall Street Journal*, June 10 and June 11, 1991.

7. Alecia Swasy, *The Wall Street Journal*, June 11, 1991, p. B1.

8. P&G news release, June 11, 1991

9. Information about P&G's internal phone search comes from Cincinnati police department memo, "Procter & Gamble Trade Secrets Investigation," Aug. 19, 1991. Information about P&G's phone system gathered in interviews.

10. Information about people questioned by security found in internal memo.

11. Artzt's questions about how to investigate Swasy were revealed in interviews with sources close to the CEO.

12. Events of search were described in police memo, Aug. 19, 1991.

13. Campaign contribution information gathered from Hamilton County records in Cincinnati.

14. Friendship between Ed Artzt and Cincinnati Bell chairman Dwight Hibbard was confirmed by Artzt.

15. Scope of first subpoena outlined in Court of Common Pleas subpoena for grand jury, June 24, 1991.

16. Additional subpoenas also dated June 24, 1991.

17. Number of phone records searched was included in numerous newspaper accounts of investigation, including Safire's essay.

18. Questions and answers found in police transcript of interrogation.

19. Some of ex-manager's comments to Armstrong were found in interviews about his talks with the police.

20. Letter from Dow Jones & Co. assistant general counsel Dick Tofel to Cincinnati Bell attorneys William D. Baskett III, Richard M. Goehler, and David C. Olson at Frost & Jacobs, Cincinnati, Aug. 9, 1991.

21. Interview with former manager, who described the conversation with Jim Jessee.

22. James S. Hirsch, "Procter & Gamble Calls in the Law to Track News Leak," *The Wall Street Journal*, Aug. 12, 1991, p. 1.

23. Review & Outlook, "What Possessed P&G?" *The Wall Street Journal*, p. A14, Aug. 13, 1991, p. A14.

24. "A Subpoena to Punish News Leaks," *The Washington Post*, Aug. 18, 1991, p. C6.

25. "P&G's Strong-arming," *Cincinnati Post,* editorial, Aug. 15, 1991.
26. Mike Peters's syndicated cartoon from August 1991.
27. Jeff Stahler's cartoon in the *Cincinnati Post,* Aug. 14, 1991.
28. Interview with David Goldberger.
29. Letter from The Society of Professional Journalists, Queen City Chapter, to Edwin L. Artzt, Aug. 12, 1991.
30. James S. Hirsch, *The Wall Street Journal,* Aug. 12, 1991.
31. Dick Rawe, "P&G Calls In Police to Probe Journal Leak," *Cincinnati Post,* Aug. 12, 1991, p. 7C.
32. Interviews with David Goldberger and Kevin O'Neill.
33. Memo from Cincinnati councilmember Tyrone K. Yates to Gerald Newfarmer, city manager, and David Rager, safety director, Aug. 16, 1991, p. 1.
34. Memo from Rager to answer Yates request, Aug. 30, 1991, p. 3.
35. Gabriella Stern, "Procter & Gamble Says Its Investigation of News Leaks Won't Lead to Prosecution," *The Wall Street Journal,* Aug. 19, 1991, p. A3.
36. Interview with former police chief Lawrence Whalen. He has since retired from that post. P&G confirmed how many officers it employed.
37. Information on Councilman Tyrone Yates obtained in interview with him.
38. Reaction by insiders gathered from interviews.
39. Letter to Swasy, signed Concerned P&G Employee.
40. William Safire, *The New York Times,* Sept. 5, 1991.
41. Interview with insider familiar with reactions from board and former CEO John Smale.
42. Letter from Artzt to employees, Sept. 4, 1991.
43. P&G news release following board meeting, Sept. 10, 1991.
44. Letter from P&G general counsel Jim Johnson to Dow Jones attorney Dick Tofel, Aug. 18, 1991.
45. Rager memo to Yates, Aug. 30, 1991.
46. Alan Farnham, "Biggest Business Goofs of 1991," *Fortune,* Jan. 13, 1992, p. 83.
47. Interview with Frederic F. Brace, Jr., Chicago attorney and P&G shareholder, who demanded a board investigation and report to shareholders, which he didn't get.

Epilogue

1. Stempel's ouster was described in Paul Ingrassia and Joseph B. White, "Stempel Quits as Head of General Motors; Workers Fear Cost-Cutting Will Quicken," *The Wall Street Journal,* Oct. 27, 1992.
2. Information on Smale's meetings, Pepper, Jager, and Artzt gathered from insiders at P&G.

3. Descriptions of Smale's reluctance to change found in numerous interviews with senior officers who served with him on the administrative committee at P&G, along with others inside P&G.

4. Smale memo to Harness as described in chapter 4, "Guerilla Marketing."

5. Information on deaths from the Centers for Disease Control in Atlanta.

6. Smale's comments about moral obligation found in his speech "Company Values Nurture Business Ethics," delivered Oct. 7, 1987, at the Deloitte Haskins & Sells annual meeting of partners.

7. Information about Andrea Kehm found in interview with her father, Mike Kehm.

8. Artzt's remarks taken from his speech at the Appeal of Conscience Foundation banquet, Oct. 8, 1992.

9. P&G's tactics regarding Florida state attorney are described at length in chapter 6, "Fear on the Fenholloway."

10. Most Admired list and information found in *Fortune* magazine, Feb. 8, 1993.

11. Information on P&G as one of the best companies in the U.S. found in *100 Best Companies to Work For in America,* by Robert Levering and Milton Moskowitz, Doubleday.

12. Employee feedback found in interviews and opinion surveys.

Appendix: Procter & Gamble Co. Products

(Source: P&G list, 1992)

United States

Laundry and Cleaning Products

Biz
Comet
Comet Liquid
Lestoil (liquid cleaner, rug shampoo, and no-wax cleaner)
Mr. Clean (all-purpose cleaner, soft cleanser)
Spic and Span
Spic and Span Cinch
Spic and Span Pine Liquid
Top Job
Bold
Cheer
Dash
Draft
Era
Gain
Ivory Snow
Liquid Bold-3
Liquid Cheer
Liquid Dreft
Liquid Ivory Snow
Liquid Lemon Dash
Liquid Tide
Liquid Tide with Bleach Alternative
Oxydol
Solo
Tide
Tide with Bleach
Cascade
Dawn
Ivory Liquid
Joy
Bounce
Downy (liquid and sheets)

Personal Care Products

Clearasil (cream and soap, stick, medicated astringent, maximum strength, adult care, double-textured pads, Clearstick, Daily Face Wash)
Noxzema Antiseptic Skin Cleanser
Noxzema Anti-Acne (Deep Cleansing Mask, Anti-Acne Pads, Regular and Maximum, Anti-Acne Lotion, Anti-Acne Spot Treatment, Anti-Acne Gel)

Analgesics

Percogesic

343

Bar Soaps

Camay
Coast
Ivory
Kirk's
Lava
Safeguard
Zest

Cosmetics

Clarion
Cover Girl
Max Factor

Denture Products

Benzodent
Complete
Fasteeth (adhesive powder, Extra Hold)
Fixodent (adhesive cream, Fresh)
Kleenite (cleanser powder)

Deodorants/ Anti-perspirants

Old Spice
Secret
Sure

Diapers

Luvs
Luvs Phases
Pampers
Pampers Phases

Feminine Protection Products

Always

Fragrances

California
Hugo Boss
Incognito
Laura Biagiotti-Roma
Le Jardin
Navy by Cover Girl
Old Spice
Toujours Moi

Gastrointestinal Products

Metamucil
Pepto-Bismol

Hair Care Product Lines/Conditioners

Pantene
Vidal Sassoon
Ivory
Prell

Incontinence Products

Attends Briefs
Attends Insert Pad
Attends Pad and Pant
Attends Undergarments
Attends Underpad
Attends Washcloth

Liquid Soap

Liquid Ivory Soap
Liquid Safeguard

Mouthwash

Scope

Oral Antiseptic/Anesthetic

Chloraseptic

Paper Tissue Products

Banner
Charmin
Puffs
Summit
White Cloud

Paper Towels

Bounty
Summit

Prescription Drugs and Physician-selected Products

Asacol (mesalamine) Delayed-Release Tablets (ulcerative colitis therapy)
Comhist (Chlorpheniramine maleate/henyltoloxamine citrate/phenylephrine hydrochloride; relief of allergy symptoms)
Dantrium (dantrolene sodium; control of skeletal muscle spasm)
Dantrium IV (dantrolene sodium intraveneous; anesthesia-related emergencies)
Didronel (etidronate disodium; treatment of bone disorders)
Entex (phenylpropanolamine HCl/quaifenesin; relief of common respiratory problems)
Entex PSE (pseudoephedrine HCl/quaifenesin; relief of common respiratory problems)
Macrobid (nitrofurantoin monohydrate/macrocrystals; urinary anti-infective)

Peridex (chlorexidine gluconate; oral rinse)

Shampoos

Head & Shoulders
Ivory
Pert Plus
Prell

Skin Care Products

Bain de Soleil (tanning products, sun protection creams, and moisturizers)
Max Factor Skin Care
Noxzema (skin cream, shaving cream, astringent, DifRinse water-rinsable cold cream)
Oil of Olay (fluid, Night of Olay, beauty bar, beauty cleanser, beauty cream, sensitive skin fluid, intensive moisture complex, foaming face wash, water-rinsable cold cream, refreshing toner, and daily UV protectant)
RainTree
Wondra

Toothpastes

Crest
Denquel
Gleem

Vicks Cough and Colds Medicines

VapoRub
Cough drops
Vatronol nose drops
Inhaler
Medi-Trating throat lozenges

Sinex
Formula 44 cough mixtures
Children's cough syrup
VapoSteam
Cough Silencers
Formula 44 cough discs
NyQuil (cherry, children's and Liqui-
Caps)
Victors cough drops
Oracin
Day-Care
Vitamin C drops
Pediatric Formula 44

Food and Beverage Products

Crisco shortening
Crisco oil
Crisco corn oil
Crisco Puritan oil
Duncan Hines Prepared Mixes (layer
cakes, muffins, brownies, cookies)
Duncan Hines Ready-to-Serve Cook-
ies
Duncan Hines Frosting
Duncans Cups Microwave
Fisher Nuts snack nuts
Folgers (vacuum packed, decaf-
feinated, special roast, gourmet
supreme)
Hawaiian Punch fruit punch
Instant Folgers (coffee crystals and
decaffeinated)
Instant High Point
Jif peanut butter (and Simply Jif)
Lincoln apple juice and other juice
beverages
Pringles
Speas Farm
Sunny Delight Florida Citrus Punch
Tender Leaf tea bags

Commercial Service Products

Coffee (Butter-Nut, Folgers, Mary-
land Club)
Shortenings and oils (e.g., Frymax,
Whirl, Professional Crisco)
Coin-vended laundry products
All-purpose cleaning products
Institutional bar soaps
Personal care amenity products
Institutional Attends

Other Product Groups

Amines
Cellulose Pulp
Fatty Acids
Fatty Alcohols
Glycerine
Laboratory Products
Methyl Esters

International Products

Arabian Peninsula

Camay soap and shower gel
Zest soap and shower gel
Drene, Head & Shoulders, Pert Plus,
Pert for Kids, and Pantene
Oil of Olay, Kamill, and Noxzema
skin care products
Clearasil
Cover Girl and Max Factor
Old Spice
Pampers and Luvs
Always
Charmin, Puffs, and Bounty
Tide, Ariel, Cheer, and Daz deter-
gents

Lenor
Fairy Liquid cleaner
Crest and Blendax
Vicks line
Chloraseptic
Metamucil

Argentina

Pantene
Old Spice
Duffy diapers
Pampers
Babysan diapers
Yes, Otros Dias, and Ladysan (feminine protection)
Tide
Downy
Vicks line
Metamucil
Pringles

Australia

Pantene
Pert Plus
Vidal Sassoon
Oil of Ulan (Oil of Olay in the U.S.)
Clearasil, Topex (acne treatments)
Max Factor
Cover Girl
Blue Stratos, Insignia, Old Spice, and Rapport fragrances
Pampers
Whisper (sold as Always in the U.S.)
Flash (cleaner)
Vicks line, Blue Throat drops, Sinex, Oracin
Metamucil
Napisan, Milgard, Infacare, and Milton infant care products
Pringles

Austria

Camay
Pantene, Shamtu, and Vidal Sassoon shampoos
O'tonic shower gel
Oil of Olaz (Oil of Olay)
Kamill skin care products
Clearasil
Credo deodorant
Pampers
Attends
Ariel, Dash, Vizur, Senso detergents
Lenor softener
Meister Proper (Mr. Clean in the U.S.)
Blend-a-med, Blendax, and Strahler toothpastes
Kukident denture adhesive
Vicks line

Belgium

Camay, Mila, and Monsavon soaps
Head & Shoulders, Hegor, Petrole Hahn, Vidal Sassoon Wash & Go shampoos. Vidal Sassoon Professional Line
Oil of Olaz, Kamill, and Mila skin care products
Clearasil and Biactol acne treatments
Old Spice
Pampers, Luvs
Always
Ariel Blue, Ariel Green, Ariel Ultra, Ariel Color, Ariel Ultra Liquid, Dash, Dash Ultra, Dash Color, Dash Ultra Liquid, Dreft, Dreft Ultra, Dreft Ultra Liquid, Tide Ultra, Vizir Ultra Liquid, Vizir Color Liquid
Lenor
Dreft Ultra dish care
Mr. Proper, Mr. Proper Super Creme,

Mr. Proper Bathroom, Spic and Span liquid cleaners

Blend-a-med and Chlorhexamed toothpastes

Blend-a-med toothbrush

Vicks line

Metamucil

Punica fruit juice

Brazil

Monica, Phebo, and Seivas de Alfazema soaps

Monica and Pert Plus shampoos

Matinal, Monica, Sandalus, Seivas de Alfazema, Seivas de Phebo, and Senior fragrances

Pinho, Phebo, Sandalus, Seivas de Alfazema, and Senior deodorants

Monica, Seivas de Alfazema talcs

Pampers

Canada

Ivory, Liquid Ivory, Camay, Zest, Safeguard, Coast

Head & Shoulders, Ivory, Pert Plus, Pantene, Vidal Sassoon

Ivory and Pantene conditioners

Noxzema, Oil of Olay, Oil of Olay cleansing products

Clearasil

Max Factor, Cover Girl, and Clarion

Secret deodorant

Old Spice, Blue Stratos, and Navy fragrances

Pampers, Luvs, Pampers/Luvs Phases

Always, Always Ultra

Attends

Royale and Dove bathroom tissues

Royalle, Facettes, and Florelle facial tissues

Royale, Pronto, and Festival Serviettes paper towels

Dreft, Tide, Liquid Tide, Ultra Tide,

Cheer, Ultra Cheer, Oxydol, Ultra Oxydol, Bold, Ultra Bold, Ivory Snow, Liquid Ivory Snow

Downy Liquid, Downy Sheets, and Bounce Sheets

Joy, Ultra Joy, Ivory Liquid, Cascade powder, liquid, and LiquiGel

Spic and Span powder and liquid

Comet, Mr. Clean, Mr. Clean Magik Spray, Supercreme

Lestoil

Scope

Crest

Fixodent and Fasteeth

Vicks line

Nyquil

Chloraseptic

Pepto-Bismol

Metamucil

Crisco, Fluffo, Golden Crisco

Crisco oil

Duncan Hines baking mixes and frosting

Pringles

Caribbean

(includes Dominican Republic, Jamaica, Trinidad, Haiti, Barbados, Guyana, Suriname, Belize, Grenada, Dominica, St. Lucia, St. Vincent, St. Kitts, Antigua, and Montserrat)

Safeguard, Zest, Ivory, Coast

Pert Plus, Pantene, Head & Shoulders

Noxzema, Oil of Olay

Clearasil

Old Spice

Max Factor

Noxzema, Sure, Secret deodorants

Pampers

Always

Charmin

Ariel, Tide, and Ace detergents
Downy
Joy and Dawn
Lestoil
Crest
Vicks line
Pepto-Bismol
Pringles

Central America

(includes Guatemala, El Salvador, Honduras, Nicaragua, Costa Rica, and Panama)

Ivory, Zest
Head & Shoulders, Pert Plus, and Pantene
Clearasil
Old Spice
Max Factor, Cover Girl
Pampers
Always
Crest
Vicks line
Pepto-Bismol and Picot gastrointestinal product

Chile

Camay and Moncler soaps
Pantene, Pert Plus, and Head & Shoulders
Babysan diapers
Ladysan feminine protection products
Ace (lemon, reforzado, ultra, liquido, con blanueador) detergents
Crest and Odontine toothpastes

China

Head & Shoulders, Pantene, Rejoice, Jiehua (herbal shampoo)

Oil of Ulan (Oil of Olay)
Whisper

Colombia

Camay
Pantene Pro-V and Pert Plus
Clearasil
Ariel, Inextra, Ya, Ya with Bleach, Unijab, Siren, Supremo, and Tris detergents
Cristal and Tras dish care products
Vicks line
Metamucil

Czech Republic/Slovakia

Camay
Vidal Sassoon Wash & Go, Head & Shoulders
Pampers
Ariel, Vizir, Tix, and Biomat detergents
Fairy and Jar dish care products
Blend-a-med toothpaste

Denmark

Vidal Sassoon
Oil of Olay
Clearasil
Desert Flower and Old Spice fragrances
Pampers
Always and Yes feminine protection products
Ariel, Jelp, Tatex, Kalk 'Vaek detergents
Mr. Proper cleaner
Vicks line
Metamucil

Egypt

Camay, Zest
Pert Plus, Head & Shoulders
Always
Ariel Low Suds, High Suds detergents
Crest

Finland

Vidal Sassoon Brown Line, Vidal Sassoon Wash & Go
Oil of Olay
Clearasil
Old Spice
Cover Girl
Pampers
Always
Ariel Ultra, liquid and color
Fairy dish care products
Spic and Span, Mr. Proper
Vicks cough drops

France

Camay, Monsavon, Roge-Cavailles, and Zest soaps
Head & Shoulders, Hegor, Petrole Hahn, Pantene, Roge-Cavailles, Vidal Sassoon Wash & Go
Oil of Olaz
Clearasil and Biactol
Pampers
Always
Ariel, Bonux, Dash, and Vizir lines of detergents
Lenor
Spic and Span, Mr. Propre, Viakal cleaners
Blend-a-med
Vicks line
Dittmeyer fruit juices

Germany

Camay
Hegor, Shamtu, Head & Shoulders, Pantene, Vidal Sassoon shampoos
Cliff, Credo, and Litamin bath/shower gels
Oil of Olaz and Kamill skin care products
Clearasil and Topexan acne treatments
Credo deodorant
Arile, Vizir, Dash 3, Rei, Sanso detergents
Lenor
Spuli, Fairy Liquid dish care products
Meister Proper cleaner
Blend-a-med, Blendi, Blendax, Blend-a-Dent toothpastes
Blend-a-Dent and Firmodent denture care products
Chlorhexamed and Dentril oral care products
Blend-a-mant, Retro-blend, Blend-a-scon, Blend-a-print, Blend-a-fill, Blend-a-dispers, Lux-a-fill, Blend-a-gum products for dentists
Vicks line
Milton infant care products
Metamucil
Punica, Valensina, Dittmeyer's Natural, Dittmeyer's Black Label fruit drinks
Orval lemon extract

Greece

Camay
Head & Shoulders, Vidal Sassoon
Oil of Olaz and Camay skin care products
Topexan acne treatments
Noxzema, Old Spice deodorants and shave foams

Pampers
Always
Attends
Ariel, Ariel Color, Tide, Bold
Fairy dish care
Viakal cleaner
Crest, Blend-a-med
Vicks line
Metamucil
Milton infant care

Holland

Head & Shoulders, Vidal Sassoon
Wash & Go
Oil of Olaz
Clearasil
Old Spice, Desert Flower, Insignia,
Blue Stratos fragrances
Pampers Phases
Always
Ariel, Dreft, Dash, and Vizir lines of
detergents
Lenor
Dreft dishwashing products
Blend-a-med and Blendi toothpastes
Kukident denture care products
Vicks line
Punica and Valensina fruit drinks

Hong Kong

Camay, Zest
Head & Shoulders, Pantene
Noxzema, Oil of Ulan
Clearasil
Max Factor
Cover Girl
Old Spice
Pampers
Attends
Crest
Vicks line
Metamucil

Pepto-Bismol
Nytolac, Mapisan, and InfaCare infant care products

Hungary

Camay
Vidal Sassoon Wash & Go
Pampers
Always
Ariel
Blend-a-med
Vicks line

India

Mediker and New Mediker shampoos
Oil of Olay products
Clearasil products
Whisper
Ariel
Vicks line

Indonesia

Rejoice and Pantene shampoos
Oil of Ulan
Clearasil
Vicks line

Italy

Camay, Zest, and Infasil soaps
Hegor, Infasil, Keramine H, Mediker,
and Pantene shampoos
Oil of Olaz and Infasil skin care prod-
ucts
Clearasil and Topexan acne treat-
ments
Pampers
Ariel, Ace, Tide, Dash, and Dora de-
tergents
Nelsen Fiatti dishwashing products
Spic and Span, Mastro Lindo, Mister

Verde, Viakal, Saleno, and Ace
cleaners
Kukident denture care products
Vicks line
Milton infant care products

Japan

Camay, Muse bar, and liquid soaps
Rejoy 2-in-1 and Pantene shampoos
Pantene Tonic, Pantene conditioner,
Pantene Treatment, Rejoy Treat-
ment hair care products
Shasta skin cream and lotion
Clearasil line
Max Factor
California for Men, Factor for Men,
Avanti, AR, Royal Regiment fra-
grances for men
Jaclyn Smith's California and Rome
fragrances for women
Pampers
Whisper
Attento incontinence products
Ultra Ariel, Super Cheer, Compact
Bonus, Monogen Uni, and Mono-
gen
Baby detergents
Super Soft Bounce
Vicks line
Colac gastrointestinal product
Milton infant bottle sterilization

Korea

Ivory, Zest
Rejoice shampoo
Old Spice
Pampers
Whisper
Blendax
Vicks Throat Drops
Pringles

Malaysia

Camay, Zest
Head & Shoulders, Pantene, Rejoice,
and Vidal Sassoon
Oil of Ulan and Noxzema
Clearasil
Max Factor, Cover Girl, and Clarion
Old Spice, Max Factor
Pampers
Whisper
Vicks line
Milton, Napisan, and InfaCare infant
hygiene products

Mexico

Camay, Escudo, Zest
Head & Shoulders, Pantene, Pert Plus
Oil of Olay line
Clearasil line
Max Factor line
Secret
Pampers
Always
Rapido, Ariel, Bold, and Don Maximo
lines of detergents
Downy
Cascade and Salvo dish care products
Maestro Limpio cleaners
Crest line
Vicks line
Picot antacid, Metamucil, Pepto-Bis-
mol line
Chocomilk milk modifier

Morocco

Camay, Zest
Pert Plus
Tide, Ariel

New Zealand

Pantene, Pert Plus, and Vidal Sassoon
Oil of Ulan
Clearasil and Topes acne treatments
Cover Girl, Max Factor
Blue Stratos, Insignia, Old Spice, and
 Rapport fragrances
Pampers
Whisper
Flash cleaner
Vicks line
NapiSan, Milgard, InfaCare, and Milton infant care products

Nigeria

Vicks VapoRub and Inhaler

Pakistan

Rejoice shampoo

Panama

Ivory soap
Head & Shoulders, Pert Plus
Clearasil
Old Spice
So Dry deodorant
Pampers
Always
Crest
Vicks line
Pepto-Bismol
Picot antacid

Peru

Camay, Moncler, Riviera, and Safeguard soaps
Pantene, Pert Plus
Clearasil

Pampers
Ace, Ariel, Sapolio, and Orvus detergents
Salvo dish care products
Crest
Vicks line

Philippines

Camay, Ivory, Safeguard
Mediker, Pantene, and Rejoice shampoos
Oil of Olay
Clearasil
Old Spice
Max Factor
Pampers
Whisper
Mr. Clean bar, Tide Ultra II and Tide
 bar, Argo, and Perla detergents
Mr. Clean
Vicks line
Star margarine and Dari Creme

Poland

Vidal Sassoon Wash & Go, Head &
 Shoulders, and Pantene Pro-V
Old Spice
Pampers
Always
Ariel and Vizir
Lenor
Mr. Proper cleaner
Blend-a-med

Portugal

Pantene, Vidal Sassoon
Clearasil
Insignia and Old Spice fragrances
Dodot diapers
Tide

Fairy dish care products
Spic and Span
Neoblanc, Neoblanc Casa bleach
Vicks line

Puerto Rico

Camay, Ivory, Safeguard, Coast, Zest
Head & Shoulders, Pert Plus, Vidal Sassoon
Noxzema, Oil of Olay
Clearasil
Clarion, Cover Girl, Max Factor
Old Spice
Sure, Secret, Old Spice deodorants
Pampers, Luvs
Always
Charmin
Bounty
Puffs
Ace, Ariel, Tide, Ivory Snow, Dash, Era detergents
Downy, Bounce
Ivory, Cascade, Dawn
Lestoil, Maestro Limpio cleaners
Crest
Scope
Fixodent, Fasteeth
Vicks line
Pepto-Bismol, Percogesic, Day Care
Crisco
Pringles
Jif
Hawaiian Punch, Sunny Delight

Russia

Camay
Head & Shoulders, Vidal Sassoon Wash & Go, Vidal Sassoon Professional Line
Oil of Ulay
Old Spice
Ariel, Tix detergents
Blendax

Singapore

Camay, Zest
Head & Shoulders, Pantene, Rejoice, Vidal Sassoon
Noxzema, Oil of Ulan, Max Factor
Clearasil
Clarion, Cover Girl, Max Factor
Max Factor and Old Spice fragrances
Pampers
Whisper
Vicks line
Milton, Infacare, and Napisan infant hygiene products

Spain

Head & Shoulders, Pantene, Vidal Sassoon Wash & Go
Oil of Olay and Litamin skin care products
Clearasil and Clearamed
Ellen Betrix and Max Factor cosmetics
Old Spice, Hugo Boss, Otto Kern, and Laura Biagiotti fragrances
Dodot and Dodotis diapers
Evax feminine care products
Ariel HS and LS, Dash, and Lenor detergents
Fairy dish care products
Mr. Proper cleaner
Profiden, Blend-a-med toothpastes
Vicks line
Praims and Victors throat drops
Milton sterilization products
Metamucil

Sweden

Clearasil, Head & Shoulders, Mediker, Pantene, and Vidal Wash & Go shampoos
Oil of Ulay, Noxzema

Clearasil
Insignia, Old Spice
Pampers
Ariel line
Yes and Yes Lemon dish care products
Dentosal toothpaste
Vicks throat drop line

Switzerland

Camay, Cliff, Kamill Foambath and Showergel, Oil of Olaz Shower and Lotion, Oil of Olaz Moisturizing Bar and Monsavon bar soaps
Pantene Hairtonic, pump and spray, Pantene Plus, Vidal Sassoon line
Kamill, Oil of Olaz lines
Clearasil, Topexan, and Moncler Derma skin care lines
Cliff Eau de Toilette, Old Spice line of fragrances and face care
Roma, Fiori, Bianchi, Uoma, Venezia, Boss, NoaNoa, Cycle, Le Jardin, Blase, Trance, Du Jour, de Soir, Street Life, and City fragrances
Pampers
Always
Attends
Ariel, Vizir, and Dash lines
Lenor
Mr. Proper
Blendax, Chlorhexamed, Kukident lines
Vicks line
Metamucil

Taiwan

Camay, Ivory
Head & Shoulders, Pert Plus line, Pantene, and Vidal Sassoon
Oil of Olay
Max Factor

Pampers
Safe & Free feminine protection products
Joy

Thailand

Pantene and Rejoice shampoos
Oil of Ulan
Clearasil
Pampers
Whisper
Vicks line

Turkey

Blendax and Rejoice shampoos
Old Spice
Prima diapers
Orkid feminine protection products
Ariel line, Alo, Mintax, and Alomatik detergents
Ace bleach
Mintax dishwashing products
Ipana, Flora, Dentafresh, and Medident toothpastes

United Kingdom

Camay, Fairy, Zest, Oil of Olay soaps
Head & Shoulders, Pantene, Vidal Sassoon line of shampoos
Delph, Oil of Ulay skin care products
Biactol, Clearasil
Cover Girl, Max Factor
Alpine, Blue Stratos, Insignia, Mandate, Old Spice, Rapport fragrances
Pampers
Always
Attends
Ariel, Daz, Bold, Fairy, Dreft, Tide, and Vizir detergents
Lenor, Bounce

Fairy dish care products
Fairy, Vortex, Flash, and Viakal cleaners
Crest
Denclen denture cleaner
Pepto-Bismol, Metamucil, and Regulan gastrointestinal products
Milton, Napisan, and Infacare infant care products
Pringles
Valensina fruit juices

Venezuela

Camay, Moncler, Safeguard
Drene, Head & Shoulders, Pert Plus, and Pantene

Drene conditioner
Oil of Olay
Clearasil
Old Spice
Pampers and Mammi diapers
Always and Tess feminine protection products
Ariel, Ace, Bold 3, and Rindex detergents
Ace Lavaplatos dish care products
Crest
Vicks line
Metamucil

Acknowledgments

Isn't this the part where I thank everyone I've ever known? Perhaps it would be easier if I did—there are so many people who helped me complete this book.

The greatest gift when writing is time. Paul Steiger, managing editor of *The Wall Street Journal,* gave me the opportunity to venture off on a book leave with the safety net of a job when I finished. Paul and former executive editor Norman Pearlstine offered unwavering support for my coverage of Procter & Gamble. They endured far too many meetings with P&G flaks, who consistently asked for my head. And Dick Tofel was a zealot in chasing away harassing Cincinnati police detectives.

Pittsburgh bureau chiefs Tim Schellhardt and Carol Hymowitz stood by me on the front line. They are two of the *Journal's* finest, and I cherish their friendship and guidance. Likewise, Atlanta bureau chief Betsy Morris was supportive and patient as I finished the book in early 1993.

Reporters and editors throughout the *Journal,* from New York to Tokyo, were helpful at every turn. Their calls to offer tips or a word of encouragement meant a lot. My friends in both Pittsburgh and Atlanta deserve medals. Even the folks in the advertising and communications departments cheered me on. Valerie Reitman, who took over the P&G beat after I left, was a good soulmate when I needed to commiserate. Former *Journal* correspondent Damon Darlin opened doors all over Seoul and provided valuable insight into the Asian markets. Shin Mee Chang was a great interpreter and research assistant during my visit. Other "Procter Watchers" at various newspapers and magazines shared their insights from their years of research. Some of their comments appear in passages on P&G's dealings with the media. Many continue to follow P&G, so their lives are difficult enough without being linked to this project. They know who they are.

In Cincinnati, Gary Rhodes at the *Cincinnati Post* gave up some weekends and lunch hours to read through a mountain of microfilm and court documents.

ACKNOWLEDGMENTS

I'm also grateful for Dr. Carol Moog's time and insightful review of P&G advertising. For more information on advertising messages, I recommend her book *Are They Selling Her Lips?*

Others volunteered their editing skills on the many drafts of the manuscript. Greg Stricharchuk, business editor of *The Dayton Daily News* and a former colleague at the *Journal*, was a tireless coach from the earliest days of my P&G work. Greg and his wife, Pat, opened up their home to me during my long visits to Cincinnati, providing a haven from the storm. I fear I was often the houseguest from hell, but they always welcomed me back. Likewise, Dean Mills, dean of the Missouri School of Journalism, has been a longtime mentor, cleaning up my copy since his family "adopted" me during my days at Penn State.

Selling the idea of a book on P&G was much easier with the help of my agent, Kris Dahl, at ICM. From our first phone call, Kris was enthusiastic about the project, and she navigated me through the mine fields of the publishing world. Gordon Kato and Dorothea Herrey at ICM were always ready to help too. At Random House, Ann Godoff sparked to the idea even before reading my book proposal. Her editing and guidance transformed a rough manuscript into the finished work. Enrica Gadler endured months of neurotic phone calls. Philip Bashe and Nancy Inglis smoothed out the final copy. James Albrecht was a diligent fact checker. And Victor A. Kovner proved that not all lawyers should be shot. I'm grateful for his patience and advice.

Of course, none of this would be possible without the men and women inside P&G. One of my favorite interviews for the book was with Howard Morgens, former CEO of P&G. Now retired in Carmel, California, Morgens still carries his P&G ID badge in his briefcase. Despite warnings from the P&G PR department, Morgens spent a day recalling his time at the company. His colorful stories of P&G's history added a lot to the book.

Likewise, former employees such as George Stults showed courage in sharing their stories. Many others still working at P&G risked their jobs by talking to me. I wish I could thank them by name, but they fear retribution. In addition, customers, competitors, and consultants familiar with P&G helped me put together the full picture. The unsung hero who called to notify me that the Cincinnati police had my phone records never stopped calling, even after his invitation to the Fraud Squad. I'm glad he has a sense of humor. Fortunately, the real sources were never discovered.

To help confirm what readers wanted in this book, a former P&G marketing expert conducted a focus group and provided quantitative research to back the anecdotal findings. The respondents' interests are reflected throughout these pages. I thank him for his efforts.

Throughout my years of covering P&G, Lou Pritchett, retired vice president of sales, was generous with his time. He spent days offering his thoughts on life at P&G. He contacted others around the globe and encouraged them to talk to me.

P&G CEO Ed Artzt labeled him an enemy because he had the guts to help me—and tell the truth about the company. And other CEOs now hire him to help fix their problems.

Even Artzt showed he had guts, breaking the traditional silence at P&G. At times, he helped me practice my favorite kind of journalism; we got to laugh and get the job done. He blessed my trip to Latin America, opening up many parts of the previously closed culture. I saw the fatherly side that wants to teach others. I also saw why employees call him The Prince of Darkness. I was disappointed when he resorted to police tactics to thwart my coverage. As a former reporter, his belief in good journalism lasts only as long as he likes the news. What's worse is that he never showed remorse for the investigation. The only thing he regretted was getting caught.

About a year into my research, he changed his mind and began to talk about his career. He was generous with his time. I wish him the best and hope he can control that often wicked temper.

Those whom P&G has tried to destroy over the years were key in my research efforts. In Iowa, Tom Riley and his family welcomed me at a July 4th bash between interviews about his work for victims of toxic shock syndrome. Tom is a brilliant lawyer who shows compassion for his clients as well as a zest for taking on giants. He is one of the few who beat P&G. The Kehm trial deserved another telling in this book because too few people read Riley's account in *The Price of a Life*, a chilling look at one woman's death after using P&G's Rely tampons. So much has come out since that trial, and too little attention has been paid to what P&G did to save its profits. Revisiting his trial offered a rare glimpse into P&G's litigious nature. I only wish Patricia Kehm—and the other victims of P&G's callous acts—could have been saved.

In Florida, Julie Hauserman, an award-winning environmental reporter at the Tallahassee *Democrat*, first uncovered P&G's destruction of the Fenholloway River. I'm grateful for her guidance during my research. She's now writing a book on Florida's environmental woes; don't miss it.

The men and women fighting P&G in Taylor County need support and prayers as they try to salvage something for future generations. Joy Towles Cummings and many others have boundless energy and won't stop until they win. Stephanie McGuire and Linda Rowland have endured far too much in their fight for justice. May they find some peace.

Through it all, my family and friends have been the biggest source of comfort and support. The entire Swasy clan—all thirty of them—endured my one-track mind during my coverage of P&G. Too many suppers and picnics were missed when I was on the road. When I was home, I'd often be distracted. But they encouraged me to forge ahead. My brother Jack Swasy, who teaches marketing at American University, has always been there when I needed him. My sister Alexis Hill was a great research assistant, transcribing scores of interviews and scouring box after box of papers for missing documents. Our mother, Maribel Allison Swasy, to whom this book is dedicated, has been a lifelong inspiration. I regret that she had to endure so much grief when the Fraud Squad came after me. It's not much fun to get phone calls from those who ask, "Did Alecia do something wrong?" It's people like Mother whom P&G forgets in its quest for success.

Finally, I'm grateful for you, the reader. I wrote this book because I thought it was important to look beyond the Ivory purity and tell the real story of P&G. You've given up some of your hard-earned cash to buy this book. Consider it an investment: I plan to share it through a journalism scholarship at Penn State, where I got my start.

Index

About
the Author

ALECIA SWASY is a staff reporter
for *The Wall Street Journal.* She
was responsible for the paper's
Procter & Gamble coverage for
three years prior to writing this
book. She lives in Pennsylvania.